Shakespeare's Curse

Conceptualizing the curse as the representation of a foundational, mythical violence that is embedded within juridical discourse, *Shakespeare's Curse: The Aporias of Ritual Exclusion in Early Modern Royal Drama* pursues a reading of *Richard III*, *King John*, and *King Lear* in order to analyze the persistence of imprecations in the discourses of modernity. Shakespeare wrote during a period that was transformative in the development of juridical thinking. However, taking up the relationship between theater, theology and law, Björn Quiring argues that the curse was not eliminated from legal discourses during this modernization of jurisprudence; rather, it persisted and to this day continues to haunt numerous speech acts. Drawing on the work of Derrida, Lacan, Benjamin and Agamben, among others, Quiring analyzes the performativity of the curse, and tracks its power through the juristic themes that are pursued within Shakespeare's plays—such as sovereignty, legitimacy, succession, obligation, exception, and natural law. Thus, this book provides an original and important insight into early modern legal developments, as well as a fresh perspective on some of Shakespeare's best-known works.

A fascinating interdisciplinary study, this book will interest students and scholars of law, literature, and history.

Björn Quiring is a Research Associate at the Peter Szondi Institute of Comparative Literature, Freie Universität, Berlin.

Discourses of Law

Series editors: Peter Goodrich, Michel Rosenfeld and Arthur Jacobson
Benjamin N. Cardozo School of Law

This successful and exciting series seeks to publish the most innovative scholarship at the intersection of law, philosophy and social theory. The books published in the series are distinctive by virtue of exploring the boundaries of legal thought. The work that this series seeks to promote is marked most strongly by the drive to open up new perspectives on the relation between law and other disciplines. The series has also been unique in its commitment to international and comparative perspectives upon an increasingly global legal order. Of particular interest in a contemporary context, the series has concentrated upon the introduction and translation of continental traditions of theory and law.

The original impetus for the series came from the paradoxical merger and confrontation of East and West. Globalization and the internationalization of the rule of law has had many dramatic and often unforeseen and ironic consequences. An understanding of differing legal cultures, particularly different patterns of legal thought, can contribute, often strongly and starkly, to an appreciation if not always a resolution of international legal disputes. The rule of law is tied to social and philosophical underpinnings that the series has sought to excoriate and illuminate.

Titles in the series:

Nietzsche and Legal Theory: Half-Written Laws
Edited by Peter Goodrich and Mariana Valverde

Law, Orientalism, and Postcolonialism: The Jurisdiction of the Lotus Eaters
Piyel Haldar

Endowed: Regulating the Male Sexed Body
Michael Thomson

The Identity of the Constitutional Subject: Selfhood, Citizenship, Culture, and Community
Michel Rosenfeld

The Land is the Source of the Law: A Dialogic Encounter with Indigenous Jurisprudence
C.F. Black

Shakespearean Genealogies of Power: A Whispering of Nothing in Hamlet, Richard II, Julius Caesar, Macbeth, The Merchant of Venice, and The Winter's Tale
Anselm Haverkamp

Novel Judgments: Legal Theory as Fiction
William Macneil

Sex, Culpability and the Defence of Provocation
Danielle Tyson

The Scene of Mass Crime: History, Film, and International Inburals
Christian Delage and Peter Goodrich

Wickedness and Crime: Laws of Homicide and Malice
Penny Crofts

Shakespeare's Curse: The Aporias of Ritual Exclusion in Early Modern Royal Drama
Björn Quiring

Visualizing Law in the Age of the Digital Baroque: Arabesques and Entanglements
Richard K. Sherwin

Forthcoming:

Crime Scenes: Forensics and Aesthetics
Rebecca Scott Bray

The Rule of Reason in European Constitutionalism and Citizenship
Yuri Borgmann-Prebil

The publisher gratefully acknowledges the support of the Jacob Burns Institute for Advanced Legal Studies of the Benjamin N. Cardozo School of Law to the series *Discourses of Law.*

Shakespeare's Curse

The Aporias of Ritual Exclusion in Early Modern Royal Drama

Björn Quiring

Translated by
Michael Winkler and Björn Quiring

Routledge
Taylor & Francis Group
LONDON AND NEW YORK

First published 2014
by Routledge
2 Park Square, Milton Park, Abingdon, Oxfordshire OX14 4RN

and by Routledge
711 Third Avenue, New York, NY 10017

First issued in paperback 2015

Routledge is an imprint of the Taylor & Francis Group, an informa business

British Library Cataloguing in Publication Data
A catalogue record for this book is available from the British Library

Library of Congress Cataloging-in-Publication Data
Quiring, Björn.
Shakespeare's Curse / Björn Quiring.
pages cm.—(Discourses of Law)
Includes bibliographical references and index.
ISBN 978-0-415-51756-0 (hbk : alk. paper)—ISBN 978-0-203-76219-6 (ebk)
1. Shakespeare, William, 1564-1616—Knowledge—Law. 2. Shakespeare, William, 1564-1616. King Richard III. 3. Shakespeare, William, 1564-1616. King John. 4. Shakespeare, William, 1564-1616. King Lear. 5. Oaths in literature. I. Title.
PR3028.Q57 2014
822.3'3—dc23

2013013956

ISBN 13: 978-0-415-70422-9 (pbk)
ISBN 13: 978-0-415-51756-0 (hbk)

Typeset in Minion
by Keystroke, Station Road, Codsall, Wolverhampton

Contents

Acknowledgements

First and foremost I want to thank my doctoral advisors, Anselm Haverkamp and Andreas Höfele, for their guidance and support. Peter Goodrich generously helped to organize the translation project, Michael Winkler did superlative work on the translation, and Matthew Vollgraff was extremely helpful during its revision. Ralf Eckschmidt helped a lot with editing and Tobias Nowotzin with formatting.

I would also like to thank the team at Routledge for their friendly patience, the German publisher, Wilhelm Fink Verlag, for their kind co-operation, and the Deutsche Forschungsgemeinschaft (German Research Foundation) as well as the Deutsche Shakespeare-Stiftung (German Shakespeare Foundation) for their support of the project.

The friends, colleagues, teachers, readers, and inspirers who also contributed to the book in one way or another are too numerous to mention. I will just name, somewhat synecdochically, Susanne Bayerlipp, Vera Beyer, Stefanie Diekmann, Tobias Döring, Stephen Greenblatt, Werner Hamacher, Michael Jennings, Margaret L. King, Anne Kockelkorn, Lester K. Little, Philip Lorenz, Julia Lupton, Christoph Menke, Winfried Menninghaus, Jane O. Newman, Claudia Olk, Klaus Quiring, Marga Quiring, Wolfgang Rapp, Claudia Richter, Nigel Smith, Goran Stanivukovic, Robert Stockhammer, Hella Tiedemann, Brian Williams, and the students in my seminars at the universities of Frankfurt, Munich, and Berlin.

Introduction

The curse is usually defined as a formula by whose mere expression its speaker seeks to inflict harm on others.[1] This definition is at once too narrow and too broad: too narrow because the person who utters a curse often does not think of the execration as a harmful act at all, but sees it, for example, in its prophetic function as an objective statement about impending events. (The medieval literature on cursing concentrates on this theme in particular.) And the definition is too broad because various performative acts such as legal judgments may also inflict harm on somebody by their mere pronouncement, but nonetheless would not normally be considered curses. The customary definition, then, is insufficient. At times, the definition is augmented by the assertion that curses are reactions to a transgression, thereby turning them into primordial acts of restituting rightful law and justice.[2] That is itself a reactive conception, for it presumes that societal structures are always already given without considering how and to what extent speech acts like curses and oaths themselves contribute to the process of constituting laws and institutions.[3] Admittedly, the heterogeneity of the phenomenon makes it difficult to find a more useful definition. Even the word's etymology is lost in obscurity: "Curse," according to the first edition of the *Oxford English Dictionary*, is "of unknown origin"; no similar word exists in the Germanic, Romance and Celtic languages.[4] The German "Fluch" seems to be derived from the Germanic root "floka-," denoting acts of striking, splitting and thrusting; but even this etymology is uncertain.[5] The words "curse" and "Fluch" are not derivable and not strictly definable. They cover several semantic fields that are separated in other languages, for example in Hebrew. The Hebrew terms that in Bible translations are rendered as "curse" essentially designate either an act of punishment by God (arûr, אָרוּר), or an appeal to His avenging justice (alah, אָלָה).[6] The concept of "curse" in this respect is overdetermined. It is exactly this semantic condensation that, since the early Middle Ages, is decisive for the prevalent Christian use of this term in Europe: malediction is at once an appeal to, and a condemnation through a punitive divine judgment, however the correlation and efficacy of these two aspects may be construed. In the culture of the Middle Ages and of the early modern era, the curse can, at best, be defined through this ambiguity.

On the one hand, the word "curse" then seems to designate the mythical entity of an exclusionary divine judgment that posits a new law and gives the world a new structure. Both Yahweh's curse upon the serpent, man and the ground in the Book of Genesis (3. 14–19), and Jesus' apocalyptic condemnation of the reprobate (Matthew 25. 14) conform to this description. Such a curse is inscribed into narratives and at times has a narrative form itself. It marks the places where the law borders on foundational myths and establishes a continuity between the two. In the myth of the Fall, for example, God's curse justifies the necessity of human work, female subordination and the inevitability of death. In this context, curses not only determine the future; they also legitimate the past and the present, and they serve as explanatory patterns. But the concept of the "curse" also designates the ritual representation of these judgments within the legal order itself, as exemplified by the Biblical obligation to repeat every seven years the curses in Deuteronomy that perpetuate the covenant with Yahweh (Deut. 27–28 and 31. 10). These curses represent a transcendental world order within the juridical system; and in this respect they do not appear as lawmaking but as law-preserving.[7] Due to this bipolarity, the relationship of curse and law amounts to a paradox: the curse institutes the law and at the same time presupposes it. Like its more courteous twin, namely the oath *qua* conditional self-execration, the curse seems to belong to the mythic, lawmaking sphere outside the law,[8] even though the law itself demands and regulates it. The curse comprises and frames the law, but the law also determines the legitimacy of cursing. Accordingly, curses appear as a significant surplus in the legal order, as a supplement of the law in Derrida's sense.[9] The term "supplement" can designate both a surplus and a substitute. Accordingly, the curse can complement and represent the law, but also threatens to dissolve and replace it. The supplement demonstrates by its necessity the deficiency of what is being supplemented: "if [the supplement] fills, it is as if one fills a void."[10] It does not, however, fill the void with anything determinable; it has no essence of its own, or rather, it is essentially derivative.[11] For a curse always refers to a mightier curse. It opens the perspective on a primordial condemnation that, like a primordial law, can only be thought of as transcendental.[12] Hence, the curse always inserts itself into a chain of curses, always extends another curse and quotes it. "It is the strange essence of the supplement not to have essentiality."[13]

This makes it difficult to define the curse in traditional categories: not only does the addressee of a curse remain a little indistinct due to this bipolarity, but also its sender nearly always remains unidentifiable due to the curse's derivative nature.[14] In the curse, self-affirmation and self-suspension of the speaker are interdependent. The execrator appeals to God and at the same time turns himself into His mouthpiece. In the empirical act of cursing, the creative power of a foundational mythic Word is referenced as a force that from the outset determines the situation in which the curser and the cursed find themselves. This suggests that the curse as an empirical speech act reduces itself to an empty, repetitive gesture: it posits what it already presupposes, forever redundant. On close analysis, even the logical position of the execrator in this arrangement is paradoxical: the condemnable deed itself, or the condemnable person, have already brought a pre-existent curse down on themselves to which the execrator merely lends his voice in repetition. Through his curse, he or she affirms an order of the world in which the accursed has already been condemned. Yet, on the other hand, the same imprecator aspires to carry out this condemnation himself through the curse, thereby insinuating that, at the moment of its utterance, judgment and world do not coincide after all. Since the curse, while denying the divergence of judgment and world, at the same time upholds this difference as its own cause and origin, it subverts itself. This performative contradiction[15] is the reason that the curse is always ahead of itself, but also that its fulfillment remains constitutively deferred. That makes the curse interminable and excessive. The temporal structure of the curse eludes the present. Since words of execration are always merely quoted by execrators, curses situate themselves within the past. But as an interminable speech act, the curse is also suspended indefinitely. In this sense, its time is that of an unending deferment, forever moving toward an unattainable future. The curse is a speech act that can neither be pronounced in a present time because it has always already been pronounced, nor bring about its effect in a present time because this effect can never be concluded. The curse is situated in an inaccessible future perfect. It is the unending announcement of a past performative.[16] The curse is the place where the first and the last verdict meet and merge.

The curse is symptomatic of an overdetermined relationship of its speaker to language. The execrator claims a position of power while recognizing that this position is denied to him. Curses thus mark the point where absolute power and complete impotence blend and become indistinguishable: the curse is a sovereign speech act that demonstrates the impossibility of sovereign speech acts. In that respect, it endangers its speaker. Curses are so constituted as to split not only the one execrated but also the execrator. The curse is always included in a fatal strategy of the law. It asserts a connection to the supreme power and, on the basis of this authority, lays claim to exerting a (re)constituting influence on the administration of justice. Curses can support existing orders and secure existing boundaries, but they can also question and subvert these arrangements. The difference is not always clear cut; often it can be determined only in retrospect. The curse is extravagant but also ritualized. It is contingent but also necessary. It marks an exception, but it is inscribed into a rule. It is precisely this irreducible ambiguity that turns the execration (just like the oath, the declaration[17], the Althusserian "interpellation"[18] and the command[19]) into a political speech act. The ensuing study concentrates on precisely this political dimension of the curse and its status within socially polarizing confrontations. In analogy to the concept of the "political oath" (as developed by Ernst Friesenhahn),[20] one might call the speech act to be analyzed here a "political curse".[21] Its historical relevance is easy to underestimate. But the legal historian Gerhard Thür goes so far as to argue that the political and juridical institutions of ancient Athens emerged from curse and oath ceremonies and their codification. According to him, the transitions between execrations and juridical verdicts were fluid during the Archaic Age.[22] Be that as it may, many indications suggest that, in the cradle of democracy, the execration (ἀρά) figured as a central public ritual. According to many sources, the members of the ancient Athenian polis committed themselves to their shared projects through oaths which contained an explicit conditional self-execration. Even extant treaties between Greek city states are sealed with prospective curses against anyone who might commit a breach of contract.[23] According to Livy, war declarations were substantiated with execrations of the enemy.[24] As late as the fourth century BC, Demosthenes mentions in a speech that every public assembly of the Athenian citizenry commenced with a herald's recitation of a curse upon the enemies of the state.[25] That the political curse is supposed to establish a precarious sort of legal security becomes palpable in such ceremonies.

The curse positions itself at the origin of Western law and asserts its binding character. The imprecatory ceremony affirms social coherence in that it addresses not merely the person cursed but also the community. Its members are expected to uphold the curse collectively, and the dismal fate of the accursed, serving as an exemplary warning, urges them to do so. By means of this feedback loop, the curse polarizes and homogenizes in equal measure.[26] One can describe the curse as marking a borderline, as inscribing the difference between an inside and an outside onto both the body politic and the individual subject. But the "outside" a curse delimits is in fact not an extraterritorial place. Due to the curse's paradoxical structure, the outside takes the form of an "interiorized outside." It is an outside that needs to be incorporated into the symbolical system that declares it to be an outside; the foreclosed exterior permeating the interior. Inasmuch as the curse must always preserve what it appears to exclude so as not to dissolve, it subverts itself and therefore needs to be constantly renewed and intensified excessively. Indeed, excessivity is the curse's *conditio sine qua non*. An execration is an interminable speech act because it obstructs its own effectiveness, and it perpetuates itself through its own failure. The curse is cursed with the need for its own endless repetition.

The blind spot of the law is the groundlessness of its foundation, a void which the ritual curse both conceals and demarcates. Luhmann's dictum that "law is what the law deems to be law"[27] implies that the justification for the law's validity depends in the final analysis on a tautological as well as violent affirmation: "Jurisdiction is done like this because it is supposed to be done like this." Since positive law lacks its own final justification, its constitution or reconstitution must take place in a space devoid of law. The curse that supplements the law represents the law's concealed, violent genesis which myth processes.[28] To draw a more precise outline of this problematic intersection of law and myth, concepts taken from Giorgio Agamben's *Homo Sacer*—inspired by Walter Benjamin's "Critique of Violence"—prove useful, especially the concept of the "inclusive exclusion" as "exception." Agamben adopts the concept of the "state of exception" via Benjamin from Carl Schmitt's *Political Theology* and makes it the center of his legal philosophy. According to Schmitt, a state of exception arises when a danger to the order of the state (for example, a coup d'état, a revolutionary uprising, a civil war, etc.) requires the suspension of civil laws. In this emergency, the validity of the law is made so precarious that the sovereign, unconstrained by laws, must first bring about by violent means "a situation in which legal prescriptions can be valid" again.[29] By proclaiming a state of exception, the sovereign may declare the order of law to be invalid without being obligated himself to invoke an existing law that would justify his decision. Schmitt reverses this definition—the state of exception is the result of a sovereign decision—and defines sovereignty as the authority both to proclaim and to end a state of exception: "Sovereign is he who decides on the exception."[30] In this respect, whoever institutes and guarantees the legal order is the one who is exempt from it and can suspend it, if necessary, in order to replace it with a "state of nature." The institution and the suspension of the law—rule and exception—are united in Schmitt's figure of the sovereign. Agamben expands Schmitt's concept by defining exception as an "inclusive exclusion."[31] Under this paradoxical inclusion of the excluded he subsumes not only Schmitt's state of exception but also phenomena that Schmitt would define quite differently. For example, a consideration of the principle of equity (*aequitas*) that supplements the law is, according to Agamben, an exception,[32] as is its Roman institutionalization through the praetorial *ius honorarium*.[33] Furthermore, even regular, codified jurisdiction takes the form of an inclusive exclusion, insofar as the legal prohibition names and consequently integrates its transgression into the law that thus "designates itself as exterior to itself."[34] Punishment by law codifies the transgression as a transgression and thereby integrates it into the legal system by excluding it. The concept of exception, when defined in such broad terms, obviously becomes the clandestine paradigm of every legal order. Consequently, jurisdiction produces nothing but "inclusive exclusions": every judgment is exclusionary, and every exclusion leaves a mark that must continue to remain legible within the marking system, and must therefore circulate within it so as not to lose its effect. This omnipresent confluence of law and exception must be ascribed to a concept of exception that does not differentiate one particular juridical structure from others but is supposed to form the comprehensive matrix of legality. Agamben declares Schmitt's figure to be the essence of any legal order: the law exists by positing itself outside of itself. In doing so it feeds like a vampire on everything it applies itself to, since it consists only of what it can absorb through inclusive exclusion.[35] Consequently, Agamben does not see the *circuli vitiosi* of violence as the opposite of the law; rather, he designates them as the law's primal form. The first manifestation of the law, therefore, is the *lex talionis*, i.e. the vengeance of an "eye for an eye" in which violence always defines itself as counter-violence: "The juridical order does not originally present itself simply as sanctioning a transgressive act but instead constitutes itself through the repetition of the same act without any sanction, that is, as an exceptional case."[36] What many theorists (Réné Girard among them) describe as the law's antithesis, unending revenge,[37] for Agamben is the law in its pure form. He presents the law as a relationship of fatal, unrepealable exchanges with mythical surplus value.

It is via the exception that the law manages to include the entirety of social life within itself and thus to coincide with pure facticity; it is unenforceable and yet always in force, it cannot be formulated and yet becomes the only valid language.[38] The omnipresent state of exception institutes "a situation that is neither one of fact nor one of right,"[39] thereby opening the space in which the positive legal order can prove its efficacy as a modifying force. But the state of exception does not recede once the legal order has been established; rather, it remains constantly present and effective in its regime. The legal order may change but only within the structure established by the exception. When seen from this perspective, the exceptional situation is the fundamental determinant of juridical forms. "The relation of exception thus simply expresses the originary formal structure of the juridical relation."[40] "Formal" in this context also means "semiotic": it is the state of exception that generates the signs with which jurisdiction operates. The state of exception produces ambiguous designations (inclusively exclusive) and thereby bestows precarious identities. It makes legal subjects determinable by means of ambiguous concepts. That is the "pure reference" of the law. The form in which its own constitutive "inclusive exclusion" is perceived by the legal subject itself is that of guilt. The identity of a legal subject is *per se* afflicted with guilt, this guilt being caused neither by deeds committed in the past nor by a sinful interiority. Instead, it represents the manner in which a subject participates in the legal system. (Agamben uses Benjaminian figures in this context as well.)[41] Hence, it is not the norm that establishes the basis of guilt; it is guilt that makes the norm and its transformations possible; guilt is their origin. "Guilt refers not to transgression, that is, to the determination of the licit and the illicit, but to the pure force of the law, to the law's simple reference to something."[42] Another term Agamben uses to describe this relationship is "ban."[43] The law puts everything and everyone under a ban by putting them simultaneously inside and outside the legal order, by abandoning them, and then by reapplying itself to them. The law's primordial form supposes a demand that it is impossible to meet insofar as its transgression is antecedent or, as it were, is *a priori*. Jurisdiction does not terminate this collective guilt but institutionalizes it. The law conquers its domains in the dynamic of the permanent state of exception.[44] Agamben's antinomian terminology strikes one as problematic and even obfuscating in that it equivocally subsumes and homogenizes very heterogeneous objects and hence implies questionable affiliations that may prevent rather than promote insight.[45] But all the same, his Benjaminian concepts of the permanent state of exception and the inclusive exclusion open new perspectives on the relationship between law, life, and language and hence also on the curse.

The curse, defined as both an appeal to and a condemnation by a divine jurisdiction, precisely circumscribes Agamben's "paradox of sovereignty" in the realm of theology: within language, it represents a zone in which it is impossible to differentiate between facticity and divine law. In God's domain, which is that of the most supreme sovereign, His eternal verdict constantly coincides with reality inasmuch as His judgment is identical with the course of the world; but by the same token, God's law also contrasts with this course. As a speech act supplementing the law, the curse expresses this ambiguous relationship, since it simultaneously posits and negates the difference between the world and divine judgment. In this respect, the curse functions as the verbalization of a "ban" (in Agamben's sense) that God as the sovereign imposes upon mankind through his representatives. The "pure reference" of divine law is the medium whose sole appropriate message is the eternal curse that assigns to the subjects their appropriate paradoxical place in creation. It is exactly this paradoxical, interminable status of the curse which forces subjects to be involved in its problematic nature. Similar to the way in which, according to Foucault, the unending confession assumes a decisive role in constituting modern subjects,[46] one can attribute a generative effect on the formations of subjectivity to the entanglement in the curse. Curse and oath split the speaker and the addressee, pitting each against him- or herself. But this split allows them a specific form of self-reference that is mediated through the binding word. Curses belong to the set of instruments that power employs to divide and rule, by objectifying the subject.[47] This can be seen, for example, in the attempt, initiated by state and church authorities during the early modern age, to engage by way of curses and oaths in the serial production of subjectivity *qua* guilt.[48]

In Christian contexts, the power to curse depends on acknowledging God's primordial maledictions—free-floating, quasi-ontological curses that cannot be ascribed to empirical persons—even if these divine curses may merely provide the frame and ritual form for any actual execration. Only the speaker who takes up a divine imprecatory threat hovering over everyone's head and representatively repeats it is capable of pronouncing an effective curse. Subjects may damn their opponents, but only by quoting the word of God. Thus, in every concrete speech situation a curse is re-activated, varied at best, but not invented; in that respect, the curse is a conventional act. Austin's speech-act theory developed in his book *How To Do Things With Words* helps provide a better understanding of those peculiarities of its employment resulting from its paradoxical structure. The curse is doubtless a performative in Austin's sense, it is "doing something by saying something."[49] But due to the ambiguity of the "something" which the curse performs, curses do not fit neatly into Austin's theoretical framework. Austin himself classifies the curse as a "behabitive".[50] According to his definition, it is by means of behabitives that one reacts to the behavior of another and expresses one's attitude toward him or her. The motivation for this uncommented categorization appears to be that the curse is normally seen as a reaction to deeds that the curser considers damnable. But it may be argued that the curse does not necessarily react to the behavior of an antagonist and that, granted the requisite qualifications, it can also be subsumed under the other four of Austin's speech-act categories. The "verdictive" utterance, for example, consists of "the delivering of a finding, official or unofficial, upon evidence or reasons as to value or fact,"[51] as in the rendering of a verdict by jurors. The Bible's first curse, the one pronounced on the Serpent, satisfies, when read in Spinoza's sense,[52] the criterion of a verdictive: "Because thou hast done this, thou art cursed above all cattle, and above every beast of the field" (Gen. 3. 14).[53] God utters the verdict that the Serpent has turned into an accursed animal because it has seduced Eve to eat of the apple. Austin's third speech-act category is the "expositive." Expositive utterances expound arguments and facts, as when one makes a descriptive statement or develops an interpretation.[54] In the curse, however, "world-to-word direction" and "word-to-world direction" are inseparable. The speaker gives a directive by describing something that does not depend on his utterance. The effect and sense of the utterance are obviously correlated; curses situate themselves exactly at the place where these two factors are supposed to converge. That is why the curse often assumes the form of a representation of facts. But maledictions can also, fourthly, be considered "exercitive" speech acts, a term Austin defines somewhat imprecisely as "exercising of powers, rights or influence."[55] The difference between verdictive and exercitive is reduced to that between the jurors' verdict and the sentence of the judge.[56] If one defines the curse as condemnation through divine judgment, one classifies the curse as an exercitive utterance. Consequently, Austin himself subsumes the verdict of excommunication under the exercitives.[57] Lastly, "commissive" speech acts are also contaminated by the curse, commissives being utterances by which one declares an intention or enters into an obligation.[58] If a witness swears an oath in a court of law, he performs a commissive, and an oath, as mentioned above, is a conditional self-condemnation. Curses resist Austin's schema: while derivatives of it can be put into all five of his categories (which are obviously derived from juridical procedures), the curse itself does not really fit into any one of them. That this result also applies to oaths, which are classifiable as a subset of curses, could be easily demonstrated. Austin himself points to the porosity of his categories, but this degree of multivalence of a speech act is unusual. An explanation of its exceptional status will emerge from a more detailed analysis of Austin's theory.

Austin defines the conditions under which a performative act can come about as follows:

> There must exist an accepted conventional procedure having a certain conventional effect, that procedure to include the uttering of certain words by certain persons in certain circumstances, and further, the particular persons and circumstances in a given case must be appropriate for the invocation of the particular procedure invoked.[59]

This statement asserts that performatives are always related to institutions and conventions which legitimize them.[60] This estimation seems incomplete insofar as performatives also contribute to the establishment of institutions and conventions. For example, declarations of independence are instrumental in the constitution of some nations, while decrees help to establish binding norms of behavior, e.g. for judges and juries. One performative, then, supports another performative; they form chains. Can final links in these chains be detected? Austin continues his enumeration of criteria for successful speech acts as follows:

> The procedure must be executed by all participants both correctly and completely. Where, as often, the procedure is designed for use by persons having certain thoughts and feelings, or for the inauguration of certain consequential conduct on the part of any participant, then a person participating in and so invoking the procedure must in fact have those thoughts or feelings, and the participants must intend so to conduct themselves, and further must actually so conduct themselves subsequently.[61]

Particularly the topic addressed in the last sentence—the quality of the performative to obligate its speakers both internally and externally—implies the problematics of the oath and the law. In the final analysis, the speech act guarantees its own effectiveness: it is commissive with regard to itself. When seen from this angle, every performative looks like an oath. Consequently, the term "performance" originally designated, at its inception in the early modern era, the ceremonial execution or discharging of an obligatory action.[62] Curse and oath are thus implicitly intrinsic to the very term "performative act". Oath and curse alike appear as "performatives of the second order". They add themselves, obligatorily and obligingly, to other speech acts and, when uttered explicitly, heighten their performative potential. It can be observed that, as a general practice, their proclamation is added to other speech acts whose perlocutionary effectiveness is in some way problematic, e.g. insofar as they are new and have not as yet been firmly established within the social sphere or, on the contrary, are already outdated.[63]

In the second half of *How To Do Things With Words*, Austin puts forward that performativity is not one particular kind of language use that can be separated from others, but rather underlies all linguistic utterances as their "illocutionary" force. Accordingly, the binding word in its two manifestations could be designated not only as the common property of a certain class of institutionalized or institutionalizing pronouncements but also as the foundation for any authoritative, responsible use of language. Not the extra-linguistic, objective world but the curse/oath implicit in it guarantees the coherence and social relevance of language.[64] Serious utterances generate themselves by solemnly vouching for themselves. Communication in society functions on account of this promise of coherence. Since language makes this pledge of itself, thereby positing itself as an already given entity, it too bypasses the present time in its act of self-constitution. The curse is the reverse side of the never-present unity of language. Modern theories of language with a political orientation frequently emphasize the connective, consensual and consensus-building dimension of language. (Habermas' work could serve as the prime example in this context.)[65] But this bond also latently supposes an exclusionary aspect of language: its persistence as the threat which the curse formulates.[66] It is therefore problematic to suppose a determinable perlocutionary effect of curses: on account of their paradoxical openness, they cannot have any effect that is univocally demonstrable as well as determinable by language. Absolute power and absolute impotence converge in the curse as well as in language. For this reason, it is structurally impossible to disprove or to prove the effectiveness of curses empirically. The failure of a malediction remains forever uncertain because its success can remain hidden or lie in the future. A curse is indeterminable in precisely the same measure that it does not determine. Insofar as the possibility that a speech act fails is one of its constitutive conditions,[67] the curse is not so much a typical speech act as the horizon of all speech acts. Perhaps the political relevance of curses in the modern era has diminished not so much because of their increasing obsolescence and their replacement by more rational speech acts, but because the curse is now taken for granted anyway, as a horizon persisting in latency.

According to Austin, subjects performing a speech act are both internally and externally bound by the performative: "[they] must in fact have those thoughts and feelings [. . .] and further must actually so conduct themselves [as stated]." But Austin is ambivalent in his ranking of inwardness and outwardness. At first, the speech act seems to refer above all to an interior state, insofar as Austin emphasizes that the speaker must consider what he or she has said with an awareness that all its consequences are binding before a performative can be "felicitous." But immediately thereafter he states that the performative does not at all depend on the sincere intentions of the speaker, calling any reference to inwardness "fictitious."[68] For a baptism or a marriage ceremony, even when it is conducted with the best of intentions, is invalid unless the person performing it is authorized to preside over the ceremony. And even though an oath may be sworn erroneously or with fraudulent intent, it nonetheless remains a binding oath: "our word is our bond."[69] It is not the inner attitudes of the speakers but their words and the institutional structures in which these words are embedded that are the decisive factor. However, the apparatus of a binding force inherent in words can only be sustained when, despite this indifference toward subjective attitudes, an inner accountability is posited as a form of addressability, in other words: as a point of reference for an actualizable guilt formulated in the curse. Speech-act theory is a theory about the generation of responsibility. It is, in the end, a theory of how the subject, language, and the law relate to each other.[70]

Insofar as performatives cannot be controlled by their speaker, always say more than one can comprehend, and have unpredictable results (as discussed by Derrida in *Limited Inc*)[71], their theory also describes the limits of responsibility. What takes place beyond these limits? Austin himself declares the theater to be a paradigmatic case of the "unserious" use of performatives since a speech act delivered as part of a dramatic performance binds nobody. The theater and irony are therefore outside the territory Austin has marked as relevant; he excludes them from his theory.[72] But one cannot overlook the fact that in establishing this exclusion of unseriousness he repeatedly quotes from dramatic works. Citing, for example, a remark from Euripides' *Hippolytus*, Austin explains the problematic status of oaths as it pertains to the way they put inwardness and outwardness in relation to each other.[73] He does so even though, following his own argument, the example he uses should be "void."[74] Beyond that, Austin's own text is saturated with theatrical metaphors: for example, he refers to presumed personae that act only within the pure inwardness of the psyche as "offstage performers" "who would duplicate the play,"[75] and designates the hollowing-out of performatives in the theater with Shakespeare's term "sea-change."[76] Drama, then, is inclusively excluded from Austin's theory. Or does his theory rather include itself in a drama? Even if we ignore the fact that "unserious" theater and the most serious of rituals are nowhere cleanly separable from each other—the borderline case of the Eucharistic representation will be discussed in Chapter 1, section 1.1—one circumstance must be taken into account: since a successful performative presupposes and perpetuates existing social conventions, it quotes performative acts that have already taken place. In that respect, the performative mimetically re-enacts a model, and as such it is as dramatic as it is "parasitic."[77] The theatrical aspect that Austin seeks to exclude is, therefore, a necessary part of the performative. In most cases, it is quite impossible to clearly distinguish between the "ordinary circumstances"[78] of an utterance and its "parasitic" appropriation, especially in societies in which representation plays a crucial role (as, e.g. the courtly society of the early modern era). This reveals a fundamental problem in Austin's theory: the "ordinary circumstances," from which he wants to exclude the theater, do not (or at least not yet) exist: they are an idealized construct to which nothing in the real use of language corresponds. To this day, there exists no path that would actually lead language out of a culture's theatrical spaces of representation. The very word "speech act" implies "acting;" and it may be no coincidence that Shakespeare seems to have been the one who first used this word to denote a performance by theatrical players.[79]

Since his own theory often confronts Austin with this fact, he cannot exclude the theater completely from his reflections; hence, he surrounds it with negations[80] whose ironic dimension Shoshana Felman has analyzed.[81] In this context, where does Austin locate the significant difference between theatrical and "ordinary" rituals? Why exactly does he consider a theatrical ritual to be constitutively unsuccessful, "hollow and void?"[82] In a different context and using his conditions for success (quoted above), Austin defines various ways in which performances can fail. It is obvious that theater in a narrow sense can be designated above all as a specific form of failure. The condition that it does not fulfill is that "the particular persons and circumstances in a given case must be appropriate for the invocation of the particular procedure invoked." Without referring more explicitly to the theater, Austin calls this kind of failure "misplay":[83] a performative pattern for acting exists, but it has no binding power since the persons involved are not authorized to enact it, or the circumstances under which it is performed are the wrong ones.[84] This non-fulfillment on the stage, however, is intentional, it is indeed the very condition of theater. The boundaries between "felicity" and "misplay," then, within the theater create complex, ambiguous patterns—picture puzzles, as it were. Many of the most exemplary performative acts which Austin enumerates tend to assume key roles, for instance, in Shakespeare's plays: oaths, bequests, promises of marriage, condemnations, curses. Nearly all of these acts in one way or another turn out to be failures even within the diegetic plot, and their different types of failing determine the course of the play. In this manner, the insufficient binding power of the theatrical performatives is represented by the plays themselves, often as an insufficiency intrinsic to the speech acts themselves, so that the distinction between reality and theatrical "misplay" appears to have been shifted into the interior of the representation. Shakespeare's theater exploits the aporetic structure of linguistic obligations in a way that makes the clear boundary between "parasitic" and "ordinary" utterances dissolve. Austin's text raises the question if the play thus ceases to be a "misplay," but does not provide an answer.

Is it possible, despite the diffuse boundaries of the theater, to pinpoint a characteristic feature of the speech acts executed during a stage performance by an actor in accordance with his role? Mary Louise Pratt has taken some first steps toward an integration of the theatrical situation into speech-act theory. To this end, she demands the conceptual inclusion of the specifically theatrical "context" of such a situation, a context that would lend to performatives a qualifying index, as it were. But it is problematic that Pratt's representation of this context decisively simplifies the complicated analysis of this speech situation: she sets up a number of implicit rules that supposedly structure the relationship between the actors and their audience. This network of rules amounts to a contract whose essential agreement is the following: the spectator surrenders nearly all opportunities for interfering in a represented situation, and in return he expects to be entertained passively by the actor in order to evaluate this entertainment afterward, privately and publicly.[85] One notices again that the description of a situation in terms of Austinian speech-act theory conceptualizes it as a specific assemblage of obligations. But the insufficiency of Pratt's rules is quite obvious, too: situations outside the theater can be imagined to which Pratt's definition applies, and situations inside the theater can be singled out to which Pratt's definition does not apply. Among other things, one might point out here—as a further "parasitic" deviation—the fact that some performances of the twentieth century offensively frustrate their public's supposed demand for entertainment. More importantly, does the theatrical situation not call regularly for diverse forms of audience participation, among them the display of approval and financial support? Can the rights which the public and the actors claim for themselves in the theatrical contract really be conclusively determined? Pratt does not answer the question persuasively. Moreover, other relationships determine the theatrical speech-act situation, beside that between actors and spectators. It should be clarified, for instance, which rules regulate the behavior of actors among themselves and the behavior of spectators among themselves, how actors and their public relate to those persons and institutions who in various ways are responsible for the theater (e.g. dramatists, producers, companies), etc. This list of contexts which determine the theatrical speech situation could be extended almost indefinitely. Derrida found a formula for this problem: "context is never absolutely determinable."[86] Since every utterance has the potential of breaking with its context in order to generate its own,[87] the distinction between utterance and context collapses. Therefore, a contextualization of theatrical speech acts can take place only as a comparison with other speech acts, as their reciprocal reception history. The following investigation proceeds along this line: connections between speech acts are modeled on the basis of transmitted texts. Owing to the complexities of the topic, this project can only be carried out selectively, through a historically and geographically limited comparison of various instances of the speech-act "curse" inside and outside of what is officially designated as theater.

The following study concentrates above all on curses in Shakespeare's royal dramas, i. e. mainly his Histories, because in these plays the structures of the curse stand out with an extraordinary, almost dazzling clarity. The reason for the exemplary status of these plays can probably be found in the epistemic situation of that time, among other factors: According to Foucault's *The Order of Things*, thought in Shakespeare's time—the end of the sixteenth and beginning of the seventeenth century—is shaped by an oscillation between two ordering systems, namely the disintegrating one of similitude and the still developing one of representation.[88] Foucault describes the sign systems of the sixteenth century somewhat sweepingly as a network of similarities within which it is not possible to draw clear distinctions between the things of the world and the linguistic signs embedded in them.[89] As Foucault himself does not explain but his sources (among them Paracelsus and della Porta) sufficiently show,[90] it is precisely this intertwining that is also seen as a reason for the effectiveness of sacral performatives. At the turn of the seventeenth century, that is to say, at a time which Foucault refers to as "the Baroque," a different attitude becomes predominant. It no longer presumes pre-established connections between language and world, but proceeds from the assumption that their relations will first have to be constituted "through an act of cognition."[91] A dynamic, but rational order of signs differentiates itself out of the world of things and now appears as "thinking *per se*." Language no longer is a signature pervading and governing objects; it is a system by which one can compare what exists and arrange it within a mental tableau, i.e. represent it.[92] It is through the correct arrangement of the signs in a representational tableau that the true order of the world reveals itself. In the background of this *episteme*, however, an unresolved tension is at work: on the one hand, the signs are supposed to open a completely transparent view on the things they represent so that the represented seems to rest at the very core of the representation, but, on the other hand, the representing sign must nonetheless indicate that it is nothing more than a sign and not the thing itself.[93] This unresolved conflict between presence and reference pervades the order of representation: it "is at the same time *indication* and *appearance*; a relation to an object and a manifestation of itself."[94] In the seventeenth century, exactly this tension between referring and appearing is being enacted in diverse self-representations of power, as Foucault shows by way of Velázquez's *Las Meninas*.[95] During the Baroque, the space of representation in general becomes the place where truth is performed,[96] and *The Order of Things*—as Foucault himself puts it—retroactively provides the "dramaturgy" for this performance.[97] During the transition from the sixteenth to the seventeenth century, however, when representation has not yet fully separated itself from similitude, the new stage of truth often appears merely as a disconcerting and somewhat ghostly hall of mirrors. The illusory status of similitude as well as the self-contradictory status of representation become apparent in this time of transition. By this phenomenon, Foucault tries to explain the Baroque fascination with allegory and the *mise en abyme* which express themselves, for example, in the insistent figure "of the theater that duplicates itself by representing another play."[98] It seems logical that the ambiguous structure of the theater as well as that of the curse stand out most distinctly at this point of epistemic fracture, where old conditions of performative acts become visible in new ways.

Stephen Greenblatt's "New Historicism," and especially his *Shakespearean Negotiations*, concentrate on the analysis of this implicitly theatrical tension of public discourses at the turn of the seventeenth century, and on the consequent overdetermined status of Shakespearean theater. It is perhaps for this reason that Greenblatt has repeatedly named Foucault as a decisive influence on his work.[99] Greenblatt examines the complex of tensions between signification and manifestation in Shakespeare's theater, comprehending their oscillation as a symptom of diverse cultural exchange and appropriation processes.[100] These processes which also elevate the theater into the position of a prominent absolute metaphor,[101] he attributes to England's social development (whereas Foucault in *The Order of Things* is notably reticent about such political contextualizing). Accordingly, under the auspices of emerging capitalism (which induced the emergence of commercial theater) feudal, liturgical, and other obligations perpetuate themselves despite their obvious obsolescence or mutual incompatibility. Therefore, these obligations are best understood as theatrical affairs. For example, representational festivities and props of royal sovereignty as well as the spectacular punishment of public enemies are the foundation for Tudor and Stuart claims of divine kingship.[102] At the transition point of post-Reformation theater, these untimely obligations are, on the one hand, exposed as empty; on the other, their tenacious forms and formulas are perpetuated and given a new home, which keeps them both problematizable and profitable. Accepting Greenblatt's suppositions, the following study conceptualizes Shakespeare's dramas as repositories of excessive and transitional performatives, adding to this the assumption that the plays systematically exhaust the representational potential of these symbolic actions. To put it schematically, Shakespeare's strategy consists first of marking out the boundaries between theater and non-theater as often as possible and then of overstepping them—within the drama and by way of the drama. Orders of representation or similitude are appropriated and sublated by their mirroring in the play. In this respect, Shakespeare is "*bon à penser*"[103] due to an attitude that Keats has called his "negative capability,"[104] but that one could also, somewhat less romantically, designate as the "overwhelming opportunism" of his dramas. This opportunism, essential for the theater's survival during the early modern era, Shakespeare strategically pushes to an extreme which makes it possible to test the capacities of the institution. This implies that the plays do not simply depict societal developments taking place elsewhere. Instead, they should be regarded as strategic interventions in an unstable political and epistemic situation which unfolds in the drama, becoming recognizable in the process.

Above, it has been implied that the curse *per se* can be seen as an eminently theatrical speech act insofar as it affirms the course of the world and at the same time denies it, that is to say: it "performs" it by way of recontextualization. Its ambiguous representation within Shakespeare's plays not only makes it possible to understand the curse as theatrical, but also implies that, in many respects, the ritual of execration might be seen as a dark precursor of theater itself, indicating, for instance, that the latter has evolved to a high degree through an engagement with the problem of the curse and its derivatives. It is this relationship of mutual dependence which is displayed in the drama of the early modern era; both the curse and theatrical speech under these circumstances appear as paradoxical and marginal entities that nonetheless constitute a horizon of binding performatives. Hence, when one examines the history of ceremonial cursing and its relation to the process of secularization in the early modern era, one is persistently confronted with the problem of the curse's reception and adaptation in the developing theater form. In this context, another question arises: to what extent can the curse assume a new role in the social conflicts of the modern era, not despite but precisely because of its questionable, aporetic and theatrical status?

The study concentrates on Shakespeare's royal dramas (that is, the Histories as well as *King Lear*, *Macbeth* and *Hamlet*), because these plays deal with the problems that the curse raises in a particularly intense and pregnant manner.[105] As supplemental background material, diverse literary, juridical, religious, and political sources will be used. In this connection, it may be remarked that the topic of cursing is a relatively neglected area of research. To be sure, the typology and terminology of execrations in ancient and medieval literature have been investigated.[106] But there is still much to be said about their use in the modern era, post-Reformation England providing exemplary material for their analysis under the auspices of speech-act theory. At the time in question, curses function as remainders which, after the abolition of the rites into which they were firmly integrated, i.e. after the dissolution of the English Catholic Church, become apparently placeless and redundant, but continue to play an important role precisely in their marginalized position. After the Reformation opposes the spiritual monopolies of the Roman Church, secured through its power of excommunication, sacral speech acts like curses are characterized in Protestant pamphlets and polemics as somewhat disreputable, powerless, and ridiculous instruments.[107] But at the same time, curses are redistributed over the social field and re-embedded in customs and institutions, which in novel ways divide them into legitimate and illegitimate, persecuting the latter. In this course, various societal powers try to impose different divisions, as the studies by Keith Thomas and others have shown.[108] Curses, even more so than during the Middle Ages, become a religious, political, and epistemic problem, since they situate themselves in a yet more insecure and embattled epistemic field. Particularly in English theologico-political literature of the sixteenth and early seventeenth centuries, there is a proliferation of texts containing curses or pertaining to curses, while at the same time questioning their efficacy and intensifying attempts to control them *extra ecclesiam*.[109] The question of who is and is not allowed to curse elicits a controversial discussion in which maledictions are not only refuted or forced back, but also cited and employed in exactly this problematic form and in exactly these attempts to suppress them. The curse is appropriated and used in new contexts where, despite its obvious dysfunctionality and hollowness, it is carried along by contemporary discourse. It may be a symptom of this apparent ambivalence that even the rhetorical literature of that era contains detailed treatments of cursing—for the first time in the history of rhetoric.[110] While the rhetorical literature of the ancient world and that of the Middle Ages pays only short and superficial attention to cursing, the English rhetoricians of the Renaissance, above all Henry Peacham, define the pronouncement of a curse as a figure of speech in its own right.[111] It seems appropriate that Sir Philip Sidney concludes his *Defense of Poesy* with a pedagogical and redundant curse directed against those who disdain the arts of language and poetry.[112]

In the course of these problematizations, rearrangements, incorporations and negotiations, the curse finds its true locus in Shakespearean theater: it appears there in its true form as a revenant residue, its own specter, so to speak, the symptom of a persistent, unending past.

In the early modern speech situation,[113] this theatrical curse is ideally suited to unfolding the aporetic, crypto-theatrical structures of christologically legitimated kingship and of a jurisdiction supported by theology. In that symptomatic function, Shakespeare seizes on various curse forms, appropriates them and their history for his use, and reworks them. This study considers these reworkings as pragmatic projects: theater is not to be understood as a free arena for the activity of the poetic genius, in which Shakespeare's all-encompassing spirit can reveal and redeem the virtuality of early modern humankind; rather, theater is to be seen as an institution that must arrange and embed its speech acts in very specific ways if it wants to survive and perpetuate itself. For this reason, the following discussion will focus on the productive constraints imposed on the commercial theater of the Elizabethan epoch—in accordance with the Foucauldian supposition that the theatrical situation constitutes itself first and foremost in relation to these constraints. Hence, Shakespeare's curse texts can be studied not only as historical documents that more or less accurately depict independently unfolding social developments, among them transformations of liturgy and jurisdiction. Rather, the plays can be read as strategic interventions within these processes.[114] Theater is an arena in which power constitutes itself. In this respect, it is a supplement of law, not its polar opposite. Shakespeare's theater has to work against the traditional apparatuses of power, but it must also (in part mimetically) connect with them in order to stay in business. The plays can be described, as will have to be shown, as resultants of the interplay of these compulsions, above all from the interconnected pressures exerted by three vectors: the court, the church, and the market. Shakespeare, one of the first capitalist dramatists (in the playwright Heiner Müller's formulation: a "Shakespeare Factory"),[115] uses the theater to produce the need for more theater, and for this purpose appropriates the speech acts of other institutions, actualizing them in the process despite their undeniable obsolescence. Thus, Shakespeare's plays mark an important point of articulation in the history of cursing, which from its very beginning has been a reception history.

Even though other plays by Shakespeare and his contemporaries will be occasionally referred to, the following study is devoted primarily to *Richard III*, *King John* and *King Lear*[116] because the aforementioned shifts in the use of cursing during the late sixteenth and early seventeenth century can be shown most distinctly in these three plays. They enact an increasing dispersion and deregulation of the curse in which the removal of fixed liturgical formulas leads to the unfolding of its paradoxical structure and finally to its reification in the form of "fateful stage props." As Shakespeare represents this modernization, his dramas undergo a retrograde movement in time, from the nearly contemporaneous king Richard III through the John of the High Middle Ages to Antiquity's Lear, as if the depiction of the curse as a deprivation of the present made increasing parts of the future and the past collapse into each other. The study of this process will be structured by the various forms and formulas of maledictory speech acts, most of them closely connected or overlapping. Each speech act is provisionally apportioned to a *dramatis persona*, or rather vice versa: the protagonist stands in for the functions and the theatrical potential of his or her assigned speech act, rather than the other way around. As incarnations of the curse, the Devil, the fateful stage prop, and the theater itself will also make appearances and articulate unresolved political paradoxes and religious mortgages of the modern era in the (after-)life of the malediction. Again and again, surprising links between the history of theology, of theater and of law will become observable and show that Shakespeare's performances of the curse can serve as ideal index fossils[117] of a secularization overpowered by its mythic latencies.

Notes

1 Karl Beth, 'Fluch', in Hanns Bächtold-Stäubli (ed.), *Handbuch des deutschen Aberglaubens*, vol. 2, Berlin/Leipzig 1930, p. 1636; Michael Belgrader, 'Fluch, Fluchen, Flucher', in Kurt Ranke (ed.), *Enzyklopädie des Märchens*, vol. 4, Berlin/New York, NY 1984, p. 1316; Kenneth Gross, *Shakespeare's Noise*, Chicago, IL/London 2001, p. 162.

2 Wolfgang Speyer, 'Fluch', in Theodor Klauser (ed.), *Reallexikon für Antike und Christentum*, vol. 7, Stuttgart 1969, p. 1161; Jan Assmann, 'When Justice Fails. Jurisdiction and Imprecation in Ancient Egypt and the Near East', *Journal of Egyptian Archaeology* 78, 1992, pp. 149–162.

3 See Jacques Derrida, 'Declarations of Independence', translated by Tom Keenan and Tom Pepper, *New Political Science* 15, 1986, pp. 7–15.

4 James Augustus Henry Murray, Henry Bradley [et al.] (eds), *The Oxford English Dictionary*, first edition, vol. 2, Oxford 1933, p. 1273.

5 Eckhard Meineke, 'Fluch', in Johannes Hoops (ed.), *Reallexikon der Germanischen Altertumskunde*, vol. 9, Berlin/New York, NY 1995, p. 239–240.

6 See John S. Kselman, 'Curse and Blessing', in Paul J. Achtermeier (ed.), *Harper's Bible Dictionary*, San Francisco, CA 1985, p. 198.

7 On these concepts, see Walter Benjamin, 'Critique of Violence', in *Selected Writings*, Michael Jennings (general ed.), vol. I, translated by Edmund Jephcott, Cambridge, MA 1996, pp. 238–252.

8 Even Thomas Hobbes, for example, still considers the taking of an oath as the only possibility of arriving at a binding consensus in places where the law is not yet firmly established. (Thomas Hobbes, *Leviathan*, Oxford [et al.] 1998, p. 94.)

9 Jacques Derrida, *Of Grammatology*, translated by Gayatri Spivak, Baltimore, MD 1976, pp. 144–145.

10 Derrida, *Of Grammatology*, ibid.

11 Derrida, *Of Grammatology*, op. cit., p. 314.

12 The oath also always refers to another oath (e.g. the New Covenant) and is situated between creation and affirmation.

13 Derrida, *Of Grammatology*, op. cit., p. 314.

14 The impossibility of clearly attributing biblical curses to specific speakers is discussed with exemplary lucidity in Norbert Lohfink, 'Moab oder Sichem – Wo wurde Dtn. 28 nach der Fabel des Deuteronomiums proklamiert?', in F. García Martínez and A. Hilshorst (eds), *Studies in Deuteronomy. In Honor of C. J. Labuschagne on the Occasion of his 65th Birthday*, Leiden/New York, NY/Cologne 1994, pp. 139–153.

15 On this concept, see Jürgen Habermas, 'Discourse Ethics: Notes on a Program of Philosophical Justification', in *Moral Consciousness and Communicative Action*,

Cambridge, MA 1990, section III: 'Discourse Ethics and Its Bases in Action Theory', pp. 43–115; 80.

16 This means that the curse, being both ahead of itself and its own presupposition, always produces a surplus of meaning that makes it uncontrollable. On a similar figure, see Werner Hamacher, 'Afformative, Strike: Benjamin's Critique of Violence', in Andrew E. Benjamin and Peter Osborne (eds), *Walter Benjamin's Philosophy: Destruction and Experience*, London/New York, NY 1994, pp. 110–138.

17 Derrida, 'Declarations', pp. 10–11.

18 Louis Althusser, 'Ideology and Ideological State Apparatuses', in *Lenin and Philosophy and Other Essays*, translated by Ben Brewster, New York, NY/London 1971, pp. 173–175.

19 Marcus Twellmann, *Das Drama der Souveränität*, München 2004, pp. 59–61.

20 Ernst Friesenhahn, *Der politische Eid*, Darmstadt 1979.

21 Alternatively, the concept of the "ritual curse" is used, even though the very broad concept of "ritual" allows little differentiation, given the current status of its theoretical discussion. I use "ritual" as well as "ceremony" above all to designate institutionalized acts that involve a reference to the deity. The heritage that colors the concept both of ritual and of ceremony during the early modern age also has to be considered in this context: the terms "ceremony" and "ritual" emerge during the Reformation and are first used in an altogether pejorative sense: they designate the empty sacred acts of the members of other confessions. (Edward Muir, *Ritual in Early Modern Europe*, Cambridge 1997, p. 167.)

22 Gerhard Thür, 'Oaths and Dispute Settlement in Ancient Law', in Lin Foxhall and Andrew D. E. Lewis (eds), *Greek Law in its Political Setting*, Oxford 1996, pp. 57–72.

23 Daniel Ogden, 'Binding Spells: Curse Tablets and Voodoo Dolls in the Greek and Roman Worlds', in Bengt Ankarloo and Stuart Clark (eds), *Witchcraft and Magic in Europe*, vol. 2, *Ancient Greece and Rome*, London 1999, p. 78.

24 An example is the Athenians' curse on Philip V of Macedonia: "the people passed a motion [. . .] that the public priests, as often as they offered prayers [. . .] should so often curse and execrate Philip [. . .]." (Livy, *History of Rome*; vol. IX (Book xxxi–xxxiv) Cambridge 1967, pp. 127–128.)

25 "To show you that he also lies under your curse [. . .] – recite the curse laid down by the law. Take it and read it – [the text of the curse itself has not been preserved] – that's what the herald prays on your behalf, as required by law, and also in the presence of the Boulé, whenever it sits." (Demosthenes, *On the False Embassy (Oration 19)*, translated by Douglas M. MacDowell, New York, NY 2000, p. 80.)

26 For this reason the curser uses rhetorical devices to make the curse appear as a collective undertaking. Curses are seldom uttered in the first person singular ("I curse you . . .); generally, neutral, indicative or optative forms are preferred, most often a passive perfect participle ("Cursed is/be . . .").

27 Niklas Luhmann, *Law as Social System*, Oxford/New York, NY 2004, p. 157. A surprisingly affirmative reference to Benjamin's 'Critique of Violence', albeit with a "sociologist's general reservation" can be found in Luhmann's 'Die Theorie der Ordnung und die natürlichen Rechte', *Rechtshistorisches Journal*, Heft 3, 1984, p. 145.

28 Benjamin, 'Critique of Violence', op. cit., p. 248.

29 Carl Schmitt, *Political Theology. Four Chapters on the Concept of Sovereignty*, translated by George Schwab, Cambridge/London 1985, p. 13.

30 Schmitt, ibid. p. 5.

31 Giorgio Agamben, *Homo Sacer. Sovereign Power and Bare Life*, translated by Daniel Heller-Roazen, Stanford, CA 1998, p. 21.

32 Agamben, ibid. p. 17.

33 Agamben, ibid. p. 23.

34 Agamben, ibid. p. 18.

35 Agamben, ibid. p. 27.

36 Agamben, ibid. p. 26.
37 René Girard, *Violence and the Sacred*, translated by Patrick Gregory, Baltimore, MD 1977.
38 Giorgio Agamben, *The Time that Remains. A Commentary on the Letter to the Romans*, translated by Patricia Dailey, Stanford, CA 2005, pp. 105–106.
39 Agamben, *Homo Sacer*, op. cit., p. 18.
40 Agamben, *Homo Sacer*, op. cit., p. 19.
41 Walter Benjamin, 'Fate and Character', in *Selected Writings*, vol. I, translated by Edmund Jephcott, pp. 201–206.
42 Agamben, *Homo Sacer*, op. cit., p. 27.
43 Agamben, *Homo Sacer*, op. cit., pp. 28–29.
44 According to Agamben, the order established by positive law increasingly reduces itself in modernity to the bare mask of the state of exception, which the latter threatens to take off in order to reveal its face of absolute violence. Agamben sees the extralegal space of the camp (above all the National Socialist concentration camp) as paradigmatic for this development in that the camp is the place where no law other than the pure form of the law, i.e. the state of exception, rules (Agamben, *Homo Sacer*, op. cit., pp. 166–180).
45 For example, in an essay from 1995 Agamben dignifies the frustrated perplexity of leftist Italian intellectuals after the rise of Berlusconi by approximating it to the traumatized silence of Auschwitz survivors. With such ideologemes Agamben's thought takes rather dubious forms. See Giorgio Agamben, *Means Without End: Notes on Politics*, translated by Vincenzo Binetti and Cesare Casarino, Minneapolis, MN 2000, p. 121.
46 Michel Foucault, *The History of Sexuality*, vol. I: *An Introduction*, translated by Robert Hurley, New York, NY 1978.
47 Michel Foucault, 'The Subject and Power', in Hubert L. Dreyfus and Paul Rabinow (eds), *Michel Foucault: Beyond Structuralism and Hermeneutics*, Chicago, IL 1983, p. 208.
48 See Chapter 1, section 1. 3.
49 John Langshaw Austin, *How To Do Things With Words*, Cambridge, MA 2003, p. 6.
50 Austin, ibid. p. 160.
51 Austin, ibid. p. 153.
52 Benedict de Spinoza, *Theological-Political Treatise*, translated by Michael Silverthorne and Jonathan Israel, Cambridge 2007; see Chapter 4: "On the divine law", especially pp. 62–63 and 65.
53 All quotes from the Bible will follow the King James Version in order to accentuate possible assonances between Shakespeare's dramas and the biblical texts. This translation has closer affinities to Shakespeare's own time than, for example, such already publicly circulating (and in essential parts identical) versions as the Geneva Bible and the Bishop's Bible.
54 Austin, op. cit., p. 161.
55 Austin, op. cit., p. 151.
56 Austin, op. cit., p. 155.
57 Austin, op. cit., p. 155.
58 Austin, op. cit., pp. 151–152.
59 Austin, op. cit., p. 14–15.
60 This institutional dimension is a bit neglected but not superseded in Austin's re-classification of speech acts in his later lectures as locutionary, illocutionary and perlocutionary.
61 Austin, op. cit., p. 15.
62 Jean-Christophe Agnew, *Worlds Apart. The Market and the Theater in Anglo-American Thought, 1550–1750*, Cambridge, MA 1986, p. 82.
63 On this, see Brenda Danet and Bryna Bogoch, 'Whoever Alters this, May God Turn His Face from Him on the Day of Judgment', *Journal of American Folklore*, 105 (416), 1992, p. 144.

64 On a similar idea, see Agamben, *The Time that Remains*, op. cit., pp. 131–133.
65 Jürgen Habermas, *The Theory of Communicative Action*, translated by Thomas McCarthy, Boston, MA 1984–1987.
66 See for example Geoffrey Hartmann, *Saving the Text*, London 1981, pp. 118–120.
67 Austin, op. cit., pp. 14–16, and passim.
68 Austin, op. cit., p. 10.
69 Austin, op. cit., p. 10. Stanley Cavell has already pointed out the "fatal curse" implicit in this constellation. See Stanley Cavell, *Philosophical Passages. Wittgenstein, Austin, Derrida*, Oxford/Cambridge, MA 1995, p. 62.
70 Jacques Derrida, *Limited Inc*, translated by Samuel Weber, Evanston, IL 1988, p. 97.
71 Derrida, *Limited Inc*, ibid. and passim.
72 Austin, op. cit., p. 22.
73 Austin, op. cit., p. 9.
74 Cavell shows that Austin himself must have been aware of this inner tension in his theory. See Cavell, op. cit., p. 79.
75 Austin, op. cit., p. 10.
76 Austin, op. cit., p. 22. On this and further examples, see also J. Hillis Miller, *Speech Acts in Literature*, Stanford, CA 2001, pp. 35–36.
77 Austin, op. cit., p. 22; again, see Derrida, *Limited Inc*, op. cit., passim.
78 Austin, op. cit., p. 22.
79 Agnew, op. cit., p. 98.
80 Sigmund Freud, 'Negation', in *The Standard Edition of the Complete Psychological Works of Sigmund Freud*, vol. xix, translated by James Strachey, London 1953, pp. 233–239.
81 Shoshana Felman, *The Scandal of the Speaking Body. Don Juan with J. L. Austin, or Seduction in Two Languages*, translated by Catherine Porter, Stanford, CA 2003.
82 Austin, op. cit., p. 22.
83 Austin, op. cit., pp. 17–18.
84 Austin, op. cit., pp. 15/17.
85 Mary Louise Pratt, *Toward a Speech Act Theory of Literary Discourse*, Bloomington, IL/London 1977, p. 113.
86 Derrida, *Limited Inc*, op. cit., p. 3.
87 Derrida, *Limited Inc*, op. cit., p. 12.
88 Michel Foucault, *The Order of Things. An Archaeology of the Human Sciences*, New York, NY 1970, p. 51. On the decline of similitudes, see also Anselm Haverkamp, *Metapher. Die Ästhetik in der Rhetorik*, München 2007, pp. 127–128. On the epistemic situation in Shakespeare's time according to Foucault, see also Malcolm Evans, *Signifying Nothing. Truth's True Contents in Shakespeare's Texts*, Hemel Hempstead 1989, p. 106.
89 Foucault, *The Order of Things*, op. cit., p. 66.
90 Hans Blumenberg, *Die Lesbarkeit der Welt*, Frankfurt a. M. 1986, pp. 69–70.
91 Foucault, *The Order of Things*, op. cit., p. 59.
92 Foucault, *The Order of Things*, op. cit., p. 79.
93 Foucault, *The Order of Things*, op. cit., p. 65. See also François Wahl, 'Die Philosophie diesseits und jenseits des Strukturalismus', in François Wahl (ed.), *Einführung in den Strukturalismus*, Frankfurt a. M. 1973, p. 346.
94 Foucault, *The Order of Things*, op. cit., p. 65.
95 Foucault, *The Order of Things*, op. cit., pp. 3–16.
96 Foucault, *The Order of Things*, op. cit., p. 95.
97 Michel Foucault, *Dits et Écrits II. 1976–1988*, edited by Daniel Defert and François Ewald, Paris 1994, p. 574.
98 Foucault, *The Order of Things*, op. cit., p. 51.
99 See for example Stephen Greenblatt, 'Towards a Poetics of Culture', in H. Aram Veeser (ed.), *The New Historicism*, London/New York, NY 1989, p. 1.
100 Stephen Greenblatt, *Shakespearean Negotiations*, Berkeley/Los Angeles, CA 1988, pp. 8–10.

101 On the concept of "absolute metaphor," see Hans Blumenberg, *Paradigms for a Metaphorology*, translated by Robert Savage, Ithaca, NY 2010, pp. 5, 14–17.
102 Greenblatt, *Shakespearean Negotiations*, op. cit., p. 64.
103 See Claude Lévi-Strauss, *Le Totémisme aujourd'hui*, Paris 1965, p. 128.
104 John Keats, 'Letter to George and Tom Keats, December 1817' in *The Major Works*, Oxford 2001, p. 370.
105 It can only be pointed out here that sequences of execrations are also found frequently in other literary genres of that time, for example in John Donne's poem 'The Curse', in *The Complete English Poems*, London 1996, pp. 50–51.
106 See, for example, Daniel Ogden, op. cit.; Willy Schottroff, *Der altisraelitische Fluchspruch*, Neukirchen-Vluyn 1969; Lester K. Little, *Benedictine Maledictions. Liturgical Cursing in Romanesque France*, Ithaca, NY/London 1993.
107 See Chapter 1, section 1.2.
108 Keith Thomas, *Religion and the Decline of Magic. Studies in Popular Beliefs in Sixteenth- and Seventeenth-Century England*, London 1991. See Chapter 1, section 1.2.
109 See Ashley Montagu, *The Anatomy of Swearing*, Philadelphia, PA 2001, pp. 159–161: "The printed works against swearing published between 1601 and 1650, from broadsides to books, numbered many hundreds."
110 See for example George Puttenham, *The Arte of English Poesie*, Kent, OH 1970, pp. 23, 71–72.
111 Henry Peacham, *The Garden of Eloquence*, Historisch-kritische Einleitung, edited and translated by Beate-Maria Koll, Frankfurt a. M. 1996, p. 68; Dietmar Till, 'Execratio', in Gert Ueding (ed.), *Historisches Wörterbuch der Rhetorik*, vol. 3. Tübingen 1996, pp. 181–182.
112 Philip Sidney, 'The Defense of Poesy', in Gavin Alexander (ed.), *Sidney's 'Defense of Poesy' and Selected Renaissance Literary Criticism*, London 2004, p. 54.
113 On this concept of "Sprachsituation," see Hans Blumenberg, 'Sprachsituation und immanente Poetik', in *Ästhetische und metaphorologische Schriften*, Frankfurt a. M. 2001, pp. 120–135.
114 This study will devote only limited attention to the question how accurately Shakespeare's rewriting of history portrays the ancient and medieval periods during which his monarchs reigned. The following discussions are not concerned with "how it really was" in Richard's III time, for example, not even for the purpose of denouncing Shakespeare's propagandistic manipulations. It may be interesting in places to thematize the difference between the representation of history in the plays and in current or ancient historiography; the effort of systematically unraveling these differences, however, would be of limited value for several reasons, foremost among them the fact that Shakespeare's plays themselves indicate that their historical sources are only used as processed material. (See e.g. Ivo Kamps, *Historiography and Ideology in Stuart Drama*, Cambridge/New York, NY 1996, p. 110 ff.)
115 Heiner Müller, *Shakespeare Factory 1*, Berlin 1996.
116 The dramas are quoted from the Arden edition. In cases of textual uncertainty, I have also consulted *The Norton Shakespeare* and *The First Folio of Shakespeare. The Norton Facsimile*; in the analysis of *King Lear* I focus on the "darker" text of the Folio edition.
117 On this concept, see Hans Blumenberg, 'Prospect for a Theory of Nonconceptuality', in his *Shipwreck with Spectator. Paradigm of a Metaphor for Existence*, translated by Stephen Rendall, Cambridge, MA/London 1997, p. 82: "[. . .] metaphors are fossils that indicate an archaic stratum [. . .]."

CHAPTER 1

Richard III and the ostracized heritage of theater

1.1 Anne and the supplement of the Eucharist

When the protagonists of Shakespeare's *Richard III* utter curses, they often emphasize the fact that these maledictory formulas have been approved or instituted by a higher authority; they even try to assimilate themselves to this process of institution. In I. iii, for example, Richard states that his father's legitimate curses against Margaret coincide with the Almighty's curse, so that they announce as well as execute a divine judgment:

> RICHARD: His curses then, from bitterness of soul
> Denounc'd against thee, are all fall'n upon thee,
> And God, not we, hath plagu'd thy bloody deed.
>
> (I. iii. 179–181)

As the following discussion will explicate, this form of officially establishing a curse points back to a figure of institutionalizing legitimate imprecations that dominated Shakespeare's time, namely Christ's founding of the Church by way of the Last Supper. Just like the illocution of the curse, so the illocutionary component of the "*Hoc est corpus meum*" in the worship service is overdetermined: through transubstantiation it changes bread and wine into the body of God's son and thereby ritually repeats a foundational act that not only institutes a continuum between God and man, but is also supposed to unify the Christians among themselves. Through the covenant of communion, the Church establishes itself as Christ's body which virtually comprises all of mankind. (This universal metonymy is itself denoted by a metonymic concept, since "Eucharist" means "giving thanks" and originally referred to the prayer of thanksgiving that preceeded communion.)[1] In spite of its claim to originality, this performative act, foundational for many theological and legal conventions, quotes and perpetuates older conventions (especially the Jewish Passover meal). The Eucharist, no less than the curse and the blessing, is always derivative: it echoes old covenants and tries to absorb them metonymically. It functions as a sacrament and as the origin of all sacraments; but insofar as it institutes a "primordial signifier,"[2] it is also the indirect origin of the historically variable dogma to which the faithful are sworn when they take communion.[3] In the Eucharist, the word is instituted through the Word, and the body of the congregation closes itself around this act of institution.

But an act of expulsion supplements this sanctifying institution. Besides the inclusionary, blissful workings of the Eucharist, an exclusionary, condemning dimension of its efficacy is implied. Bread and wine serve as bearers of Christ's spirit, and their consumption fills the faithful with this spirit. But if members of the congregation are unworthy to receive the Eucharist, they become guilty and God's Supper turns into a divine judgment that makes them ill or kills them, as Paul had already pointed out in his first letter to the Corinthians:

> Wherefore whosoever shall eat this bread, and drink this cup of the Lord, unworthily, shall be guilty of the body and blood of the Lord. But let a man examine himself, and so let him eat of that bread, and drink of that cup. For he that eateth and drinketh unworthily, eateth and drinketh damnation to himself, not discerning the Lord's body. For this cause many are weak and sickly among you, and many sleep.
>
> (1 Cor. 11. 27–30)

"Sleep" in this context is a euphemism for "death."[4] And it is in accordance with this doctrine that the Gospel narratives on the institution of the Eucharist were always interpreted: all disciples participated in the Eucharist, but Judas only received it to his ruin.[5] This official reading combines Matthew 26. 18–29 and John 13. 20–30, interpreting the following verses from the Gospel of John as a report of the Eucharist's institution:

> And when he had dipped the sop, he gave it to Judas Iscariot, the son of Simon. And after the sop Satan entered into him. [. . .] He then having received the sop went immediately out: and it was night.
>
> (John 13. 26–27/30)

Accordingly, the Eucharist shows similarities with ordeals, i.e. with codified tests of innocence that can also be found in the Old Testament. Numbers 5. 16–28 gives an example of how the suspicion of marital infidelity could be repudiated: water, but also wine,[6] mixed with dust off the Temple's floor had to be drunk. This liquid was thought to be harmful to sinners and hence to condemn them. According to the theory of several Church Fathers, Judas was not excluded *from*, but *by* the Eucharist. His condemnation was not seen as an argument for refusing the Eucharist to grave sinners, but as evidence that Christians who receive it in a state of unworthiness will be punished by it.[7] This is exactly what necessitates a self-examination in order to prevent the curse. During the time of Elizabeth I, the priest who administered the sacrament for this reason was enjoined through *The Book of Common Prayer* to warn those among the congregants who are living in sin, and to urge them not to participate in the Eucharist: "Come not to this holy table, lest after taking of that holy sacrament the Devil enter into you, as he entered unto Judas, and fill you full of all iniquities, and bring you to destruction both of body and soul."[8] That statements of witnesses and contractual obligations are confirmed through partaking of the Eucharist goes back to this conception of the feast as an ordeal by poison. This is the reason why, during the Tudor era, certain people often would take communion in order to absolve themselves of a suspicion.[9]

The Eucharist, then, represents the outpouring both of a curse and of a blessing. But a logical problem arises when one understands the Feast as a verdict and as the verdict's execution. If the Eucharist turns into a fateful court of law for the accused transgressor, how can it be a form of punishment to withhold it from him through excommunication? This exclusion of the person excommunicated from the Eucharistic community, codified already in early Christendom, is by no means an act of mercy because excommunication is always understood as an act of punishment and expulsion from the realm of salvation. An unresolved ambivalence in the relationship between divine and ecclesiastical law becomes apparent here: the Eucharist establishes a new covenant and a new law (*Recht*) that henceforth regulates access to the Eucharist itself. The Church, according to Benjamin's notion of the tendential decline of law-preserving violence,[10] seems to be turning against the lawmaking violence that institutes this Church.

Consequently, the Church has an ambivalent relationship to lawmaking curses in the Old Testament that likewise seem to supplement the covenant and law. The Passover meal, for example, affirms a divine covenant but also makes it possible for the Lord to find his designated victims (Exodus 11–12). Also, Yahweh's explicit covenant with Israel in Leviticus and Deuteronomy ends with curses against its transgressors (Lev. 26. 14–45; Deut. 28. 15–68). The commandment to love your enemy and the sacrificial death of Christ that he, as God's son, takes upon himself voluntarily, seem, according to ecclesiastical rhetoric, to suspend these covenant curses and make them superfluous once and for all. The Gospels and apostolic epistles accordingly promulgate repeated commandments to bless and not to curse (Luke 6. 27–28; Romans 12. 14); they even forbid swearing (Matthew 5. 33–37). On the other hand there is abundant swearing and cursing in the New Testament. Jesus himself, for example, curses the fig tree in a fit of anger, apparently for no good reason (Mark 11. 12). Paul curses "those who pervert the Gospel" by deviating from orthodoxy (Galatians 1. 8). And Revelation ends with an execration of its falsifier (Rev. 22. 18–19), which means that the Bible ends with a curse. This ambivalence is given its most succinct expression in a much-discussed formulation of the Letter to the Galatians:

> For as many as are of the works of the law are under the curse [ἀρά]: for it is written, Cursed is every one that continueth not in all things which are written in the book of law to do them. But that no man is justified by the law in the sight of God, it is evident [. . .]. Christ hath redeemed us from the curse of the law, being made a curse for us: for it is written, Cursed is every one that hangeth on a tree.
>
> (Galatians 3. 10–11/13)

In the figure of Christ the Accursed, the Pauline equivocation allows for the congruity of curse and law while apparently denouncing both. An antinomian interpretation seems to impose itself, a short-circuit of the law's logic of sacrifice, which makes the passage problematic and in need of exegesis. Its most influential reading is that of Augustine who comments on it in an anti-Manichean polemic: sin is accursed, both the transgression itself, and, metonymically, the punishment resulting from it. For since original sin has made punishment necessary, punishment too is accursed. But only insofar as Christ has taken this punishment upon himself despite being free of guilt, can one say that he is accursed.[11] This reading of the death on the cross rejects law and curse only in order to restitute the logic of sacrifice by positing, in the very act of its rejection, a new difference between guilt—that of fallen mankind as the murderer of God—and innocence—that of the Redeemer and his institutions; a differentiation that is immediately followed by its legal codification. The cross does not make the curse superfluous but universalizes it. Through Judas' expulsion, the Church reposits the very exclusion which it claimed to suspend through Christ's sacrificial death. A very flexible system of guilt emerges. Its guiding principle is: no subject is any longer exempt from the curse from which it has been redeemed—not even God's son.

The ecclesiastical Eucharist consists of a representation of the act of its institution. It points to its biblical origin and thereby also demonstrates the prominent position of the priests as successors and imitators of Christ.[12] In the Middle Ages laymen experienced the Eucharist almost exclusively through seeing (the host) and hearing (the transubstantiating words), but not through touching or tasting: the Eucharist is above all a *spectaculum*.[13] Accordingly, English theater tradition begins in the late Middle Ages by referring to the Eucharist. The sacrament is expanded to become the "*Corpus Christi* play," the host at that time being known as the "*corpus Christi*." This explains the name of the feast day and of the plays performed on its occasion. (Originally, i.e. in Paul, this term also refers to the community of Christ, whereas "*corpus mysticum*" designates the host and only after 1150 begins to denote the community that is united through the Eucharist.)[14] The "*Corpus Christi* plays" were not staged, however, on Holy Thursday, the traditional feast day of the Eucharist's institution. Instead, Pope Urban IV in the fourteenth century created the new feast day of *Corpus Christi* in order to celebrate the Eucharist separately as the redemption of mankind, arguing that Maundy Thursday immediately precedes Good Friday. In other words, this feast day takes place in fearful anticipation of the death on the cross so that no joy commensurate with the day's occasion could arise. The first Thursday after Trinity Sunday was established as the date for this new festivity.[15] The religious performances on this day, extending other religious festivities, were staged by the guilds of many cities. The plays present the entirety of biblical history, albeit in extremely condensed form, as a *theatrum mundi* from the Creation to the Apocalypse, with the life of Jesus as its center. The focal point of the entire performance was a staging of the Last Supper, which forever raised the question: Is this dramatized Eucharist a genuine ecclesiastical feast? Is the bread that the actor portraying Jesus designates as His body and thereby consecrates truly consecrated?[16] On the one hand, this is a moot question since the role of Jesus is normally played by a layman; on the other hand, the theater is indeed used to create sacramental evidence: A pastor in the sixteenth century, for example, refers to the "*Corpus Christi* play" as evidence to buttress his biblical stories and Church dogma: "If you believe not me then for a more sure and sufficient authority, go your way to Coventry, and there ye shall see them all played in Corpus Christi play."[17] The sacred plays confirm the ecclesiastical Eucharist by mirroring it, adopting its formulas, etc. But their confirmation also creates suspicion by displaying their mediated character and at the same time polemicizing against the illusions of the world.[18] They direct the spectators' attention to the way in which manipulative representations and signs structure the world.

During the Reformation, the debate on the Eucharist's relative importance intensifies. The fact that one segment of the Church breaks with another is sufficient to jeopardize the idea of universal communion. Luther, Calvin, Zwingli, and the Catholics mutually exclude each other from the Christian community as heretics, their conflicts being decisively concerned with the problematical nature of the Eucharist. The resultant virulent discussion about the real presence brings with it a general dispute about the relevance of representations. Zurich and Geneva draw the most radial consequences from the arising doubts: For the Swiss reformers, bread and wine are commemorative symbols, not real presences of Christ. Zwingli is of the opinion that the "*est*" in "*Hoc est corpus*" means "*significat*." In that respect, he interprets the Eucharistic formula as a trope, in his analysis as a metonymy.[19] In this argumentation, the host appears as a sign that is a figuration of Christian truth.[20] Thomas Cranmer also understands the words of institution as "figurative speech," thus more or less directly questioning transubstantiation.[21] Under Edward VI, Cranmer enforces this interpretation of the Eucharist as the official doctrine of the Anglican Church.[22]

The counter-constructions of the Catholics in defense of transubstantiation insist on the primacy of the mystery and hence burden their opponents with the onus of proof. This strategy is given its most precise formulation in the Grammar of Port-Royal that posits the Eucharistic "*Hoc est corpus meum*" as the "matrix for every other sentence."[23] Luther's concept of the Eucharist oscillates between that of the Catholics and the Calvinists. In his writings, the sacrament appears above all as a divine social contract the object of which is forgiveness of sins and acceptance into Heaven. The Eucharist is represented as a political act in which taking communion actualizes the communicants' membership in the *civitas dei*.[24] Hence, the Lutheran position often describes the Eucharist in juridical and contractual terms, Luther himself referring to the sacrament of bread and wine "as a letter and seal"[25] while at the same time emphasizing the identity of bread and wine with Christ's body. As for the Catholics, so also for Luther the Eucharist continues to be a condemnatory act as much as an act that creates community. The right faith is a condition for receiving the blessing, but the sacrament itself is being accomplished in any case: if bread and wine are taken by unbelievers, they receive the body and blood of Jesus not as a blessing but as a curse.[26] Calvin, however, rejects this Lutheran "*manducatio impiorum*;" in his opinion, the unworthy do not receive the Redeemer's body in the Eucharist, be it as a blessing or as a curse.[27] The Anglican Church takes up an undecided position on this issue but accepts an at least similar-sounding doctrine into its Articles of Faith and into the *Book of Common Prayer*. The reformed Church breaks apart over this contentious question, among other issues.[28] Swiss as well as radical English Protestants reject ecclesiastical blessings, exorcisms, consecrations, and curses. They assume their futility, arguing that the accursed either have broken God's law, in which case God himself has already accursed them, or they have kept it, in which case the ecclesiastical curse is impotent.[29] Hence, the liturgy seems to be a redundant mirror image of a process of salvation that is taking place anyway, which makes the Geneva doctrine of the Eucharist appear as an appropriate complement of the Calvinist doctrine of predestination.

In many reformed territories, the princes and kings try to settle the conflict between the Protestant doctrines about the Eucharist through decrees of the secular sovereign and through the imposition of Church hierarchies. The question of the Eucharist thus turns into a State affair, especially in England. The reason for this may be found not only in Elizabeth's policy of compromises with the Catholics but also in the fact that England's first push for Reformation was primarily Lutheran, while the second one has a predominantly Calvinist imprint. Under James I it is even demanded of immigrant subjects, as a condition for their naturalization, that they participate in the Anglican Eucharist.[30] In 1661, under Charles II, this is made a condition for holding any public office.[31] The "Test Act" of 1678 decrees furthermore that all candidates for an office have to swear not only the "Oath of Supremacy" and the "Oath of Allegiance" but also a "Declaration against Transubstantiation" that begins: "I [. . .] profess, testify, and declare, that I do believe that in the Sacrament of the Lord's Supper, there is not any Transubstantiation of the elements of bread and wine into the Body and Blood of Christ, at or after the consecration thereof by any person whatsoever."[32]

In the Elizabethan worldview, the monarch is accorded the status of a mediator between Heaven and Earth, which applies also to the problem of sacramental speaking. To conceptualize this connection, one should consult above all the construction of "the king's second body" (as studied by Ernst Kantorowicz) that duplicates the monarch's earthly body with an immortal one.[33] According to Kantorowicz, the "immortal body" of kings is created when the Church's "*corpus mysticum*" is made temporal—a process in which this "mystical body" is being changed from the synchronously existing community of the faithful into the diachronic community of monarchs who replace one another in an orderly succession.[34] This idea is taken up by Elizabeth I and James I themselves.[35] In this respect, the English Renaissance continues a medieval tradition in which the "pneumatic position"—for Paul an inheritance of every Christian—is monopolized by the Pope and later by the monarchs.[36] Since Henry VIII, the "*corpus mysticum*" of the English Church has been absorbed by the "*corpus politicum*" of the State.[37] The rituals of the monarchy and of parliament borrow from the liturgy. Royal processions, pageants and other State ceremonies go back to ecclesiastical prototypes, and like these they are eminently theatrical.[38]

A further complication arises from the fact that, particularly in England, the king is thought of not only as a transcendent being but also, at least since the Magna Carta, as *primus inter pares.* Beyond that, royal rule over the Church is decidedly not sacerdotal. Already Henry VIII as "Supreme Head" does not claim any priestly authority, only the absolute administrative *imperium* over the English Church.[39] Elizabeth I even declines to be called "Supreme Head of the Church" but chooses "Supreme Governor" instead, which is also a concession to the Catholics.[40] But if neither the Pope nor the King is the spiritual head of England, and neither is the clergy, who is? The ambiguities are intensified by a prevailing rhetoric that makes the royal office sacred by referring, for example, to Exodus 22. 28: "Thou shalt not revile the gods, nor curse the ruler of thy people." Hence, *lèse majesté* is considered blasphemous under Elizabeth.[41] But the relationship between the curse and the full powers of the English king in this context has not been determined unequivocally. There also exists no official royal power of execration that the king might exercise beyond his juridical function. Yet both Elizabeth[42] and especially James I (e.g. in his letter to the Dutch government against the theologian Vorstius)[43] pronounce royal execratory prophecies as threats of punishment. But at the same time, and in accordance with Anglican doctrine, they refer to God's will, which is unfathomable and cannot be influenced. Therefore, these execrations sound more conjectural than papal maledictions.

Long-established overdeterminations of the Eucharist and of the power structures legitimated by it become an urgent problem in the sixteenth century; contradictory exegeses that could exist side by side during the Middle Ages enter into perpetual conflict after the Reformation. Under these circumstances, transubstantiation and real presence cannot simply be eliminated from the discourse in favor of pure reference: and the theater provides one of the places where the resulting conflict plays out latently. This appears appropriate insofar as the theater itself constitutively finds itself in a similar tension between thing and sign, presence and reflection, a tension that characterizes representation in Shakespeare's theater. It is an institution that establishes its place between timeless, ritual drama *sub specie aeternitatis* and references that are specific in space and time.[44] Does theater merely refer to a historical situation that has come to its end and as such is separated from the theater, or is it in the theater that history becomes present and palpable? Shakespeare's theater plays with this duality and with the shock that lets the one understanding abruptly change into the other.

In *Richard III*, the question of how sacred signs and things relate to each other is negotiated with particular urgency and irreverence. In this negotiation, the intriguer Richard appears as master of the signs. This mastery institutes him as the "laughing third" beside the despotic Edward IV and the Christ-imitating royal martyr Henry VI. It establishes choreographies in which intrigue lays down the rhythm for any political action.[45] Under Richard the question of the signifying and sign-establishing power of the sacrament is redefined: he takes up the conventional sacraments (the Protestant ones of Baptism and Eucharist, but also Catholic sacraments such as Marriage), instrumentalizes and parodies them by demonstrating their emptiness. But they retain their eminent power nonetheless and are reduced to a game only for those who have the power to institute them. Especially the murder of Clarence, royal brother and heir to the throne, "wash'd to death with fulsome wine" in I. iv, is an inversion of baptism instituted by Richard and attributed to King Edward, a "new-christening in the Tower":

> RICHARD: O, belike his Majesty hath some intent
> That you should be new-christened in the Tower.
>
> (I. i. 49–50)

This murder also alludes to a Eucharistic subtext,[46] and not only because wine has replaced holy water as the medium of immersion: baptism and the Eucharist, the two sacraments that survived the Reformation due to their biblical precedence, are being parodied in their conjunction. The murder is staged as a sacramental act that unfolds in accordance with the Christian Paradox which explodes the traditional logic of sacrifice only to reinstitute it by way of this explosion. The murderers hired by Richard thematize these religious and paradoxical implications of their deed by repeatedly describing it both as the punitive judgment on a second Judas (cf. e.g. I. iv. 194) and as a figuration of Christ's sacrifice:

> SECOND MURDERER: A bloody deed, and desperately dispatch'd.
> How fain, like Pilate, would I wash my hands
> Of this most grievous murder.
>
> (I. iv. 261–263)

True to his role as a figuration of Christ, Clarence is assigned the place of the (Eucharistic) host:

> FIRST MURDERER: Take him on the costard with the hilts of thy sword, and then throw him into the malmsey-butt in the next room.
> SECOND MURDERER: Oh excellent device! And make a sop of him.
>
> (I. iv. 146–149)

It is worth remembering that the bite Jesus passes to Judas (in John 13) is also called a "sop" in the *King James Bible*, a motif that is taken up again after Clarence wakens and the second murderer addresses him as "my lord":

> CLARENCE: Where art thou, Keeper? Give me a cup of wine.
> SECOND MURDERER: You shall have wine enough, my lord, anon.
>
> (I. iv. 153–154)

At this "supper of our lord," Clarence is given wine (*genitivus subiectivus*), but he himself is the redeeming and damning bread (*genitivus obiectivus*). The theological dispute between Clarence and his murderers that delays the deed appropriately circles around the relevance of the sacrament as divine judgment and the legitimacy of its restitution by Richard. This legitimacy seems both to be confirmed and to be contested by an elusive legal authority: in confronting his murderers, Clarence refers to a constantly shifting court of law, first calling on the proper, official jurisdiction, sanctioned through God's blood:

> CLARENCE: What is my offence?
> Where is the evidence that doth accuse me? [. . .]
> Before I be convict by course of law,
> To threaten me with death is most unlawful.
> I charge you, as you hope to have redemption,
> By Christ's dear blood, shed for your grievous sins,
> That you depart and lay no hands on me [. . .].
>
> (I. iv. 171–172/176–180)

The murderers counter by invoking the sovereignty of the royal order that has the force of law:

> FIRST MURDERER: What we will do, we do upon command.
> SECOND MURDERER: And he that hath commanded is our King.
>
> (I. iv. 182–183)

Clarence then refers to divine law as being superior to royal edicts:

> CLARENCE: Erroneous vassals! The great King of kings
> Hath in the table of His law commanded
> That thou shalt do no murder. Will you then
> Spurn at His edict, and fulfil a man's?
> Take heed! For He holds vengeance in His hand
> To hurl upon their heads that break His law.
>
> (I. iv. 184–189)

The murderers counter by designating the impending execution itself as a divine judgment, reminding Clarence of the blasphemous dimension of his violent perjury against Henry VI. And they especially emphasize the fact that this oath had been secured by the Eucharist:

> SECOND MURDERER: And that same vengeance doth He hurl on thee,
> For false forswearing, and for murder too:
> Thou didst receive the sacrament to fight
> In quarrel of the House of Lancaster.
> FIRST MURDERER: And like a traitor to the name of God
> Didst break that vow, and with thy treacherous blade
> Unrip'st the bowels of thy sovereign's son.
> SECOND MURDERER: Whom thou wast sworn to cherish and defend.
> FIRST MURDERER: How canst thou urge God's dreadful law to us,
> When thou hast broke it in such dear degree?
>
> (I. iv. 190–199)

Clarence appears as an archtraitor who murdered the "sovereign's son," as a second Judas who is no longer in a position to appeal to any law and who for this reason can hope for nothing but elimination. In his person, the functionally analogous roles of Christ and Judas appear to be so tightly intertwined as to defy unraveling. Clarence thereupon enacts another aboutface. Now it is again—in a kind of legal ballet—precisely the secular sovereign and his will that he invokes in order to justify his transgression of divine law:

> CLARENCE: Alas, for whose sake did I that ill deed?
> For Edward, for my brother, for his sake.
>
> (I. iv. 200–201)

But this king has already been revealed in the murderers' argumentation as a usurper, which also makes their own reference to the "king's command" null and void. The two sides become entrapped more and more in the contradictions of their position; hence, their exchange becomes ever more circular. The argumentation slides into an infinite regress. Divine law refers to secular law and vice versa, in an unending chain. Thus, the murder is not a consequence of a moral or legal verdict that emerges from the discussion, but enacts an attempt to escape from the horns of a theological-political dilemma. Thus, a son of the royal family is consumed in a lawmaking act as a substitutive "*corpus Christi*."

In its frequent references to the competing English noble houses and their royal lineage (cf. I. iv. 156/193/210), scene I. iv alludes to an additional motif that permeates the early royal dramas and in which remnants of the Eucharist are involved. According to the Christological conception of the monarchy, as analyzed by Kantorowicz, the bloodlines of the rulers and nobles establish a community analogous to that of Christ's blood since the noble "house" is understood to be a diachronous form of the *civitas dei*.[47] Henry VI in particular is insistently designated as a successor to the Savior throughout the York tetralogy. But even he appears to be rather a parody of Christ: he may be peace-loving, forgiving and pious, but he is also gullible, bigoted, narcissistic, and ineffectual. His sanctification is sealed when he is assassinated by Richard, a murder which retrospectively elevates the incompetent king to the status of a martyr. Complementing Richard's role as the King of Intrigue, the dead King Henry takes on the role of the royal sacrifice whose blood miracle the community of theatergoers repeatedly consumes with their eyes. The first opportunity to do so presents itself during the murder scene in the third part of *Henry VI*:

> HENRY: And thus I prophesy: that many a thousand
> Which now mistrust no parcel of my fear [. . .]
> Shall rue the hour that ever thou wast born. [. . .]
> RICHARD: I'll hear no more. Die, prophet, in thy speech. (*He stabs him.*)
> For this, amongst the rest, was I ordained.
> HENRY: Ay, and for much more slaughter after this.
> O, God forgive my sins, and pardon thee! (*He dies.*)

> RICHARD: What – will the aspiring blood of Lancaster
> Sink in the ground? I thought it would have mounted.
> See how my sword weeps for the poor king's death.
> O, may such purple tears be always shed
> For those that wish the downfall of our house!
>
> (*3. Henry VI*, V. vi. 37–38/43/57–65)

Since the king is God's deputy on earth, regicide is considered the worst of crimes in the early modern era; it is repeatedly described as a second murder of Christ.[48] Henry's rhetoric first establishes this sacral subtext, including the Christian gesture of forgiveness. Richard parodies it by reducing the *topos* of the holy blood to its political dimension. The use of "aspiring" as well as "mount" and "ordained" obscures the boundary between the secular will to power and transcendental aspirations. Social climbing is equated with the Ascension; secular and divine power again refer to each another in a circular way.

This blood motif in *Richard III* is further developed through numerous allusions to royal communion. Some of the most prominent ones are found in I. ii, the scene of Henry's obsequies. Here, Henry's daughter-in-law enters with a small procession that carries his body to its grave. The funeral is not an affair of State but a very private "maimed rite," since Henry had been declared a usurper. On Anne's order the procession is interrupted, his corpse is set down and displayed, and Anne begins to intone a semi-official, rhetorically polished lament (I. ii. 3) that both invokes Henry's ghost ("be it lawful that I invocate thy ghost," I. ii. 8) and denounces his murder. Anne refers to Henry with obvious Christological assonances as "holy king" (I. ii. 5), "holy load" (I. ii. 29), and "dear saint" (IV. i. 69), calling his body "poor key-cold Figure of a holy king" (I. ii. 5), in other words, a royal figuration, as if he were his own effigy.[49] She forcefully laments his shed blood and his wounds ("these windows that let forth thy life," I. ii. 12). Linda Charnes argues that this scene quotes the "ocular communion" during Catholic rituals of lament such as "Easter Sepulchre," a visual Eucharist on the occasion of which the faithful, especially women, would congregate around a representation of the bleeding Christ in imitation of the Three Marys. It was believed that their contemplation as a group would strengthen the identification with the Redeemer and the community.[50] In continuing this tradition, Anne addresses Henry as synecdoche of the Lancastrian bloodline, as "virtuous Lancaster" (I. ii. 4) and as "bloodless remnant of that royal blood" (I. ii. 7). In these formulations, "blood" refers to the real liquid flowing from the violently murdered body, to the mystery of lordly descent that constitutes a nobleman's nobility, and to the sacramental blood of the Redeemer. The various ensuing dialogues play with the ambiguities inherent in the relationships between these three significations: the three foundational qualities that legitimate the rule of lords, that is, divine judgment, noble descent and life-or-death combat, are designated by the same word and are approximated to each other through the evidential figure of the Eucharist. Shedding blood thus legitimates the noble blood, the murderous as well as the murdered blood, which makes each of the murders committed in *Richard III* appear to be a sacrificial rite. Lord Rivers alludes to this constellation in his farewell speech before his execution:

> RIVERS: And for more slander to thy dismal seat,
> We give to thee our guiltless blood to drink. [. . .]
> Be satisfied, dear God, with our true blood,
> Which, as thou know'st, unjustly must be spilt.
>
> (III. iii. 13–14/22–23)

It is not only through the term "true blood" that Rivers here invokes the vocabulary of an *imitatio Christi.* To designate one's own body as "*corpus Christi*" seems to be a prevalent strategy among the nobility. Even Richard refers to his self-sacrifice in the interest of the House of York and of his royal brother with the same formula:

> RICHARD: To royalize his blood, I spilt mine own.
> MARGARET: Ay, and much better blood than his, or thine.
>
> (I. iii. 125–126)

And indeed, throughout the play Richard is spoken of as "bloody Richard" (III. iv. 103), the "bloody King" (IV. iii. 22), with his "bloody mind" (I. ii. 101) and his "bloody deeds" (V. iii. 172) "to worry lambs, and lap their gentle blood" (IV. iv. 50), transgressions that can be stayed only with his "bloody end" (IV. iv. 195) When Anne speaks of Richard's "bloody mind," this designation is applicable in several respects: for example, he is also obsessed with the pedigree of his House (cf. I. iii. 263–265 and passim). Richard's successor, Richmond, takes up these ambiguities in his speech against Richard:

> RICHMOND: A bloody tyrant and a homicide;
> One rais'd in blood, and one in blood establish'd [. . .].
>
> (V. iii. 247–248)

On the occasion of Richard's coup-d'état-like accession to his royal office, this figure of speech is parodied in a legitimating speech given by Buckingham:

> BUCKINGHAM: [. . .] we heartily solicit
> Your gracious self to take on you the charge
> And kingly government of this your land,
> Not as Protector, steward, substitute,
> Or lowly factor for another's gain,
> But as successively, from blood to blood,
> Your right of birth, your empery, your own.
>
> (III. vii. 129–135)

The ironic ambiguity of "from blood to blood" must be obvious to all who participate in this ceremony of proclamation. Such a play with double meanings is also a play with the obligatoriness of abstraction levels, a heritage of the theater. Supported by this interim result, we may return to Act I, scene ii, where Anne also supplements her communion with Henry by a curse, echoing the Eucharist:

> ANNE: O, cursed be the hand that made these holes;
> Cursed the heart that had the heart to do it;
> Cursed the blood that let this blood from hence.
> More direful hap betide that hated wretch
> That makes us wretched by the death of thee
> Than I can wish to adders, spiders, toads,
> Or any creeping venom'd thing that lives.
> If ever he have child, abortive be it:
> Prodigious, and untimely brought to light,
> Whose ugly and unnatural aspect
> May fright the hopeful mother at the view,
> And that be heir to his unhappiness.
> If ever he have wife, let her be made
> More miserable by the death of him
> Than I am made by my young lord, and thee.
>
> (I. ii. 14–28)

There are good reasons why Anne's lament can seamlessly transform into a curse. The relation of lamentation to curse is similar to that of wailing (*Klage*) to indictment (*Anklage*). Female mourners are traditionally considered to draw a fair amount of political power from their rites of mourning.The ruling powers tend to look at their elaborate wailings and flailings with suspicion because they may trigger violent acts of recrimination. In Greece and Italy, for example, the traditional mourning ceremonies after politically motivated murders, vendettas, etc. threaten to turn into campaigns of revenge and revolutionary uprisings even well into the modern age. It is mostly the widows and mothers of the murder victims who start these events in order to incite the community to avenge the death of their relatives. For this reason, ceremonies of mourning are generally controlled and, if necessary, suppressed by the State.[51] Keith Thomas and others have shown that the potentially political power of the mourners and their curses also was a force to be reckoned with in the England of the early modern age. Thomas quotes court transcripts that mention execration ceremonies performed by bereaved women kneeling in the middle of the street—rituals which, though unofficial, imitate juridical proceedings.[52] These curses appear to be related to lamentations in that the cursing woman prospectively assigns the deprivations that her lament recounts to an individual accused of being their cause. Most curses also share structural connections with ceremonial lamentations, both being defined in Shakespeare's time (e.g. by George Puttenham[53]) by their purgative properties: they enumerate sufferings, draw up catalogues of good and bad fortunes and are often structured as an anaphora ("Where are . . . /Where are . . .," "Cursed the . . ./ Cursed the . . ."). The matrix of most Christian mourning and cursing formulas can be found in the Book of Psalms, many of which are also quoted at appropriate occasions in the liturgy. The anaphoras and parallelisms of the Book of Psalms (cf. Psalm 109. 17) have been incorporated into excommunication formulas that often consist of anaphoric sequences beginning with "Cursed."[54] Anne herself does not quote the liturgy directly but varies the structural elements of liturgical and biblical formulas, for example in the symploces of I. ii:

> ANNE: O God! which this blood mad'st, revenge his death:
> O earth! which this blood drink'st, revenge his death [. . .].
>
> (I. ii. 62–63)

But Anne's curses are more worldly than the liturgical formulas she modifies. In I. ii. 8 Anne not only appeals to God but also to the earth and to the dead king himself. She insists on secular evidence, even when it comes to the punishments meted out by divine judgment. Her curses reach their apex not in the pronouncement of eternal damnation and the expurgation of the sinner's name from the book of life, but in the denial of immortality in this world through the absence of heirs who could continue the bloodline.[55]

But in the course of the next scene and of the whole play thereafter, the divine power to which Anne appeals in her *maledictiones* becomes less and less distinguishable from secular violence. As in I. iv, both refer to one another in a vicious circle. Yet no living, active figures are left alive who represent legitimate juridical power and whom the curser would acknowledge. Hence, Anne is speaking to an absence but also in its stead.[56] She occupies the place of this absence, which she cannot hold as an empirical person and thus merges into a symbolic vacuum. In this context, cursing once more appears not only as an excluding but also as a contaminating form of speaking. Since the curse by its very nature cannot be brought to an end, it must rebound on the curser as well as on itself.

The Eucharistic subtext of I. ii becomes conspicuous again when blood starts to flow from the wounds of the displayed (un)dead Henry after Richard's entrance. That the murdered king is giving a miraculous sign through his sacred blood is one of the folkloristic elements that Shakespeare took over from Holinshed's chronicles.[57] But Shakespeare emphasizes the status of this blood miracle as divine judgment, that is, as a production of condemning evidence: a "deluge most unnatural" of the excluding sacred blood:

> ANNE: O gentlemen! See, see dead Henry's wounds
> Open their congeal'd mouths and bleed afresh.
> Blush, blush, thou lump of foul deformity,
> For 'tis thy presence that exhales this blood
> From cold and empty veins where no blood dwells:
> Thy deed inhuman and unnatural
> Provokes this deluge most unnatural.
>
> (I. ii. 55–61)

Richard responds to this accusation with a countercharge that denounces Anne as Unchristian for her cursings:

> RICHARD: Lady, you know no rules of charity,
> Which renders good for bad, blessings for curses.
>
> (I. ii. 68–69)

Richard not only swears by the apostle Paul (I. ii. 36; I. iii. 45; III. iv. 76; V. iii. 217), he also repeatedly paraphrases the latter's Christian commandment to "bless, and curse not" (Rom. 12. 14). In his dialogue with Anne he practices this precept by answering every one of her curses with a blessing. The forms of address that both sides use contain a strongly religious charge ("saint" vs. "dreadful minister of hell," "angel" vs. "devil"). In this way the interdependency of Heaven and Hell, good and evil, blessing and curse gradually turns into the interdependency of Anne and Richard.[58] It is part of Richard's rhetorical strategies to appeal to Christian values in a manner that functionalizes these values in an openly cynical and parodistic way, but nonetheless confronts his opponents with a theological problem. In the present case, it is the question of the merit of forgiveness. Conventional formulas and regulations such as the appeal to leave vengeance to God are unconvincing, because the situation is unfolding inside a vicious circle of divine and secular power. What dimension are forgiveness and mercy supposed to have in this context, and should they be measured at all? Several frequently quoted passages from the Gospel give a negative answer to the second question and demand of any Christian a universal, loving forgiveness beyond all bounds (Matt. 6. 44; Matt. 18. 35; Mark 11. 25; Luke 23. 34). In the subsequent dispute, Richard's insistence on universal forgiveness assumes an increasingly erotic connotation, the merciful acts blending into "*dons de merci*." Richard himself qualifies their dialogue as a "keen encounter of our wits" (I. ii. 119) and thus transforms the tragic into a comedic rhetoric. That ruse also serves to move sexuality and marriage rather than death into the dialogue's compass. Richard turns the lamentation into a stichomythia which also makes use of symploces and parallelisms. Both speakers imitate and invert the choice and sequence of their opponent's words in a way that recalls comedies of conflicted codependency like *Much Ado About Nothing*.[59] The dynamics of ritual speech patterns force Anne to play her part in a game that plays sentences and binary oppositions off against each other:

> ANNE: O wonderful, when devils tell the truth!
> RICHARD: More wonderful, when angels are so angry.
> Vouchsafe, divine perfection of a woman,
> Of these supposed crimes, to give me leave,
> By circumstance, but to acquit myself.
> ANNE: Vouchsafe, diffus'd infection of a man,
> Of these known evils, but to give me leave,
> By circumstance, to curse thy cursed self.
>
> (I. ii. 73–80)

An erotic tension is created by the very theological polarization of codependent antagonisms.[60] With a gesture that likewise has Christian antecedents, Richard next marshals the platitude that a curse will return to its perpetrator. Using several *topoi* of love poetry, he shifts Anne in I. ii into the position of her curse's recipient:

> ANNE: Black night o'ershade they day, and death thy life.
> RICHARD: Curse not thyself, fair creature; thou art both.
>
> (I. ii. 135–136)

By blaming all his acts of violence on Anne's beauty, Richard outlines a new image of society in the immobile center of which the Lady herself stands as an angel of destruction. What Richard offers Anne is a gruesome vision of her own body as the body politic. On this basis, he validates her curses, lends them performative force, and manipulates her into the position of judge and executioner by forcing her to either forgive him or to put him to death on the spot:

> RICHARD: If thy revengeful heart cannot forgive,
> Lo here I lend thee this sharp-pointed sword,
> Which if thou please to hide in this true breast,
> And let the soul forth that adoreth thee,
> I lay it naked to the deadly stroke,
> And humbly beg the death upon my knee.
>
> (I. ii. 177–182)

Richard feigns to grant her the opportunity to convert her curses into an execution. And precisely this pretense makes it obvious that these curses are constitutively excessive and arise from a placeless vacuum, thus showing the absolute untenability of her position. For he makes her play the role of a demonic exterminating angel and turns his proposed execution into a sacrificial death, once more with Christian undertones. In this way, Anne is raised into a figure of the very history under which she has to suffer. She is forced to commit the same violence that she has experienced, and hence to perpetuate it. The alternative is a type of mercy that, due to the eroticized sacrificial situation, already is equated with a "*don de merci*," including its sexual as well as Christological connotations. On this basis, Richard appropriates from Anne first the power to interpret for the dead, then the dead body of Henry VI, and finally Anne's own body, whose obligation as Henry's heir it is to assume this sacrificial function:

> ANNE: Within so small a time, my woman's heart
> Grossly grew captive to his honey words,
> And prov'd the subject of my own soul's curse,
> Which hitherto hath held my eyes from rest [. . .].
>
> (IV. i. 78–81)

In the final analysis, only one person disposes of the Eucharist's heritage of bankruptcy more successfully than even Richard, namely his successor on the throne. As Richard usurps power over ceremonies and bodies by strategically employing sacred speech acts, so Richmond legitimizes his advancement to supreme power by means of Eucharistic, lawmaking *topoi*. According to Richmond, the fight against Richard is a holy war, the victory over him is a triumph of God (V. iii. 253–255). Richmond's proclamation of himself as the new king is as sacral as circumstances permit; he stages it as a ceremony that re-establishes the continuity of divine and royal power. The declaration again begins with an announcement of the obsequies for the war dead (now elevated to the status of martyrs) and an invocation of the Eucharist, an appeal in which political power and the sacrament legitimate one another through the linguistic merger of *optative* and *indicative*. The Eucharist has finally been transmuted into a State ceremony:

> RICHMOND: Inter their bodies as become their births.
> Proclaim a pardon to the soldiers fled
> That in submission will return to us;
> And then, as we have ta'en the sacrament,
> We will unite the white rose and the red.
> Smile, heaven, upon this fair conjunction,
> That long have frown'd upon their enmity.
> What traitor hears me and says not Amen?
>
> (V. v. 15–22)

Richmond concludes the play with a "Prayer for the Monarch," thus repeating a theatrical convention of the Elizabethan era; however, these supplicatory epilogues usually were not integrated into the plot.[61] His prayer involves the audience and thereby arrogates to itself an additional, meta-dramatic level of the play. But Shakespeare adds signs of situational irony to the prayer as well as to its introduction. The sacramental reconciliation of the red and white rose (i.e. the Houses of York and Lancaster) through Richmond's marriage with Elizabeth of York has the effect of an ironic pseudo-ending since Richard's notoriously unhappy union with Anne had already united the white rose and the red. (Anne as a Neville was a member of the House of Lancaster.) This makes Richmond's act not only an empty gesture but also a redundant imitation of Richard's under the guise of corrective righteousness. Richard's removal and the installation of Henry VII do not suspend but affirm the logic of sacrifice that has kept the mechanism of the drama in motion until that point. All the more so as the blessing of England and her monarch, safeguarded by the sacrament, is supplemented by a prospective curse on their traitors[62] which ends the drama:

> RICHMOND: O now let Richmond and Elizabeth,
> The true succeeders of each royal House,
> By God's fair ordinance conjoin together,

And let their heirs, God, if thy will be so,
Enrich the time to come with smooth-fac'd peace,
With smiling plenty, and fair prosperous days.
Abate the edge of traitors, gracious Lord,
That would reduce these bloody days again,
And make poor England weep in streams of blood.
Let them not live to taste this land's increase,
That would with treason wound this fair land's peace.
Now civil wars are stopp'd; peace lives again.
That she may long live here, God say Amen.

(V. v. 29–41)

This declaration echoes Richard's speeches in the first half of the play in several respects. The concluding prayer, for example, contains an announcement of peace using the imagery of propitious seasons ("with smooth-fac'd peace, with smiling plenty, and fair prosperous days," V. v. 33–34) that suggest a parallel to Richard's announcement opening the play:

RICHARD: Now is the winter of our discontent
Made glorious summer by this son of York; [. . .]
Grim-visag'd War hath smooth'd his wrinkled front [. . .].

(I. i. 1–2/9)

Prominent in both speeches is the "now" that creates immediacy and at the same time distance, the shifter (linguistically speaking) indicating the theater's potential for generating time frames, establishing epochs, and allowing representations to coexist with real presences. Theater is the medium in which kings become comparable and hence are being connected in a new way. It is their use of metaphors as well as their content and their symmetrical positioning, that establish connections between Richard's speech and that of Richmond. The similarity of their names and the symmetry of the scenes in which they share the stage brings them closer together and thereby puts an ironic twist on their statements. As is true of other Shakespearean dramas, the ending of this play is a pseudo-ending inasmuch as the curses pronounced by and over Richard III apparently continue to be in effect in the kingdom of the Tudors. In the final analysis, Richmond is a shadow of Richard; he imitates him, less strongly but benefiting from Richard's preparatory work. Blurring the differences between holiness, lineage, and warfare has prepared the ground on which Richmond can justify his bloody usurpation.

The kings in *Richard III* (Henry VI, Richard III, Henry VII and also Edward IV, as will be shown in Chapter 1, section 1.3) appropriate the tropes of the Eucharist for the new communion of the State. The hollow patterns of the ancient faith are displayed, remainders of the Eucharist's consecration are functionalized and at the same time ironised. The differences between Richard and the others are gradual rather than substantive in this respect. What dominates all their shifts in the struggle for power is the question of representation—that Shakespeare's theater in the end decides for itself. It claims to provide what communion promises: to be the medium in which social conflicts are given their adequate representation and potential reconciliation. When the kings steal communion from the Church, the theater steals communion from the kings.

1.2 Margaret and the excommunication of the old liturgy

During the early modern age, excommunication represents the most visible institutionalized act of condemnation by divine judgment. A ceremony of excommunication is the expulsion of a parishioner from the congregation of the faithful by the clergy. The ecclesiastical performative of the major excommunication, the anathema, can be understood as a juridical act. Its name refers, however, to a supplement of the juridical: the Septuagint uses the term "anathema" (ἀνάθεμα) to translate the Hebrew "cherem" (חֵרֶם).[63] Paul (1 Cor. 16.22) may also have adopted the concept from this source. The word "cherem" is the Hebrew equivalent of Latin "sacer": it designates what through consecration has entered into the realm of the sacred, i.e. that which has been handed over to God, both what has been cursed and expelled from human society and the sacred.[64] It may profit the theoretical elaboration of this concept to go back to the Roman figure of the *homo sacer* who, has recently been elevated to the status of an absolute metaphor by Agamben and who is produced through a paradigmatic act of "inclusive exclusion."[65] In terms of the history of law, however, one finds oneself on shaky ground here: on the question of the *homo sacer*, early Roman authors refer to a questionable legend about a custom that, was already abolished in the time of the kings. It demanded that whoever killed a member of his own clan was to be expelled from his community. The clan no longer protected him; hence, he could be killed by anybody without fear of retribution. But he was not to be sacrificed since in a certain way he already had been sacrificed—in that he had been excluded from both secular and divine law.[66] But the sources do not permit one to attribute a juridical status to this construction: the *homo sacer* seems to have been a phantasmatic reconstruction from his very inception, a supposedly pre-juridical concept through which logic is to be retrospectively introduced into law.[67] It points to a clan structure of society that, already by the quasi-mythical time when the Twelve Tablets were written, no longer existed.[68] Upon closer observation, the figure of *homo sacer* dissolves in the darkness of speculation.[69] The tenacity with which Agamben combines Jewish and Roman law, folklore, philosophy, literature, archaic myths, and contemporary political developments reveals, however, that he uses *homo sacer* above all in order to outline a philosophical thought figure that complements his transcendental concept of exception. This figure denotes a living being that is so completely subjugated to divine as well as to secular law that it is reduced to "bare life." For this reference to a "foreclosed" organism, the Roman term *homo sacer* serves only as a Freudian "screen memory."[70] Consequently, Agamben's concept remains rather unspecific, requiring his recipients to specify it when they apply it to specific historical phenomena. This is what the following discussion will undertake for excommunication in early modern England.[71]

During Christianity's formative years, the concept of *homo excommunicatus* and the rituals generating him are also only hazily discernible. Paul's use of the concept as well as the exclusions he advocates in his letters remain vague as to their institutional circumstances and practical consequences. Historical evidence concerning disciplinary measures and administrative exclusions from early church communities likewise provides no precise outlines.[72] This only changes some time after Christianity has become an official State religion. Extant documents describing the history of excommunication in late antiquity and the early Middle Ages suggest that it was one of systematic hierarchization and monopolization. These processes turn excommunication into one of the Church's dominant judicial tools.[73] The theoretical frame for the resultant legal practices which remained valid for centuries was developed in the Supplement to Thomas Aquinas' *Summa Theologica*: among the clerics, only bishops and higher prelates have juridical authority ("can bind a human being in respect not only to God but also to other humans"), and for that reason only they can excommunicate. Parish priests can do so only on instruction; at best they inform their congregations of excommunications, unless a case of emergency occurs.[74] An excommunication is a strictly hierarchical process: the excommunicator can excommunicate only people in a position below his own, but not superiors or his equals, not even himself.[75] Extra-juridical, extra-ecclesiastical cursing is considered pagan and forbidden to laymen by decree.[76] The Old Testament justifies this law and the Church's monopoly on execrations. Not only Deuteronomy (18. 9 ff.) but also Exodus (22. 27) and Leviticus (24. 10–23) condemn curses not sanctioned by Yahweh as both ineffectual and contemptuous. The ecclesiastical discourse about this topic regularly (e.g. in the writings of Gregory the Great) contrasts curses that are to be rejected for their lowly personal motivations with the Christian curse that is necessary as an instrument of justice.[77] Thomas also worked out this point dogmatically in the *Summa Theologica*. He separates the legitimate curse that refers to the eternal, transcendent law from the illegitimate curse that erupts from a curser's thirst for revenge and from his spitefulness. The Church certainly does use the curse, but insofar as it has justice and the best interests of the accursed in mind, its curse is not subject to any injunction.[78]

Four variants of ecclesiastical exclusion emerge in the course of the Middle Ages. Among them are, first, two versions of territorial ostracism: the *generale interdictum terrae* and the *clamor* (which lends emphasis to the interdict through additional ceremonies, thereby, in fact, taking over the function of an *interdictum maior*).[79] These excommunications of a whole territory—one could characterize them briefly as an "ecclesiastical strike"—will be discussed only indirectly, since their history has largely ended in the Middle Ages. Thereafter, they have been subsumed under the other forms of exclusion.[80] More interesting for the present context are the two variants of personal excommunication: *excommunicatio minor* and anathema (*excommunicatio maior*). Other relevant terms would be "ban" (*bannum*) and "malediction" (*maledictio*). Both denote overriding concepts that can be applied to all four types of execration. The difference between major and minor excommunication and the association of "anathema" with the former did not exist from the very beginning; it was established as a juridically relevant distinction in a ninth-century canon.[81] These forms of excommunication differ in their applicability and in their degree of punishment: anathematization punishes mortal sins (apostasy, sodomy, murder, etc.); minor excommunication is imposed even on minor transgressions (e.g. the forbidden contact with a person anathematized). The lesser is concerned with religious contacts, the greater with all social contacts.[82] The latter excludes from the community of the Eucharistic body, i.e. above all from participation in the Lord's Supper; the former adds to this the removal from the congregation of the faithful. Again it is Thomas who worked out the theory of this differentiation: through baptism the person baptized, first, is accepted into the congregation and, second, is authorized to share in the sacraments. The withdrawal of the sacraments defines the minor form of excommunication; the revocation of both privileges is the result of its major version.[83]

Excommunicatio maior is the severest form of punishment that ecclesiastical courts may impose. Its legal consequences are far-reaching. The person anathematized may not offer or receive any sacrament; he has no right to a church burial or to handle any sacred objects. He may also not participate in the administration of the church, e.g. in ecclesiastical jurisdiction or in the election for a church office; he may not serve in such a position or receive income from church revenues.[84] But major excommunication is not a purely ecclesiastical sanction inasmuch as it also denies the condemned any kind of association with the community of the faithful. Under the threat of minor excommunication, Christians are forbidden from eating, praying, or working with anyone excommunicated.[85] The verdict of anathema does not include the loss of authority over one's inferiors, e.g. vassals, servants, spouse, and minor children whose right to consort with him is in no way restricted. But as an *excommunicatus vitandus,* he must be shunned by anybody outside this group of subordinates.[86]

Excommunication is imposed by the clergy but is also executed by the State. Since the early Middle Ages, secular and ecclesiastical courts worked together to enforce this verdict.[87] Under pressure from the Pope, the Emperor Frederick II in 1220 added the Ban of the Empire to the major excommunication.[88] Beyond that, a person anathematized is forbidden from instituting legal proceedings or to stand before a court as a witness or an advocate.[89] The arguments for it are in part sacramental: plaintiffs have to affirm the truth of their accusation by swearing an oath on a sacred object, usually the Bible. Since excommunicates are enjoined from handling consecrated objects, they cannot be granted this privilege.[90] Subsequently, Pope Lucius III (1181–1185) decreed that such people are to be admitted at least as defendants lest their status turn to their advantage.[91]

Even though the anathematized person has been excluded from the Christian community and its privileges, he remains a member of it and foregoes none of his duties. Clearly, this puts him into a worse position than a Jew or a heathen since he is integrated and excluded at the same time,[92] a point that is also explicated in Thomas' *Summa*: through baptism a human being has been indissolubly received into God's community; hence an excommunicate continues to be a member of the church, and the church does not lose its jurisdiction over him. In this respect, he differs from heathens and infidels, who do not share in the sacrament.[93] For Thomas, excommunication is a spiritual chain that binds no less than the chain of the law.[94] In this context, Agamben's figure of the inclusive exclusion practically imposes itself on one's mind: Thomas reflects that inclusion and exclusion in the state of excommunication are interdependent and reinforce one another.

The performative act of excommunication is part of the liturgy; its announcement (which is subject to major local differences of formula and frequency) is incorporated into the church service before the Lord's Supper, between the *Pater Noster* and the *Pax Domini*.[95] The excommunication formulas that are to be pronounced at this stage tend to assume the form of cosmic catalogues; these lists begin with an appeal to the Trinity as the source of the execration. From there, they progress from one circle of Heaven to the next down to Earth, where the body and the life world of the excommunicate are cursed in profuse detail. A famous example of this is the five-part "Curse of Rochester;" it is based on French prototypes and for a long time was circulated in English anti-Catholic pamphlets. In Laurence Sterne's *Tristram Shandy*, Walter Shandy induces the Catholic Dr Slop to declaim it.[96] These liturgical execration formulas were collected in compilations of canon law, e.g. in the *Libri duo de synodalibus causis et disciplinis ecclesiasticis* of Regino of Prüm (c. 845–915).[97] They were not freely invented by the clergy but consist almost entirely of shifted, refunctionalized, and rearranged biblical and patristic quotes. Passages from the Old Testament are frequently incorporated into the execration formulas, e.g. Deut. 18. 23: "And thy heaven that is over thy head shall be brass, and the earth that is under thee shall be iron."[98] In its Christian context, this formulation implies that neither Heaven nor Earth will receive the execrated person.[99] In addition to these extensive formulas, the ritual of the major excommunication involves sacred objects. This is what the phrase "bell, book, and candle" refers to: it evokes three forms of symbolically murdering the accursed. First, at the end of the excommunication ceremony, the clergymen frequently extinguish candles that represent the anathematized person's light of life. According to Prüm, 12 priests are to gather around the excommunicating bishop, each holding a burning candle in his hand. After the anathema has been pronounced, they throw these candles to the ground and stamp on them.[100] Second, the ceremony includes the ringing of bells[101] "in churches throughout the city," some legends suggesting that they imitate funereal knells.[102] Third, the ritual of excommunication involves the forceful closing of a holy book, mostly a Bible or a Book of Psalms.[103] This seems to symbolize a blotting out from the "book of life" (*liber vitae*), i.e. from the roll of the blessed that God keeps.[104] The parish membership registry that many churches keep appears to be a metonymy of this divine book.[105] These registries are frequently exhibited on the altar as liturgical paraphernalia, and it is emphasized that the clergy prays for the souls of the persons listed in them.[106] The ritualistic blotting out from the book of life goes back to a rabbinical tradition,[107] presumably even as far back as the execration in Psalm 69, verse 28: "Let them be blotted out of the book of the living, and not be written with the righteous." The figure of the "book of life" appears repeatedly in the Bible, and in nearly all cases in connection with threatened erasures. An example is Exodus 32. 33: "And the Lord said unto Moses, whosoever hath sinned against me, him will I blot out of my book." Paul adopts this figure (Phil. 4. 3; Heb. 12. 23), but it also plays a major role in Revelation: at the Last Judgment, whoever is not enrolled in the book of life will be thrown into the lake of fire (Rev. 20. 15, presumably based on Daniel 12. 1). The execration is once again not to be understood as a undoing of marks but as a supplementary marking.[108] According to these ceremonies, the rite of excommunication ends with the words "Amen," "Fiat, fiat" or "Anathema sit." All members of the congregation speak these words, thereby sealing their consent the way an oath seals a contract.[109]

The anathema can be rescinded if the accursed promises to do penance and undergoes a ceremony of absolution. Fixed liturgical formulas that regulate the return of an excommunicated sinner, also collected by Regino of Prüm, have existed since the beginning of the tenth century: The excommunicate throws himself down before the excommunicating bishop at the church door, confesses his guilt, asks for forgiveness and promises to do penance. The bishop leads him into the church and recites a number of blessings over him that invert the preceding curses.[110] Metaphors of light play a significant role here. But the ceremony of absolution appears to be paradoxical at least insofar as the anathema has been pronounced rhetorically with attributes of irreversibility. For example, one common formula of the major excommunication is: "*Sic extingatur memoria eorum in secula seculorum.*"[111] Many collections of canon law adopt a phrase from the 845 Council of Meaux that defines anathema as *aeternae mortis damnatio.*[112] That a suspension of the ban is nonetheless possible in the course of time implicitly questions this rhetoric of eternal punishment. Once again, a logical irreconcilability in the relation of time and eternity results when the curse both equates human and divine law and separates them from each other.

The same problem also causes a difficulty in the relation between excommunication and the Lord's Supper. This issue is not resolved by claiming that the exclusion of the excommunicate from the Eucharist simply expresses the Douglasian idea that the holy has to be kept separate from the unholy.[113] As was explained in the last section, it is the Eucharist itself that should perform this function insofar as it metes out the fateful punishment of the accursed. But when the Eucharist punishes the transgressor in this way, how can it be punishment to withhold the Eucharist from him or her through the anathema? The excommunication complements the verdict of the Eucharist and at the same time obstructs it; it functions as an ecclesiastical supplement of divine judgment. Consequently, the anathema is perceived, to be sure, as a "separation from God."[114] But even so, it remains obvious that excommunication does not necessarily represent a manifestation of divine justice. A decree by Innocent III in the thirteenth century states that a woman, if she knows but cannot prove that her marriage is illicit, should refuse marital concourse even when this may lead to her excommunication, such punishment being preferable to incurring mortal sin.[115] Thomas Aquinas thinks of the relationship of Eucharist and excommunication as one of "imitation": in the act of excommunication, the Church imitates God's judgment.[116] But even when this act is not justified, Thomas says, it is to be considered legally valid. A person so punished may ask the excommunicator for absolution but is not permitted to ignore the excommunication, as this would be a mortal sin.[117] Whoever does not accept it as binding has deserved the verdict in any case, even if it may be unjustified.[118]

The ambivalence in the relationship between divine justice and ecclesiastical jurisdiction also becomes relevant in the conflict between Church and State. The superior political position of the medieval popes vis-à-vis the secular rulers is based in part on their power to excommunicate. The dispute over lay investiture in the eleventh century, for example, was solved temporarily when Gregory VII excommunicated the emperor, Henry IV.[119] In the late Middle Ages, however, as new States are being created and consolidated, secular and spiritual jurisdiction are necessarily at odds again. In the France of the fourteenth century, royal officials are often excommunicated as a result. The king's "parlements" attempt to rescind these verdicts, and at least one case is known in which one parliament responds to a ban with a kind of counter-ban that prohibits any association with the excommunicating dean and his chapter.[120] During the times of its growing power, the State would try to limit the Church's authority to *excommunicatio minor* and either to abolish the *excommunicatio maior* or usurp it. Hence, figures of the ecclesiastical excommunication are occasionally imitated in official statements. Especially during the sixteenth century—in part even before the Reformation—secular power takes over the rhetoric of execration. In 1521, for example, the Mayor of Lincoln publishes "a formal curse on those who had improperly removed the records and books of the Common Council."[121]

The Reformation speeds up this development with attacks on the papal power of excommunication. Already in the Middle Ages, the Popes were occasionally criticized for their excessive use of the anathema. The reformers take up this issue and in their propaganda represent the Pope as the unprincipled author of horrible execrations and hence as a heretic. The first Protestants (as well as the Puritans later) denounce this papal practice as blasphemous arrogance insofar as it claims that the bishops can command God to impose a penalty, i.e. that they can direct God's will as they wish.[122] Luther first and foremost elaborates this *topos* even before his own excommunication in 1521. But the ban imposed on all the important reformers and their adherents obviously makes this issue still more relevant. Many Protestants plead for abolishing the practice because they see it as blasphemous and believe that no Christian may exclude anybody from the universal community of Christ. Luther describes the anathema not only as blasphemy but also as an illicit interference in secular jurisdiction:

> We maintain that the "great" excommunication, as the pope calls it, is a purely secular penalty and does not concern us who serve the church. However, the "small" (that is, the truly Christian) excommunication is that public, obstinate

> sinners should not be admitted to the sacrament or other fellowship in the church until they improve their behavior and avoid sin. The preachers should not mix civil punishments together with this spiritual penalty or excommunication.[123]

On the other hand the reformers use the Bible to develop their own ceremonies and formulas of execration; elements of the these even enter into their own denunciations of the papal power to excommunicate. In his polemics against the Pope as a blasphemous execrator, Luther himself often uses phrases taken from excommunication formulas:

> The other [papal] punishments and penalties – [. . .] lightning, thundering, cursings, damnings, and the rest of these devices – should be buried ten fathoms deep in the earth so that their name and memory not be left on earth.[124]

Luther justifies such curses by saying that a curse is implied in every prayer and blessing, as there is a negation in every determination:

> Whoever prays, also curses, as for example when I say: 'Hallowed be thy name', I curse Erasmus and all those who fight against the word.[125]

But does this justification not also falsify Luther's own polemic against papal bans? Luther does emphatically distinguish between true and false imprecations, but *de facto* he relinquishes all criteria that in case of doubt would make it possible to maintain this difference. The only criterion he accepts is God's imperceptible approbation of the curse. No wonder that the anti-reformation propaganda of the Catholics often represents Luther as an unrestrained execrator and blasphemer.[126] In the territories reformed according to Luther's creed, it is nonetheless only the *excommunicatio minor* that is retained as an ecclesiastical disciplinary measure. It excludes persistent sinners and those who are contemptuous of the sacrament from the congregations. But they can be readmitted into the fold after a confession of their sins. In the final analysis, Luther thereby secularizes the anathema, because many sovereigns henceforth make use of the right to *excommunicatio maior* and withhold it from the clergy; the boundary between secular and ecclesiastical jurisdiction remains blurred until excommunication is ultimately absorbed into secular punishment.[127]

The controversies about excommunication in sixteenth-century England take a similar course. The papal ban receives special attention insofar as Henry VIII (1533) and Elizabeth I (1570) are excommunicated after breaking with Rome and for a long time rule under a ban. Under Henry VIII (in part as a reaction to this ban), the Catholic Church is dissolved and the Pope's power to excommunicate is declared null and void.[128] In 1534, the Act of Supremacy is published that demands of all officials and the clergy to swear an oath of loyalty to the king as the head of the English Church. In the same year, execration ceremonies that promulgate papal bans are removed from the liturgy.[129] While the ecclesiastical ban loses its disciplinary effectiveness due to decrees issued by the State, Puritanical tracts keep evoking its horrors through the translation and distribution of extensive quotes from ecclesiastical anathemata: the Reformation starts a tradition of polemically quoting from Catholic bans, a practice that continues until the nineteenth century. Especially at times when English Protestants fear a Catholic usurpation of the throne, medieval or contemporary excommunication formulas are circulating in anti-papist propaganda. From such a pamphlet (first published in 1681 and reprinted in 1745), titled *The Popes Dreadfull Curse*, originates the previously mentioned text of the ban quoted in Sterne's *Tristram Shandy*.[130] The tradition seems to have started as early as with John Foxe who, in his *Acts and Monuments* (i.e. the widely read *Book of Martyrs*), gives an extensive quote of a papal curse:

> Accursed may they be, and given body and soul to the devil. Cursed be they, he or she, in cities and towns, in fields, in ways, in paths, in houses, out of houses, and in all other places, standing, lying, or rising, walking, running, waking, sleeping, eating, drinking, and whatsoever thing they do besides. We separate them, him or her, from the threshold, and from all the good prayers of the church; from the participation of holy mass; from all sacraments, chapels and altars; from holy bread and holy water; [. . .] and we give them over utterly to the power of the fiend [. . .].[131]

English Protestants close to the government also attribute to the Papists a curse on James I and the Anglican Church that, they claim, originated at the time of the "accursed powder-plot."[132] They repeatedly denounce "Popery" itself as a curse.[133] This denunciation of the papal power to execrate is given its theoretically most advanced form in Thomas Hobbes' *Leviathan* (1651). In his critique, Hobbes reduces excommunication to only one of its components, i.e. to the constative announcement of God's judgment, thereby approximating it to the Eucharist:

> The power of excommunication [. . .] is not in its own nature a punishment, but only a denouncing of punishment, that Christ shall inflict, when he shall be in possession of his kingdom, at the day of judgment [. . .].[134]

Excommunication and interdict are especially loathed as ecclesiastical and papal means of exerting political pressure in Elizabethan England, where the Church's monopoly on execrations has officially been suspended.[135] Ecclesiastical jurisdiction in general has in Shakespeare's time already outlived its relevance; it does continue to exist, but in a state of decrepitude since its competencies and resources are being increasingly curtailed.[136] But once again, excommunication returns in the form of its suspension and appears to be merely restructured rather than abolished. Once more, it first becomes symptomatically discernible in the secularization of the *excommunicatio maior*: under Elizabeth, the anathema is by statute[137] subordinated to secular jurisdiction, in particular to the courts of chancery where it is largely absorbed into their normal procedures.[138] Richard Hooker's *On the Laws of Ecclesiastical Polity* provides the justification for this:

> In a word our estate is according to the pattern of God's own ancient elect people, which people was not part of them the Commonwealth and part of them the Church of God, but the selfsame people whole and entire, were both under one chief Governor, on whose supreme authority they did depend.[139]

Excommunicatio minor remains at the clergy's discretion, but is rarely implemented. It seems, however, that one does not want to do away with the ecclesiastical ceremony of excommunication altogether: as early as the 1540s, a reformed execration ritual is introduced into the Anglican ceremony. This rite is free of all "papist" features and instead conforms to biblical precedent. At first, it merely consists of a reading from *Deuteronomy* 28; then, in 1549, the "Commination Service" is instituted and, in 1552, is included in the *Book of Common Prayer*.[140] In order to distinguish it from Catholic execration practices, "Commination," is expressly identified as a petitionary prayer, not as a command with automatic effectiveness.[141] The day designated for this liturgical service is Ash Wednesday, but, if required, the service can also be performed at other times of the year. The minister introduces the ritual in a speech that declares it to be a replacement for the ceremonies of atonement practiced by the early Christians:

> In the steede wherof until the saide desciplyne maye bee restored agayne (whiche thynge is muche to bee wished), it is thoughte good that at thys tyme (in your presence) shoulde bee read the general sentences of goddes cursyng agaynste impenitente sinners, gathered out of the xxvii. Chapter of Deuteronomie, and other places of scripture. And that ye should aunswere to every sentence. Amen.[142]

The minister next recites the curses against the idolater, the one disobeying father and mother, the one who moves boundary markers, the incestuous, the sodomite, the adulterer, the drunkard, the murderer, the one who takes bribes, and the one who perverts justice. To all this, the congregation responds by saying "Amen."[143] These responses make the execration resemble a litany, i.e. a prayer of supplication that is codified in the liturgy and in which the appeals of a prayer leader are given an unchanging reply.[144]

The Anglican Church is only one religious group among several in post-Reformation England, and it does not succeed in establishing its claim to an execration monopoly. Curses become free-floating, and several competitors claim them for themselves: besides the Church of England, these rivals include the King, the Pope (represented by those Catholics who have stayed in England), but also the leaders of more or less radical groups. Puritans and other sects use excommunication ceremonies in their congregations as an instrument of power, making no effort to codify the causes and forms of cursing. Puritan preachers, for example, tend to execrate unruly members of their community spontaneously; Quaker leaders imprecate their enemies and collect legends about the subsequent divine judgments.[145] These competitive relationships bring a variety of attempts to control and discipline the practice of rebellious cursing, which in the sixteenth and seventeenth centuries was regulated and punished more severely than during the Middle Ages.[146] This policy is enforced predominantly by the church authorities, but also by secular jurisdictions. Beyond that, one can discern in the reformed territories a proliferation of sermons, pamphlets, street ballads, etc. which exhort their adressees to refrain from cursing *extra ecclesiam* and at the same time question the efficacy of execrations.[147] It is at this time that splinters of excommunication ceremonies find their way into the secular theater. One can generally observe that the Elizabethan theater establishes itself by appropriating existing conventions and ceremonies and by reshaping them in accordance with its own interests and those of its controlling organizations.[148] During the controversies surrounding imprecations, Shakespearean drama appropriates many a shred of anathema and of other rites to its own use, a process during which these adoptions often assume the form of parody. The ambivalence of excommunication and its problematic, waning efficacy is demonstrated in *Richard III* and, less subtly in *Doctor Faustus*. In Christopher Marlowe's drama, Faustus visits the Vatican on his travels with Mephistopheles, renders himself invisible, steals, unseen, the Pope's food from his plate and wine from his mouth and beats him on the head. A cardinal thinks Faust is a "ghost crept out of purgatory" who has to be exorcised or excommunicated with "bell, book, and candle" (III. i. 73–76/83).[149] In an aside, Faust lets it be known that he does not fear the anathema:

> FAUSTUS: Bell, book, and candle, candle, book, and bell,
> Forward and backward, to curse Faustus to hell.
> Anon you shall hear a hog grunt, a calf bleat, and an ass bray,
> Because it is Saint Peter's holy day.
>
> (III. i. 84–87)[150]

Thereupon an excommunication ceremony is staged that Faustus and Mephistopheles disrupt with more slaps at the clerics' heads and by setting off fireworks. The ineffectivity as well as the selfish and worldly minded nature of papal curses is represented in this scene. However, during Marlowe's time, Catholic ceremonies, even when performed on stage and played with parodic intent,[151] are frowned upon—all the more so since here, provocatively and as an exception in a Protestant drama, the devil is not declared the clandestine lord of the Catholic Church, but appears in the role of a reformed anti-cleric's minion.[152]

In *Richard III*, no complete excommunication ceremony is performed, but there are many fragmentary quotes from execration formulas among the play's numerous curses, and they are clearly marked as such. Imprecation litanies and formal particularities of the ban are frequently referred to in the play, if only in extra-ecclesiastical connections. In this way, an appropriation and secularization of these liturgical formulas is integrated into the appropriation and secularization that the theater itself enacts. One can find the most conspicuous example of this manner of handling a ritual exclusion in a remark by Queen Elizabeth: after Richard has been execrated by the Duchess of York in IV. iv, Elizabeth approves of the curse in an obvious allusion to the structure of the imprecation litany in the Commination Service:

> ELIZABETH: Though far more cause, yet much less spirit to curse
> Abides in me; I say "Amen" to her.
>
> (IV. iv. 197–198)

Otherwise, explicit references to the rite of excommunication are rare, but the rite is a latent source for numerous utterances especially of the former queens. Margaret, the widow of Henry VI, no doubt is the most prominent execrator in *Richard III*: the bride of the Christ-King Henry[153] pronounces, in her two scenes on stage, almost nothing but curses and laments; even her "gentle counsel" assumes the form of a ban that she articulates in order to polarize the Court (I. iii. 289–294). As a monument to outmoded power relations[154] she floats through the play like a curse incarnate. She has turned into a revenant who cannot be located in the symbolic system and who is defined by an already inapplicable signifier ("Queen Margaret"):[155]

> MARGARET: Ay, little joy enjoys the Queen thereof:
> For I am she, and altogether joyless. [. . .]
> If not, that I am Queen, you bow like subjects,
> Yet that by you depos'd you quake like rebels.
>
> (I. iii. 155–156/161–162)

Even more than the other persons she treats herself as an abstraction; her actual existence has been suspended. She speaks from an insistent past that is her only reality. The historical Margaret, according to Holinshed and Hall, died in France in 1482, meaning that at the time in which *Richard III* takes place, she was already no longer alive.[156] Shakespeare weaves this death-in-life into the diegetic plot: in *Henry VI, Part 3*, after the murder of her son by Richard, Margaret had begged the sons of York for her death but had been denied (V. v. 67 ff.). Thereafter, she memorializes the trauma of the War of the Roses as an undead, spectral apparition. Accordingly, she often describes herself as dead and shattered into fragments, thus introducing the metaphors of the fall that permeate the entire play:

> MARGARET: They that stand high have many blasts to shake them,
> And if they fall, they dash themselves to pieces.
>
> (I. iii. 259–260)

Quoting snippets of excommunication formulas and their biblical precedents, Margaret directs her curses above all against the Yorkists. They reach their most prominent and richly allusive fury in I. iii, during her major execration of the entire attendant court:

> MARGARET: Though not by war, by surfeit die your King,
> As ours by murder, to make him a king.
> Edward thy son, that now is Prince of Wales,
> For Edward my son, that was Prince of Wales,
> Die in his youth, by like untimely violence.
> Thyself, a queen, for me that was a queen,
> Outlive thy glory like my wretched self:
> Long may'st thou live to wail thy children's death,
> And see another, as I see thee now,
> Deck'd in thy rights, as thou art stall'd in mine;
> Long die thy happy days before thy death,
> And, after many lenghten'd hours of grief,
> Die neither mother, wife, nor England's Queen.
> Rivers and Dorset, you were standers-by,
> And so wast thou, Lord Hastings, when my son
> Was stabb'd with bloody daggers. God, I pray Him,
> That none of you may live his natural age,
> But by some unlook'd accident cut off.
>
> (I. iii. 197–214)

This curse (as well as the one pronounced by Anne) contains an abundance of parallelisms, anaphoras, epiphoras, and symploces—figures of concatenation that mirror the *lex talionis* of the chain of curses. But beyond that, allusions on the level of form as well as content evoke the great curse of the Covenant in Deuteronomy 28 that, as mentioned, is a favored source of excommunication formulas even in the Anglican Church. The threat, for example, that the execrated one will survive his children and die in loneliness, is reminiscent of Deut. 28. 32 ff.; the proclamation that the execrated one will be forced to relinquish his position to a usurper, of Deut. 28. 43 ff. But even stronger than the influence of Deuteronomy is that of the Psalms. Many execration psalms use series of phrases and figures that also structure Margaret's speech:

> Let his children be fatherless, and his wife a widow. [. . .] Let his posterity be cut off; and in the generation following let their name be blotted out.
>
> (Psalm 109. 9/13)

As a figure of levelling justice, there also appears, both in execration psalms and in excommunication formulas,[157] the constant tit-for-tat of transgression and vengeance that is characteristic of Margaret's curses:

> As he loved cursing, so let it come unto him: as he delighted not in blessing, so let it be far from him.
>
> (Psalm 109. 17)

Margaret uses the same rhetorical strategies in an even more plain and formal way during her second scene:

> MARGARET: I had an Edward, till a Richard kill'd him;
> I had a husband, till a Richard kill'd him:
> Thou hadst an Edward, till a Richard kill'd him;
> Thou hadst a Richard, till a Richard kill'd him. [...]
> Thy Edward he is dead, that kill'd my Edward;
> Thy other Edward dead, to quit my Edward; [...]
> Thy Clarence is dead, that stabb'd my Edward [...].
>
> (IV. iv. 92–97)

In this scene she also employs the "ubi sunt" motif in quoting a medieval *topos* that likewise goes back to the psalms and is important in the history of the elegy:[158]

> MARGARET: Where is thy husband now? Where be thy brothers?
> Where are thy two sons? Wherein doest thou joy?
> Who sues, and kneels, and says "God save the Queen"?
> Where be the bending peers that flatter'd thee?
> Where be the thronging troops that follow'd thee?
> Decline all this, and see what now thou art [...].
>
> (IV. iv. 92–97)

It is the imitation of traditional patterns that structures the speeches in the first half of IV. iv, a fact that can be explained primarily by Margaret's formalizing, traditionalizing influence: the curses and laments that Margaret and the other former queens (i.e. the Duchess of York and Elizabeth) pronounce subvert the dialogic situation and dissolve it into conventional ceremonies of mourning and cursing.[159] Their speakers are exponents not only of outdated power relations but also of outmoded forms of representation. Even Margaret's informal asides (at the beginning of I. iii and IV. iv) turn the controversy into a ceremony by rhyming with the laments of the assembled court:

> ELIZABETH: Small joy have I in being England's queen.
> MARGARET: (*Aside*) And lessen'd be that small, God, I beseech thee:[160]
> Thy honour, state, and seat is due to me.
>
> (I. iii. 110–112)

Margaret enters with a rhyming curse that makes an imperfect rhyme of the official queen's preceding words and in this way binds them to her own utterance. The same scheme of the triple rhyme is repeated in IV. iv:

> DUCHESS: Edward Plantagenet, why art thou dead?
> MARGARET: (*Aside*) Plantagenet doth quit Plantagenet:
> Edward, for Edward, pays a dying debt.
>
> (IV. iv. 19–21)

Rhymes are rather infrequent in Shakespeare's dramas of this time; this might have something to do with the circumstance that they were a characteristic feature of the Mystery Plays, which had been recently suppressed because of their association with Catholicism.[161] In this respect, rhymes are also part of the repertory of historically charged poetic and liturgical forms that the lamenting queens dip into. As one *telos* of their wails, they identify an odd form of inverted hegemony: in the *agon* of their agony, the queens compete with one another for the title of the one who bears the greatest pain, as if this were a special distinction. Sorrow and lament, like the curse, seem to be signs of a paradoxical sovereignty:

> MARGARET: If ancient sorrow be most reverend
> Give mine the benefit of seigniory,
> And let my griefs frown on the upper hand.
> If sorrow can admit society [. . .]
>
> (IV. iv. 35–38)

According to Margaret, "sorrow" can even be "usurped" (IV. iv. 109–110). But her stance as a lamenting and cursing "Woman of Sorrows" is far from affording her a prospect of institutional restitution, social recognition, or real political power. Her curses cement her status as an outcast instead of ameliorating it. She insists on a lost sovereignty and on the outmoded forms which are its emblems. What is notable about her maledictions, however, is the fact that both the curser and the cursed are being defined by terms of deprivation: loss of position, loss of social connections and loss of perlocutionary power. In this representation, the curse appears as a congregation created by violent degradations in which the position of the excommunicate largely coincides with that of the excommunicator: curses are received and passed on in concatenated series in which the execrators are at the same time the execrated. Once more it is obvious that, due to its constitutive interminable nature, the curse always extends to the curser. If sovereign power constitutes itself with the help of an ambivalent reference to divine judgments, then, in times of uncertain and contested legitimacies, the dynastic lineages of royalty and nobility do not complement those of the accursed congregation, but will often tend to coincide with them. Curses serve as a way to articulate obsolete, "untimely" powers which have not been completely annihilated and deposed by their opponents but but rather been kept in indefinite suspension. Like Poe's *Purloined Letter* that passes from one hand to the next, such curses are signs of power and at the same time the circulating evidence of a traumatic transgression.[162] Margaret is not the first link in this chain of curses, as Richard is the first to point out: he refers, in a passage already quoted, to the curse that his father York has pronounced against Margaret before she had him executed:

> RICHARD: The curse my noble father laid on thee
> When thou didst crown his warlike brows with paper,
> And with thy scorns drew'st rivers from his eyes,
> And then to dry them, gav'st the Duke a clout

Steep'd in the faultless blood of pretty Rutland –
His curses then, from bitterness of soul
Denounc'd against thee, are all fall'n upon thee,
And God, not we, hath plagu'd thy bloody deed.

(I. iii. 174–181)

That this curse too is not only charged with Christological allusions but also perpetuates another royal curse, namely that of Richard II, can only be stated here. Another thing that Richard, characteristically, does not emphasize is that York has tied his curse on Margaret to the crown:

YORK: There take the crown – and with the crown, my curse [...].

(*3 Henry VI*, I. iv. 165)

Richard merely mentions, but does not actualize this curse that derives its authority precisely from this indirectness. Its effect is to unite the royal House of York against Margaret in an antiphony on the topic of God's justice. In this as well as in its parallelisms, it resembles the curses and laments of later scenes (I. iii. 183–187). It is a passage that reminds the spectator of the fact that Margaret in *Richard III* constantly invokes God's name, but that her deeds in the three parts of *Henry VI* were not godlier than those of Richard. Once again, the sanctifying performatives of all parties are subverted by an inherent irony. Margaret's curses only appear superior by virtue of the fact that she subordinates herself explicitly and entirely to the fateful dynamics and the aporetic structure of this speech act. It is the Protestant problem of all cursing queens, however, that the man they curse is already cursed by his deeds, which makes their work seem tautological. In Anne's words: they "curse [the] cursed self" (I. ii. 80). Margaret seems to be the only one who is cognizant of this redundancy and whose utterances are informed by this awareness. Her curses against Richard are prophetic only insofar as they are repetitive, enumerating Richard's past sins again and again:

RICHARD: Foul wrinkled witch, what mak'st thou in my sight?
MARGARET: By repetition of what thou hast marr'd:
That will I make, before I let thee go.

(I. iii. 164–166)

Hence, Margaret's curses are as often descriptive as they are prescriptive. She condemns Elizabeth, for example, to the loss of a royal status she has denied her from the beginning (I. iii. 155–156/209). In this way, she also adapts to the structural necessity that a curse must always quote a past curse. But the play demonstrates that it is this very past that is being constructed by the antiphony of free-floating curses. Margaret's portrayal of history is highly tendentious as becomes obvious when one compares her utterances with the events depicted in the first three parts of the York tetralogy; the persistent past she constructs from a melange of narration and prophecy is a simulacrum.[163]

All this makes it seem not too farfetched to understand Margaret and her outmoded and undead rituals as an allegory of English Catholicism in decline. But that would overly simplify the dramatic constellation: just like all of Shakespeare's characters, Margaret represents a theatrical potential that can at best be overdetermined by political parables. Representations of diverse social tendencies coalesce in this placeless personification of a past that is marked as a simulacrum. The Puritans too, for example, constantly refer to a purer, biblical past that they emulate in the conduct of their lives; and an aristocracy already in decline likes to invoke phantasms of its glorious past. And many of their subjects who have lost their old status during England's transformations in the early modern era do the same, as Margaret's title of "witch" presages. According to Keith Thomas' ethno-historical studies, the presumed maledictory power of every "foul wrinkled witch" consists of her claim on a persistent past. Thomas sees the witch trials of the sixteenth and seventeenth centuries as a symptom of emerging capitalism and of the resultant social conflicts: the medieval village community demanded of its members that they give economic support to their indigent neighbors, among them destitute widows. With the emergence of a market economy, these social rules lose their obligatory power and come back as vague, inexplicable threats that seem demonic, and against which the villagers protect themselves with accusations of witchcraft. Thence, those women, who continue to depend on the community's old obligations of mutual support and remain on the periphery of the new social order, are often declared witches. Above all, this concerns marginal figures of the lower class—elderly remnants whose claim to support has previously been secured by religious traditions, but who are now felt to be a threat to the new societal and economic structure.[164] According to this notion, the witch is not an antagonist of the traditional symbolic order but its very personification, and persecuting her is a symptom of the early modern emergence of economic individualism. All these possibilities of representing tradition, seized by the Church, the aristocracy and various marginalized groups, converge in Margaret and her curses.[165] The parties involved do not, however, enter into a new harmony as a result of this convergence, as much as E. M. W. Tillyard may want to read Shakespeare's dramas optimistically by conceiving Margaret and her curses as figures of destiny with the help of which the invisible hand of history will reunite England.[166] The quasi-dialectical movement of reintegration that Tillyard emphasizes is constantly being frustrated by undialectical figures of persisting conflict and its unendingly circulatory and self-perpetuating repetitions that produce nothing but simulacra of harmony. The reckoning that unfolds in Margaret's curses is no process of healing and restoration but the articulation of a catastrophic zero-sum game, an accounting in which incompatible positions are balanced according to debit and credit until all entries have been eliminated. The horizon of this unfolding *lex talionis* is total destruction since the pure logic of vengeance can find no other end. Margaret herself recognizes this constitutive excess of her maledictory inventory:

> MARGARET: Think that thy babes were sweeter than they were,
> And he that slew them fouler than he is:
> Bettering thy loss makes the bad-causer worse.
> Revolving this will teach thee how to curse.
>
> (IV. iv. 120–123)

The redundant surplus of Margaret's curses does not restitute, but parodies destiny and divine justice. Her harsh representation of history makes balancing acts of justice appear as an eternal return of the same annihilation:

> MARGARET: Thus hath the course of justice whirl'd about
> And left thee but a very prey to time [. . .].
>
> (IV. iv. 105–106)

When Margaret characterizes the present political situation, her disquisitions, especially in IV. iv., revolve around the metaphor of a parodistic *theatrum mundi*, in which satire and *vanitas* motifs easily coalesce:

> MARGARET: A dire induction am I witness to,
> And will to France, hoping the consequence
> Will prove as bitter, black, and tragical. [. . .]
> Thy Clarence he is dead, that stabb'd my Edward;
> And the beholders of this tragic[167] play,
> Th'adulterate Hastings, Rivers, Vaughan, Grey,
> Untimely smother'd in their dusky graves. [. . .]
> I call'd thee then vain flourish of my fortune;
> I call'd thee, then, poor shadow, painted queen,
> The presentation of but what I was;
> The flattering index of a direful pageant; [. . .]
> A sign of dignity; a breath, a bubble;
> A queen in jest, only to fill the scene.
>
> (IV. iv. 4–6/67–70/82–85/90–91)

These lines portray the present as a travesty of the past. The "repetition" on which Margaret insists appears as a theatrical reenactment, which explains why an abundance of words with theatrical connotations such as "induction,"[168] "consequence,"[169] and "tragic play" are used to describe it. Also, the identical names of the various Edwards, Henrys, Richards and Plantagenets serve in Margaret's speeches as indications that the play's characters act on the world stage as nothing but the degenerate doubles of other characters. In her depiction, theater is reduced to an unending loop, apishly repeating an idealized past. Margaret is not primarily the allegorical representation of a certain historical personage or group but, like

Richard, the historically overdetermined representation of a theatrical potential. This representation quotes old rites but introduces them into a new context in which they must appear as deficient—as outmoded, but endlessly repeated approximations to a mythic past. That seems to be the reason why Margaret so strongly irritates Richard, who uses theater as a force of progress.[170] Richard apparently tries to escape from Margaret's presence; at least that is what seem to suggest her repeated orders to him not to leave the stage:

> MARGARET: Ah, gentle villain! do not turn away. [. . .]
> RICHARD: Have done thy charm, thou hateful wither'd hag.
> MARGARET: And leave out thee? Stay, dog, for thou shalt hear me.
> (I. iii. 163/215–216)

At times, Richard displays almost timid reactions toward Margaret, for example in his oddly childish interruption of her cursing tirade (I. iii. 234). He seems to be in awe of her liturgical curses against him and apparently wants to prevent their propagation:

> RICHARD: Why should she live to fill the world with words?
> (*3 Henry VI*, V. v. 43)

> RICHARD: A flourish, trumpets! Strike alarum, drums!
> Let not the heavens hear these tell-tale women
> Rail on the Lord's anointed. Strike, I say!
> (IV. iv. 149–151)

Richard proves to be Margaret's antagonist on many levels, not least in his role as a governmental reformer of canon law. Various scholars have enumerated the parallels between the coups of Shakespeare's Richard and the reformatory martial laws of Henry VIII.[171] Richard and his cronies, for instance, suppress mourning and funereal ceremonies, just like Henry.[172] Buckingham and Richard pressure the Archbishop of Canterbury in III. i to break the right of refuge in the sanctuary (III. i. 47–54), which amounts to abolishing *de facto* the Church's right of asylum, as Henry VIII did on the political stage.[173] And like Henry, Richard is a master of emergency decrees.[174] In his official speeches, he repeatedly evokes states of public emergency to which a firm and instantaneous reaction is urgently needed. He decides on the state of exception without having been declared king. In this respect, he is a Schmittian sovereign even before his coronation, and as such he cannot tolerate any competing power in the State:

> RICHARD: What, think you we are Turks or infidels?
> Or that we would, against the form of law,
> Proceed thus rashly in the villain's death,
> But that the extreme peril of the case,

The peace of England, and our persons' safety,
Enforc'd us to this execution.

(III. v. 40–45)

The antagonists Margaret and Richard do agree, however, on one decisive point: both absolutize the metaphor of the *theatrum mundi*, even though this metaphor for both connotes diametrically opposed implications. Richard thinks of the "theater of the world" as the persistent abduction of history, opening onto his own glorious future;[175] Margaret sees in it the ritual continuation of a mystifying past. It turns out that their conceptualizations are dependent on one another: Margaret's retrograde zero-sum game of justice takes the form of an apocalyptic excess, whereas Richard's dramatical emergency decrees feed on bygone rituals (such as excommunication) and in the end are overtaken by them.[176] The ambivalence of the church ban and of its problematic post-Reformation afterlife appears in the theater as an unresolved tension that gives rise to discourses circling between the poles of a traumatic past and a traumatic future.

1.3 Edward IV, the oath, and the performance of the social contract

The constitutive openness of the curse makes it possible to use it preventively; thus it can prospectively be turned against all members of a community. This potential is realized most prominently in the case of oaths which play a significant role in the ceremonies of *Richard III*. Oaths are a conditional self-execration; by their utterance, subjects submit themselves to a legal order and thereby come to perpetuate it. Whoever swears an oath, accepts through this act that he will be under a curse if he transgresses certain boundaries. Perjury provokes God's eternal curse on the perjurer's body and soul, which is clearly expressed in the formulas oath-givers are required to recite before a court in the early modern era—be it by Common Law, by *ius civilis*, or by canon law.[177] Formulas of Christian oaths often contain cosmic catalogues of conditional curses, proceeding from all the powers of creation and resembling the catalogues of excommunication formulas.[178] In the New Testament, the oath is often designated by the term ἀνάθεμα.[179] But beyond that, many passages express reservations about ceremonies of oath taking, most prominently in Jesus' well-known prohibition of swearing in the Sermon on the Mount (Matthew 5. 33–37). Consequently, the early church did not require a loyalty oath of its members and in general disapproved of oaths. Only with the ascent of Christianity to the status of the Empire's official religion does the sacramental oath constitute itself as an ecclesiastical ceremony that regulates the handling of secular affairs.[180] Consequently, the injunction against swearing in the Gospel of Matthew is modified. For example, Saint Jerome interprets the words of the Sermon on the Mount in the sense that it is only forbidden to swear by things created, but that it is permitted to swear by God.[181] Afterwards, the Christian oath becomes a part of juridical proceedings. This development continues until the early modern era; it almost always considers as its origin a definition by Augustine, according to which an oath is an appeal to God as witness and judge of a statement.[182] This formulation attaches itself to the jurisdiction of the Roman Empire insofar as in Republican Rome the parties engaged in a lawsuit were put under oath at the start of judicial proceedings.[183] In the liturgy as well as in Christian jurisdiction, God acts as supreme oath-taker. In the early Middle Ages (around 630), perjury is accordingly declared a sacrilege.[184] The usual punishment for perjury is exclusion from the Eucharist; later, in Gratian for example, it is even the *excommunicatio maior*.[185] During the Middle Ages, legal deliberations about perjuries are generally the prerogative of ecclesiastical courts.[186] Most of the time, oaths are also solicited by them or by institutions which they have authorized, and in important cases they are secured by the obligation of those who are put under oath to take communion. This difference between oath-takers and oath-givers reveals an important factor in the theory of oaths. Since the early modern age, contractual theories have tended to proceed from the assumption that the relationships among those who participate in an oath are free and symmetrical. But *de facto* this holds true only in exceptional cases. Traditionally, an oath does not establish a social relationship but consolidates and expresses it. And most of the time, this relationship is strictly hierarchical. It is power that institutes the act of swearing: the ruler receives an oath, and his inferior gives it. Exactly this hierarchical gradation becomes particularly apparent in medieval oath ceremonies: in Western Europe, the oath primarily affirms existing dependencies, for example in the way the oath of fealty is formulated. Consequently, the occasions for oaths are in large part firmly institutionalized. After a while, however, it becomes problematic that even officials of the highest rank have to be sworn in, since this is a prerequisite for assuming royal as well as priestly office in many kingdoms, for example in England.[187] One could in fact see the coronation oath as the *point de capiton*[188] that ties the king's two bodies together. The obligations the king enters into through this oath, however, are formulated ambiguously enough; through his coronation oath an English king, for example, is "bound to justice's salvation," the ambiguity of the genitive being presumably apparent to the oath's authors.[189] But even this option becomes increasingly problematic. Whenever possible, the highest authorities are exempt from vowing ceremonies. According to most legal sources and starting in the thirteenth century, after kings have sworn their coronation oath, they are absolved from swearing any further oaths.[190] This is no doubt a consequence of the king's "pneumatic," sacred status.[191] But it soon turns out that this royal exemption from swearing cannot be sustained in everyday political life insofar as the promissory oaths of sovereigns prove to be an important tool of diplomacy.[192]

In the course of the Reformation and with reference to the above-quoted passage in Matthew, oaths are frequently criticized for instrumentalizing the sacred for secular purposes. Already the Lollards and Wyclif as well as the Anabaptists formulate these reservations.[193] Luther likewise argues against oaths, at first primarily against those taken by bishops.[194] As in the case of curses, this polemic does not lead to the abolition of oaths but to their redistribution: in the early modern age, the State becomes the principal recipient of oaths, whereas the purely ecclesiastical oath is being discredited.[195] According to Thomas Beade, no other nation consequently instituted as many State oaths as England, where vows of loyalty are considered a prerequisite of the sovereign State.[196] Their proliferation is a direct consequence of the Reformation under Henry VIII, spearheaded by the Oath of Supremacy of 1535, which was to be sworn on demand by all subjects. Those who refused to swear this oath were executed for high treason. The most prominent victim of this legislation was Thomas More, whose refusal to submit to the loyalty oath should be understood as an advocacy of Catholic universalism in opposition to the emerging idea of the nation State.[197] After an interruption due to Mary's awkward attempt of returning England to Catholicism, the tradition of the supremacy oath is continued under Elizabeth and further expanded under James I. The Oath of Allegiance, obligatory as of June 22, 1606, binds those who swear it not only to royal supremacy but also to the "divine right of kings" and the invalidity of papal excommunications.[198] The less stable the rule of the king becomes in the course of the early seventeenth century, the more detailed and numerous these obligatory oaths do grow. The loyalty oath of 1643, for example, requires the additional renouncing of belief in transubstantiation, Purgatory, and other articles of faith.[199] During the time of the Civil Wars, this development reached its apex with an abundance of State-mandated ceremonies instituted by Parliament.

Until the Reformation, the feudal oath before the English king was not a commitment of the subject's conscience but of his or her reputation. By contrast, the post-Reformation loyalty oath is largely aimed at the individual's moral conscience.[200] During the early modern era, it is inner attitudes rather than verifiable actions that increasingly become the objectives of the required oaths.[201] The significance of such ceremonies that encroach upon the subject's inwardness underlines once more how strongly power in the early modern era depends on rites of representation—an issue that the New Historicism has already repeatedly analyzed in detail.[202] The developing modern State has been shown to require public displays of power, especially in England. The kingdom's lack of a fully developed executive made it advisable to veil the State's instability and precariousness, respectively to install power in the king's subjects themselves.[203] But the ceremonial representation of interiority soon has to struggle with logical problems: during the Civil Wars, English subjects are forced in short order to swear exclusive and eternal loyalty to ruling powers that are competing with each other. The consequence of this is that oaths in general lose a fair amount of their prestige. Thomas Hobbes in *Leviathan* (among others) describes swearing as a highly problematical tool for creating consensus in spaces unregulated by law. He sees it as the paradoxical nucleus of society:

> The force of words, being [. . .] too weak to hold men to the performance of their covenants [. . .] there is nothing can strengthen a covenant of peace agreed on, [. . .] but the fear of that invisible power, which they every

> one worship as God [. . .]. All therefore that can be done between two men not subject to civil power, is to put one another to swear by the God he feareth: which *swearing*, or OATH, is a *form of speech, added to a promise; by which he that promiseth, signifieth, that unless he perform, he renounceth the mercy of his God, or calleth to him for vengeance on himself.* Such was the heathen form, *Let* Jupiter *kill me else, as I kill this beast.* So is our form, *I shall do thus, and thus, so help me God.* [. . .] It appears also, that the oath adds nothing to the obligation. For a covenant, if lawful, binds in the sight of God, without the oath as much as with it: if unlawful, bindeth not at all; though it be confirmed with an oath.[204]

Hobbes' theory of sovereignty which is based on this diagnosis, indirectly articulates a general contradiction inherent in the use of oaths: without a central power that enforces their execution, oaths are difficult to imagine, but they are also supposed to precede and constitute this power. The oath is, like the curse, a performative act of great theatricality, and similarly involves a paradox: the obligatoriness an oath is meant to create is the condition for its very existence. In order to be meaningful, an oath presupposes that those involved in it acknowledge common symbolic, mostly religious, obligations and submit themselves to them, but also that they constitute obligatoriness by way of the oath. The oath seems to belong to the law-positing sphere outside the law, even though the law itself demands and regulates it. Oaths may create structural frameworks, but they also reaffirm existing frames; hence they can be described by Derrida's concept of the supplement, too. Swearing an oath is therefore both voluntary and obligatory: Slavoj Zizek cites the case of a Yugoslav draftee from the previous century who declined to swear an oath on the flag, arguing that an oath of allegiance was a free act and that he for this reason was also free to refuse it. However, he declared himself willing to swear the oath if he were given an order to do so. His superiors explained to him that they could not give him an order in this matter since an oath was indeed a free act, but that his refusal nonetheless would result in punishment. And the draftee was in fact subsequently sentenced by a court of law.[205] The oath is always a *double bind* insofar as it compels the one swearing it to accept an obligation voluntarily. This paradox, if it is formulated at all, is mostly evaded by historicizing it. The corresponding strategy claims that the ceremonious oath is merely meant to explicate and actualize a long-established obligation that loses itself in the darkness of time. As a curse refers to another curse, so also an oath always refers to another oath, just as, for instance, the New refers to the Old Covenant. Therefore, in this arrangement the position of the empirical person swearing an oath, *qua* transitory being, is a marginal one. Through his oath, he must locate himself in a subject position that has been determined for him from the beginning of time. Based on its descent from the execration, the oath also renders the subject determinable as a point of reference, particularly within the referential system of the law.[206] It is not by swearing an oath that a person becomes subject to the law, but by this performative act he explicitly assumes the place to which the oath-taking power has already implicitly assigned him: he takes upon himself the curse that society proclaims against the transgressor. Insofar as the figure of an *a priori* guilt is, according to Agamben, the basis of every system of law,[207] the oath produces a field of culpability even when it is not broken. And there is still another dimension to this technology of power: oaths not only attribute actualizable guilt to their speakers but also absolve their recipients of any such guilt. For instance, by calling the wrath of God down on himself if he should commit perjury, a witness or defendant in court obviously exonerates the judges and the community in the case of an injustice committed in course of the trial. By subordinating himself to the oath, the oath-swearer conditionally suspends his own existence and at the same time posits it anew as a legally addressable subjectivity. The oath no less than the curse establishes a boundary between friend and enemy that traverses the oath-giver himself. The dispositive of the oath splits the swearer against himself, and by this fatal strategy constitutes a subject that the sovereign power can approach with expectations of coherence, which means that this person must have a conscience. Through the loyalty oath, the State apportions to each subject an inner life to which the State's representatives have, by definition, the right to appeal.

Due to political power struggles as well as economic developments in the course of the sixteenth and seventeenth centuries, the oath devolves and coagulates into a contractual form. The rise of capitalism entails the rise of contractual law.[208] The resulting hegemony of the contract—understood as a mutual transfer of rights—means that the obligation liberates itself from old forms. New forms are established which to a large extent are no less hierarchical, but more flexible. Unlike the oath, which affirms a timeless obligation, a contract is by its very nature temporally limited. It expires when the partners have fulfilled their commitments. Even in the late Middle Ages, contracts remained strictly incorporated into and reglemented by the traditional hierarchies upheld by oaths to church or State. At that time, many trade contracts are sealed by oaths sworn during ecclesiastical ceremonies. As a result, they are approved and secured by the church's authority.[209] That the conditional curse is still operative in contractual oaths of this time can be gleaned from the fact that an excommunicate is not allowed to sign trade contracts: a contract too "is binding," and since no excommunicate may bind another person, every contract with him is null and void.[210] Occasionally such rules are bad for business, and in such cases the church repeatedly gets in its own way. In the thirteenth century, for example, Innocent IV opposes the exclusion of excommunicates from trade since this could also work to the detriment of the faithful. The problem is acute for this pope inasmuch as the troops of the Fourth Crusade, set for departure from Italy, depend on business transactions with excommunicate Venice.[211] The issue remains controversial throughout the Middle Ages; it is decided case by case, the church definitively relinquishing its control of oaths and contracts only after the middle of the sixteenth century at the Council of Trent.[212] Henceforth, contracts no longer require ceremonies of confirmation.[213] This is also a consequence of economic developments, in particular of the need for dependable laws regulating trade relationships between different confessions: consensual agreements that are not secured by religious rituals must be able to become legally binding. Otherwise, trade between parties of different faiths (such as Protestants and Catholics) would be impossible. Attorneys close loopholes in the law with natural law constructions like that of the *obligatio naturalis*.[214] A situational, reciprocal contract replaces the absolute oath. Carl Schmitt has defined this development as follows: "The *oath* is a characteristic sign of the existential engagement with the entire person. As such, it must disappear from a social order based on free contract."[215] The Creed and the faith in oaths is replaced by Credit, the financial instrument that is the prerequisite for the conclusion of free contracts. Credit thus makes the world of business and the new economic order possible. An English merchant of the Tudor era remarks: "If goods were lost much were lost; if time were lost more were lost; but if credit were lost all were lost."[216]

Against this background, the proliferation of State oaths can also be read as a symptom of their decline. Accordingly, at the time of its rampant increase, the transcendent State oath is often legitimized as an exponent of the pragmatic trade contract, instead of going about the subject inversely, as before. For this purpose, natural law theorists (such as Hobbes, Grotius, Pufendorf, and Thomasius) refer to the contract as the to primal, community-creating tie, as the foundational building block of society. They no longer make the contract dependent on the godhead but on its self-referential function; that is, they try to make contracts self-supporting. The *causa sui* is watered down from a substance to an act. The ritualized oath before God, while not losing all its power, is considered a special form or a facultative component of the trade contract; the conclusion of a contract, conversely, is no longer seen as a special form of the oath ceremony. Some Puritans, for example, draw an analogy between God's covenant and a trade agreement.[217] In the argumentations of natural law theorists like Pufendorf and Hobbes, these rearrangements turn the oath into an insignificant act that adds a purely decorative religious aura to a word of honor.[218] But the idea of a self-referential basis for contracts has had to struggle with aporias ever since the earliest attempts to formulate it. Again, Hobbes is a good example. He considers contracts the atoms of society and attempts to synthesize from them the supreme power that guarantees them by enforcing a radical representative contractualism.[219] To this end, he constructs the sovereign as Leviathan whose installation makes the founding social contract and the contract of governance coincide in the *commonwealth*:

> The only way to erect such a common power, as may be able to defend them from the invasion of foreigners, and the injuries of one another, and thereby to secure them in such sort, as that by their own industry, and by the fruits of the earth, they may nourish themselves and live contentedly; is, to confer all their power and strength upon one man, or upon an assembly of men, that may reduce all their wills, by plurality of voices, unto one will: which is as much as to say, to appoint one man, or assembly of men, to bear their person; and every one to own, and acknowledge himself to be author of whatsoever he that so beareth their person shall act, or cause

> to be acted, in those things which concern the common peace and safety; and therein to submit their wills, every one to his will, and their judgments, to his judgment. This is more than consent, or concord; it is real unity of them all, in one and the same person, made by covenant of every man with every man, in such manner, as if every man should say to every man, *I authorize and give up my right of governing myself, to this man, or to this assembly of men, on this condition, that thou give up thy right to him, and authorize all his actions in like manner.* This done, the multitude so united in one person, is called a COMMONWEALTH, in Latin CIVITAS. This is the generation of that great LEVIATHAN, or rather (to speak more reverently) of that *Mortal God*, to which we owe under the *Immortal God*, our peace and defence. For by this authority, given him by every particular man in the commonwealth, he hath the use of so much power and strength conferred on him, that by terror thereof, he is enabled to conform the wills of them all, to peace at home, and mutual aid against their enemies abroad. And in him consisteth the essence of the commonwealth: which (to define it) is *one person, of whose acts a great multitude, by mutual covenants one with another, have made themselves every one the author, to the end he may use the* strength *and means of them all, as he shall think expedient, for their peace and common defence.*[220]

The "as if" already calls attention to the fact that the genesis of this primordial agreement of representation is an ideal construction. It need not have taken place in empirically ascertainable history in order to be considered obligatory. The social contract is as much a fiction as is the Leviathan himself. The problem of this fiction is its paradoxical status: Hobbes emphasizes, by way of contrast, that the State, its authority and the validity of State-instituted norms are based on the binding social contract of all citizens. On the other, he accents the fact that words *per se* are powerless:

> The bonds of words are too weak to bridle men's ambition, avarice, anger, and other passions, without the fear of some coercive power; which in the condition of mere nature, where all men are equal, and judges of the justness of their own fears, cannot possibly be supposed.[221]

If a contract has no force until the sovereign can threaten with punishments if it is not complied with, then how can a contract empower the sovereign to threaten with punishments? In other words: how can the contract's validity generate itself? This obviously involves a paradox of time: a contract must precede the Leviathan temporally and logically but the Leviathan, reversely, must precede the contract temporally and logically. Hobbes tries to solve this dilemma by allowing the Leviathan to constitute himself in a space and time that relate ambivalently to the space and time of the empirical subjects who enter into the social contract. This means in effect that the paradox is resolved by a further paradox: the impossibility of emancipating oneself from the state of nature is sublated by making the sovereign represent the state of nature. For the sovereign himself, as Hobbes emphasizes, is not subject to the social contract:

> The right which the commonwealth (that is, he or they that represent it) hath to punish, is not grounded on any concession, or gift of the subjects. But I have also showed formerly, that before the institution of commonwealth, every man had a right to every thing, and to do whatsoever he thought necessary to his own preservation; subduing, hurting, or killing any man in order thereunto. And this is the foundation of that right of punishing, which is exercised in every commonwealth. For the subjects did not give the sovereign that right; but only in laying down theirs, strengthened him to use his own, as he should think fit, for the preservation of them all: so that it was not given, but left to him, and to him only [. . .].[222]

Even if the sovereign were to swear an oath that would limit his sovereignty and subject him to a positive law, this oath would by definition be invalid and not bind him, who marks the point where state of nature and commonwealth become indistinguishable.[223] The paradox of sovereignty[224] is made incarnate in the Leviathan. In the sovereign, who as the representative of the social contract is not a partner in the same, the state of nature is sublated within the commonwealth, that is, terminated as well as sustained. In the Leviathan's realm, both the state of nature and the commonwealth persist, even though they exclude one another. Due to this paradoxical structure, Hobbes' society is in constant decomposition.[225] But this paradox and the resultant ambiguity of the sovereign figure also nourish his authority and performative strength; the terror at the sovereign's disposal is the monopolized and authorized terror of the anarchic state of nature. Hobbes evades this problem by various maneuvers, one of which is to explicitly exclude the curse, which is the symptom of a constant decomposition of social obligations, from language and hence from the political sphere: "for cursing, swearing, reviling, and the like, do not signify as speech; but as the actions of a tongue accustomed."[226]

In other cases, Hobbes deals with the paradoxical constitution of the social contract by exploiting the polyvalence of the concept of representation. The use of this concept in *Leviathan* undergoes a latent shift: it is introduced in its purely juridical meaning (as an agreement of authorization on the one side, and of acting as proxy on the other). But in certain contexts he also uses it in its artistic denotation, as an actor's "acting" vis-à-vis a dramatist's "authoring", as if no difference existed between these two relationships.[227] Defining the contract of installation in such theatrical terminology makes it possible for Hobbes to let the sovereign's declaration take place outside of historical time. The conclusion of the contract is a dramatic fiction, as Hobbes makes explicit by characterizing, for example, the preceding war of all against all as an ideal construction and as a mental experiment about the complete absence of sovereign power, a mind game that is fostered by experiences of the Civil War:

> It may peradventure be thought, there was never such a time, nor condition of war as this; and I believe it was never generally so [...]. Howsoever, it may be perceived what manner of life, there would be, where there were no common power to fear; by the manner of life which men that have formerly lived under a peaceful government, use to degenerate into, in a civil war.[228]

The installation of the Leviathan did not take place; it can only be represented as having already taken place in the performatives of *Leviathan*, i.e. as a necessary history play in which the book's actors represent its readers. A theatrical structure is the condition that makes Hobbes' sovereignty possible; he bases his fundamental political contractualism on a theater metaphor. In his subsequent argumentation, Hobbes demonstrates, among other things, that the natural person is merely a special category of the "artificial person," that is, of the representative as "actor":

> The word person is Latin: instead whereof the Greeks have πρόσωπον, which signifies the *face*, as *persona* in Latin signifies the *disguise*, or *outward appearance* of a man, counterfeited on the stage; and sometimes more particularly that part of it, which disguiseth the face, as a mask or vizard: and from the stage hath been translated to any presenter of speech and action, as well in tribunals, as theatres. So that a *person* is the same that an *actor* is, both on the stage and in common conversation; and to *personate* is to *act* or *represent himself*, or another; [...] and he that acteth another, is said to bear his person, or act in his name; [...] is called diverse occasions, diversely; as *representer*, or *representative*, [...] an *attorney*, a *deputy*, a *procurator*, an *actor*, and the like.[229]

In the area of representation, Hobbes explicitly introduces the person as a metaphor ("the [...] outward appearance of a man, counterfeited on the stage [...] hath been translated to any representer of speech and action"), even though he repeatedly speaks against the use of metaphors as the root of all confusion.[230] In fact, he avails himself of metaphors to dodge the ambiguity of his concept: a person is a human being, but a person is also a mask. The actor is someone who engages in acts, but in particular the one who represents someone else in his acts, for example, the actor on the stage. "To personate is to act or represent oneself, or another" implies that every act of a juridical and/or literary person is an act of representation. A person represents somebody or something else, and if he does not do this but acts nonetheless, then he represents himself. The person who represents someone else is an "artificial person"; the person who represents himself is a "natural person."[231] Consequently, there is no "natural person" who could be detected behind the "artificial person" as the ground for the representation. Insofar as representation structurally precedes the distinction between artificiality and naturalness, the natural person is rather a species of the theatrical person. There is no face behind the masks of society. One can derive a similar result from what Hobbes says about the author: he too appears both as the one who writes texts and as the one who, as a person represented in the juridical or political sphere, is represented by a representative:

> Of persons artificial, some have their words and actions *owned* by those whom they represent. And then the person is the *actor*; and he that owneth his words and actions, is the AUTHOR; in which case the actor acteth by authority.[232]

Hobbes allows "authorship" and "authorization" to merge and connects them through the common denominator of intellectual property, that is, the ownership of words and actions.[233] But the concept of property is also inscribed into Hobbes' *circulus vitiosus* of the social contract's constitution: property is something that becomes possible only through the installation of the sovereign, "where there is no coercive power erected, that is, where there is no commonwealth, there is no property; all men having right to all things."[234] Thus, claiming the property of words and actions and thereby the possibility of representation is a logical impossibility before the social contract has been ratified. Hence, neither the "author" nor the "actor" as such can precede the theater of the Leviathan.[235]

In *Leviathan*, sovereignty appears as a theatrical supplement of society: the Leviathan is a mask which represents the commonwealth and thereby generates it, but he also represents and generates the state of nature and allows both of them to merge seamlessly into each other. And the same comprehensive representativeness, which is self-positing in its very suspension, the book *Leviathan* also claims for itself: the only feature that allows Hobbes to distinguish the state of the commonwealth from the state of nature is the *Leviathan* as a text with perlocutionary intent. To put it more precisely, it is the book's phantasmal performativity which is made possible by the interlocking of two prolepses. As Matthias Bohlender has shown, *Leviathan* has a double orientation: on the one hand, the book presents a theory that claims the objectivity of the natural sciences; on the other hand, it requires of its readers that they accept this theory, that is, to allow the Leviathan to represent them, or rather to acknowledge that he has represented them all along. The salient point in Bohlender's analysis is the fact that this acceptance of the theory, that is, the success of Hobbes' perlocutionary speech acts, is the precondition for the objective correctness of the theory itself: "Hobbes's owl of Minerva fabricates its own dusk so as finally to be able to spread its wings and take flight."[236] The reason for this is that Hobbes derives the superiority of his theory over the other political theories of his time (which refer to revelation, reason, etc.) from its being objectively founded on the nature of things, which is external to theory. But it is only the universal acknowledgement of Hobbes's sovereign that constitutes this foundation. This means that his sovereign becomes objective only through the acceptance that Hobbes' theory demands. In the final analysis, the social contract that Hobbes insinuates is one between himself and his readers, which may be the reason why the image of the Leviathanic ruler on the first edition's famous frontispiece bears Hobbes' own face.[237] The center of Hobbes' theory contains a supreme logical loop: the recursive self-reference of the Leviathan.[238] This place is the place of a representation that does not require a pre-existent object. At the base of Hobbes' representation is a simulacrum, and it is exactly on this foundation that *Leviathan* locates the political theory of modernity.[239] This is how Hobbes modernizes the oath and, through the figure of Leviathan, veils its fateful logic in a new way. "Leviathan – the sovereign person as well as its language – is a fetish. It denies and at the same time confirms a nothingness it has defined as the opposite of its existence."[240] Perhaps its spectacle of sovereignty is subjugating precisely because it is nothing but a spectacle.[241]

In the early modern era, ritual oaths that are compents of a theatrical representation often meet with hostility because of their corrupting lack of seriousness.[242] But Hobbes sees the theater, more than anything else, as a place of extreme seriousness since it is the only space in which the Leviathan can be generated. Shakespeare's theatrical politics is certainly not that of Hobbes, but it unfolds the latter's aporias *avant la lettre.* The reason for this is primarily to be found in the circumstance that Hobbes' problem, i.e. the problem of representation and its obligations, has been virulent since the time of Elizabeth, and that several similarly circular solutions for its remedy have already been proposed in that period.[243] The contours of Leviathan, as they develop from the Christian thought on the Covenant,[244] already begin to take shape in Shakespeare's Histories.

In the York tetralogy, oaths appear at first in their traditional, medieval role: they actualize and perpetuate the hierarchies of honor whose foundation is the Christian God *qua* supreme ruler. However, in this function they take the form of empty ceremonies which are effective only by virtue of this very emptiness. Even if an oath is not broken intentionally, it emerges as an enormously problematic form of utterance, as a self-subversive act, for example in this double bind from the second part of *Henry VI*:

> WARWICK: As surely as my soul intends to live
> With that dread King that took our state upon Him
> To free us from his Father's dreadful curse,
> I do believe that violent hands were laid
> Upon the life of this thrice-famed Duke.
>
> (*2 Henry VI*, III. ii. 153–157)

This oath invokes the absolution from a curse of eternal damnation, which it unavoidably continues to allege by its very form. Consequently, the oath enters a vicious circle that makes the sacrificial deaths of Christ and of the "thrice-famed" Duke of Gloucester—whose *post mortem* display in this scene again calls the "Easter Sepulchre" to mind[245]—seem equally futile. Analogously, oaths are used in *Richard III* to justify morally questionable, dishonorable acts in the name of honor, e.g. when Brakenbury fends off the intervention of the three queens in the preparation of the princes' murder by referring to his oath of office:

> BRAKENBURY: No, madam, no: I may not leave it so.
> I am bound by oath; and therefore pardon me.
>
> (IV. i. 26–27)

The honor that an oath installs and through which it legitimizes itself already appears as subverted by its functionalization. Therefore, oaths in *Richard III* appear as a fatal double bind and as the machinery of doom. This topic unfolds above all in II. i, where Edward tries to regulate the intrigues at his unruly court by instituting an eucharistically charged oath ceremony, obligatory for all parties. Thus, the Yorkists bind themselves by means of a ceremony which they, within the diegetic action, have already nullified and reduced to a mere theatrical performance. For an unbroken chain of perjuries has structured their political careers. The decisive battle for the victory of their party was won after York had broken his holy oath of loyalty against Henry VI at the insistent urging of both Edward and Richard. Edward himself has in this context proclaimed:

> EDWARD: But for a kingdom any oath may be broken.
> I would break a thousand oaths to reign one year.
>
> (*3 Henry VI*, I. ii. 16–17)

Brother Richard supplies an equally circular juridical justification of the perjury:

> RICHARD: An oath is of no moment being not took
> Before a true and lawful magistrate
> That hath authority over him that swears.
> Henry had none, but did usurp the place.
> Then seeing 'twas he that made you to depose,
> Your oath, my lord, is vain and frivolous.
> Therefore to arms – and, father, do but think
> How sweet a thing it is to wear a crown,
> Within whose circuit is Elysium
> And all that poets feign of bliss and joy.
>
> (*3 Henry VI*, I. ii. 22–31)

The Yorkists withdraw from their oath, arguing its illegitimacy, while they must be well aware that legitimacy is not a concept that is still applicable to their situation. The uncertain situation of the Wars of the Roses make it impossible to decide who indeed is the legitimate king since none of the candidates satisfies all criteria. The competing parties in fact take recourse to a combination of military power and the insignia of sovereignty when they designate the monarch. And the loyalty oath of the subjects is part of these insignia. The ruler legitimates himself through the general acknowledgement of his legitimacy. It is this circularity in the institution of rulers that Richard uses to legitimate perjury, though he and his clan are perfectly aware that kings *de facto* have never any greater problems in making themselves also kings *de jure* (even if they have to refer back to mythic times, as the Tudors did[246]). But even so, none of the protagonists in the York tetralogy seems to be willing to altogether renounce faith in the divine approbation of the anointed king. Their pragmatic cynicism never principally questions the royal justification by way of holy insignia. That is the fetishism of the society in which Richard lives: it believes in the validity of eternal systems of divine order and at the same time manipulates them in the pursuit of personal interests. The society Shakespeare portrays is full of actors who cling to obsolete power relations, and of *personae* who lend an undead half-life to these relations. This fetishistic employment of ceremonies and of the need to safeguard them through religion are already strongly evident in the vocabulary of II. i. This scene of reconciliation is announced as an "atonement" (I. iii. 36), a term that connotes Christ's propitiatory sacrifice. Plus, various other religious phrases are subsequently applied to the ceremony, among them "blessed labor" (II. i. 53) and "holy day" (II. i. 74). In many productions, this scene begins with a celebration of the Eucharist,[247] a ritual which the text of Shakespeare's scene seems to require insofar as its introductory remark ("Why so: now have I done a good day's work," II. i. 1) would otherwise remain mysterious. And as Edward, facing his impending death, claims to institute a new covenant, he does indeed describe it in terms that resonate with formulations taken from the story of the Last Supper:

> EDWARD: You peers, continue this united league.
> I every day expect an embassage
> From my Redeemer, to redeem me hence;
> And more in peace my soul shall part to Heaven,
> Since I have set my friends at peace on earth.
>
> (II. i. 2–6)

The oath Edward institutes is meant to have the effect of a transcendental peacemaker among the interest groups at court. But in this function it veils the aporias of royal power most ineffectively and, for that very reason, excessively. A symptom of this excess are the demands Edward makes as early as the beginning of the scene:

> EDWARD: Rivers and Hastings, take each other's hand;
> Dissemble not your hatred: swear your love. [. . .]
> Wife, love Lord Hastings, let him kiss your hand:
> And what you do, do it unfeignedly. [. . .]
> Dorset, embrace him; Hastings, love lord Marquess.
>
> (II. i. 7–8/21–22/25)

The oath ceremony is meta-theatrical insofar as it forces the oath-givers to take on a prescribed role. The requirement, however, is the all-round love of every Yorkist for every other, a demand in which Christ's commandment of mutual love, from the description of the Last Supper in John 15. 12, appears to reverberate. The king's conceptualization of love, however, is modern in that it not only connotes mutual loyalty but also an impassioned interiority, i.e. the emotional intensity of free affect.[248] The double bind inherent in the oath thereby becomes explicit: Edward orders spontaneous affections; he demands of his subjects not merely to accept a role but to be identical with it. The commandment "dissemble not" forbids the subjects to play-act; they are being ordered to accept a role as their reality and thus to represent the unrepresentable. But Edward is not the only one who perceives the affects of the nobility as something that can be commanded; nobody else seems to notice that such a free love given on demand is an oxymoron. The *raison d'état*, formulated by Lord Grey and others, implies that the survival of the kingdom and the king depends on this permanent method acting:

> GREY: In that you brook it ill, it makes him worse;
> Therefore, for God's sake entertain good comfort,
> And cheer his Grace with quick and merry eyes.
>
> (I. iii. 3–5)

The supreme power not only demands loyalty from its subjects but also an immediate affection that transcends symbolic obligations. The final outcome of this is a mingling of the law and its institutionalized transgression. (The double bind resulting from this mixture, by the way, is a basic structure in many of Shakespeare's history plays, as will be shown later on.) Even though the resulting oaths are promissory, they undermine themselves at the very moment of their declaration; they are self-parodies.

The popular distinction between "horizontal" oaths (contractual agreements between equals) and "vertical" oaths (one-sided obligations of a subaltern towards his master)[249] cannot always be drawn clearly. In this scene, it is in the interest of the ruler not to suppress the horizontal in favor of the vertical oath but to pass the one off as the other. The scene of the oath, to be sure, establishes a hierarchy since the oath-givers submit to their sovereign's will. But the oath is also meant to serve as an agreement among people of equal rank. The sovereign's will is being imputed to partners in an alliance who unite by his dictate. The one in power compels through a free social contract. Invoking the divine judgment, Edward gives orders to form a voluntary association:

> EDWARD: Take heed you dally not before your King,
> Lest He that is the supreme King of kings
> Confound your hidden falsehood, and award
> Either of you to be the other's end.
>
> (II. i. 12–15)

The ruler's performative pomp is contextualized in a way that voids its metaphysical legitimation. A resultant symptom is that, as punishment for perjury, this same perjury is designated ("award either of you to be the other's end"). For how would the breach of the promise of peace between Rivers and Hastings be imaginable if not as a potentially deadly aggression of the one against the other? At the same time, any future reconciliation is made impossible insofar as the oath has made a taboo of their differences so that they can henceforth only be enunciated by way of negation. This fateful oath has a strictly "anti-perlocutionary" effect in that it prevents what it seeks to accomplish (like the command to swear that the ghost in *Hamlet* gives, who by this very speech act continuously sabotages its execution, I. v. 148–191). Apel and Habermas have developed the normative "principle of the avoidance of performative contradiction." This contradiction "occurs when a constative speech act *k(p)* rests on noncontingent presuppositions whose propositional content contradicts the asserted proposition."[250] In *Richard III*, there is almost no performative without performative contradiction, and the more fundamental a speech act is, the more contradictory it seems to be.

The court accedes to the king's incongruous demands with elaborate oaths, evoking transcendental forms of misfortune that encompass both worldly misery and the fall from divine grace. In their self-execrations, material and spiritual punishment coincide (see e.g. II. i. 32–34). The oaths have to be so emphatic and oscillate so elaborately between this world and the beyond, because what has been demanded by the king is self-contradictory and because this self-contradiction has to be drowned out. The participants have to say too much simply because they can say nothing . In this way, they produce an excess of significance that afterwards can be used in the interpretation of fatal events: nearly all oaths return in retrospect as prophetic self-execrations. (The next section will come back to this aspect.) The problem of excessive significance is not limited, however, to the oath-givers; the king says more than he means, too:

> EDWARD: There wanteth now our brother Gloucester here
> To make the perfect[251] period of this peace.
>
> (II. i. 43–44)

In this Freudian compromise formation, the ambiguities intertwine: "period of this peace" designates both the fulfillment and the end of peace, "wanteth" suggests the lack of Gloucester's presence and Gloucester's subjective "wish" (for the end of peace). Two ambiguities that support one another produce two contradictory and yet complementary statements: Gloucester's absence prevents a perfect peace settlement, but Gloucester also endeavours to end a questionable peace, thus definitively putting it into the perfect tense. The complex interweaving of these two aspects is almost reminiscent of Raymond Roussel's constructions. In his "perfect period," Richard himself uses ambiguity more strategically and consciously: he formulates the oath that is demanded from him so ambivalently that, first, it dissipates and, secondly, he can keep it by surpassing it:

> RICHARD: Among this princely heap – if any here
> By false intelligence or wrong surmise

Hold me a foe –
If I unwittingly, or in my rage,
Have aught committed that is hardly borne
By any in this presence, I desire
To reconcile me to his friendly peace [. . .].

(II. i. 54–60)

In this scene, it can once more be observed that Richard does not institute ritual acts but uses their equivocal surplus as material for his "dangerous plots." In his ambiguous conditional construction Richard, while avoiding a genuine oath formula, makes allowance for two cases: first, that the other nobles may consider him an enemy due to false reports or misdirected speculations; second, that he has offended one of them unwillingly or in anger. If, however, as is in fact the case, "intelligence" and speculations have not been misdirected but are completely true, and if his offending acts are not based on anger and ignorance but on cool calculation, then this sentence does not obligate him to anything. But even in case of his obligation, the result envisioned in his main sentence would be nothing more than a "reconciliation to their friendly peace," a locution that is likewise doubly ambiguous: it attributes peace only to the opposing party, and, since "peace" also connotes expiration, it indirectly articulates the desire that his enemies may rest in peace. The derogatory description of the court society as a "princely heap" additionally sabotages the official performative. But it needs to be pointed out nevertheless that Richard subverts the oath ceremony without, strictly speaking, using perjury. His speech fully remains within the boundaries set by the sovereign and articulates their suspension only through its ironic ambiguities. Richard pursues this strategy further with his reference to Clarence's death at the very moment when the latter is also to be included in the staged reconciliation and when its language thereupon takes on an exceptionally Christian tone:

ELIZABETH: A holy day shall this be kept hereafter;
I would to God all strifes were well compounded.
My sovereign lord, I do beseech your Highness
To take our brother Clarence to your grace.
RICHARD: Why, madam, have I offer'd love for this,
To be so flouted in this royal presence?
Who knows not that the gentle Duke is dead?

(II. i. 74–80)

Richard's news articulates a suppressed truth ("who knows not"), namely the fact that the sovereign oath of fraternization is based on nothing since the invoked affective unity of the royal house belongs, at best, to an idealized past. In the present situation that oath comes about, as it were, only over its own dead body. Moreover, Richard's utterance imputes the informed consent of the court to this murder, thus attributing a share in the guilt to all who are present. If one considers the parodistic sacramental circumstances of both Clarence's demise[252] and of Edward's ritual of reconciliation, then Richard's question exposes the exclusionary dimension of all Eucharistic and oath-taking ceremonies. When seen in this light, the social contract imposed by Edward can be understood as the perpetuation of a fatal Christian heritage. This provokes a defensive reaction from the king which, however, only entangles him deeper in his lethal strategies: he prophetically announces a divine condemnation of this trial and laments Clarence as the paragon of Christian self-sacrifice. (II. i. 103–105) In several respects, this leads to the dissolution of the assembly: the king dies soon after, apparently out of grief, and the alliance he brought about by coercion will hereafter haunt its members as a curse.

In scene II. i, a last attempt is made to force the contractual agreement under the control of the oath, which is exactly what reveals the finality of the rupture between the two as well as the oath's obsolescence. This obsolescence is the condition of theater becoming the place appropriate for the oath. When perjury becomes inevitable, the oath becomes theatrical. To the challenge of making successful use of oaths under these new dramatic circumstances, Richard proves himself, in the long run, unequal. (This is most clearly discernible in scene IV. iv. 366–396 and will be demonstrated extensively in section 1.7.) Shakespeare develops these problems further in the subsequent royal dramas. In *Hamlet*, for instance, perjury becomes locatable only within the space of commercial (meta-)theater, a fact that becomes apparent especially in the meta-theatrical oath (including a detailed self-execration) of the Player Queen:

> PLAYER QUEEN: In second husband let me be accurst;
> None wed the second but who killed the first. [. . .]
> Nor earth to me give food, nor heaven light,
> Sport and repose lock from me day and night,
> To desperation turn my trust and hope;
> An anchor's cheer in prison be my scope.
> Each opposite that blanks the face of joy
> Meet what I would have well and it destroy,
> Both here and hence pursue me lasting strife
> If, once a widow, ever I be wife.
> HAMLET: If she should break it now!
>
> (*Hamlet*, III. ii. 161–162/198–204)

That this oath can at the same time be broken and kept (Gertrude indeed "weds the second who killed the first," etc.), is precisely the point of the meta-drama *The Mousetrap*, as it is also, at least according to Lacan, the secret kernel of the drama *Hamlet*.[253]

This complex of themes is also taken up in the late Histories, oaths likewise providing a structuring element in the Lancaster tetralogy. The Lancastrians manage to employ oaths functionally and successfully again, adapted to their circumstances. The cleverest givers and takers of vows among Shakespeare's sovereigns are, without doubt, Henry V and his brother John. The majority of the utterances by Bolinbroke's princes appear to consist of commissives. They unfold and use the paradoxical structure of oaths in a way that seems to come straight out of Hobbes. Their successful handling of this performative is due to the fact that they situate their sovereignty in a theatrical space from the very beginning. In his discussion of the Lancaster tetralogy in "Invisible Bullets," Stephen Greenblatt has shown under what conditions power feeds on its inauthentic and histrionic nature, on its symbiosis with the theater.[254] The king's divine authority in this arrangement depends, as does the theater, on its falsification.[255] As Greenblatt demonstrates, the paradoxical and broken oath itself can become an instrument of dominion that does not delegitimize but seals the king's sovereignty.[256] Dissimulation and pragmatic betrayals only strengthen the politically astute ruler; open and unpunished perjury makes the king more convincing since it is a sign of his sovereignty that stands above the law. The Percies declare that the perjury of Henry IV, who has falsely assured the deposed Richard II of freedom from bodily harm, is the cause of their rebellion, but Henry IV counters even this accusation with an act of perjury:

> WORCESTER: I told him gently of our grievances,
> Of his oath-breaking, which he mended thus:
> By now forswearing that he is forsworn.
> He calls us 'rebels', 'traitors' and will scourge
> With haughty arms this hateful name in us.
>
> (*1 Henry IV*, V. ii. 36–40)

This double perjury is amortized in *2. Henry IV* with a new act of perjury. Prince John swears in his father's name that the rebels in Gaultree Forest will be given satisfaction:

> JOHN: And swear here, by the honor of my blood,
> My father's purposes have been mistook,
> And some about him have too lavishly
> Wrested his meaning and authority.
> My lord, these griefs shall be with speed redressed;
> Upon my soul they shall.
>
> (*2 Henry IV*, IV. i. 281–286)

It is symptomatic that he swears his oath not on his soul but on the honor of his blood. That "blood" in this context denotes violence as well as loyalty toward one's lineage soon becomes apparent: John has the rebels, who trusted his oath and disbanded their troops, apprehended as traitors and executed. When they accuse him of disloyalty on their way to the "block of death," he refers to the wording of his oath:

> JOHN: I promised you redress of these same grievances
> Whereof you did complain; which, by mine honour,

I will perform with a most Christian care.
But for you rebels, look to taste the due
Meet for rebellion and such acts as yours.

(*2 Henry IV*, IV. i. 339–343)

The satisfaction his oath guaranteed them reaches the condemned only as a mockery. Next follows the slaughter of the troops raised and then disbanded by the rebels, a confrontation so asymmetrical that even Sir Falstaff can distinguish himself in it (*2. Henry IV*, IV. ii). Prince John attributes the success of his cynical strategy to God's judgment:

JOHN: Strike up our drums, pursue the scattered stray.
God, and not we, hath safely fought today.

(*2 Henry IV*, IV. i. 347)

But the submission to divine jurisdiction, as which war was described in the early modern age,[257] has not taken place in this scene; John has cleverly prevented it. Fighting has indeed been done "safely," that is, with empty words as the weapons of peace. The God to whom John refers is already a functional part of the sovereign machinery. The princes, like the "Mortal God" Leviathan, are not under the social contract and hence are released from all oaths they swear in their political roles. It is the king's privilege not to be bound by his word; the royal presence for that reason no longer excludes, but assimilates the traitor. That sovereign speech acts, for example in the use of oaths, subvert themselves under these circumstances no longer causes the throne of the monarch to shake. Instead, his power seems all the more comprehensive because it can no longer be attacked by means of logic. Such power forces its subjects into a *credo quia absurdum*, which means that the crown can be played as a joker in the contractual power games. In this respect, the oaths of the princes John and Hal already reveal contours of the new Leviathan: oath and contract can be interwoven again via perjury, and thus they form a theatrical picture puzzle in which their genesis remains paradoxical and the order of their priority undecidable.

1.4 Hastings and the fateful prophecy

In late antiquity and during the Middle Ages the church condemns any malediction not integrated into liturgical ceremonies as an unchristian act to be avoided both by the laity and the clergy. In this context, various biblical curses are re-examined and declared legitimate since they are judged to merely have the form of curses, but actually to be prophecies through which God or the saints announce divine justice. John Chrysostom, for example, in the fourth century describes biblical curses as "prophecies in the guise of imprecations."[258] Augustine uses the same *topos*, stating that Jesus directed the curses in Psalm 109[259] against Judas and that they predict the punishment of the godless even though their speaker entertains no evil wishes against them.[260] This distinction makes it possible to separate illegitimate from legitimate cursing: the latter agrees with the world's course as determined by God and revealed to his prophets, the former repudiates this course of the world. It is a *topos* that survives well into the modern era. For example, John Donne explains in one of his sermons that the curses in the Psalms are "prophetical" and "always conditionall":

> Not that David in his owne heart did wish all that upon Iudas; but only so, as foreseeing in the Spirit of Prophesying, that those things should fall upon him, he concurred with the purpose of God therein, and so farre as he saw it to be the will of God, he made it his will, and his wish. And so have all those judgements, which we denonce upon sinners, the nature of Prophecies in them [. . .].[261]

The transitions between a prophecy and a curse are fluid; both break down the boundary of expositional and exercitive speaking and turn out to be ambiguous and aporetic.

In Renaissance England, prophecies are an influential genre. Old prophetic writings, such as the well-known "Prophecy of Merlin" in Geoffrey of Monmouth's *Historia Regum Brittaniae*, are frequently cited. Like curses, these predictions form series by pointing to other predictions. In the "Prophecy of Merlin," one can detect, first and foremost, echoes of the Bible's prophetic books, especially Daniel. The resulting prophecies consist for the most part of formulas that are emblematic, enigmatic, and hence irrefutable. The following passage can serve as a representative example:

> A Hedgehog loaded with apples shall re-build the town and, attracted by the smell of these apples, bird will flock there from many different forests. The Hedgehog shall add a huge palace and then wall it round with six hundred towers. [. . .] The Hedgehog will hide its apples inside Winchester and will construct hidden passages under the earth. In that time the stones shall speak. [. . .] Next a Heron shall emerge from the Forest of Calaterium and fly round the island for two whole years. By its cry in the night it will call all winged creatures together and assemble in its company every genus of bird. They will swoop down on to the fields which men have cultivated and devour every kind of harvest. A famine will attack the people and an appalling death-rate will follow the famine. As soon as this terrible calamity has come to an end, the accursed Bird will transfer its attention to the Galabes Valley and raise it up into a lofty mountain. On its highest peak the Heron will plant an oak and on the branches of the oak it shall build its nest. Three eggs shall be laid in the nest and from them will emerge a Fox, a Wolf and a Bear. The Fox will devour its mother and then put on an Ass's head. Once it has assumed this monstrous guise, it will terrify its brothers and drive them away to Normandy. In that country they will in their turn stir up the tusky Boar.[262]

The inscrutability of the future is integrated into the prophetic utterance by making it opaque. The language of such prophecies is at times so dense as to be incomprehensible: it is language *qua* language, script *qua* script, beyond semantics, that comes to the fore on these occasions.[263] Many prophecies project a series of mysterious emblematic figures (among them the frequently mentioned "Dreadful Dead Man" on the English throne),[264] and the interpreters assign them to specific historical persons as needed. Both the Yorkists and the Lancastrians used the "Prophecy of Merlin" during the War of the Roses in order to legitimize their aspirations to the throne.[265] Later, some Anglican bishops, among them John Bale, analogously discover foreknowledge of the break with Rome in many a popular prophecy, especially in the "Prophecy of Merlin." Consequently, these prophecies are often treated as works of divine inspiration, the Reformation itself being seen as a work of providence.[266] In the sixteenth and seventeenth centuries, even the monarch resorts on occasion to such formulas. James I in particular often pronounces execratory prophecies that complement his juridical power (e.g. in the Preface of *Basilikon Doron*).[267] But he supplements these statements by again referring to God's will, which can be neither grasped nor influenced. One among numerous examples is James' letter of October 6, 1611 to the Dutch authorities concerning the heretic theologian Vorstius, in which he writes:

> For these respects therefore have Wee cause enough very heartily to request you, to roote out with speede those Heresies and Schisms, which are beginning to bud foorth amongst you, which if you suffer to have the reines any longer, you cannot expect any other issue thereof, then the curse of God, infamy throughout all the reformed Churches, and a perpetuall rent and distraction in the whole body of your State.[268]

The authority of the prophetic admonition that here fluctuates between royal interpretive power and divine executive power affirms the authority of the sovereign as much as that of the wishes he attributes to God. In order to saturate this verbal hegemony, secular power strives for a monopoly over prophecy: in post-Reformation England prophecies not approved by the sovereign are increasingly criminalized. Clandestine prophecies and interpretations of prophetic texts that are not sanctioned by the State or the Anglican Church are officially considered as *per definitionem* "vain," on the one hand, and as "the very foundation of all rebellion," on the other.[269] The Tudor monarchy uses severe juridical and political measures against unsolicited prophets. One reason for this is the regular practice of referring to prophecies in order to legitimize revolts, for which Keith Thomas gives copious examples.[270] Already a statute of 1532 defines prophecies about the ruling king's death as high treason.[271] In 1580, the Act Against Seditious Words and Rumours Uttered Against the Queen's Most Excellent Majesty is adopted, which imposes the death penalty for prophecies (especially about the demise of Tudor rule) as well as for curses pronounced against Elizabeth.[272] James continued this form of censorship and persecution of prophetic activities.[273]

Like the curse, the prophecy is an ambivalent instrument of authority. It can legitimize and preserve existing power relations but it can also question and attack them. It is frequently impossible or only retrospectively feasible, to distinguish between subversive and conformist prophecies, not only because they are usually ambiguous, but also because they are often pronounced in situations in which the distribution of power is indistinct or shifting. The problematic differentiation between edifying and dangerous prophecies again involves the religious ambiguity of a prophecy's efficacy: does the prophecy infringe on divine order or merely articulate it? The relation between actively fixing the world's course, on the one hand, and passively pronouncing the future consequences of a deed, on the other, must remain unclear because both prophecy and curse refer to a destiny of which they also seem to be a paradoxical supplement. They themselves inflict the destiny to which they are subjected. Being thus ambivalent, prophecy and curse instigate the work of fate in Walter Benjamin's sense. For according to him, "fate is not a purely natural occurrence any more than it is purely historical"; it is the ruling power in history, and its field is defined by the guilt that came into the world as the curse of original sin: "Fate is the entelechy of events within the field of guilt."[274] The decisive element in defining the problematic nature of fate in early modern times is the overdetermined significance attributed to primal guilt—that is, to original sin. The sixteenth century formulates the question of guilt against the background of the Protestant doctrine of predestination. The origin of sin is one of the central problems of its dogma because original sin appears as "both necessary and voluntary,"[275] as the point where man's own will deviates from God's plan and by this very fact confirms it. The problem, which despite spirited discussions finds no satisfactory solution, can be stated thus: if original sin is intrinsic to God's plan for creation, then man, in the final analysis, is free of guilt; if it is not, then this fact appears to challenge God's sovereignty.[276] Religious predeterminism relies on a paradoxical point of undecidability at which the transcendental guilt of original sin, as the fateful inheritance of the subject, is inscribed into the myth of the law's genesis. The sovereign defends his authority to control and to elucidate this point against the competition from false prophets. The official discourse of Elizabethan England keeps the question of the relationship between original sin and predestination unresolved;[277] the issue of prophecy appears likewise suspended in ambiguity. The prophetic speech act shifts between activity and passivity and through this very ambiguity binds its subjects to a narrative of their fate.

The ambivalence of prophecy is connected to the latent presence of the curse within it, whose paradoxical, withdrawn temporality was already addressed in the Introduction. The form of interaction that the prophetic curse intends to produce is always already presupposed as futurity, a performative that forever "will have been." Its temporal structure retreats from the present into a permanent future perfect tense: from out of time immemorial, prophetic speech brings tidings of coming events to which one may never attain. In this way, prophecy formulates a history that binds future and past together in the figure of fate, at the exclusion of the present moment. In Maurice Blanchot's words: "When words become prophetic, it is not the future that is given to us; but it is the past that is taken from us, including any possibility of a firm, steadfast, and lasting present."[278] Prophecy does not so much anticipate or signal the future as subtract it from the present, making the latter incomplete and subjecting it to its own narrative. This narrative is the fate inflicted on man by God, "because the word *Fatum* comes from nowhere but *à fando*, which means from speaking, and *Fatum*, in essence, is nothing but a word and command of God."[279]

Shakespeare's Histories maintain complex relations with the doctrine of fate. One should first keep in mind that prophecies represent a prominent class of speech acts in all royal dramas. They also play a central role in E. M. W. Tillyard's interpretation of the Histories, a study that is still influential in spite of the numerous objections it has provoked. Tillyard describes the events of the York tetralogy as a chain of transgressions and of the curses that follow and punish them.[280] According to this reading, fate in the Histories is always and everywhere the instrument of God's vengeance. Consequently, the theater reduplicates and stages fate, while the inverse is also true: the idea of fate makes the world theatrical, turning it into a stage where a pre-written drama runs its course according to plan. In this way, Tillyard establishes an ideological univocity that neglects to account for the ambivalences of Shakespeare's theater. In contrast, Nicholas Grene and Wolfgang Iser have argued that prophecies and omens do not actually consolidate the Histories into one massive monument of Fate Triumphant. Instead, they guide the spectator's perception on different levels from one event to the next, make it skip from this perspective to another, without providing an end point to this movement.[281] The curses and prophecies do not converge but rather diverge and conflict with one another; they articulate incompatible historiographies as interpretations of events that elude them:[282]

> Between them, the strategies of inversion, reversal and foreshadowing unfold a network of connections that draw the spectator into the play. We tend always to look at one character's situation through the eyes of another: we see the court from Richard's viewpoint, then Richard from that of the court; we have Richard's perspective on the citizens of London, then theirs on him. And we even see the murderers through their victims' eyes and vice versa (with the murderer's view of their employer as well). [...] With this overturning, virtually all the positions lose their stability. [. . .] It is impossible to establish any frame of reference, let alone an ideal, that might allow some kind of integration of positions and hence a conceivable counter image.[283]

Prophecy in Shakespeare's dramas speaks in many voices: every prediction quotes a previous one but also competes with it, usurps its place and overwrites it, so that palimpsests of utterances seem to emerge. This creates not one but many chains of prophetic curses. These chains of curses become readable for different subjects under divergent circumstances, revealing contrasting perspectives on history. The catastrophic developments of the Histories are not inexorable and fated in the traditional sense; their contingency is emphasized in key scenes, though without completely excluding the idea of fate. Instead, the situations appear to be oversaturated with predictions that refer to them and mutually exclude one another, so that one of them must inevitably be justified by the course of events. The idea of providence in Shakespeare is not subverted by the idea of contingency, but neither does the relationship of free will and predestination become a question of perspective, as it has sporadically since Boethius.[284] Instead, the work of providence is made dependent on a semantic oversaturation whose position cannot be clearly situated within the polarity of contingency and predestination and whose metaphysical status remains uncertain. This surplus of prophecies serves as raw material for fabricating ideological constructions of history. In *Richard III*, Shakespeare demonstrates the criteria whereby various parties select and use this material. The first principle of selection is that the persons involved remember only those prophetic curses that seem to come true, while the inapplicable ones are forgotten. For example, not all the curses pronounced by Margaret, who calls herself a "prophetess" (I. iii. 301), hit their mark: Dorset, for one, survives the War of the Roses even though he and his mother have been cursed:

> MARGARET: Thyself, a queen, for me that was a queen,
> Outlive thy glory like my wretched self:
> Long may'st thou live to wail they children's death,
> And see another, as I see thee now,
> Deck'd in thy rights, as thou art stall'd in mine;
> Long die thy happy days before thy death,
> And after many lengthen'd hours of grief,
> Die neither mother, wife, nor England's Queen.
> Rivers and Dorset, you were standers-by,
> And so wast thou, Lord Hastings, when my son
> Was stabb'd with bloody daggers. God, I pray Him,
> That none of you may live his natural age,
> But by some unlook'd accident cut off.
>
> (I. iii. 202–214)

But the fact that Dorset, and with him also Queen Elizabeth, elude Margaret's curse, has not been registered by most scholarship. Instead, the secondary literature usually states that all of Margaret's curses are devastatingly effective.[285] This is all the more surprising since Elizabeth herself refers to Margaret's curse immediately before Dorset's successful escape:

> ELIZABETH: Go: hie thee, hie thee from this slaughter-house
> Lest thou increase the number of the dead,
> And make me die the thrall of Margaret's curse:
> Not mother, wife, nor England's counted Queen.
>
> (IV. i. 43–46)

Generally speaking, prophetic curses can be determined as such only in retrospect; it is their fulfillment that makes them prophetic; their effects are always interpretations. Similarly, events become omens only through their consequences. The fate of Lord Hastings offers illustrative material for both facts: He first accounts for Margaret's curse and for events such as his unexpected encounter with a priest and the tripping of his horse on their way to the Tower as contingent and meaningless. But in the time between his condemnation by court-martial for high treason and his execution, these events reappear to him as portentous omens:

> HASTINGS: Woe, woe for England; not a whit for me –
> For I, too fond, might have prevented this.
> Stanley did dream the boar did raze his helm,
> And I did scorn it and disdain to fly;
> Three times today my footdcloth horse did stumble,
> And started when he look'd upon the Tower,
> As loath to bear me to the slaughter-house.
> O, now I need the priest that spake to me [. . .].
> O Margaret, Margaret, now thy heavy curse
> Is lighted on poor Hastings' wretched head.
>
> (III. iv. 80–87/92–93)

One can never be certain that a prophecy has in fact come true. Its materialization is always also interpretable as accidental: "footcloth horses" with low-hanging blankets do trip from time to time; the statistical chances of meeting a priest on the way through London are quite good; and Margaret curses because she has nothing better left to do. But the prediction is located beyond the zone of meaningful, rational proof. In this "beyond" the prophetic curse serves as explanatory framework and as final metaphysical consolation. It is a reservoir of meaning that, as needed, can integrate the traumatic present into the workings of fate and thereby alleviate the trauma. This is how the curse perpetuates itself and in the process proliferates, since its manifestation justifies new prophetic curses. Accordingly, Hastings joins the choir of maledictory prophets after he has inserted his impending execution into a Tillyardian explanatory schema:

> HASTINGS: O bloody Richard! Miserable England,
> I prophesy the fearfull'st time to thee
> That ever wretched age hath look'd upon.
> Come, lead me to the block: bear him my head.
> They smile at me who shortly shall be dead.
>
> (III. v. 103–107)

One should note the ambiguity of "shall," which here indicates the future tense as much as a wish. The auxiliary verb "shall" originally marks obligations, but during the Renaissance "shall" and "will" take on a new function as designators of the future. Since that time, the use of "shall" to indicate futurity in many cases still suggests obligation and an optative dimension.[286] This ambiguity pervades the prophetic curses of the entire play and is a good example of the subtle designation of proliferating curses as factors that are "both necessary and voluntary." For instance, when Vaughan, Rivers, and Grey are led to their executions, they see this as partial fulfillment of Margaret's curse. It is for this reason that they reassert it, likewise using "shall":

> VAUGHN: You live, that shall cry woe for this hereafter. [. . .]
> GREY: Now Margaret's curse is fall'n upon our heads,
> When she exclaim'd on Hastings, you, and I,
> For standing by when Richard stabb'd her son.
> RIVERS: Then curs'd she Richard, then curs'd she Buckingham,
> Then cursed she Hastings. O remember, God,
> To hear her prayers for them, as now for us [. . .].
>
> (III. iii. 7/15–20)

This proliferation is already taken account of in Margaret's curses: her prophetic curse as a "meta-malediction" announces new curses:

> MARGARET: The day will come that thou shalt wish for me
> To help thee curse this poisonous bunch-back'd toad.
>
> (I. iii. 245–246)

And so it happens:

> ELIZABETH: O thou didst prophesy the time would come
> That I should wish for thee to help me curse
> That bottled spider, that foul bunch-back'd toad. [. . .]
> O thou, well skill'd in curses, stay awhile
> And teach me how to curse mine enemies.
>
> (IV. iv. 79–81/116–117)

The prophetic curse perpetuates itself, then, not through an unquestioning acceptance of its magic effectiveness, but through its ability to charge traumatic contingencies with meaning. But even though the curse's fulfillment in *Richard III* can always be read as accidental, the play, in the final analysis, does not provide a determining perspective that would permit an objective decision about the efficacy of curses. The supplement renders all positions uncertain without establishing an alternative order. Since all perspectives and positions in *Richard III* constantly reverse themselves, as Iser and Grene have observed, and since every statement of the play is being referred back to protagonists who are in conflict with each other, it is impossible to integrate the dramatic events into a comprehensive symbolic frame of reference. The prophecies of the York tetralogy articulate this semantic exuberance in the form of ambiguities. But while the self-fulfilling prophecies in *Richard III* (as well as in *Macbeth*) mainly work by way of equivocations, Shakespeare in the preceding prophecies of *Henry VI* primarily uses amphibology, that is, a type of ambiguity deriving from grammatical constructions. He even quotes the textbook example of an amphibology from the *Annals* of Ennius, namely the oracle's answer to Pyrrhus: "Aio Aeacidam, Romanos vincere posse" (*2. Henry VI*, I. iv. 57). "Romanos" can be read both as the subject and the object of this *accusativus cum infinitivo*; Shakespeare finds an English equivalent:

> ASNATH: The Duke yet lives that Henry shall depose,
> But him outlive, and die a violent death.
>
> (*2 Henry VI*, I. iv. 29–30)

The structure of this sentence leaves open who deposes whom and who survives whom. Amphibolic and equivocal prophecies allow contrary interpretations, from which the subjects select according to their needs at any particular time. Richard, at the beginning of *Richard III*, is fully aware that he manipulates this semantic surplus of "drunken prophecies" (I. i. 33) by interpreting an equivocal prophetic verdict according to his own interests:

> RICHARD: And if King Edward be as true and just
> As I am subtle, false, and treacherous,
> This day should Clarence closely be mew'd up
> About a prophecy, which says that "G"
> Of Edward's heirs the murderer shall be [. . .].
>
> (I. i. 36–40)

It remains unclear who launched this prophecy which leads to Clarence's incarceration.[287] Due to its ambiguity, it is also applicable to Richard, and in this respect it is accurate. But that is not a problem for him so long as he can appropriate the semantic surplus and, through its use, convince the sovereign of an interpretation in his favor:

> RICHARD: Plots have I laid, inductions dangerous,
> By drunken prophecies, libels, and dreams,
> To set my brother Clarence and the King
> In deadly hate, the one against the other [. . .].
>
> (I. i. 32–35)

The term "induction" in this passage is normally read as referring to "preparations" and "first steps."[288] But could it not also suggest the Aristotelian concept of logical induction, i. e. the derivation of general statements from a number of particular observations?[289] This is how Richard derives the danger Clarence presents from a series of ambiguous signals. In this context too, he is a man of interpretation *qua* reduction of complexity. In accord with Lacan's dictum that sense and meaning constitute themselves through breaks,[290] Richard supplies interpretations through interruptions. He cuts short the words of both friends and foes, prematurely terminates ceremonies and juridical procedures, thus fixing their meaning:

> MARGARET: O, let me make the period to my curse!
> RICHARD: 'Tis done by me, and ends in "Margaret".
>
> (I. iii. 238–239)

In the asides of the play's first half, Richard with neat regularity predicts the course the drama will take. He can do this because he manipulates the other figures by way of their aspiration to make sense of the world. Even his own body is one of the semantically oversaturated quantities that Richard has at his disposal: he uses the *topos* that designates his body as the prophetic sign of a curse.[291] When he presents his arm, crippled since birth, as index and evidence, this free-floating curse is freely assigned to a specific target:

> RICHARD: Then be your eyes the witness of their evil.
> See how I am bewitch'd! Behold, mine arm
> Is like a blasted sapling wither'd up!
> And this is Edward's wife, that monstrous witch,
> Consorted with that harlot, strumpet Shore,
> That by their witchcraft thus have marked me.
>
> (III. iv. 67–72)

For the same purpose Richard repeatedly (e.g. in III. vii. 171) refers to fate, most prominently in the second courtship scene in which he attributes the murder of the princes to the "doom of destiny" (IV. iv. 216–219). That he appears unconvincing here and remains unsuccessful, is a first indication that something is going wrong after his coronation: Richard's has relapsed into legitimistic thinking and into a fetishistic belief in the crown,[292] and subsequently his manipulations of the semantic surplus no longer work. Richard himself begins to become intoxicated with the reservoir of meanings the "drunken prophecies" provide and to inscribe himself into them as a subject. For example, almost immediately after he has become king, he brings up various prophecies concerning Richmond in a dialogue with Buckingham:

> RICHARD: I do remember me, Henry the Sixth
> Did prophesy that Richmond should be King,
> When Richmond was a little peevish boy.
> A king . . . perhaps . . . perhaps – [. . .]
> Richmond! When last I was at Exeter,
> The Mayor in courtesy show'd me the castle,
> And called it Rougemont, at which name I started,
> Because a bard of Ireland told me once
> I should not live long after I saw "Richmond".
>
> (IV. ii. 94–97/101–105)

This reference to prophecies certainly has a practical perlocutionary function, insofar as Richard tries to drown out Buckingham's demands by his ruminations. But this and subsequent similar utterances by Richard (e.g. V. iii. 281) allow the conclusion that his newly acquired fetishism goes hand in hand with a new belief in prophecies. In this scene and the following ones, Richard falls behind the dramatic logic with which he has kept pace before. His preoccupation with prophecy appears as idolizing adoration of the semantic surplus of which he could dispose sovereignly before his coronation.

In the theater, prophecy turns into usable material, and Shakespeare displays it *as material*. Just as there is not too little but too much legitimacy, so there are also not too few but too many prophecies. They serve as a reservoir of surplus meaning. This semantic excess can irritate any univocal representation of the world, even against the speaker's will. It makes positions so uncertain that no subject can any longer simply be identical with him- or herself. As one of the citizens puts it: "I promise you, I scarcely know myself" (II. iii. 2). But exactly because of this uncertainty, a new form of power takes shape: a regime of the theater whose defining figure is that of irony. That the theater must include irony is a quality of the very medium itself. The basic meaning of "irony" is "dissimulation," the Greek word εἴρων denoting someone who dissembles, including the actor. Irony at the same time posits and undermines. It is not limited to saying *x* and meaning *y*, but displays what is meant and what is said as opposites, emphasizing the distance between the two. Irony points to different levels of meaning that it simultaneously affirms as incompatible and relates to each other.[293] The perspective on persons and on history in *Richard III* is ironic:[294] all characters exist only in a state of acute instability. The events that determine their "fate" are characterized by ironic reversals and depend so strongly on their ambiguous interpretations that they remain ungraspable. Every moral the dramas appear to convey is at the same time negated by its ironic implications. Prophecy in the theater reveals itself as irony, as the perpetual convergence of incompatible perspectives.

In his prophetic curses, Shakespeare interweaves psychological-creaturely and metaphysical concatenations, which allows him to avoid any polarizing judgment on their transcendent effectiveness. This strategy has also made it possible for both materialists and those with religious convictions to claim him as their own. Shakespeare effectively brackets both discourses by using the theater as an ironically contextualizing interregnum. Providence and contingent causality seem to refer to each other and to harmonize; but the plays have been arranged in such a way that the question of their rank remains unanswerable. As Walter Benjamin has pointed out, "what is characteristic of Shakespeare is precisely that both aspects are equally essential."[295] The paradigms of divine justice and this-worldly psychological (and respectively societal) regularities play into each others' hands by way of the curse, without enabling anyone to univocally determine their relationship and hierarchy. This constellation causes uncertainty and accordingly torments the characters in *Richard III* rather than assuring them of their human dignity. It is therefore all the more surprising that this fact does not play a role in Benjamin's reflections, though it could serve to confirm some of the theses he advances in his *Trauerspielbuch*. Among the protagonists of *Richard III*, the perception of the world also wavers frighteningly between "enigmatic allegorical references" and "dust."[296] "This uncovers the instability of all positions, but since the changes never lead to any fixed point, with even the most powerful positions being overturned when they come into contact with others, the result is a constantly unfolding event which canot be kept under control."[297] Iser considers precisely these indeterminable events the stuff that history is made of.

And as the characters lose control over events, even though all their conduct aims at mastering the vicissitudes of situations, history becomes an experience. The very fact that the spectator is denied the reference point that would link the toppling positions with one another proves to be a strategy for turning history into into an experiential reality. History, then, is no longer perceived as a given, controllable reality, but as something that emerges from actions performed by those who try to gain control over the situation.[298]

The agents of social processes use decrees, interpretations or force in order to gain mastery over the ambivalences and ambiguities proliferating all around them. They are all taken in this unsuccessful process of restructuring that itself defies control. According to Iser, this process is what is meant by history since Shakespeare's time. Shakespeare, then, makes it possible to experience history; he "discovers" it in the fullness of its uncontrollability.[299]

Each of the Histories depicts no more than a snippet of history that, when taken by itself, does not necessarily represent the whole and even casts doubt on the notion that there is such a totality. That is what distinguishes them from mystery plays and the Christian chronicles.[300] Instead, the emphatically fragmentary character of the Histories promises serial continuations, since sequential plot elements connect the plays with each other. Every Shakespearean History is both a self-doubting means of representing reality and publicity for all other Shakespearean Histories, a situation that is thematized explicitly, for example, in the plea for "acceptance" in the epilogue of *Henry V*:

> CHORUS: Henry the Sixth, in infant bands crowned king
> Of France and England, did this king succeed,
> Whose state so many had the managing
> That they lost France and made his England bleed,
> Which oft our stage hath shown – and, for their sake,
> In your fair minds let this acceptance take.
>
> (*Henry V*, Epilogue 9–14)

Richard also delivers similar announcements at the end of the third part of *Henry VI* (e.g. *3 Henry VI*, V. vi. 85–92). The chain of Histories can be continued at will into the future and into the past, and the question about the meaning of history, for example its relationship to salvation, can thus be postponed indefinitely. The Histories present history as the promise of a closure, but they leave this promise unfulfilled. Shakespeare's theater offers no meaning of history but arouses and sustains the desire for it while at the same time ironizing it. The theater is the locus of this indefinite postponement and openness, in which only apparent and preliminary conclusions exist. In this respect, the theater opens a new horizon: the purposed end of history is the vanishing point toward which all dramas move. But they do not reach it; they don't even get closer. The dramas describe a "testing ground,"[301] but it is the test for a play that lies outside the frame of representation. For the performance of the Last Judgment is excluded from the outset in Shakespearean theater, be it for no other reason than that the direct translation of eschatology into theater no longer has a place on the stage after the prohibition of the mystery plays.[302] There is no event in the Histories, not even Richard's death, that inaugurates a truly new era; their final scenes mark themselves as ironic pseudo-conclusions. And this is exactly what constitutes history as history: in the dramas, history takes place by virtue of the fact that the protagonists work toward a salvation that is institutionally inaccessible, but whose traces recommend the Histories for consumption.[303]

Shakespeare discovers history as an interminable performance that appropriates the past by selecting from it according to its current needs. This appropriation of the past goes hand in hand with the historicization of a present that the drama represents as indelibly marked by history. The historical drama pushes present and past into each other: Jeremy Tambling has pointed out that in the York tetralogy Shakespeare writes not only the history of the fifteenth but also that of the sixteenth century;[304] he writes both into one constellation and makes them visible as interdependent constructions. Shakespeare's Histories are full of symptoms of a temporal oversaturation, resulting from their semantic surfeit: the plays charge the past and the present with each other, which is probably the reason for their occasionally claustrophobic atmosphere.[305] The "giddy world" that Shakespeare's royal dramas unlock, then, would also be one that is filled to excess with too many times. This is the context in which to consider a well-known phenomenon that characterizes Shakespeare's theater as a chronologically oversaturated medium: the use of numerous anachronisms, the striking of the clock in *Julius Caesar* (II. i. 192) and the reference to billiards in *Antony and Cleopatra* (II. v. 3) being only the most prominent examples. In *King Lear*, the invocation of Merlin's prophecy whose proclamation lies in the play's future (III. ii. 95–96) is likewise one of these distancing, ironic effects which emphasize that the drama's plot is enacted in a retroactively constructed past. (This circumstance will be treated more extensively in Chapter 3.) Richard too avails himself of anachronisms, for example by "unhistorically" mentioning Machiavelli in a diegetic time that precedes the latter's birth:

> RICHARD: I can add colours to the chameleon,
> Change shapes with Proteus for advantages,
> And set the murderous Machiavel to school.
>
> (*3. Henry VI*, III. ii. 191–193)

Richard himself is characterized as a figure not of his time; the word "untimely" hovers around him and his deeds (I. ii. 4; I. ii. 21; I. iii. 201; II. iii. 35; IV. iv. 70).

Furthermore, there are contradictory statements about how this "untime" is to be understood, e.g. whether he was he born abnormally late or abnormally early:

> RICHARD: Deform'd, unfinish'd, sent before my time
> Into this breathing world scarce half made up [. . .]
>
> (I. i. 20–21)

> DUCHESS: Art thou so hasty? I have stay'd for thee,
> God knows, in torment and in agony.
>
> (IV. iv. 163–164)

It is equally uncertain whether he grew abnormally fast or slowly:

> DUCHESS: He was the wretched'st thing when he was young,
> So long a-growing, and so leisurely
> That if his rule were true, he should be gracious.
>
> (II. iv. 18–20)

> YORK: Marry, they say my uncle grew so fast
> That he could gnaw a crust at two hours old [. . .].
>
> (II. iv. 27–28)

Insofar as Richard as the sovereign personifies history,[306] he first and foremost personifies its ambiguities. Since he himself appears as an anachronism, without a determinable place in time and hence without a genuine identity, he embodies the theater's untimely regime. His asides directed to the audience should also be seen in this context. Richard, then, does not appear as a Tillyardian figure of fate but as the figure of a semantic oversaturation that Shakespeare's dramas carry within themselves and which sustains their reception to this day. Karl Kraus for one, citing the Histories, calls Shakespeare a "forward looking anachronist"[307] and in this sense a prophet who has "foreknown everything."[308] Of course, this perspective that reads Shakespeare's Histories as prophecies is no less retroactive; but it thereby confirms that the varieties of semantic surplus preserved in Shakespeare's dramas are imperiously efficacious, now as ever.

1.5 Henry VI and the standing army of the dead

Christian tradition attributes the origin of death to the curse of God (Gen. 3. 19). St. Augustine even suggests that the concepts of "curse" and "death" are equivalent insofar as death was brought into the world by the curse.[309] Death is the primordial punishment for the primordial transgression and hence the prototype and supra-legal guarantor of the law. The legislative power assumes the divine right to create death and, as appropriate, to overcome it through Christian mercy. According to Benjamin, capital punishment is the partial representation of the lawless foundation of the legal system. Its purpose is less to punish than to reaffirm the law and its establishment by violence.[310] Capital punishment and pardon are primarily the expression and regeneration of the State's *vitae necisque potestas.*

This raises the question of exactly how the State's power over life and death is related to its divine prototype. Does the secular punishment coincide with God's judgment or does it diverge from it? Even in the Bible this relationship is equivocal; at least scholars are divided whether executions by stoning, for example those demanded in Leviticus, should be read as expiatory readmittance of the condemned into the community or as a definitive expulsion.[311] And even in the early modern era there is uncertainty whether a public execution anticipates the punishments of hell or is their propitiatory substitution.[312] The question cannot be answered definitively and unequivocally precisely because the execution situates itself at the border of lawmaking and law-preserving, because it not only carries out a punishment but also lets the primordial act of lawmaking "jut manifestly and fearsomely into existence."[313] The execution complements the staging of the sovereign as *legibus solutus.* In *Discipline and Punish*, Foucault, with reference to Kantorowicz, sees the delinquent in public execution ceremonies as "the symmetrical, inverted figure of the king"[314] in the State's body. According to this view, the delinquent about to be executed and the king are in a mirror relation, in which the legitimacy of the one and the illegitimacy of the other reciprocally support one another and reactivate power. Through the punishment ceremony, a "plus de pouvoir" [surplus power] on the one side imposes its claim on a "moins de pouvoir" [lack of power] on the other. The execution serves as an evidentiary means with which re-inscribe sovereignty into the body politic. Hence it is exactly the community of those who attend the execution as spectators and potential victims that forms the modern body politic. Agamben's dictum, formulated with reference to Hobbes, could also be applied *mutatis mutandis* to this situation: "The absolute capacity of the subjects' bodies to be killed forms the new political body of the West."[315] This may be another reason why Elizabethan executions are public and theatrical, and therefore "decked out" for spectators.[316] Foucault himself repeatedly refers to public executions in the early modern era as "spectacles."[317] Through the spectacular execution, the sovereign proves to himself and others his own wholeness, that is, his coincidence with sovereign violence. In this respect and also because the wholeness he claims must remain structurally impossible, he appears as a "survivor" in Canetti's sense.[318] The elaboration of the doctrine of the two bodies depends from the beginning on the denial of the sovereign's mortality. This denial is used in the Middle Ages above all in order to deal with the political and juridical problems specific to the uncertain period between a ruler's death and his successor's coronation, e.g. to establish an interregnum *in effigie.*[319] Due to this disavowal of the inevitable, the king's two bodies cannot avoid impeding each other; to that extent, the monarch is constitutively torn in two[320]—a fact that the execution transfers onto the inverted mirror image of the monarch: the sovereign can overcome death only on the field of representation, by representing death *qua* execution as posited by himself.

In order to conceal the fact that the sovereign's legal power inherently depends on the figure of the doomed convict, a short episode is often incorporated into the early modern ceremony of condemnation and execution. In this scene, the man about to die, knowingly or unawares, is made to pronounce his own verdict. The transgressor is not only condemned but is also coaxed into affirming the justice of the law that executes him.[321] Often the whole execution is arranged around this obligatory self-condemnation; in many cases, the killing of the felon is preceded by his or her detailed public confession, followed a request for execution. His torture-unto-death often mirrors his crime. In this case, his execution is "carried out at the very place where the crime had been committed" and "with the same instruments."[322] According to Foucault, the execution effectuates an officially sanctioned restatement of the crime in the interest of retributively balancing justice. This mirror construction seems to turn the guilty man into his own executioner, and the role of legal violence (*Rechtsgewalt*) seems to be reduced to the staging of an eternal and just judgment of God. In the following execution, then, divine power and sovereign authority appear not as directly identical but as coordinated. That in the early modern era God's judgment continues to survive latently in the execution can be observed, for example, in the controversy on the question whether a delinquent should be pardoned "if the execution happened to fail"[323] due to the executioner's incompetence. This coordination of divine judgment with the sovereign's judgment makes implementing the punishment an all the more exemplary and representative act. Only for as long as the sovereign can maintain this conjuncture with divine judgment can the execution fulfill its regenerative purpose. Otherwise, and especially in the Christian context of the crucified divinity, the execution runs the danger of elevating its victim to martyrdom and thus immortalizing him. To prevent the creation of a new sublimely sovereign body, quasi a limb of the *corpus Christi*, by the symbolically precarious execution of the criminal's body, the ruling power must arrogate to itself the sole authority to interpret the meaning of dying and the language of the dead, which is never possible without restrictions. In this respect, even dead delinquents continue to be an administrative problem.

But this is no obstacle to the strong emphasis on the paradigmatic dimension of capital punishment in early modern jurisdiction. Even much milder punishments appear sometimes as figurations of the death penalty, as though it were the essence of all legal activity. During the Elizabethan era, some condemned persons as well as "outlaws" who have evaded a warrant for their arrest, are declared *civiliter mortuus*, that is to say, the law treats them like dead bodies: they do not have the right to institute legal proceedings or to inherit property. Their possessions are confiscated and passed on to their heirs or to the crown.[324] Several disciplinary punishments also involve public or semi-public enactments in which living delinquents are symbolically turned into dead people,[325] a process that Shakespeare occasionally incorporates in the Histories: in *2 Henry VI*, for example, the Duchess of Gloucester has arranged a necromancy and prophecy to ascertain how long Henry VI will rule. For this, she is banished after the judicial theatrics of "three days of open penance." Her fellow conspirators are executed. She does this penance as "a wonder and a pointing-stock" (*2 Henry VI*, II. iv. 47–48), wrapped in a white sheet (II. iv. 17), as if she herself were a ghost, and using otherworldly metaphors to describe the punishment she herself approves of:

> DUCHESS: Trowest thou that e'er I'll look upon the world,
> Or count them happy that enjoys the sun?
> No, dark shall be my light, and night my day;
> To think upon my pomp shall be my hell. [. . .]
> My joy is death – [. . .]
> Stanley, I prithee go and take me hence.
> I care not wither, for I beg no favor.
>
> (*2 Henry VI*, II. iv. 39–42/89/92–93)

Thereupon she becomes prophetic and announces Gloucester's impending death (II. iv. 49–58), which indeed occurs two scenes later.

Excommunication likewise in many aspects assumes the form of a symbolic execution.[326] The excommunicate is regularly equated with a corpse.[327] As a person deceased yet alive, suspended between death and life, he is like an undead revenant. The ghost of popular tradition is itself most often the result of an ecclesiastic or private curse: the revenant is a dead person who cannot enter the next world because by God's decree he must first insist on atonement for a guilt that manifests itself in him.[328] Hence the ghost testifies on behalf of the divine law, whether as a transgressor or as the victim of a transgression; in these two roles he is functionalized. What is the social function of the belief in ghosts? Keith Thomas emphasizes that this superstition affirms the validity of traditional norms, especially in times of crisis.[329] Ghosts protect symbolic bonds, including the oath which for this reason is often sworn on a grave.[330] By its mere existence, the specter declares the central importance of traditional institutions and laws, thus perpetuating them.

Thomas sees the specter primarily as a proponent of late medieval traditions. But he barely thematizes the fact that ghosts are closely related to writing, and increasingly also to the printed word,[331] even though his own examples point in this direction.[332] Indeed writing, as the bearer of tradition, appears in some discourses of the early modern age as the medium in which ghosts persist. Historians of the sixteenth century often use the *topos* of the book as an object that keeps the dead alive. Edward Hall, for example, states:

> Writing is the keye to enduce vertue, or represse vice. Thus memorie maketh menne ded many thousande yere still to live as though thei wer present: Thus fame triumpheth upon death, and renoune upon Oblivion, all by reason of writyng and historie.[333]

To be sure, the commonplace that writing assures the survival of the dead is not a modern invention. Many ancient epitaphs articulate explicitly that they are based on a similar motivation. Since the grave is perceived as the place of eternal rest and hence as the image of unchangeable permanence, the epitaph is likewise considered an inscription that immortalizes and perpetuates the dead man's fame or his disgrace. In *1. Henry VI*, the epitaph assumes precisely this political function in the fields of the Hundred Years' War:

> TALBOT: Bring forth the body of old Salisbury
> And here advance it in the market place,
> The middle centre of this cursèd town.
> Now have I paid my vow unto his soul:
> For every drop of blood was drawn from him
> There hath at least five Frenchmen died tonight.
> And that hereafter ages may behold
> What ruin happened in revenge of him,
> Within their chiefest temple I'll erect
> A tomb, wherein his corpse shall be interred –
> Upon the which, that everyone may read,
> Shall be engraved the sack of Orléans,
> The treacherous manner of his mournful death,
> And what a terror he had been to France.
>
> (*1 Henry VI*, II. ii. 4–17)

The tomb in this scene serves not only to memorialize and represent the dead hero, but also to mark an enduring interior boundary.[334] The epitaph is an instrument of propaganda that, as it blesses the departed "old Salisbury," is also meant to articulate the eternal condemnation of his French opponents. Thus it perpetuates a tradition of curse epitaphs, a tradition that extends from antiquity into the modern era.[335] These inscriptions announce divine punishment on the dead man's enemies in general and especially on those who violate the tomb or the inscription itself. Epigraphs in which the memorialized person speaks in the first person are also part of this genre: Timon's epitaph (*Timon of Athens*, V. v. 71–78) is an example, and so is the inscription on Shakespeare's own tombstone that is usually attributed to him:

> Good friend for Jesus' sake forbear,
> To dig the dust enclosed here:
> Blest be the man that spares these stones,
> And curst be he that moves my bones.[336]

The common notion that the dead are being increasingly marginalized in the course of the Reformation,[337] should be qualified. It is true that some rites for the dead are suppressed after the English Reformation. The existence of Purgatory is denied as part of an effort to separate England from its Catholic tradition, and perhaps also in order to strengthen incipient absolutism. Funerals become shorter, less ceremonial, and increasingly shift from the public into the private sphere.[338] But do the theater and the printing press not fill the vacuum created by this reduction? It is of interest in this context that at the end of the sixteenth century, beside the Bible, John Foxe's *Book of Martyrs* is the most widely read book in England and that in many churches it is treated like a sacred text.[339] One can observe that during the Renaissance printed epitaphs, elegies, and other written forms of remembering the dead designate themselves more and more as the medium of immortality and the place of transcendence. Shakespeare's sonnets offer numerous variations of this *topos* in which poetry appears as the truly eternal monument for the dead. A prominent example can be found in Sonnet 55:

> Not marble nor the gilded monuments
> Of princes shall outlive this powerful rhyme,
> But you shall shine more bright in these contents
> Than unswept stone besmeared with sluttish time.
>
> (*Sonnet 55*, 1–4)

The same *topos* is rendered even more explicitly in Sonnet 18:

> Nor shall death brag thou wander'st in his shade
> When in eternal lines to time thou grow'st.
> So long as men can breathe or eyes can see,
> So long lives this, and this gives life to thee.
>
> (*Sonnet 18*, 11–14)

Similar formulations appear in the so-called *Funeral Elegy* of 1612 that was apparently written by Shakespeare and distributed by his publisher Thomas Thorpe. In its commemoration of William Peter, this elegy not only announces itself as the medium of immortality whose "eternal characters" preserve the fame of the departed; the hope for the afterlife in Heaven here seems to be not only supplemented, but altogether replaced by the hope of posterity's remembrance, safeguarded by writing. One should no longer expect to be rewarded for good deeds in the next world, but rather to find one's compensation in the praise of succeeding generations:

> Respective titles or a gracious style,
> With all what men in eminence possess,
> Are, without ornaments to praise them, vile:
> The beauty of the mind is nobleness.
> And such as have that beauty, well deserve
> Eternal characters, that after death
> Remembrance of their worth we may preserve
> So that their glory die not with their breath.
> Else what avails it in a goodly strife
> Upon this face of earth here to contend,
> The good t'exceed the wicked in their life,
> Should both be like obscured in their end?
> Until which end, there is none rightly can
> Be termed happy, since the happiness

> Depends upon the goodness of the man,
> Which afterwards his praises will express.[340]
>
> (*Funeral Elegy*, 467–482)

The rites for the dear departed, then, do still appear to be of decisive importance even after the Reformation. But the performances and hopes associated with them increasingly migrate into texts as though the dead themselves were entering into a kind of symbiosis with writing. Of course, the deceased cannot be made present again, but they can be represented in the sign. Huston Diehl has sketched the connection of this new relationship with the dead and the reformed understanding of the Eucharist: in both cases the real presence is replaced by figuration.[341] Diehl sees the same symbolically mediated relationship with the dead incorporated and propagated in the drama of the early modern age, especially in the revenge drama, which includes an implicit critique of the belief in the real presence.[342] This view is both confirmed and qualified by the fact that the advocates of early modern theater describe it with the same representative resurrection metaphors that the defenders of various types of printed literature on historical subjects and on obsequies also use. Thomas Nashe in "Pierce Pennilesss," for example, refers to Shakespeare's *Henry VI* when he justifies the theater as a mediated communion with all the English heroes and conquerors who died for the motherland:

> Nay, what if I prove plays to be no extreme, but a rare exercise of virtue? First, for the subject of them: for the most part it is borrowed out of our English chronicles, wherein our forefathers' valiant acts, that have lain long buried in rusty brass and worm-eaten books, are revived, and they themselves raised from the grave of oblivion, and brought to plead their aged honours in open presence: than which, what can be sharper reproof to these degenerate effeminate days of ours?
>
> How would it have joyed brave Talbot, the terror of the French, to think that after he had lain two hundred years in his tomb, he should triumph again on the stage, and have his bones new embalmed with the tears of ten thousand spectators at least, (at several times) who, in the tragedian that represents his person, imagine they behold him fresh bleeding![343]

It should be noted that history books and grave monuments are here characterized as deficient in comparison with the theater. The subsequent passages in Nashe's text retain these resurrection metaphors ("hopes of eternity") with their Eucharistic assonances ("fresh bleeding"). A historical character thus also appears on the theatrical scene as a revenant; drama shows the living dead and affirms the debt owed them by the living. The actor appears as the equivalent of a piece of writing insofar as his representation keeps the dead alive: "Like the alphabetic signifier, like the letter, the actor himself is not inspired or animated by any particular language. He signifies nothing. He hardly lives, he lends his voice."[344]

The Richard of *Richard III* represents less a dead person than death itself; whoever dies in this drama dies more or less indirectly through Richard. His sovereignty is upheld by executions and by the power to interpret them; it seems to subsist on those executions and falls apart when no further prominent victims are at his disposal. It is therefore only logical that his surviving and subjugated victims in their lamentations and curses demonstratively identify with the departed. Especially the former queens (Margaret, the Duchess of York, and Elizabeth) seem to position themselves on the border between the realm of the living and that of the dead insofar as they have survived their own symbolic death. Above all, the ghostly Margaret identifies with an obsolete signifier ("Queen Margaret") that defines her while she persists as the incarnation of a traumatic past. Margaret's rhetorical anticipation of her own death has already been discussed in section 1.2, but until now it has only been briefly indicated that her successors follow her in this rhetorical strategy. In their lamentations, they present themselves not only as undead specters, but also as written documents of heinous crimes (the "abstract and record of tedious days"):

> DUCHESS: Dead life, blind sight, poor mortal living ghost;
> Woe's scene, world's shame, grave's due by life usurp'd;
> Brief abstract and record of tedious days,
> Rest thy unrest on England's lawful earth,
> Unlawfully made drunk with innocent blood.
> ELIZABETH: Ah, that thou wouldst as well afford a grave
> As thou canst yield a melancholy seat,
> Then would I hide my bones, not rest them here.
>
> (IV. iv. 26–33)

That every life under the rule of Richard is a life-in-death is a permanent motif in the drama. It is accentuated in locutions that conflate the womb and the grave (see also IV. iv. 296–298/422–425):

> DUCHESS OF YORK: O ill-dispersing wind of misery!
> O my accursed womb, the bed of death! [. . .]
> MARGARET: From forth the kennel of thy womb hath crept
> A hell-hound that doth hunt us all to death:
> That dog, that had his teeth before his eyes,
> To worry lambs and lap their gentle blood;
> That excellent grand tyrant of the earth,
> That reigns in galled eyes of weeping souls;
> That foul defacer of God's handiwork
> Thy womb let loose, to chase us to our graves.
>
> (IV. i. 52–53; IV. iv. 47–54)

As the production of ghosts is coupled with the distribution of curses, so too the life of the court, outlived and marked by death, appears as the bearer and agent of a contaminating curse. All the protagonists of *Richard III* are accursed, and precisely for this reason they are the living dead. The curse marks them as dead and yet allows them to participate in life. In this context, the play repeatedly alludes to the motif of the Dance of Death. In the late Middle Ages, the Dance of Death was a theatrical performance akin to the Morality Plays before it became a pictorial subject.[345] The performance traditionally took place on All Souls' Day in the churchyard: a monk first gave a short sermon on the inevitability of death. Then a number of figures dressed up as skeletons entered from the charnel house, invited actors playing emperors, cardinals, noblemen, and commoners to purgatory, and led them away. Another sermon concluded the performance.[346] Of course, references to this practice in *Richard III* can be found most prominently in the ghost scene on All Souls' Day (V. iii. 119–177), but the frequent mention of St Paul's Cathedral also alludes to it indirectly: in the old church of St Paul's there existed a well-known fresco showing a dance of death.[347] Anne accompanies Henry VI from St Paul's to the place of his burial (I. ii. 30) until Richard wrests control of his corpse from her. After the execution of Hastings, justice is performed in St Paul's as a macabre revival of the same farce: the public reading of the bill of indictment takes place there. It declares that Hastings is to be executed for high treason pursuant to accusations for which he had not even been apprehended when the document was formulated:

> SCRIVENER: Here is the indictment of the good Lord Hastings,
> Which in a set hand fairly is engross'd,
> That it may be today read o'er in Paul's.
> And mark how well the sequel hangs together:
> Eleven hours I have spent to write it over [. . .]
> And yet within these five hours Hastings liv'd,
> Untainted, unexamin'd, free, at liberty.
>
> (III. vi. 1–5/8–9)

Both Paul and the cathedral are repeatedly referred to metonymically. Alistair Fox has pointed out that Richard in *Richard III* swears a total of five times (six times in the Quarto version) by the apostle Paul and that this oath appears nowhere else in Shakespeare. In the same article, he also traces the origin of the oath back to Thomas More's biography of Richard III.[348] Paul is perhaps the saint who is most appropriate for Richard, since he is a great promulgator of "death in life" (Romans 6. 3–13; Colossians 3. 3).

The ghost scene V. iii almost seems redundant in a play that swarms with the living dead and whose series of executions resembles the procession of a *danse macabre*. But this episode is as necessary as "The Mousetrap" is for *Hamlet*: as a mirror image of the drama, it opens the play on to a meta-theatrical level. For the dead perform an abridged version of the play: their entrances are chronologically arranged according to the point in time at which they were killed, and their accusations repeat the plot development of *Richard III*. Ghostly apparitions often introduce this meta-theatrical dimension in Shakespeare's dramas; they are not only histrionic themselves, but also direct the spectator's attention to the theatrical character of reality by pointing towards a different scene, "*ein anderer Schauplatz*."[349] Like the play *Richard III* itself, the drama of the revenants which allegorizes it poses the question of the relationship between representation and reality without providing a definitive answer.[350] This fact is indicated, for instance, in the ambiguous status of the ghostly apparitions that wavers between dream and reality. Many indications suggest that these apparitions are an objective fact, among them the blue-burning candle flames, which are traditionally thought to be the sign of a spectral presence:

> RICHARD: The lights burn blue. It is now dead midnight.
>
> (V. iii. 181)

Furthermore, by the time-condensing continuity of the fifth act's plot it is suggested that the precise time for the entrance of the ghosts is the midnight of All Souls' Day (V. i. 10–12), which is exactly the hour of the year that popular tradition considers most propitious for supernatural apparitions. But all these signs are also ambiguous because they might as well be read as "residues of the day"[351] which excite dreams, and thus be explained psychologically. Both Richard and Richmond refer to the apparition of the ghosts as a dream. Only the congruence of the two dreams, perceivable exclusively by the play's spectators, would be somewhat unusual, although such a coincidence could be read as the symptom of a spiritual affinity between the dreamers, rather than as proof of a supernatural intervention. Again, mundane psychic or societal laws and the paradigm, which regards existence as the enactment of divine justice, work into each other's hands, while their hierarchical relationship cannot be characterized unequivocally.

Other dreams in *Richard III* are also ambiguously prophetic, and they always announce death: Clarence dreams an allegory of his death after his death sentence has been signed, i.e. when he has already died symbolically (I. iv. 1–65), and Lord Stanley's dream (III. ii. 9–17) seems to prophesy Lord Hastings' death. These premonitory dreams too can be read as manifestations of repressed affections no less than as transcendent messages. And it is precisely through this ambiguity that they tie the dreaming subjects to the official narrative of their "fate." According to Benjamin, ghosts are manifestations of this fate, understood as a hypostatizing remodelling of temporality:

> [There exists a] widespread notion that at this hour [midnight] time stands still like the tongue of a scale. Now since fate, itself the true order of eternal recurrence, can only be described as temporal in an indirect, that is, parasitical sense, its manifestations seek out the spatio-temporal dimension. They stand in the narrow frame of midnight, an opening in the passage of time, in which the same ghostly image constantly reappears.[352]

Fate as "the eternal recurrence of the same" finds its most succinct incarnation in the figure of the revenant. Its existence beyond time is that of an eternal calamity.

In this connection it once more becomes obvious that the apparition scene reproduces the entire play in an intensified abbreviation: not only the concept of fate becomes ambiguous, but this scene clearly sets forth that temporality at a standstill is a general condition of the theater. For instance, in the dialogues of V. iii, which surround the apparitions of the ghosts, time is a constant concern:

> RICHARD: What is't o'clock?
> CATESBY: It's supper time, my lord; it's nine o'clock. [. . .]
> RICHARD: It is now dead midnight. [. . .]
> RICHMOND: How far into the morning is it, lords?
> FIRST LORD: Upon the stroke of four. [. . .]
> (*The clock striketh.*)
> RICHARD: Tell the clock there! Give me a calendar –
> Who saw the sun to-day?
> RATCLIFF: Not I, my lord.
> RICHARD: Then he disdains to shine, for by the book
> He should have brav'd the east an hour ago.
> A black day will it be to somebody.
>
> (V. iii. 48–49/181/235–236/276–281)

By these exchanges, Shakespeare directs attention to the fact that the time of the royal drama is not the time of the clock: in a scene whose performance lasts at most 30 minutes, a whole night is enacted, a time of at least nine hours. The use of such quick-motion effects which also distinguishes the rest of the play and sometimes creates oddities[353] is one method by which to demonstrate how the theater concentrates and abbreviates time. For this very reason, the play by definition takes place in the witching hour; theater time is a time in which history condenses and solidifies. In the fated time–space of this stasis it is always midnight and "All Souls' Day," even in the night before the battle of Bosworth Field that took place in August, that is, two months before All Souls'.[354]

The entrance of the dead in V. iii. is more ceremonious than was customary in the Elizabethan theater.[355] The ghosts dialogue neither with each other nor with the living; instead, they recite formulas. The stereotypical and only superficially varied exhortation "Despair and die!" in all ten cases is combined with a "Think on . . ." formula that is a reminder of the speaker's murder. Often, but not consistently, two other locutions occur: "Let me sit heavy on your soul" and "Let fall thy sword." The formulaic character of these utterances seems to suggest liturgical performatives; the scene of the ghosts is a kind of sacrificial mass with references to the ecclesiastical excommunication ceremonies discussed in section 1.2. Together with the dead, a dead ceremony returns. But in contrast to the mass, the revenant dead do not testify to anything beyond themselves. They demand neither their own deliverance nor Richard's eternal damnation; or other interventions of divine powers. All they insist on is commemoration and the defeat of Richard, resulting from his awareness of former guilt. The ghosts are, as it were, "enlightened" ghosts who already take into consideration their own possibly phantasmatic, status as personified pangs of conscience:

> RIVERS, GREY, VAUGHAN: Our wrongs in Richard's bosom
> Will conquer him [. . .].
>
> (V. iii. 145–146)

However, this wish involves a slight paradox: the dead insistently demand commemoration even though the dream in which they appear must itself be understood as a form of this commemoration. The princes make this dilemma explicit by cursing Richard with a bad dream in which they themselves appear:

> PRINCES: Dream on thy cousins, smother'd in the Tower.
>
> (V. iii. 152)

Since Richard is experiencing this very dream at the very same moment, the curse wishes for something that is already happening; in other words, it is redundant, even more than usually. On the occasion of the meta-theatrical mass of the dead, Shakespeare again plays with the fact that the utterance of fateful speech acts in a time of ambiguous signs is both impossible and inevitable. His theater sublates the concept of fate and shows that it derives from a semantic overdetermination. An excess supply of meaning articulates itself in the diverging voices of the cursing ghosts whose political claims remain unreconciled behind the façade of a ritual unvocity; their curse is less a communal than a serial act. (According to the stage directions of the Folio, never more than three ghosts have to be on stage at the same time.) Contrary to Tillyard's dictum,[356] this scene, then, does not signal the inception of a new epoch of theologico-political unity. The revenants do indeed echo each other but without actually speaking in harmony: polyphonic notes tending toward dissonance are softly audible in their chorus. They continue to speak as Yorkists and Lancastrians, and it is precisely the residual claims to legitimacy on the two competing sides which lend performative strength to their curses. Several of Richard's victims who were at best ambivalent figures in life could not present themselves as martyrs without this legitimation: Henry VI could not refer to his "anointed body [. . .] full of deadly holes" (V. iii. 125–126) and Clarence could not count the murdered Yorkists among the "good angels" (V. iii. 139). The dead do not articulate a law but an abundance of mutually exclusive obligations. They escape becoming completely functionalized by remaining, like writing itself, supplementary and ambiguous. Consequently, the curse pronounced on Richard remains overdetermined, and Richard's subsequent defeat remains a matter of interpretation: it can be ideologically appropriated, but it has no indisputable meaning beyond itself. For precisely this reason, his death does not establish a truly new social order. The fatal logic of sacrifice which has driven the drama's mechanism up to this point is not disrupted by Richard's execution and Richmond's victory—it is rather confirmed. From this perspective, Richmond appears as a pale revenant of Richard, whose sovereignty and power of interpretation, despite his murderous evidentiary procedures, can in the end also only rely upon their continuous decomposition.

1.6 Clarence and the diabolical allegory

Since late antiquity, Christian theology has represented unsuccessful pretenders to God's monarchical position as devils. God's absolute rule is affirmed not only through the downfall, but also through the allegorization of these competitors. According to Benjamin, Christian allegoresis of pagan traditions is a method of Christianization that seeks to exorcise the remnants of polytheism.[357] This process turns the pagan gods, especially those of classical antiquity, into allegories of evil and hence into figurations of Satan.[358] But allegoresis not only exorcises the pagan gods; it also preserves them, since in general it both mortifies and saves at once.[359] The divinities are inclusively excluded and in this way subjected to the "originary formal structure of the juridical relation."[360] As devils, they are subject to God's judgment: that means they bear guilt and keep God free of it. This guilt does not depend on specific deeds but merely marks the fact that its bearers live under the signifiers of the eternal system of law. Allegoresis implies guilt: "The allegorically significant is prevented by guilt from finding fulfillment of its meaning in itself."[361] In this state of affairs, the devil must be accursed; as the primordial outcast, he is the accursed one *par excellence*. In exorcism, the cursing and casting out of the devil is ritually repeated at regular intervals. One of the essential Christian ceremonies of the late Middle Ages is this constant exorcism. Baptism already includes an exorcism in which the devil is addressed as "maledicte diabole" and is expelled from the body of the person to be baptized.[362] Other specific ceremonies of exorcism are components of all threshold rituals (confirmation, wedding, funeral, etc.). Beyond that, routine exorcisms, the Eucharist among them, take place for the same purpose.[363] Also penance and the subsequent absolution are frequently considered exorcizing acts.[364]

The curse sends all the accursed into that godforsaken zone to which the devils have also been banished. In the end, the place reserved for the fallen is Satan's sphere, namely hell. According to Irenaeus, hell was created to punish Satan, a reference to Matthew 25. 41: "Depart from me, ye cursed, into everlasting fire, prepared for the devil and his angels." By which he means to indicate that eternal fire is not primarily prepared for man but for the tempter who caused man to sin and for the originator of apostasy and his angels who together with him became apostates; to this fire quite rightly also they will be forfeited who like them persevere in their evil deeds without penance and without changing their ways.[365]

But strangely enough, in the medieval iconography of hell at the latest, Satan functions not as its primordial victim but as its chief supervisor and master torturer; he is not punished in hell but rather executes the punishments God has imposed. He appears less as accursed and more as the curse put to work. This state of affairs shows that the paradoxes of the diabolic converge with the paradoxes of the curse. In the orthodox depiction of the anathema, they support one another:

Thomas Aquinas writes that the devil has been given greater power over the excommunicate than over the regular member of the parish.[366] But he also states that an excommunication is meant to exact chastisement; its purpose is not to ruin the excommunicate but to save him from apostasy.[367] Hence, the devil affirms divine law by transgressing it. As late as in the Morality Plays, Satan justifies his role as the eternal executioner of apostates by referring to God's justice, even though he himself is the first apostate.[368] The devil enforces the curse that was pronounced upon him more than anyone else: he is at the same time God's servant and rebel. In precisely this ambivalence, the devil is a figuration of the law as demonic entity that in its very form institutes injustice. He incarnates retribution, that is, punishment for a transgression that becomes definable as transgression only through its punishment.[369]

It has often been asserted that the devil is given greater power over man in the discourses of the Reformation than in those of the Middle Ages.[370] Since sin is one of the central topics in the theology of early Protestantism, its representative is also of higher importance. Satan as sovereign over this world is an integral component of Reformation rhetoric.[371] The ritual means that parish members can use to protect themselves from the devil, however, are both characterized as ineffective and prohibited, especially in England where Catholic ceremonies are being fought resolutely: rites of exorcism are forbidden, the veneration of guardian angels and of saints is strongly curtailed, and the statues of protective saints are no longer included in the English processions of the late sixteenth century, while those of their diabolical antagonists are.[372] During this time, there are ever more explicit suggestions made that it is the function of the devil and his demons to impose political discipline. One can recognize tendencies in this direction in utterances by Joseph Glanville[373] and James I, who calls the devil "God's hangman."[374] But once more it is Hobbes who rigorously reduces this motif to its basic, most pragmatic form. He sees a political dimension in the demonic insofar as the early legislators knew how to utilize the belief in demons in the State's interest "by establishing that demonology [. . .] to the public peace, and to the obedience of subjects necessary thereunto."[375] This means that the commonwealth becomes possible only through demons, which function as precursors of the sovereign Leviathan. For Hobbes, even the modern sovereign is in the final analysis a logically necessary demon (even if, as all demons, an artificial one). It is precisely his demonic and demonically ambivalent status that gives him his executive power.[376]

As an illegitimate pretender to the throne of the supreme ruler, the devil is the father of lies and, in Tertullian's formulation, "God's monkey" (*simia dei*).[377] As an archetypal imitator and illusionist, he is also considered the forefather of actors. This increase in the power of the devil and of representation during the early modern age entails that enemies of the theater see it more and more as a terrain in which Satan is at work with particular relentlessness. In the antitheatrical polemics of the Puritans, the theater becomes the anti-church, the performance a black mass. William Prynne, for example, writes: "Stage-plays are the cup and table of Devils."[378] As if the theater were the Antichrist in person, the Puritan John

Northbrooke sees the fact that the stage is more popular than the pulpit as a sign that the Day of Judgment is close at hand.[379] Above all, the Puritans criticize the theatrical representation of dissolute behavior and of depraved persons, an especially precarious issue being the portrayal of Lucifer himself. If the Devil is essentially nothing but an imitator, is his imitation not already his reality? Are satanic conjurations within a theatrical frame true conjurations or merely their representations? Especially in *Doctor Faustus*, Christopher Marlowe plays with this ambivalence (as would have to be demonstrated elsewhere).[380] Consequently, rumors arose around 1594 that an additional devil had appeared during a performance of *Faustus* along with the actors dressed up as devils, whose presence nobody was able to account for and who terrified spectators as well as actors.[381] The way Shakespeare deals with the diabolical exposes him much less to these problems: first it should simply be noted that neither angels nor devils appear in the Histories and that not even unequivocally supernatural interventions are depicted. However, mundane circumstances and persons are frequently paralleled with heavenly and hellish circumstances and persons, the latter being moreover addressed, invoked and denounced abundantly. God's workings and those of the devil are recognized everywhere; most protagonists of the Histories describe history as a theater of war where the good angels battle the fallen angels. Once more, Tillyard paraphrases such statements and passes them off as Shakespeare's conception of history.[382] But the question whether sacral speech acts in Shakespeare's dramas are indeed validated by transcendent authorities cannot be answered quite so easily: references to God's eternal decree that are ambivalent or merely motivated by mundane interests are too prominent in the plays. As mentioned, Shakespeare lets the paradigm of divine justice and secular laws work in unison without clarifying their hierarchy.[383] Especially in the late dramas, this equivocal ranking causes a rhetorical amalgamation which lets hell and the kingdom of heaven coalesce on earth: the world of angels and demons and this material world are not kept apart, but penetrate each other. This convergence is given poignant expression in utterances such as the following:

> JESSICA: Our house is hell, and thou, a merry devil [. . .].
> (*The Merchant of Venice*, II. iii. 2)

> GIACOMO: Though this a heavenly angel, hell is here.
> (*Cymbeline*, II. ii. 50)

> ARIEL: Hell is empty, / And all the devils are here.
> (*The Tempest*, I. ii. 215–216)

It can be shown that these three locutions are neither solemn, sacral references nor conventionalized, "athrophied" metaphors where "hell" would simply stand in for "unpleasant existential circumstances." These utterances are situated between both poles, which is also suggested by the fact that the three speakers are threshold figures (a Jewess on the brink of conversion, an intriguer, and a "spirit of the air" under the control of a Renaissance magician). In the third part of the York tetralogy, Richard introduces the same *topos* when he decides to see the world as hell and the dream of the crown as heaven:

> RICHARD: I'll make my heaven to dream upon the crown,
> And whiles I live, t' account this world but hell,
> Until my misshaped trunk that bears this head
> Be round impalèd with a glorious crown.
>
> (*3 Henry VI*, III. ii. 168–171)

In this statement, the hierarchy between this world and the next, hence the direction of the allegoresis, also remains unclear: is hell used as a trope for Richard's life in this world, or is this life used as a trope for hell? This ambiguity extends to the laments of his victims, who call him a devil that transforms the earth into hell by filling it with curses:

> ANNE: Foul devil, for God's sake, hence, and trouble us not;
> For thou hast made the happy earth thy hell,
> Fill'd it with cursing cries and deep exclaims.
>
> (I. ii. 50–52)

Again and again, the accusations of the four queens describe Richard as a representative of hell. But the denunciations of Margaret, Elizabeth, Anne, and the Duchess do not accord on the issue whether he should be understood as the sovereign of hell or as an agent in its service ("minister," I. ii. 46; "intelligencer," IV. iv. 71, etc.). Once more it remains impossible to decide if hell depends on Richard or Richard depends on hell:

> MARGARET: Hie thee to hell for shame, and leave the world,
> Thou cacodemon: there thy kingdom is. [. . .]
> Thou that wast seal'd in thy nativity
> The slave of Nature, and the son of hell [. . .]
> Sin, death, and hell have set their marks on him,
> And all their ministers attend on him. [. . .]
> Richard yet lives, hell's black intelligencer,
> Only reserv'd their factor to buy souls
> And send them thither.
>
> (I. iii. 143–144/229–230/293–294; IV. iv. 71–73)

It is emphasized frequently that Richard is a figure of diabolical fate. However, this fate is mainly diabolical because it is grounded in a surplus of "enigmatic allegorical references" whose status must remain ambiguous.[384] Richard takes possession of the *terrain vague* of this ambiguity: as a "born actor"[385] he is a psychologically comprehensible individual and at the same time an allegorical figure. That Richard's *persona* exhibits distinct features which recall the devil of the Mystery Plays and the "Vice" of the Morality Plays is a cliché since Benjamin at the latest.[386] It is, however conspicuous, that these allegorical vestiges, as remnants from medieval traditions, do not stand in the way of the requirements for a psychologically credible depiction of his character. On the contrary, they appear to strengthen this credibility. Various authors have already noticed that Richard strikes one as artificial as soon as he drops his diabolical role (e.g. when he awakens from the ghostly dream in V. iii), and that he is psychologically convincing whenever he is absorbed by it (as in his dialogue with Anne in I. ii).[387] Richard does not only mark the boundary between character portrayal and type casting;[388] in his role both aspects seem to be so tightly interwoven as to become indistinguishable. This phenomenon is explicable through Richard's relation to specific characteristics of the diabolical type: his declared strategy for success is a theatrical one, namely a dissimulation bordering on protean essencelessness in courtly life:

> RICHARD: Why, I can smile, and murder whiles I smile,
> And cry "Content!" to that which grieves my heart,
> And wet my cheeks with artificial tears,
> And frame my face to all occasions. [. . .]
> Deceive more slily than Ulysses could,
> And like a Sinon, take another Troy.
> I can all colours to the chameleon,
> Change shapes with Proteus for advantages [. . .].
>
> (*3 Henry VI*, III. ii. 182–185/189–192)

The very fact that his character aspires to characterlessness leads to his merging with the diabolical type:

> RICHARD: And seem a saint, when most I play the devil.
>
> (I. iii. 338)

Both "seem" and "play" in this line denote dissimulations, implying that there is no face behind the mask of the saint but another, diabolical mask. Richard does not identify with the devil; he plays the saint and the devil as needed. But this is precisely what makes him diabolical—insofar as the devil is the primordial actor, the man without a face behind his masks.[389] Richard's theologically skilful handling of the Devil figure institutes a kind of "meta-diabolism" in which the diabolic character and the devilish type appear to represent each other in an endless loop. In this game, Richard outplays his opponents by bidding on his knowledge that the devil, through his ambivalent function as both anti-godly demon and avenging angel-*cum*-instrument of destiny, holds a very strong hand. For example, the diabolization of Richard makes it impossible or redundant to threaten him with hellish punishments (especially when hell is already on earth). A kind of helplessness in the face of this ambivalence is already discernible in Anne's first vilification of him:

> ANNE: What, do you tremble? Are you all afraid?
> Alas, I blame you not, for you are mortal,
> And mortal eyes cannot endure the devil.
> Avaunt, thou dreadful minister of hell!
> Thou hadst but power over his mortal body,
> His soul thou canst not have; therefore begone.
>
> (I. ii. 43–48)

The use of this figure gets her into logical difficulties precisely because Richard does not deny his diabolical status (I. ii. 71–74) but plays with its ambiguity. Richard justifies his murders, for example, by averring that he sends those he kills to heaven and hence does them a favor. By thus presenting himself as an instrument of destiny—"part of that force which would/ Do ever evil and does ever good"[390]—he thwarts Anne's laments about Henry VI and mocks her to boot:

> ANNE: God grant me too
> Thou mayst be damned for that wicked deed.
> O he was gentle, mild, and virtuous.
> RICHARD: The better for the King of Heaven that hath him.
> ANNE: He is in Heaven, where thou shalt never come.
> RICHARD: Let him thank me that holp to send him thither,
> For he was fitter for that place than earth.
>
> (I. ii. 104–110)[391]

With this justification of the devil, Richard utilizes a religious commonplace that an orthodox believer cannot easily rebut. The woman so addressed is reduced to repeating instead her rhetorically enfeebled demonization (I. ii. 111). Allegorizing religious positions are exactly the ones from which Richard is unassailable.

The ambivalent attitude toward the devil in the early modern age is connected with the problem of the right to resist the bad ruler and tyrant. Contrary to the classical tradition, many theoreticians of political theology in the sixteenth and seventeenth centuries do not grant the subject of the State the right to resist an abuse of power by the ruler. The doctrine of the sovereign's second body in this connection also serves to vindicate apologias of emerging absolutism: even the tyrant who abuses his power has divine legitimacy and is called "to punish the sinfulness of humankind" by his deeds.[392] Benjamin writes that the reverse side of this absolutism, as propagated by the State church, is a deep fear of catastrophe. It is overcome by granting the sovereign active authority over the catastrophe *qua* state of exception.[393] Shakespeare implies that in this case the devil is necessarily exorcized with the help of Beelzebub, as it were. Tillyard, by contrast, accepts Richard's justification of the diabolical tyrant without thinking through its theological implications:[394] if the king is God on earth who by definition can do no wrong and who punishes the innocent for the sins of their fathers, what does that tell us about the conception we are supposed to have of God? Do not God and the devil become indistinguishable on the political stage? And does this not also turn Richmond's uprising into an illegitimate usurpation? Persistent aporias undermine the distinction between good and evil, subverting the subsumption of the world by steadfast moral categories. Richard's success derives from his exploitation of the forced, fetishistic belief of his antagonists in the world's religiously mediated intelligibility, a belief he himself does not want to share.[395] The fact that he does not posit a rigorous distinction between truth and deception[396] enables him to instrumentalize the power of exegesis completely; he uses the ambivalence of natural signs by providing their commodious interpretation:

> RICHARD: mark'd you not
> How that the guilty kindred of the Queen
> Look'd pale when they did hear of Clarence' death?
> O, they did urge it still unto the King [. . .].
>
> (II. i. 136–139)

It is to be noted that Richard's insinuating analyses are often neither true nor altogether false. (Perhaps the Queen's relatives have indeed pushed for Clarence's murder, and perhaps their pallid faces can also be attributed to this; Richard never states explicitly that they are responsible for Clarence's death.) Just as there is no face behind his masks, no truth can be detected behind his deceptions. Precisely this untraceability of any original identity is the condition for Richard's theater. Richard is working on an absolute allegory, insofar as it is the allegorical that lends strength to his courtly drama.[397] George Puttenham in his taxonomy of rhetoric calls "allegoria" the "Courtly figure" precisely because the court implies dissimulation, "when we speake one thing and thinke another, and that our wordes and our meanings meet not."[398] Allegoresis is a desideratum of a world without a final valid reference, a world in which every thing can mean any other thing. This ability of the thing to refer to any other extracts it from its habitual context, but also raises its status by charging it with an excess of potential allegorical significations.[399] There is no way of deciding unequivocally whether the practice of this semantic agglomeration is left to the arbitrary will of the allegorist or follows clandestine sympathies. It leads to contradictions in any case: the allegorizing method creates opacity by providing an abundance of possible interpretations that seem to be mutually exclusive. As an activity of sowing obscurity and contradiction, the creation of allegories itself seems increasingly diabolical.

In the early modern age, allegoresis, for having given a position to the devils, is attributed to the devils themselves; according to some authors, it is a Satanic temptation.[400] When allegorical exegesis of the Bible departs from the dogmatic consensus, the danger of heresy is always present; the antinomian sects of the sixteenth and seventeenth centuries are often accused of allegorical distortions of the Bible.[401] In this conception, the devil assumes the procedure through which he became addressable as his own deed: it is Satan who tempts mortals to see everything as allegorically meaningful. Through this method of allegoresis, Benjamin writes, the devil designs the illusion of an absolute spirit that frees itself of all stable divine essences in order to penetrate matter and gain discretionary power over it. But matter denies this hubris any access to truth: the data of bottomless diabolical profundity will not unlock either power or knowledge.[402] For matter exceeds the grasps of allegoresis: "Matter [. . .] scorns its allegorical 'significance', and mocks anyone who believes he can pursue it into the depths with impunity."[403] The allegorical image for this endless secession of the allegorist is the fall of the damned. "For it is the characteristic of all virtue to have an end before it: namely its model, in God; just as all infamy opens up an infinite progression into the depths."[404] As the allegory of allegoresis, the fall into the abyss figures the fact that the symbolic field is bottomless. In exactly this function it is also used in *Richard III*, its emphasis having shifted to the political realm: the hubris responsible for this fall will be less the search for knowledge than the pursuit of power and advancement stripped of any obligations. Since the "untimely fall of virtuous Lancaster" (I. ii. 4) the image of the fall of the damned appears to be ever present; a political lack of orientation, the fear of social decline, of death, and of God's judgment all conjoin in it (e.g. in V. iii. 61–63). In Margaret's denunciations of courtly hubris, the tradition-laden image of the fall is utilized extensively as she lets ascent and descent seamlessly merge:

> MARGARET: They that stand high have many blasts to shake them,
> And if they fall, they dash themselves to pieces. [. . .]
> One heav'd a-high, to be hurl'd down below [. . .].
>
> (I. iii. 259–269; IV. iv. 86)

In a moralizing tone, Hastings takes up the motif after he has been deprived of his power:

> HASTINGS: O momentary grace of mortal men,
> Which we more hunt for than the grace of God.
> Who builds his hope in air of your good looks
> Lives like a drunken sailor on a mast,
> Ready with every nod to tumble down
> Into the fatal bowels of the deep.
>
> (III. iv. 96–101)

The image's diverse allegorical implications are unfolded most extensively in Clarence's visionary dream before his execution. And this dream is legible, once more, both as a transcendent message of doom and as a concentrated representation of the repressed knowledge of a psychologically determinable individual:

> CLARENCE: Methought that Gloucester stumbled, and in falling,
> Struck me (that thought to stay him) overboard,
> Into the tumbling billows of the main.
>
> (I. iv. 18–20)

Then follows the description of an allegorical fall into allegory, i.e. into the damnation of an afterlife inextricably intertwined with this temporal world. This damnation is first described as a paradoxical state of living death, above all a death with open eyes:

> CLARENCE: What sights of ugly death within my eyes!
> Methoughts I saw a thousand fearful wrecks;
> Ten thousand men that fishes gnaw'd upon;
> Wedges of gold, great anchors, heaps of pearl,
> Inestimable stones, unvalu'd jewels,
> All scatter'd in the bottom of the sea.
> Some lay in dead men's skulls, and in the holes
> Where eyes did once inhabit, there were crept –
> As 'twere in scorn of eyes – reflecting gems,
> That woo'd the slimy bottom of the deep,
> And mock'd the dead bones that lay scatter'd by.
> BRAKENBURY: Had you such leisure in the time of death
> To gaze upon these secrets of the deep?
>
> (I. iv. 23–35)

The inventory of this dream sequence presents itself as an unorganized assemblage of things lost in an indistinct depth ("slimy bottom of the deep"), a fragmented mixture ("wrecked" and "scattered") of significant precious objects and human remains. Their combination yields emblems of death as much as insignia of political power—just as the sea in which Clarence drowns figures both as the source of power for a "seafaring nation"[405] and as the bringer of a premature death. This passage is more than simply an elaboration of the concept of *vanitas*; it depicts a state between death and life that amounts to a kind of travesty of life, representing the quasi-living power of dead over living things. Precious metals and gems appear strangely enlivened; as the real protagonists in this submarine spectacle, they are equipped with the capacity of "creeping," "scorning," "wooing," and "mocking." Conversely, that same fetishism reduces the dead, as an arrangement of *capita mortua* and bones, to the role of emblematic stage props.[406] Some phrases Clarence uses to describe his catastrophic vision imply that it is a self-portrait. The "reflecting gems" in the eye sockets of the skulls mirror his own face. As Benjamin suggests, it is in the *caput mortuum* that the objects of the allegorical gaze form a mirror image of the allegorist.[407] Insofar as Clarence hovers between life and death during his contemplative "leisure in the time of death," the enlivened skulls can accept him as one of their own. The gaze at the life of dead things is itself the gaze of a corpse: "sights of ugly death within my eyes" can be read both as an objective and as a subjective genitive. Clarence's vision represents his life flashing before his eyes, the eyes of a dying man. In this abbreviation, English history, and not only that of the Wars of the Roses, appears as "one single catastrophe, which keeps piling wreckage upon wreckage."[408] "Everything about history that, from the very beginning, has been untimely, sorrowful, unsuccessful, is expressed in a face – or rather in a death's head."[409] The resulting image of history is compounded of allegorically charged props that amount to the allegorist's dead life. Consequently, his vision denies Clarence a liberating death; his body and his soul remain tied to each other:

> CLARENCE: often did I strive
> To yield the ghost, but still the envious flood
> Stopp'd in my soul, and would not let it forth
> To find the empty, vast and wand'ring air,
> But smother'd it within my panting bulk,
> Which almost burst to belch it in the sea.
>
> (I. iv. 36–41)

Without resolving this situation, the report almost cinematically leaps into a new dream sequence. Clarence's dream is "lengthen'd after life" (I. iv. 43), but his subsequent descent into the underworld only prolongs his fall through ambiguous, allegorical signs. For this nether realm is allegorical as well; it is a mirror image of this world, its continuation by other means. What is remarkable in this context is above all the accumulation of monarchical characterizations of hell, such as "the kingdom of perpetual night" (I. iv. 47) and "this dark monarchy" (I. iv. 51), terms that can also refer to the England of the Wars of the Roses. And just like England, Clarence's underworld is also a split kingdom. Clarence sinks into a realm of the dead between Hades and hell in which pagan and Christian elements are not synthesized into a new unity, as in Dante, but persist in an irreconcilable conflict. But nonetheless, there is an introductory allusion to Dante: Clarence describes his passage through Acheron's "melancholy flood" with Charon, the "sour ferryman which poets write of" (I. iv. 45–46), whom Dante has Christianized in Canto III of *Inferno*.[410] At the opposite shore, he encounters Warwick and Prince Edward who indict him, sentence him on the spot, and hand him over to the underworld's executioners (I. iv. 48–61). Are these two dead men among the damned? Why then do they appear to hold the power of divine judgment? If Clarence's underworld is Hell and not Hades, it remains unclear what Prince Edward, completely passive throughout the York tetralogy, but arousing the very best expectations, is doing in this place, "with bright hair dabbled in blood." One need only compare, for example, the description Richard gives of him in a monologue:

> RICHARD: A sweeter and a lovelier gentleman,
> Fram'd in the prodigality of Nature,
> Young, valiant, wise, and no doubt right royal,
> The spacious world cannot again afford.
>
> (I. ii. 247–250)

Oxford, comparing Prince Edward to Henry V, sounds the same bugle:

> OXFORD: O brave young Prince, thy famous grandfather
> Doth live again in thee! Long mayst thou live
> To bear his image and renew his glories!
>
> (*3 Henry VI*, V. iv. 52–54)

This is how things stand when Richard and his brothers stab Prince Edward to death near Tewkesbury. Should he then not dwell in heaven rather than in hell? Or might he have risen to the rank of a judging archangel? Out of their unclear speech situation, the two dreamed dead men raise the same accusations against Clarence that Richard will raise against himself after his dream in scene V. iii: charges of perjury and of murder (cf. V. iii. 197–198). First Warwick takes up the indictment for perjury (I. iv. 50–51), and then Edward adds murder. His indictment smoothly merges into the verdict and then into punishment:

> CLARENCE: A shadow like an angel, with bright hair
> Dabbled in blood; and he shriek'd out aloud,
> "Clarence is come: false, fleeting, perjur'd Clarence,
> That stabb'd me in the field by Tewkesbury!
> Seize on him, Furies! Take him unto torment!"
> With that, methoughts, a legion of foul fiends
> Environ'd me, and howled in mine ears
> Such hideous cries, that with the very noise
> I trembling wak'd, and for a season after
> Could not believe but that I was in hell,
> Such terrible impression made my dream.
>
> (I. iv. 53–63)

At the conclusion of this passage, the motif of the here-and-now reappears that cannot be distinguished clearly from the hellish Beyond. But this conflation is not developed as extensively as the tension between Christian and pagan elements: on the one hand, the demons that attack Clarence are addressed as Furies, i.e. as the Latinized Erinyes of Greek antiquity. On the other hand, Clarence uses Christian concepts to describe the same beings: the "legion of foul fiends" seems to refer to Mark 5. 9 and Luke 8. 30 as well as to the designation of the devils as "fiends," in common usage since Tyndale's translation of the Bible.[411] This condensation also has a predecessor in Dante's *Comedia*, namely in Canto IX of *Inferno*, where the Erinyes, as inhabitants of Hell, appear for the first time within a Christian context.[412] But once again Shakespeare's combination is more problematic and fractured: in Clarence's dream, devils, angels, souls of the dead and furies are condensed into an image that does not accomplish a synthesis, but rather displays unsublatable contradictions. A self-contradictory trial is opened in which conscience, God's judgment, and blood vengeance—mundane, celestial, and chthonic jurisdiction—are inconveniently entangled. The overdetermined act of Clarence's sentencing supercharges semantics and breaks out in a scream. Edward's "shriek" fades into the "cries" and "howls" of the infernal legions; the victim's scream and the executioners' roar become indistinguishable. The Furies actually do not seem to carry out the customary penalties of hell, but limit themselves to unleashing polyphonic, punishing howls. Beyond this auditory impression, Clarence does not describe the Furies, perhaps he does not even perceive them, as if they consisted of nothing but a cacophony of inarticulately damning screams ejaculated by the ghosts of the dead, appearing as divine executioners. Are the Erinyes thus allegorical curses as well? To identify the avenging divinities with the curse would by no means constitute a new and original interpretation; it preserves the legacy of both classical antiquity and of Christianity, reducing it to its lowest common denominator. The Erinyes are called ἀραι (curses) as early as in Aeschylus' *Oresteia*:

> Χορός: ἀραὶ δ᾽ἐν οἴκοις γῆς ὑπαὶ κεκλήμεθα
> CHORUS: Deep in the halls of Earth they call us Curses.[413]

Are the Erinyes of the *Oresteia*, then, already allegorical figures? Nothing prevents us from interpreting them as such. More exactly, they mark the boundary between allegory and myth, insofar as the *Oresteia* itself enacts allegoreses of mythical figures in the course of its development. In Aeschylus' drama, not only is the transition between the curse and the demons fluid, but so is that between them both and the Pelopids involved in the curse. In Cassandra's vision, for example, the dead children of Thyestes appear as Erinyes (*Agamemnon*, 1186–1189), and in Clytemnestra's dialogue with the Chorus after Agamemnon's murder she herself lays claim to the role of the curse, as the avenging spirit who has haunted the House of Atreus (*Agamemnon*, 1475–1504).

It is worthwhile pursuing this parallel a little further. In the *Oresteia*, the fate of the House of Atreus appears in the form of an illimitable demand for retribution according to the law of blood vengeance. The representatives of this law are the Erinyes, who claim two concurrent authorities: to cause the killings and to exact vengeance for the same. This dual role of the Furies puts Orestes under a double bind: Apollo threatens him with the Erinyes if he does not avenge his father upon his mother (*Libation Bearers*, 283–290), and after his murder of Clytemnestra they pursue him as a matricide. The infringement of the blood law with its demand for retribution in this case does not occur "unwittingly"[414] but without alternatives, despite its ambiguity—thus, it is "fated." According to Benjamin, the protagonist in ancient tragedy escapes fate's "demonic jurisdiction" by "reflecting [his guilt] in his consciousness of himself," absorbing it into himself and thereby, paradoxically, extinguishing it as a general fatality.[415] The solution of the *Oresteia*, however, produces less a definitive defeat of the archaic cursing power than its containment: as would have to be shown elsewhere, the political transformation of the *Eumenides* does not really entail the extinction of the curse, but amounts to its bureaucratization and nationalization.[416] The allegoresis does not lead to redemption but to the centralization of fate. This implies that even ancient tragedy is contaminated with what Benjamin calls "Trauerspiel." For in *The Origin of German Tragic Drama*, he defines the difference between tragedy and *Trauerspiel* by stating that there are no tragic protagonists in the *Trauerspiel*, which means there are no heroes who overcome fate. Instead, the curse unfolds in the social field; it is not dissolved, but passes from one constellation over into the next: "the *Trauerspiel* therefore has no individual hero, only constellations."[417] Seneca's tragic closet dramas, which likewise involve the Erinyes, match this description better than the Greek tragedies. Seneca's plays seem to be located, as it were, halfway between tragedy and *Trauerspiel*. Shakespeare most probably did not know the *Oresteia*,[418] but it is all the more likely that he was familiar with Seneca's *Thyestes*, a popular play during the Elizabethan era. In emulating Aeschylus, this drama also has a Fury appear as an excessively cursing personification of the malediction on the House of Atreus, and as a voice proclaiming hell on earth.[419] In *Thyestes*, however, the contours of the tragic protagonist dissolve: Thyestes is no hero, he does not belong to the last but to the penultimate generation, and he suffers under the curse without overcoming it. The fall of Atreus' posterity is prefigured in him, but postponed, by his curse on his brother's house[420], until the next generation, the redemptive "last generation" of Orestes that will restrain the power of the curse. For this reason, Fate in the form the "malicious chance" can continue to unfold and spread in this drama, proclaimed by the triumphant Fury. The Christianization of the Erinyes in the *Divina Comedia* sublates this complex and preserves it in the ambiguity of diabolical allegoreses. Even in a Christian context, the theological aporia of the demonic figure still appears as identical with the aporia of the curse. Shakespeare's theater acts out precisely this pathlessness; the "last generation" of his Histories, however, has vanished into a phantasmatic time that can only be aped, on the stage as elsewhere.

1.7 Buckingham and the grounds of theater

The church legitimates itself through its function of testifying for Christ. Its consequent task consists of representing at various levels the redemption accomplished by Jesus. For Paul this already holds good for the mission of the apostles: "We are made a spectacle [θέατρον] unto the world, and to angels, and to men" (1 Cor. 4. 9). For ecclesiastical ritual, the representation of redemptive acts is of central importance as well, not only in the form of a recurrent reproduction of the Last Supper (figuring Christ's death on the cross), but also in the form of sermons, hymns, etc. Against this background one could surmise that the church's hostility toward the theater is based on the repression of a similarity and clandestine competition between the two institutions. Especially the admission of actors to share in the Eucharist has often been a problematic issue for the orthodoxy: Augustine, Cyprian, Lactantius and Arnobius plead for excluding professional comedians from receiving communion. As late as the Middle Ages, this view has legal force in a few places.[421] In Shakespeare's time, actors may take communion, but Puritans like Phillip Stubbes rigorously oppose this practice.[422] It should be emphasized here that contrary to the often-quoted opposition of Anglicans and Puritans to the theater, a good number of English Protestants put high hopes in drama during the first phase of the Reformation. During this period the boundaries between the Anglican clergy and theatrical troupes are much more open than has long been assumed: many priests participate in secular performances of plays, not merely as spectators but also as actors and authors.[423] John Foxe considers the stage alongside Protestant itinerant preachers and the printing press as the third medium that is called upon to resist the Pope's hegemony. All three of them he designates "a triple bulwark against the triple crown of the Pope, to bring him down."[424] (This statement also intimates that both the converting forces of the Reformation and the theater of the Renaissance are supported by the indirect power of language and signs.) Hostility toward the theater, especially among the religious rigorists, surfaces only after the consolidation of the Reformation. During the Elizabethan and Jacobean period it is the Puritans who launch the most vehement polemics against the theater, claiming that the new social order must be protected from it. They assert that the actor, by taking on many roles, contradicts the God-given precept that every subject has been accorded one, and only one, place in society.[425] This motif can be traced back to Plato's *Politeia* in which the banishment of actors from the ideal city is demanded for the same reason: in Plato's state every citizen has to play a specific role corresponding to his place in the hierarchy. The actor's constant change of roles undermines this notion of identity that is mandatory for the polis. The stage play, like any mimetic art, is a lie: actors pretend to be someone they are not—hence they are deceivers, hence criminals, and ought to be kept from doing what they do.[426] In sixteenth-century England, these reasons are still included among the central charges in the indictment of theater.[427] Just at the time when emerging capitalism begins to rearrange the social strata, Calvinist elements (which contribute to this change themselves) insist on an already illusory stability of societal roles. In this context as well, hostility toward the theater seems to arise in part from a sense of inappropriate proximity and unconscious competition: not only do actors under Elizabethan circumstances have to become entrepreneurs, but also conversely, as Jean-Christophe Agnew has shown, the new market becomes perceived as a theatrical institution, with the merchants as actors.[428] There is a good reason that, for instance, the writer John Hall declares in the seventeenth century: "Man in business is but a Theatricall person, and in a manner but personates himselfe."[429] One indication that the Puritans are closer to the theater than they would like to admit may be the fact that many noblemen of high standing in the 1670s and 1680s simultaneously support both the theater and the Puritan movement.[430]

Robert Weimann describes the Reformation as a "crisis of authority," traceable to the collapse of the church's monopoly on knowledge, caused first and foremost by the development of the printing press and of a non-itinerant theater.[431] This view is somewhat imprecise, not least because Weimann downplays the fact that in England the State largely controls both the theater and the printing of books, as well as the Reformation, and that it can saturate its authority through this control in many respects. The effect is rather a shifting of authority from the church to the State. Part of this rearrangement is a juridical integration of the theater into the performances of the State. In 1572 a law is passed ("Acte for the punishment of Vacabondes"[432]) that forces actors' troupes to put themselves under the licensing protection of a noble patron; otherwise, they will be arrested and punished as vagabonds. Hence the theater as an institution starts to depend on the court and, in the long run, on the monarch.[433] For the protected troupes, this change means an improvement of their market position. Oftentimes, the licensed actors and writers even offer their services to the authorities, as knowledgeable inquisitors and judges over their illegitimate competitors.[434] Henceforth, the theater obtains its legitimization from its official charge of fabricating appreciation of the State.

The "Queen's Men," for example, are from the very beginning conceived as a troupe of propagandists who are to spread royalist enthusiasm.[435] That stage plays affirm "England" as a collective identity is a motif that apologists of the theater like Thomas Heywood are pleased to take up:

> What English blood seeing the person of any bold English presented and doth not hug his fame and hunny at his valour, pursuing him in his enterprise with his best wishes and as being wrapt in contemplation, offers him in his heart all prosperous performance, as if the performer were the man personated? So bewitching a thing is lively and well spirited action, that it hath power to new mould the hearts of the spectators.[436]

The *New Historicism* has investigated theatrical elements in the self-representation of the early modern nobility and of the monarch, and has shown that both buttress their power to a considerable extent by stagings of their mastery.[437] In this context, Christopher Pye quotes Holinshed quoting a description of Elizabeth's first public procession:

> If a man would saie well, he could not better term the citie of London that time, than a stage, wherein was shewed the wonderfull spectacle of a noble hearted princesse towards hir most loving people, and the people's exceeding comfort in beholding so worthie a sovereigne.[438]

The sovereign presence must be staged and turns social life into stagecraft, rendering urban space theatrical. Monarchs are dramatic figures whose appearance is decisive for their being. Both Elizabeth and James use the commonplace metaphor depicting monarchs as actors who spend their life on the stage of the *theatrum mundi*, before the eyes of the whole world.[439] Kantorowicz has analyzed the medieval Christological concepts resonating in such statements: according to the anonymous author of the twelfth-century treatise *De consecratione pontificum et regum*, the anointed kings of the Old Testament prefigured the royal Christ. The kings who rule after the Ascension of the Savior appropriately play the role of his "shadows." For this writer, Christian rulers are χριστόμιμηταὶ, the impersonators of Christ's dual nature.[440] Precisely because the monarch is a sovereign ruler, he can mime Christus-Pantokrator. That he is not subject to any command but can issue commands qualifies him to *imitatio dei*. Kantorowicz writes that the Church Father Theodoret of Cyrus was the first to expound that man's godlike nature refers neither to body nor soul but to rulership (τὸ ἀρχικόν): man is like God insofar as the natural world is subject to his will.[441] In the king's rule, the ties that hold the *theatrum mundi* together are crossed and re-crossed. Perhaps for this reason, Shakespeare's Histories are all named after the monarch ruling during the diegetic time, even if said ruler is not on the stage all that often. (If the *persona* playing the major part were to provide the play's title, *Henry IV* would, for instance, have to be called "Prince Hal" or "Falstaff.")

The fact that the dramatic performance of dominion is so essential to the Tudors and Stuarts is largely due, writes Greenblatt, to the heightened instability of their executive power. According to this view the English State of the sixteenth and seventeenth centuries lacks the disciplinary institutions, in part already developed on the Continent, of a modern polity (such as a standing army, a police force and a functioning bureaucracy); hence England needs all the more urgently to stage royal executive power (through pageants, masques, public executions, etc.) in order to disguise its precarious status.[442] For this reason, the State also places hopes in the theater; on the part of the rulers, there do not seem to be any marked fears of contact. Especially in the "pageants" and "masques" the boundary between stage and spectators becomes at times so porous that performance and courtceremonial can merge seamlessly. The climax of the masque at the Elizabethan and Jacobean court occurs when the costumed actors step down from the stage to mingle with the spectators and select dancing partners from among them. The illusion of power on the stage enters into the illusion of power *tout court*.[443]

The monarchy of the Renaissance legitimates itself through the theater, among other things, and keeps it free of competitors as much as possible. Nevertheless, the State-controlled kingdom of representation is nagged by sundry irksome rivals, especially in Elizabethan times: a large number of illegal impersonators of royal, divinely legitimated authority irritate the univocity of the State's spectacle. Prophets who announce the return of Edward V or Edward VI or others will subsequently often feel called upon to take on the role of the missing king themselves in order to support their statements. The yeoman Robert Blosse who on one of these occasions portrayed Edward VI, is executed in 1581, his indictment reading "Impersonation of the King."[444] In his wake, there appears during the Elizabeth's reign "a small army" of commoners who declare themselves to be members of the royal family, Christ, apostles, or "Lord of Lords and King of Kings" and for this are sentenced to prison, the stocks, or execution.[445] Often they threaten unbelievers with punitive curses.[446] In 1591 the "illiterate and bankrupt ex-serving-man" William Hacket, for example, declares that he is the Messiah and has come to judge the world. He begins to hand opponents over to divine judgment, reciting declamations that display similarities to ecclesiastical cursing ceremonies. When in this connection he declares the Queen deposed and the Privy Council dissolved, he is arrested and executed for high treason.[447] Another impersonator, fashioning a particularly astounding figure of sacral royalty, declares himself the son of Elizabeth I, whom she has conceived by God the Father.[448] Keith Thomas lists numerous further examples and points out in conclusion that the descent from Brutus, the State-founding grandson of Aeneas, to whom the Tudors trace back the legitimacy of their rule, is no less phantasmatic.[449]

The theater appears to be an absolute metaphor[450] of the English Renaissance, as reflected in the abundant use of expressions constellated around the locution "theater of the world." One of the most often-quoted elaborations of this motif is surely Jacques' declamation "All the world's a stage" from *As You Like It* (II. vii. 138–165). It is, to be sure, not a particularly modern metaphor, having been used occasionally as early as antiquity and through the Middle Ages. But what is new about its early modern employment, according to Jean-Christophe Agnew, is the motivation underlying its usage: in the Middle Ages, the propagation of the *theatrum mundi* metaphor was sustained by the notion of the vanity of worldly affairs. During the Renaissance, however, this image rather conveys the circumstance that many of the most important traditional bonds (feudal relationships, the bindingness of liturgical forms, obligations between members of a community) are slowly becoming obsolete, without disappearing from social life. The reason for this obsolescence can be found, first and foremost, in the restructuring processes driven by emerging capitalism.[451] The metaphor of the world as theater had been used in the Middle Ages to produce an "alienation effect" in one's view of the world. During the Renaissance, which is to say, during a time when the old social structures already displaced by the structures of the developing free market still retain their binding power, the same metaphor is also used; but now it denotes an increasing alienation within social life itself, and becomes used as a prop to keep pace with this estrangement.[452] It is perhaps for this reason that the State seeks to obtain a monopoly on the theater, even against the church, whose very theatrical potential is being curtailed and partially taken over by the court. Remnants of the mystery and miracle play traditions do survive even into the seventeenth century, and Shakespeare sometimes alludes to them. But the government prohibits and suppresses them due to their association with Catholicism.[453] The theater of Shakespeare and his contemporaries appropriates what remains of this English theatrical tradition; affinities between their plays and the morality plays have been noticed frequently.[454] This expropriation often takes on the hostile form of satire. It is obvious that the stage at times parodies the old liturgy, as in Marlowe's Faustus' rude interruption of the anathema carried out in the Vatican.[455] When James I came to Cambridge in 1615, the university staged "a play containing an episode mocking the whole procedure of [Catholic] exorcism."[456] Accordingly, some see in theater a potential exponent of "popery," i.e. of (crypto-)Catholic elements infiltrating public life. Samuel Harsnett's identification of exorcism and theater, which Greenblatt has analyzed, belongs in this context, as well as the denunciation of the Catholic Church as "the Pope's playhouse" for its elaborate ceremonies.[457] Sacral speech on stage is generally viewed with skepticism, as one can also gather from a Jacobean statute of 1606 that forbids not only cursing but also using the names of God and of Jesus Christ on the public stage.[458]

The drama of Shakespeare's time appropriates as its capital the significant surplus of outdated, "undead" rituals, above all those of the church. In this respect, it might be considered emblematic that most theaters north of the Thames (e.g. Holywell, Whitefriars, and Blackfriars) were built on the site of plundered monasteries.[459] The theater dynamizes this heritage, nominally submitting it to the State's authority while preserving its old forms. The ambiguity of this situation is mirrored in the way the theater itself constructs ambiguities. Under Elizabeth and James, the political impetus of the theater becomes more implicit and ambiguous, and hence capable of satisfying divergent societal forces in equal measure. The rhetorical education of many Elizabethans in the grammar schools is a condition for this development. Mastery of the *argumentum in utramque partem*, that is, the ability of speaking persuasively for two diametrically opposed positions, is a particular professional necessity for dramatists and actors; it exerts a formative influence on the drama of the time.[460] Summarizing, Greenblatt suggests that Shakespeare's theater could be considered as something like an "enlightened Church": the old, quasi-magical power of language is employed in a new, more rational context, but not simply superseded.[461] As "*hoc est corpus meum*" transforms bread and wine, so "even here in Bosworth Field" changes the stage into an other scene. But on stage this transformation, which continues to be theater's strange attractor, is marked as an illusion and can be problematized, discussed and variegated.

By Austin's dictum, performatives within a theatrical context are empty speech acts ("hollow and void");[462] but in Elizabethan drama, and especially in Shakespeare's plays, this "emptiness" is integrated into the plot and forms a crucial part of it. Within the diegetic action, ritual acts are performed in such a way that the hollow fetishism underlying them is exposed; they are marked as inherently unsuccessful and as dependent on deceptive staging. Shakespeare's early plays are haunted by the shadows of failed, ineffective, and obsolete rituals. But oftentimes Shakespeare also presents performances that, their emptiness notwithstanding, appear to be opportune and necessary: despite (or even precisely because of) this ineffectuality they fulfill an important function. Many of the curses in his dramas can be considered among these speech acts. Shakespeare's works frequently revolve around situations in which powerlessness represents itself as power and vice versa. Insofar as curses inhabit the zone where power and its opposite are seen as interdependent,[463] their theatrical efficacy in these situations is evident. By appropriating the curse—whose various facets have been described in the preceding chapters—Shakespeare turns the theater into an institution that (always already) rules without power. The form of the ban that it delineates lends the theater its latent force of legitimacy. Shakespeare lets the theater converge with the void at the heart of society by integrating into the play the very categories that separate reality from play. For this type of theater, the question of truth becomes topical only under the sign of deception.

The same way of handling the limits of the theater can also be observed with reference to the difference between representing and represented time: the "untimely" character of diegetic time itself is thematized in Shakespeare's plays. The theater that is publicly presenting history is a new institution that sees as its task the revivification of the past *as* past. Consequently, in *Richard III*, a past is portrayed which portrays another past: The society represented in the play is full of characters who cling to outdated relations, who cannot escape obsolete obligations and endow them with an undead half-life. The York tetralogy is largely about people who, in a twofold sense, live in the past. The fate of being doubly outmoded, however, falls not only on the characters but also on the stage props. The theater of sixteenth-century England becomes a place of discarded sacral objects: as a result of the Reformation and the dissolution of the monasteries, the Catholic clerical vestments, pluvials, ornates, etc. are sold to acting companies.[464] It is highly probable that the two bishops flanking Richard in scene III. vii. were wearing authentic bishop's robes in the early performances. One may presume that the players banked on a certain *frisson* caused by this appropriation of symbolic prestige, even though these vestments have been reduced to the status of stage props not just in Shakespeare's but also in Richard's staging. The theatrical character of Richard's acclamation (III. vii.) has been pointed out frequently; that the silent bishops are being instrumentalized for the purpose of lending some legitimacy to the proceedings is suggested by Buckingham's ironic locution describing them as "props of virtue" (III. vii. 95). Already within the diegetic situation, the priest's robe is a commodity that goes to the highest bidder. Something similar is true, as can be observed throughout the play, of the status symbols of the secular nobility.[465]

The theater is a site haunted by the ghosts of dead ceremonies which cannot be conclusively exorcised since the symbolisms of society still depend on them, even in the very gesture of exorcism. It is in this function above all that theater in the modern age becomes the "setting for the enactment of history."[466] In this capacity, the theater does not describe historical processes from the outside; it is inscribed into these processes and performs them. In Wolfgang Iser's terms, history can be defined in this context as the perpetually backfiring attempt to overcome the ambivalences of one's own and others' actions through the exercise of power.[467] But while it becomes a problem for the monarch that his methods of tackling ambiguities constantly generate new ambiguities, the dramatist can tally this dilemma into the books as his guarantee of employment. In commercial Histories, history is turned into a commodity. Shakespeare's theater, as a service enterprise and joint venture company that prepares history for consumption, comes out of this transaction with great success: Shakespeare is one of the first litterateurs who can live from the sale of their products in the marketplace.[468]

The theater (re)constitutes history in the field of tension between court and marketplace. It serves as a compromise formation between economy and ceremony, a middle ground that must be capable of satisfying opposing social forces through its ambiguities. For while the troupes are institutionally bound to act out the ceremonious representations of a decaying court culture, economically they are dependent on the contractual representations and joint venture company structures of the emerging capitalist market. The theater stands at the threshold of both forms and must accommodate itself in both directions, thereby relating both to each other. Drama participates in both ceremonial and commercial representation; it relates one to the other by displaying the differences between the three institutions of court, church, and market, while at the same time linking each with the other two. The theater criticizes the new time of the new market as much as the old hierarchical structures, and in these very criticisms, it subordinates itself to both. *Richard III* can be regarded as an ideal figuration of this tense arrangement. Using Richard as *point de capiton*,[469] Shakespeare transforms the legitimizing ceremonies of decomposing feudal power structures into the form of consumable commodities and portrays this transformation within the very merchandise he proffers for sale. It is the intermediate status of the curse, floating between temporalities, between institutions, and between power and subordination, which renders it analogous to the theatrical form and interesting to the theater of the early modern period. As developed in the preceding chapters, the curse appears in Shakespearean drama in many respects as a theatrical speech act. The stage in these plays establishes itself as the representative locale of a sovereign irony, where the curse can circulate in infinite suspension, holding a reservoir of sense. Through the curse, the indefinitely suspended verdict on the world theater is delivered. And it is this property which reveals the floating curse as a paradigm of societal cohesion; it strikes the entire social field, by supplementing Elizabethan sovereignty. Figures on the stage become symptoms of this fact. First and foremost, Richard assumes his position as curse incarnate exactly by assuming his function as a meta-dramatist. A. P. Rossiter and others have discussed before how in Richard the public *persona* of the Elizabethan actor and stage director seems to be reproduced within the drama itself.[470] With his skill at appropriating rituals and at the same time ironically subverting them by taking on various roles, Richard represents the theater onstage. Within the diegetic plot, he brings about what the drama *Richard III* does in the public arena, and in this respect he appears on stage as an allegory of the Shakespearean History.

Rossiter's approach, however, needs specification: Richard is not alone in taking on the role of an actor within the diegetic frame of *Richard III*. It is a characteristic of nearly all figures, positive or negative, that they depend on stagings and dissimulation to achieve their goals. Buckingham, Catesby, Stanley, Margaret, and Elizabeth are particularly zealous players. (The court's pitiable festivals of reconciliation under the direction of Edward IV have already been discussed.) Even the Lord Mayor, a scrivener, diverse clergymen, and various citizens of London are drawn into the performances and are forced to actively participate in them. The remaining figures, too, do not simply identify with a certifiable social position. The remark made by the second citizen in scene II. iii. may be paradigmatic of this fact:

> SECOND CITIZEN: I promise you, I scarcely know myself.
>
> (II. iii. 2)

What he formulates here is a fundamental mood that is constantly present in *Richard III*, namely the insecurity about one's own place and identity ("I scarcely know myself"), trying continually to find self-assurance through commissive utterances ("I promise you") but unable to secure anything but insecurity itself. And since the citizen does not know his position, he also cannot say where he is going ("whither away," II. iii. 1), even if he was summoned to appear in court (II. iii. 46). The royal court is likewise reduced to playing its reality since the kingdom's survival in such uncertain times depends on its method acting. Pivotal for this theme, beside the oath scene in II. i. (analyzed in section 1.3), is the scene of acclamation (III. vii), a far more skillfully and convincingly arranged play-within-the-play. All citizens and noblemen gathered on the stage are perfectly aware, as is their audience, that this *mise-en-scène* of a crisis prevention is a universal farce; none of the persons involved is deceived or participates out of conviction. But all the same, everybody plays the role Richard and Buckingham have assigned them to the hilt, believing that this will be to their advantage. Even the London citizens in front of Baynard's Castle are in no way convinced of Richard's legitimacy; rather, they enter into an alliance with the illusionists fully aware of the deception: Buckingham's story of the gathering in Guildhall (III. vii. 1–40) makes it clear that the people of London do not believe the myth Richard fabricated to prove his legitimacy. But they would not stand in front of Baynard's Castle a few hours later if they would not intend to support him; and since they do not do this out of conviction, their motives most likely are opportunism and political calculation. Subjects, no less than the nobility, are no mere passive bystanders to the performances that help Richard procure the throne. As helpers who are privy to what is going on, they act in minor roles and as co-authors.

Their non-identity with themselves turns all the characters, not only Richard, into actors and stage directors. Consequently, more complex reasons must exist as to why Richard occupies a privileged position in this play. What indeed sets him apart is that he seems to be the only person for whom the theater is an absolute: he does not think in the Platonic categories of original and imitation but in terms of simulacra.[471] If one compares his utterances with those of his helper Buckingham, it becomes apparent that both do indeed behave like stage directors and actors, but that Buckingham speaks of their play as a clever fraud and playful deception, whereas Richard seems to see no difference between truth and lie. In scene III. v. 71–93, for example, Richard orders Buckingham to denounce the princes, the king and the queen dowager. Truth and falsehood intermingle in Richard's instructions, for he does not keep them apart but uniformly uses the stereotypical "tell them" and "infer," which allow no judgments about the truth of what is said. Richard examines its content only for plausibility and possible effects. Buckingham, by contrast, uses words like "counterfeit" (III. v. 5) for their performances, which Richard never does. The same difference can also be observed in others of their interactions, which permits the general conclusion that Buckingham in contrast to Richard deduces deception from truth and subordinates it to the latter.[472] It is in keeping with Buckingham's realistic attitude that he (in contrast to Richard's ambivalence in this matter) denies the efficacy of cursing:

> BUCKINGHAM: curses never pass
> The lips of those that breathe them in the air.
>
> (I. iii. 285–286)

It is only as a result of his fall that Buckingham comes to revise his opinion: in order to come to terms with the traumatic news, he declares his impending execution in scene V. i. to be the judgment of a heavenly court of law.

He is able to charge this situation with new sense by way of his oath in Act II, scene i, as well as of Margaret's maledictions: the farcical oath now seems to turn against him as a curse. Subsequently, play and reality become inseparably confused for him:

> BUCKINGHAM: That high All-seer which I dallied with
> Hath turn'd my feigned prayer on my head,
> And given in earnest what I begg'd in jest.
> Thus doth He force the swords of wicked men
> To turn their own points in their masters' bosoms.
> Thus Margaret's curse falls heavy on my neck [. . .].
>
> (V. i. 20–25)

For Richard, by the same token, the difference between deception and reality has never been anything but relative. In the final analysis, every role in this world is an arrogated role. Like Iago, Richard is "not what he is" (*Othello*, I. i. 65), meaning that he is not self-identical. His declaration that not only his bigoted dissemblance but also the diabolical tactic hidden beneath it are equally to be understood as role-playing (I. iii. 338) has already been quoted in section 1.6; there is no face to be detected behind Richard's masks. This is also the context in which to place his often discussed predilection for ironic utterances, in which strategically placed, ambiguous truths become a component of deceptive behavior. In I. i, for example, he consoles Clarence by announcing the latter's imminent demise which Richard has instigated:

> RICHARD: Well, your imprisonment shall not be long:
> I will deliver you, or else lie for you.
>
> (I. i. 114–115)

When Richard calls the prince "my thoughts' sovereign" (in III. i. 2), he gives an indication that the latter's elimination has occupied him for a long time, and he offers him a warm "welcome" above all because the resulting plot can now be carried out.[473] His irony points toward two incompatible levels of meaning and condenses both. He speaks ambiguously but his ambiguous speech is distinguished not merely by the fact that another, latent interpretation is possible besides the obvious one, but that their relationship may reverse itself; that depending on one's perspective and circumstances, one of them may at any point shift into latency. By thus positing and at the same time undermining, his irony is the figure of theater. It is appropriate to the simulacrum and lends it a verbal form. In the process, Richard does not really deceive any of the *dramatis personae* in the sense that they would accept his lies as truths. That the execution of Clarence, for example, is to be attributed to Richard and not to the king, all three former queens take for granted without discussion in scene IV. iv (IV. iv. 46/145/281). But up to that point, nobody has voiced an accusation against Richard in this matter. Before his coronation, Richard consistently succeeds in manipulating situations through the equivocal use of linguistic, juridical and religious forms in such a way that even those who are not taken in by him cannot move against him. Richard starts to run into problems with the coherence of his utterances only when he himself loses the beat and begins to sabotage his own projects. He ceases to be sovereign the moment he becomes king, and it becomes ever more obvious that the reason for this loss of power lies in his diminishing capacity for irony. That he considers the *theatrum mundi* to have ended and "true reality" to have dawned after he has gained the crown can be detected as early as in his policy statement from *Henry VI*:

> RICHARD: And whiles I live, t' account this world but hell,
> Until my misshaped trunk that bears this head
> Be round impalèd with a glorious crown. [. . .]
> Why, I can smile, and murder whiles I smile, [. . .]
> And frame my face to all occasions. [. . .]
> Can I do this, and cannot get a crown?
> Tut, were it farther off, I'll pluck it down.
> (*3 Henry VI*, III. ii. 169–171/182/185/194–195)

Causa efficiens and *causa finalis* of Richard's stagings is the crown. After he has reached this place of his destiny, the performance of the infernal world theater has come to its happy end for him. In contrast to the earlier/later kings of *Realpolitik*, Henry IV and Henry V, Richard is still a believer: he believes in the sacredness of the crown. He considers it the unmoved center of history (the earthly Paradise, "Elysium," *3. Henry VI*, I. ii. 30) and the king's name "a tower of strength" (V. iii. 12). The crown is not the stake in the game Richard set up, but its *telos* and source. In this regard as in others, he conforms to Benjamin's description of the intriguer in tragic drama (*Trauerspiel*), who submits himself to the insignia of royal sovereignty, crown and scepter, yet not to the person of the ruler, toward whom he proves disloyal. Hence, the court is subjected to the law of the *Dingwelt*, the world of things.[474] The crown functions as Richard's fetishistic, fixated *object a*, a pure nothing and everything, around which his subjective reality structures itself.[475] Richard knows that the crown bestows no power insofar as he is already in the sovereign position to determine the state of exception well before his coronation; and yet he does not know this because he fetishizes the crown. More than his amorality, it is this perverse faith in a fixed point in the universe that proves his undoing.

Iser writes that Richard after his coronation tries to consolidate through the production of dynastic legitimacy the position he has conquered by political means, and so to doubly safeguard himself.[476] But the text of the drama rather suggests that Richard reverts from thinking in terms of political strategy to thinking in purely dynastic terms. His political intelligence appears to decline rapidly. He attempts to legitimize his position irreversibly by either murdering or marrying all other legitimate pretenders to the crown. But he goes about this project with so much political clumsiness that he comes to resemble his predecessor more and more. Like Edward IV, he involuntarily establishes double binds (e.g. in IV. ii. 442–455), and begins to harken after "drunken prophecies" (IV. ii. 94–105). In the process, he neglects the realm of politics as if it had grown irrelevant in the new "dark monarchy." When he hears of the attack by the new pretender to the throne, who lacks real dynastic legitimacy, he seems genuinely confused:

> RICHARD: Is the chair empty? Is the sword unsway'd?
> Is the King dead? The empire unpossess'd?
> What heir of York is there alive but we?
> And who is England's King but great York's heir?
> Then tell me, what makes he upon the seas!
>
> (IV. iv. 469–473)

Richard's use of language also flattens out. For example, all he has at his command to counter the vivid accusations of the three queens in scene IV. iv. are frighteningly conventional commonplaces in the style of Edward IV. He seems to have foresworn ambiguities: "Be not so hasty to confound my meaning" (IV. iv. 262), he demands of Elizabeth in the course of a tepid stichomythia. Since his identification with the crown induces him to distance himself from the ambivalence of his earlier *personae*, he becomes ever more vulnerable, for example, to the strategical play-acting of Elizabeth, who, in order to deflect the orders he issues, refers to the prevalence of divine law:

> RICHARD: Tell her the King, that may command, entreats.
> ELIZABETH: That, at her hands, which the King's King forbids.
>
> (IV. iv. 345–346)

Such appeals can be used effectively only since Richard no longer plays the role of the simulator of a simulating devil.[477] But since Richard has already ironized the position he is trying to occupy, he cannot rid himself of his masks; his abandoned ability to speak in many voices continues to haunt him, most prominently during the entrance of the "shadows" in scene V. iii. Contrary to repeated claims by scholars, the spectral apparitions of Richard's victims do not "subjectivize" him.[478] On the contrary, it can be gathered from the text that the appearance of the ghosts, representing the diverse lineages of undead royalty, provokes an occultation of the singular crown fetish as his fixed point of orientation and, as a consequence, causes his desubjectivization. Despite Tillyard's dictum, the ghosts do not reanimate a stable theologico-political univocity, but represent incompatible and obsolete claims on symbolic positions of power.[479] Hence, Richard does not only see the dead as personifications of his moral conscience belatedly raising its voice but also as exponents of his many-tongued, fragmented consciousness:

> RICHARD: My conscience hath a thousand several tongues,
> And every tongue brings in a several tale [. . .].
>
> (V. iii. 194–195)

The use of the word "conscience," however, allows for both meanings, and both meanings unfold in the space of his nocturnal monologue. He not only calls himself a "villain," but also describes how he disintegrates into his roles and consequently turns against himself:

> RICHARD: What do I fear? Myself? There's none else by;
> Richard loves Richard, that is, I and I.
> Is there a murderer here? No. Yes, I am!
> Then fly. What, from myself? Great reason why,
> Lest I revenge ? What, myself upon myself?
>
> (V. iii. 183–187).

Richard loses himself in a professional schizophrenia that previously had not been a problem but rather a strategic condition for his success. Lacking an alternative, he insists on this split conscience even in his subsequent speech to his soldiers, in which he denounces "conscience" as "a word that cowards use" (V. iii. 310) and proclaims: "A thousand hearts are great within my bosom" (V. iii. 348). A mixed metaphor in his oration, appearing to fuse the holy dragon slayer with the dragon, is another symptom of the interior conflict that may well befall any sovereign who seeks to cut his ties to the *theatrum mundi* with the help of a stage prop:

> RICHARD: Our ancient word of courage, fair Saint George,
> Inspire us with the spleen of fiery dragons!
>
> (V. iii. 350–351)

The alienation which enabled him to gain the crown dismembers the identity Richard envisioned obtaining through the crown. The rest is the operation of motor reflex functions in the last battle.

Insofar as some of his utterances have an ironic dimension that he himself fails to notice, the play *Richard III* ironizes even Richard the ironist. Irony is a quality intrinsic to the medium of theater itself, as the most radical exponent of an endlessly shifting representation. No subject can truly master this irony; instead, it surreptitiously overwhelms the retrospectively accursed subjects in the form of historical calamities. In this respect, as Benjamin has suggested, irony also appears as a variant of the allegorical.[480] The positions in *Richard III* are ironized to such an extent that nothing but the autonomy of the signifiers remains, as the final (and empty) form of transcendence. In this history with an unreadable moral, only the ironic structure of representation itself is truly sovereign. In Shakespeare's later plays, even this last remnant of sovereignty crumbles into ashes, as will be shown in the following chapters.

Notes

1 Christoph Albrecht, *Einführung in die Liturgik*, Göttingen 1995, p. 21.
2 On this concept, see Jacques Lacan, *The Psychoses. Seminar III*, translated by Russell Grigg, London/New York, NY 1993, p. 257.
3 Hans Blumenberg, *The Legitimacy of the Modern Age*, translated by Robert M. Wallace, Cambridge, MA/London 1983, p. 112.

4 Ernst Dietzfelbinger (ed.), *Das Neue Testament, Interlinearübersetzung Griechisch-Deutsch*, Neuhausen 1998, p. 751.
5 Kenneth Hein, *Eucharist and Excommunication. A Study in Early Christian Doctrine and Discipline*, Bern/Frankfurt a. M. 1973.
6 Bernhard Lang, *Sacred Games. A History of Christian Worship*, New Haven, CT/London 1997, p. 299.
7 Hein, op. cit., pp. 47/49.
8 John E. Booty (ed.), *The Book of Common Prayer 1559. The Elizabethan Prayer Book*, Charlottesville, VA/London 1991, p. 258.
9 Keith Thomas, *Religion and the Decline of Magic. Studies in Popular Beliefs in Sixteenth- and Seventeenth-Century England*, London 1991, p. 50.
10 Walter Benjamin, 'Critique of Violence', in *Selected Writings*, Michael Jennings (general ed.), vol. I, translated by Edmund Jephcott, Cambridge, MA 1996, p. 251.
11 Augustine, *Contra Faustum Manicheum. Libri 1–19, XIV/I*, Rome 2004, pp. 224/226 [14. 4–12].
12 Yumi Dohi, *Das Abendmahl im spätmittelalterlichen Drama*, Frankfurt a. M. 2000, p. 364.
13 Edward Muir, *Ritual in Early Modern Europe*, Cambridge 1997, p. 157.
14 Ernst H. Kantorowicz, *The King's Two Bodies. A Study in Medieval Political Theology*, Princeton, NJ 1997, p. 196.
15 Glynne Wickham, *Shakespeare's Dramatic Heritage*, London 1969, p. 18.
16 Sara Beckwith, *Signifying God. Social Relation and Symbolic Act in the York Corpus Christi Plays*, Chicago, IL/London 2003, p. 73.
17 Peter Ackroyd, *The Life of Thomas More*, London 1998, p. 120.
18 Huston Diehl, *Staging Reform, Reforming the Stage. Protestantism and Popular Theater in Early Modern England*, Ithaca, NY/London 1997, pp. 98–99.
19 Muir, op. cit., p. 173.
20 Stephen Greenblatt, 'Remnants of the Sacred in Early Modern England', in Margareta de Grazia, Maureen Quilligan and Peter Stallybrass (eds), *Subject and Object in Renaissance Culture*, Cambridge/New York, NY 1996, p. 340.
21 Greenblatt, ibid p. 342.
22 Michael Davies, 'The Transubstantial Bard. Shakespeare and Catholicism', in Douglas Burnham and Enrico Giaccherini (eds), *The Poetics of Transubstantiation. From Theology to Metaphor*, Aldershot/Burlington, VT 2005, p. 33.
23 Louis Marin, *Food for Thought*, translated by Mette Hjort, Baltimore, MD/London 1997, pp. 11/18.
24 Bernd Wannenwetsch, 'Liturgy', in Peter Scott and William T. Cavanaugh (eds), *The Blackwell Companion to Political Theology*, Malden, MA 2004, p. 85.
25 Martin Luther, 'Treatise on Good Works', in *Luther's Works*, vol. 44, *The Christian in Society I*, Philadelphia, PA 1966, p. 56.
26 Ernst Sommerlath, 'Abendmahl', in Kurt Galling (ed.), *Die Religion in Geschichte und Gegenwart. Handwörterbuch für Theologie und Religionswissenschaft*, vol.1, Tübingen 1957, p. 36.
27 Johannes Calvin, *Institution of the Christian Religion [1536]*, translated by Ford Lewis Battles, Atlanta, GA 1975, IV. 17. 33–34. In his commentary on 1 Corinthians, Calvin does confirm Paul's dictum that God will punish unworthy communicants; but he does not understand this punishment to be a direct effect of the Eucharist itself. (See Johannes Calvin, *Auslegung des Römerbriefes und der beiden Korintherbriefe*, translated by Gertrud Graffmann et al., edited by Otto Weber et al., Neukirchen-Vluyn 1960, pp. 421–422.)
28 Detlef Klahr and Wolfgang Sommer, *Kirchengeschichtliches Repetitorium*, Göttingen 1994, p. 166.
29 Thomas, op. cit., pp. 59–61.
30 Act of Parliament, 7 James I, c. 2, paraphrased from Margrit Schulte Beerbühl, *Deutsche Kaufleute in London*, München 2007, p. 47.

31 Act of Parliament, 3 Charles II st. 2, c. 1 in Henry Bettenson (ed.), *Documents of the Christian Church*, second edition, Oxford 1967, pp. 293–294.
32 David Martin Jones, *Conscience and Allegiance in Seventeenth Century England. The Political Significance of Oaths and Engagements*, Rochester 1999, p. 283.
33 Kantorowicz, *The King's Two Bodies*, op. cit.
34 Kantorowicz, *The King's Two Bodies*, op. cit., pp. 312–313.
35 Kantorowicz, *The King's Two Bodies*, op. cit., pp. 147/496.
36 Ernst H. Kantorowicz, *Gods in Uniform. Selected Studies*, Locust Valley, NY 1965, p. 133.
37 Kantorowicz, *The King's Two Bodies*, op. cit., pp. 228–229.
38 Louis Adrian Montrose, '"Eliza, Queene of Shepheardes" and the Pastoral of Power', in Arthur F. Kinney and Dan S. Collins (eds), *Renaissance Historicism. Selections from 'English Literary Renaissance'*, Amherst, MA 1987, pp. 45–46.
39 Anthony W. Marx, *Faith in Nation. Exclusionary Origins of Nationalism*, Oxford/New York, NY 2003, p. 59.
40 Marx, ibid. p. 63.
41 Stephen Greenblatt, 'Shakespeare's World', in Stephen Greenblatt (ed.), *The Norton Shakespeare*, New York, NY/London 1997, p. 19.
42 See Booty, op. cit., p. 10.
43 Ralph Winwood, *Memorials of Affairs of State*, vol. 3. London 1725, p. 295. See also section 1.4.
44 Phyllis Rackin, *Stages of History. Shakespeare's English Chronicles*, Ithaca, NY 1990, p. 119.
45 Walter Benjamin, *The Origin of German Tragic Drama*, translated by John Osborne, London/New York, NY 1998, p. 97.
46 On this, see Anthony Hammond's remarks in the Introduction to the Arden edition of *Richard III*, London 2002, p. 112.
47 Kantorowicz, *The King's Two Bodies*, op. cit., p. 331.
48 Nancy Klein Maguire, *Regicide and Restoration. English Tragicomedy 1660–1671*, Cambridge 1992, p. 33. Of relevance in this context is Canto 34 of Dante's *Inferno* which banishes Brutus and Cassius, the murderers of Caesar, with Judas into the maws of Lucifer in the very center of Hell.
49 Kantorowicz, *The King's Two Bodies*, op. cit., pp. 419–421.
50 Linda Charnes, *Notorious Identity. Materializing the Subject in Shakespeare*, Cambridge/London 1993, pp. 42–43.
51 On this complex, see primarily Gail Holst-Warhaft, *Dangerous Voices. Women's Laments and Greek Literature.* London 1992. Also Katharine Goodland, *Female Mourning and Tragedy in Medieval and Renaissance Drama*, Aldershot/Burlington, VT 2005.
52 Thomas, op. cit., p. 605. Shakespeare develops this motif even more explicitly at the beginning of IV. iv, in which the three former queens, Margaret, the Duchess of York and Elizabeth, meet in order to lament the murder of the various princes and in the end form a maledictory sit-in. Shakespeare did not write the pertinent stage directions, but they follow logically from his dialogues: Their "rest on England's lawful earth" (IV. iv. 29) must take place on an open roadway since Richard reacts to it with: "Who intercepts me in my expedition?" (IV. iv. 136).
53 George Puttenham, *The Arte of English Poesie*, Kent, OH 1970, pp. 63/72.
54 Lester K. Little, *Benedictine Maledictions. Liturgical Cursing in Romanesque France*, Ithaca, NY/London 1993, pp. 3/64. See section 1.2.
55 Shakespeare used this motif often, for example in Sonnet 6.
56 Kate E. Brown and Howard I. Kushner, 'Eruptive Voices: Coprolalia, Malediction, and the Poetics of Cursing', *New Literary History* 32, 2001, 547.
57 See Anthony Hammond's commentary in the Arden edition, London 2002, p. 139.
58 See section 1.6.
59 Arthur Percival Rossiter, *Angel with Horns and Other Shakespeare Lectures*, London 1961, p. 4.

60 Charnes, op. cit., pp. 39–40.

61 John D. Cox, *The Devil and the Sacred in English Drama 1350–1642*, Cambridge/New York, NY 2000, p. 87. Wolfgang Clemen, *Kommentar zu Shakespeares Richard III. Interpretation eines Dramas*, Göttingen 1969, p. 324.

62 The criminal offense of high treason was very broadly defined in Elizabethan England, in a manner that is quite relevant for the question of who has executive authority over political representations. It can be discussed here only marginally: a statute of 1532, that will be binding for later Tudor politics, decrees, for example, that "imagining or compassing the death of the king" amounts to high treason. Mary Stuart, Essex, and Lopez are executed pursuant to this statute. (See Christopher Pye, *The Regal Phantasm*, London/New York, NY 1990, p. 117.) Illegitimate curses (as petitions to God) also are defined as high treason: the fact that the Catholic John Story was reported by witnesses to have uttered a curse against Elizabeth I every day before meals, is considered incriminating evidence in his trial of 1571. (Thomas, op. cit., p. 699.) High treason is defined as the worst of crimes, the figure of original sin (for Henry V "another fall of man," *Henry V*, II. ii. 139), but due to its mental nature it is also the least apprehensible offense (as *Henry V*, II. ii, for example, spells out in detail). The act of high treason is situated in the grey zone between imagination and deed, fact and representation (Pye, ibid. p. 119). If the law was to be applied strictly, the representation of a king's execution on the stage would also, as "imagining the death of the king," satisfy the definition of high treason. That this is not the official line is proved by the Essex verdict: the performance of *Richard II*, prompted by the conspirators before their attempted coup d'état of 1601, did not result in the punishment of Shakespeare's troupe, even though Elizabeth herself pointed out the parallel. The main reason for this leniency appears to be the fact that the troupe's spokesman could prove the exonerating and perfectly lawful monetary transactions preceding the performance. (See Stephen Greenblatt, *Will in the World*, New York, NY/London 2004, pp. 309–310.)

63 A. E. Crawley, 'Cursing and Blessing', in James Hastings (ed.), *Encyclopedia of Religion and Ethics*, vol. 4. Edinburgh 1911, p. 372.

64 Little, op. cit., p. 31.

65 Giorgio Agamben, *Homo Sacer. Sovereign Power and Bare Life*, translated by Daniel Heller-Roazen, Stanford CA 1998, pp. 21/71.

66 W. Warde Fowler, 'The Original Meaning of the Word "Sacer"', *The Journal of Roman Studies* 1, 1911, 57–63. See also Ulrich Manthe, *Geschichte des römischen Rechts*, München 2000, pp. 13–14.

67 Fabian Steinhauer, 'Gestaltung des Rechts: Agamben', in Sonja Buckel, Ralph Christensen and Andreas Fischer-Lescano (eds), *Neue Theorien des Rechts*, Stuttgart 2006, pp. 201–202; Anselm Haverkamp, *Latenzzeit*, Berlin 2004, pp. 167–168.

68 Rainer Maria Kiesow, 'Ius sacrum. Giorgio Agamben und das nackte Recht', *Rechtsgeschichte. Zeitschrift des Max-Planck-Instituts für europäische Rechtsgeschichte* 1, 2002, 62–64.

69 Some of Agamben's critics, among them Rainer Maria Kiesow (ibid.), for this reason consider his concept of the "inclusive exclusion" not only mystifying but also inapplicable to the figure of *homo sacer.* It is thought to be a aggravating circumstance that in early Rome's societal order no fully differentiated system of law existed and consequently the distinction between law and life at this time was supposedly simply senseless (ibid. pp. 64–65). It is doubtful, however, that this divests Agamben's exposition of all explanatory potential, as Kiesow assumes, and that in the final analysis Agamben can be reduced entirely to a traditional natural law thinker (ibid. pp. 61–63). Kiesow's historicizing objections bypass decisive epistemic points of Agamben's project without raising the question of what, for example, may have historically motivated the retrospective construction of the *homo sacer* during the imperial period. (It might have integrated Judeo-Christian figures into the juridical discourse of the Augustan era, in the form of original supplementariness. On this, see Haverkamp, op. cit., p. 168.) And

even though Agamben uses Walter Benjamin's 'Critique of Violence'—an essay that in places sympathizes dangerously with concepts of *ius naturalis* (see e.g. Benjamin's largely uncommented embellishment of lynch mob killings as "the crowd's divine judgment on a criminal," Benjamin, 'Critique of Violence', op. cit., p. 252)—the "inclusive exclusion" is a construction with a critical rather than an affirmative relation to traditional natural law (see Chapter 3, section 3.1). On Kiesow's critique of Agamben, see also Eva Geulen, *Giorgio Agamben zur Einführung*, Hamburg 2005, pp. 19–21 and Steinhauer, op. cit., pp. 189–191.

70 Haverkamp, op. cit., p. 167; Geulen, ibid. pp. 91/152.

71 Hence, this discussion will not be concerned with Agamben's occasional references to more archaic rituals of "inclusive exclusion" such as the Hebrew and Greek scapegoat ceremonies. (See Giorgio Agamben, *The End of the Poem. Studies in Poetics*, translated by Daniel Heller-Roazen, Stanford, CA 1999, p. 107.)

72 Hein, op. cit.

73 Jürgen Stein, 'Excommunication', in Erwin Fahlbusch, Jan Milič Lochman, John Mbiti, Jaroslev Pelikan and Lukas Vischer, *The Encyclopedia of Christianity*, vol. 1, Grand Rapids, MI 2001, p. 236.

74 Thomas Aquinas, *Summa Theologica*, translated by Fathers of the English Dominican Province, London, 1915–1924, Supplement, Quaestio 22, Art. 1.

75 Aquinas, ibid. Supplement, Quaestio 22, Art. 4.

76 Little, op. cit., pp. 89/91.

77 Gregory I, *Morals in the Book of Job*, Oxford 1844, pp. 185–186, quoted by Little, op. cit., p. 98.

78 Aquinas, op. cit. Summa 2.2, Quaestio 76, Art. 1.

79 See Little, op. cit., p. 85.

80 For more detailed information on this topic, see Little, op. cit., especially pp. 20–85.

81 Françoise Monfrin, 'Anathema', in Philippe Levillain (ed.), *The Papacy. An Encyclopedia*, London 2001, p. 48.

82 Little, op. cit., p. 32.

83 Aquinas, op. cit. Supplement, Quaestio 21, Art. 1.

84 Hans Barion, 'Exkommunikation', in Kurt Galling (ed.), *Die Religion in Geschichte und Gegenwart. Handwörterbuch für Theologie und Religionswissenschaft*, vol 2. Tübingen 1958, pp. 828–829.

85 Thomas, op. cit., p. 632.

86 Aquinas, op. cit. Supplement, Quaestio 23, Art. 1.

87 Vodola, *Excommunication in the Middle Ages*, Berkeley/Los Angeles, CA/London 1986, pp. 12–13.

88 Barion, op. cit., p. 829.

89 Vodola, op. cit., p. 162. At times, the exclusion of excommunicates from secular jurisdiction had a *Catch-22* effect insofar as the quest for absolution would have meant an admission of guilt in exactly the matter that would have to be deliberated in court (see op. cit., pp. 109–110).

90 Vodola, op. cit., p. 83.

91 Vodola, op. cit., p. 112.

92 Vodola, op. cit., p. 83.

93 Aquinas, op. cit. Supplement, Quaestio 22, Art. 6.

94 Aquinas, op. cit. Supplement, Quaestio 22, Art. 3.

95 Little, op. cit., p. 188.

96 Laurence Sterne, *Tristram Shandy*, New York, NY/London 1980, pp. 122–131; cf. Little, op. cit., pp. 1–14.

97 Little, op. cit., pp. 36/38.

98 Little, op. cit., p. 60.

99 Little, op. cit., p. 9.

100 Regino von Prüm, *Libri*, Leipzig 1840, pp. 371–372. See Little, op. cit., p. 38.

101 Little, op. cit., p. 43.
102 Little, op. cit., p. 139. Even until the early modern age an analogous practice is widespread (though officially illegal), namely that of "Mortbeten," i.e. of reading funeral masses for living persons. A presumably Franciscan treatise from fifteenth-century England polemicizes, for example, against those "that [. . .] do sing mass of requiem for them that be alive, in hope that they should fare the worse [...]." (Thomas, op. cit., pp. 37–38.)
103 Jean C. Cooper, *Dictionary of Christianity*, Chicago, IL 1996, p. 23.
104 See for example the annotations by Paul Hammond and David Hopkins in John Dryden, *The Poems of John Dryden*, vol. 5. Harlow 2005, p. 561.
105 On their connection cf. Hans Blumenberg, *Die Lesbarkeit der Welt*, Frankfurt a. M. 1986, p. 23; Ludger Körntgen, *Königsherrschaft und Gottes Gnade*, Berlin 2001, p. 327.
106 Little, op. cit., pp. 195–197.
107 Jacob Taubes, *The Political Theology of Paul*, translated by Dana Hollander, Stanford, CA 2004, p. 30.
108 In this respect the rite is similar to the ancient *damnatio memoriae*: "The Roman *damnatio memoriae* worked [. . .] to *dishonor* memory, not to destroy it." Charles W. Hedrick, *History and Silence. Purge and Rehabilitation of Memory in Late Antiquity*, Austin, TX 2000, p. xii.
109 Little, op. cit., pp. 38/117.
110 Prüm, op. cit., pp. 375–376, quoted in Little, op. cit., pp. 143–145.
111 "Thus let the memory of them be forever extinguished." Excommunication formula of Saint Martial's Abbey, quoted in Little, op. cit., p. 261.
112 Little, op. cit., p. 33.
113 Stated for example in Hein, op. cit., p. 441, with reference to Mary Douglas, *Purity and Danger*, London 1966.
114 Little, op. cit., p. 32.
115 Vodola, op. cit., p. 40.
116 Aquinas, op. cit. Supplement, Quaestio 21, Art. 2. That the rite of excommunication as an imitation of God's judgment in turn has indirect effects on structures of the Eucharistic ceremony can be seen in the following: since the thirteenth century, the Pope every year publishes, besides the occasional excommunications, the bull *In coena Domini* that lists all present excommunicates. The day reserved for this festive issue is Maundy Thursday, i.e. the day that commemorates the institution of the Eucharist. (Little, op. cit., pp. 275–276.)
117 Aquinas, op. cit. Supplement, Quaestio 21, Art. 4.
118 Vodola, op. cit., p. 11.
119 See for example Wilfried Hartmann, *Der Investiturstreit*, München 2007.
120 Vodola, op. cit., p. 171.
121 Thomas, op. cit., p. 600.
122 Little, op. cit., p. 276.
123 Martin Luther, 'Concerning Excommunication', in *The Smalcald Articles*, in Robert Kolb and Timothy J. Wengert (eds), *The Book of Concord. The Confessions of the Evangelical Lutheran Church*, Minneapolis, MN 2000, pp. 297–328.
124 Martin Luther, 'To the Christian Nobility of the German Nation Concerning the Reform of the Christian Estate', in *Luther's Works*, vol. 44, Philadelphia, PA 1966, p. 182.
125 Martin Luther, 'Kirche und Gemeinde', in *Luther deutsch*, vol. 9, Göttingen 1991, p. 163.
126 Alain Cabantous, *Geschichte der Blasphemie*, translated by Bernd Wilczek, Weimar 1999, p. 20.
127 Wilhelm Maurer, 'Exkommunikation', in Kurt Galling (ed.), *Die Religion in Geschichte und Gegenwart. Handwörterbuch für Theologie und Religionswissenschaft*, vol. 2, Tübingen 1958, p. 830. See also Luther's letter to Daniel Greiser of 22 October 1543 (no. 3930 in Martin Luther, *Briefwechsel*, vol. 10, Weimar 2002, pp. 436–437).

128 David Gordon Newcombe, *Henry VIII and the English Reformation*, London/New York, NY 2003, pp. 50–51.
129 Thomas, op. cit., p. 600.
130 Little, op. cit., pp. 4–5.
131 John Foxe, *The Acts and Monuments of John Foxe*, vol. 5, London 1877, p. 21, quoted from Jane Kingsley-Smith, *Shakespeare's Drama of Exile*, Basingstoke/New York, NY 2003, p. 87.
132 Anonymous, *The Curse of Popery and Popish Princes to the Civil Government and the Protestant Church of England*, London 1716, p. 14. It begins with the words: "Let James, the Subverter of the Faith, together with his Royal issue, be confounded by the holy Influence and Approbation of the Pope." (Ibid. p. 15)
133 An example in Anonymous, ibid. p. 6.
134 Thomas Hobbes, *Leviathan*, Oxford 1998, p. 376.
135 Ian Hazlett, *The Reformation in Britain and Ireland. An Introduction*, London/New York, NY 2005, pp. 67–68.
136 George W. Keeton, *Shakespeare's Legal and Political Background*, London 1967, p. 5.
137 Act of Parliament, 5 Elizabeth I, c. 23 in William Evans, Thomas Granger and Anthony Hammond (eds), *A Collection of Statutes Connected with the General Administration of the Law*, vol. 4. London 1836, pp. 280–284.
138 Michael Questier, *Conversion, Politics and Religion in England 1580–1623*, Cambridge 1996, pp. 152–154. It is to be noted that the *Book of Common Prayer* as published in 1559, i.e. in the first year of Elizabeth's rule, still mentions excommunication as punishment carried out by ecclesiastical jurisdiction. (Booty, op. cit., p. 12.)
139 Richard Hooker, *On the Laws of Ecclesiastical Polity*, Cambridge 1989, p. 138.
140 Thomas, op. cit., p. 601. The ceremony was adopted nearly unchanged in the *Book of Common Prayer of* 1559, Booty, op. cit., pp. 316–323. (The description of the Commination Service, in keeping with the sealing function of the curse, is the final section of the *Book of Common Prayer.*)
141 It might be reiterated here that the Catholics themselves do not usually describe their excommunication ceremonies as orders issued to God.
142 Vernon Staley (ed.), *The First Prayer Book of King Edward VI*, London 1903, pp. 361–368, quoted by Little, op. cit., p. 272; Booty, op. cit., p. 316.
143 Little, op. cit., pp. 272–273; Booty, op. cit., pp. 316–317.
144 The litany is augmented by the pastor's quote of the apocalyptic curse from Matt. 25. 41: "Go ye cursed into the fire everlasting, which is prepared for the devil and his angels." (Booty, op. cit., p. 319.)
145 Thomas, op. cit., pp. 601–602.
146 Thomas, op. cit., p. 600. On parallel developments in the German-speaking world, see Heinrich R. Schmidt, 'Die Ächtung des Fluchens durch reformierte Sittengerichte', in Peter Blickle (ed.), *Der Fluch und der Eid. Die metaphysische Begründung gesellschaftlichen Zusammenlebens und politischer Ordnung in der ständischen Gesellschaft*, Berlin 1993.
147 Ashley Montagu, *The Anatomy of Swearing*, New York, NY/London 1967, pp. 128–130.
148 Walter Cohen, *Drama of a Nation. Public Theatre in Renaissance England and Spain*, Ithaca, NY/London 1985, p. 73, and passim.
149 Christopher Marlowe, 'Doctor Faustus', in David Bevington, Lars Engle, Katharine Eisaman Maus and Eric Rasmussen (eds), *English Renaissance Drama, A Norton Anthology*, New York, NY/London 2002, p. 270.
150 Marlowe, ibid. p. 271.
151 Oral information provided by Holger Schott.
152 Cox, op. cit., p. 114.
153 The situation also appears to allude to the *topos* of the *Ecclesia* as Christ's bride. On this, see for example Paul Carus, *The Bride of Christ. A Study in Christian Legend Lore*, Chicago, IL 1908.

154 On the concept of the "living monument" see Agamben, *Homo Sacer*, op. cit., p. 99.
155 She insists on her royal status, despite the fact that she, like the whole court, can trace back her lineage only to an usurper.
156 See Clemen, op. cit., p. 98.
157 Little, op. cit., p. 64.
158 E. M. W. Tillyard, *Shakespeare's History Plays*, London 1959, p. 207.
159 Margaret's laments and curses are often cut from performances since they are static and ceremonial and hence appear to contribute nothing to the story's development. For the same reasons, many directors, Laurence Olivier (1955) and Richard Loncraine (1995) among them, excise Margaret's role altogether. But this robs the play of a decisive dimension, namely its persistent captivation by the past.
160 Quarto; Folio: "Him."
161 Robert Zaller, *The Discourse of Legitimacy in Early Modern England*, Stanford, CA 2007, p. 385.
162 Jacques Lacan, *The Ego in Freud's Theory and in the Technique of Psychoanalysis. Seminar II*, translated by Sylvana Tomaselli, New York, NY/London 1988, pp. 191–205.
163 On "simulacrum," see Gilles Deleuze, *The Logic of Sense*, translated by Mark Lester with Charles Stivale, New York, NY 1990, p. 262: "The simulacrum is not a degraded copy. It harbors a positive power which denies *the original and the copy, the model and the reproduction.*"
164 Thomas, op. cit., p. 670.
165 It is remarkable that these are exactly the same groupings that also in reality are in charge of many remnants of the excommunication rite.
166 Tillyard, op. cit., p. 200.
167 Quarto; Folio: "frantic."
168 In the sense of "prologue." See Anthony Hammond's annotations in the Arden edition, London 2002, p. 275.
169 In the sense of "conclusion" (i.e. end of the play). See Stephen Greenblatt's annotations in the Norton edition: *The Norton Shakespeare*, New York, NY/London 1997, p. 573.
170 See section 1.7.
171 See John Jowett, 'Introduction', in William Shakespeare, *The Tragedy of King Richard III*, Oxford/New York, NY 2000, p. 14.
172 See section 1.5.
173 Keeton, op. cit., p. 209.
174 William A. Sessions, *Henry Howard. The Poet Earl of Surrey. A Life*, Oxford 2001, pp. 106–107.
175 See section 1.4.
176 See section 1.7.
177 See for example Andreas Holzem, 'Eid und Eidschwörer. Wahrheitssuche und Loyalitätsverpflichtung im frühneuzeitlichen Sendgericht', in Stefan Esders and Thomas Scharff (eds), *Eid und Wahrheitssuche. Studien zu rechtlichen Befragungspraktiken in Mittelalter und früher Neuzeit*, Frankfurt a. M. 1999, p. 230.
178 Wolfgang Speyer, 'Fluch', in Theodor Klauser (ed.), *Reallexikon für Antike und Christentum*, vol. 7, Stuttgart 1969, pp. 1260–1261.
179 For example in Acts of the Apostles 23. 12: "And when it was day, certain of the Jews banded together, and bound themselves under a curse [ἀνεθεμάτισαν], saying that they would neither eat nor drink till they had killed Paul."
180 Paolo Prodi, *Das Sakrament der Herrschaft. Der politische Eid in der Verfassungsgeschichte des Okzidents*, Berlin 1997, p. 50.
181 Hieronymus, *Commentarium in Matheum*, I. 5. 34, quoted by Lothar Kolmar, *Promissorische Eide im Mittelalter*, Kallmünz 1989, p. 277.
182 Augustinus, *Sermones*, 180.6–180.8, paraphrased by Kolmar, op. cit., p. 48.

183 Manthe, op. cit., pp. 18–19.
184 Speyer, op. cit., p. 1261.
185 Kolmar, op. cit., pp. 320/330.
186 Michael E. Tigar and Madeleine R. Levy, *Law and the Rise of Capitalism*, New York, NY 2000, p. 106.
187 Henry G. Richardson, 'The English Coronation Oath', *Speculum* 24, 1949, 65.
188 On this concept see Lacan, *The Psychoses*, op. cit., pp. 258–270.
189 Jones, op. cit., p. 19.
190 Kolmar, op. cit., p. 306.
191 Kolmar, op. cit., p. 307.
192 Kolmar, op. cit., p. 309.
193 Richard Firth Green, *A Crisis of Truth. Literature and Law in Ricardian England*, Philadelphia, PA 2002, pp. 287–291.
194 "Furthermore, no bishop can be confirmed unless he [. . .] binds himself with solemn oaths to the personal service of the pope. That explains why no bishop dares to act against the pope. That is what the Romanists were seeking when they imposed the oath. It also explains why all the richest bishoprics have fallen into debt and ruin." (Martin Luther, *Luther's Works*, vol. 44, Philadelphia, PA 1966, p. 148.)
195 Ernst Friesenhahn, *Der politische Eid*, Darmstadt 1979, p. 110.
196 Quoted by Jones, op. cit., p. 11.
197 Prodi, *Das Sakrament der Herrschaft*, op. cit., p. 241.
198 Act of Parliament, 3 James I, c. 4. John P. Kenyon (ed.), *The Stuart Constitution 1603–1688. Documents and Commentary*, second edition, Cambridge 1986, pp. 170–171.
199 Jones, op. cit., pp. 282–283.
200 Jones, op. cit., pp. 35/40.
201 Paolo Prodi, 'Der Eid in der europäischen Verfassungsgeschichte', in Paolo Prodi and Elisabeth Müller-Luckner (eds), *Glaube und Eid. Treueformeln, Glaubensbekenntnisse und Sozialdisziplinierung zwischen Mittelalter und Neuzeit*, München 1993, p. xx.
202 See for example Stephen Greenblatt, *Shakespearean Negotiations*, Berkeley/Los Angeles, CA 1988, p. 64.
203 In this context, see also the reference to the oath in Michel Foucault, *Discipline and Punish. The Birth of the Prison*, translated by Alan Sheridan, New York, NY 1978, p. 39. It is at this time that the concept of "representation" is expanded from the artistic and religious to the juridical and political sphere, apparently to cover this very need for signifiers. (Hanna Fenichel Pitkin, *The Concept of Representation*, Berkeley, CA/London 1967, p. 251.)
204 Hobbes, op. cit., pp. 94–95.
205 Slavoj Zizek, *The Sublime Object of Ideology*, London 1989, pp. 185–186.
206 See Introduction.
207 Agamben, *Homo Sacer*, op. cit., p. 27.
208 Tigar and Levy, op. cit., p. 69. In establishing these new forms, it is a frequent practice to appropriate the old ones. But this is a different story, though one that would be worth exploring. For example, merchants and craftsmen struggling against feudal restrictions occasionally appropriate the oath in order to organize themselves through *coniuratio* (op. cit., pp. 85/131). The emerging structures of the bourgeoisie in the growing cities remain dependent on various oaths of federation. Later, even peasants' and workers' movements constitute themselves through solemn vows. (Prodi, *Das Sakrament der Herrschaft*, op. cit., p. 314.)
209 Jean-Christophe Agnew, *Worlds Apart. The Market and the Theater in Anglo-American Thought, 1550–1750*, Cambridge, MA 1986, pp. 28–29.
210 Vodola, op. cit., p. 151.
211 Vodola, op. cit., pp. 132/152.

212 Prodi, 'Der Eid in der europäischen Verfassungsgeschichte', op. cit., pp. xix–xx.
213 Agnew, op. cit., p. 82.
214 Gerald Hartung, 'Zur Genealogie des Versprechens', in Manfred Schneider (ed.), *Die Ordnung des Versprechens*, München 2005, p. 283.
215 Carl Schmitt, *Constitutional Theory*, translated by Jeffrey Seitzer, Durham, NC/London 2008, p. 118.
216 G. D. Ramsay (ed.), *John Isham. Mercer and Merchant Adventurer*, Northampton 1962, p. 172, quoted by Thomas, op. cit., pp. 77–78.
217 Agnew, op. cit., p. 138. See also Victoria Kahn, *Wayward Contracts. The Crisis of Political Obligation in England, 1640–1674*, Princeton, NJ 2004.
218 Prodi, *Das Sakrament der Herrschaft*, op. cit., pp. 382–385.
219 Hannah Arendt has pointed out that Hobbes' social contract marks a historical transition from the old Christian thinking in terms of covenants to the new form of thinking in terms of contracts. See Hannah Arendt, *The Origins of Totalitarianism*, New York, NY 2004, pp. 186–196.
220 Hobbes, op. cit., p. 114.
221 Hobbes, op. cit., p. 91.
222 Hobbes, op. cit., pp. 205–206.
223 Hobbes, op. cit., p. 176.
224 See Agamben, *Homo Sacer*, op. cit., pp. 15–18.
225 Werner Hamacher, 'Wilde Versprechen', in Manfred Schneider (ed.), *Die Ordnung des Versprechens*, München 2005, p. 194.
226 Hobbes, op. cit., p. 41.
227 Pitkin, op. cit., p. 250.
228 Hobbes, op. cit., p. 85.
229 Hobbes, op. cit., pp. 106–107.
230 Hobbes, op. cit., p. 21, also pp. 31–32: "metaphors, and senseless and ambiguous words, are like *ignes fatui*; and reasoning upon them, is wandering amongst innumerable absurdities; and their end, contention and sedition, or contempt."
231 Hobbes, op. cit., p. 106.
232 Hobbes, op. cit., p. 107.
233 Christopher Pye, 'The Sovereign, the Theater, and the Kingdome of Darknesse: Hobbes and the Spectacle of Power', in Stephen Greenblatt (ed.) *Representing the English Renaissance*, Berkeley, CA 1988, p. 286.
234 Hobbes, op. cit., p. 96.
235 Pye, 'The Sovereign', op. cit., p. 287.
236 Matthias Bohlender, *Die Rhetorik des Politischen. Zur Kritik der politischen Theorie*, Berlin 1995, p. 161.
237 Margery Corbett and R. W. Lightbown, *The Comely Frontispiece: The Emblematic Title-Page in England 1550–1660*, London 1979, p. 224, paraphrased in Pye, 'The Sovereign', p. 300.
238 Bohlender, op. cit., pp. 160–162.
239 On the concept of the "simulacrum," see Deleuze, *The Logic of Sense*, op. cit.
240 Hamacher, op. cit., p. 187.
241 Pye, 'The Sovereign', p. 298.
242 Agnew, op. cit., p. 99.
243 Pye, 'The Sovereign', p. 281.
244 Arendt, op. cit., pp. 242–245.
245 See section 1.1.
246 Thomas, op. cit., p. 506.
247 For example, in the BBC Television production directed by Jane Howell (1983).
248 See Niklas Luhmann, *Love as Passion: The Codification of Intimacy*, Cambridge 1986, pp. 59–62.

249 See Kolmar, op. cit.
250 Jürgen Habermas, 'Discourse Ethics: Notes on a Program of Philosophical Justification', in *Moral Consciousness and Communicative Action*, Cambridge, MA 1990, p. 80.
251 Quarto; Folio: "blessed."
252 See section 1.1.
253 Jacques Lacan, 'Hamlet', translated by Franz Kaltenbeck, Susanne Hommel and Michael Turnheim, in *Wo Es War, Eine Veröffentlichung des Freudschen Feldes* 2, 1986, pp. 41–45 and passim.
254 Greenblatt, *Shakespearean Negotiations*, op. cit., p. 46, and passim.
255 Greenblatt, *Shakespearean Negotiations*, op. cit., p. 63.
256 Greenblatt, *Shakespearean Negotiations*, op. cit., p. 52.
257 See Chapter 2.
258 John Chrysostom, '*Expositiones in Psalmos 108*', in *Patrologia Graeca*, vol. 29, quoted by Little, op. cit., p. 95.
259 Psalm 109 of the *King James Bible* is counted as Psalm 108 in various other versions of the Bible.
260 Augustinus, 'Enarrationes in Psalmos 78 and 108', in *Patrologia Latina*, vol. 37, pp. 1017–1018/1431–1432, quoted by Little, op. cit., p. 96.
261 John Donne, *The Sermons of John Donne*, vol. 6, Berkeley, CA 1984, pp. 54–55.
262 Geoffrey of Monmouth, *The History of the Kings of Britain*, translated by Lewis Thorpe, London 1966, pp. 178–179.
263 In this context, see for example the prophetic anagrams of Eleanor Davies. (Esther S. Cope (ed.), Eleanor Davies, *Prophetic Writings*, Oxford/New York, NY 1995.)
264 Thomas, op. cit., pp. 481–482.
265 Thomas, op. cit., p. 471.
266 Thomas, op. cit., p. 484.
267 James VI and I, *Political Writings*, Cambridge 1993, p. 3. See Chapter 3, section 3.1.
268 See Winwood, op. cit., p. 295. Elizabeth at times avails herself of similar locutions. (See Booty, op. cit., p. 10.)
269 Thomas, op. cit., p. 479.
270 Thomas, op. cit., pp. 472–475.
271 Pye, *The Regal Phantasm*, op. cit., p. 123.
272 Mary Steible, 'Jane Shore and the Politics of Cursing', *SEL. Studies in English Literature 1500–1900* 43 (1), 2003, p. 3.
273 See for example Thomas, op. cit., p. 168.
274 Benjamin, *The Origin of German Tragic Drama*, op. cit., p. 129.
275 "Causas [. . .] necessarias sed tamen voluntarias" (Theodorus Beza Vezelius, *Volumen Tractationum Theologicarum I*, Geneva 1570, p. 176.)
276 Peter White, *Predestination, Policy and Polemic: Conflict and Consensus in the English Church from the Reformation to the Civil War*, Cambridge 1992, p. 19 and passim.
277 Contrary to an occasionally still repeated cliché, the theology of the Anglican Church under Elizabeth is not truly Calvinist; the 39 Articles of Faith, specifically those referring to predestination, are formulated so broadly that almost all schools of Protestantism and even Catholics willing to compromise can accept them as a basis for a consensus. (White, op. cit., p. 67.)
278 Maurice Blanchot, *Le livre à venir*, Paris 1959, p. 110.
279 Justus Lipsius, *Von der Bestendigkeit* [*De Constantia*], translated by Andreas Viritius, Stuttgart 1965, Book I, chapter 19, p. 57.
280 Tillyard, op. cit., pp. 60–65.
281 Nicholas Grene, *Shakespeare's History Plays*, Cambridge 2002, p. 145; Wolfgang Iser, *Staging Politics: The Lasting Impact of Shakespeare's Histories*, translated by David Henry Wilson, New York, NY 1993, p. 67.

282 Grene, op. cit., p. 150.
283 Iser, op. cit., pp. 61–62.
284 Boethius, *Consolatio Philosophiae*, Cambridge, MA 2008.
285 See for example: "What is so extraordinary in the rhapsody of cursing that follows is the exactness of the fate Margaret assigns to each of those accursed, and the rigour with which each one comes about." (Grene, op. cit., p. 152.) "In Shakespeare's plays, the curses pronounced by the characters invariably work." (Thomas, op. cit., p. 605.)
286 Norman Francis Blake, *Shakespeare's Language. An Introduction*, London/Basingstoke 1983, p. 93.
287 The sources are equally vague: the *Mirror for Magistrates.* ("George, Duke of Clarence") has: "A prophecy was found," in Lily B. Campbell (ed.) *Mirror for Magistrates*, Cambridge 1938, quoted by Anthony Hammond in his Commentary to the Arden edition, London 2002, p. 128.
288 For example in the Norton and Arden editions.
289 Aristotle, *Topica*, translated by E. S. Forster, Cambridge, MA 1989 [I 12, 105a 13].
290 Lacan, *The Ego in Freud's Theory*, op. cit., p. 284.
291 It is by this logic that the young Clifford (in *2 Henry VI*, V. i. 213) calls him a "foul stigmatic."
292 See section 1.7.
293 See Wayne C. Booth, *A Rhetoric of Irony*, Chicago, IL/London 1975.
294 See Rossiter, op. cit., p. 20.
295 Benjamin, *The Origin of German Tragic Drama*, op. cit., p. 228.
296 Benjamin, *The Origin of German Tragic Drama*, op. cit., p. 229.
297 Iser, op. cit., p. 67.
298 Iser, op. cit. Translation slightly modified.
299 Iser, op. cit., pp. 67–68.
300 Benjamin, *The Origin of German Tragic Drama*, op. cit., p. 78.
301 Benjamin, *The Origin of German Tragic Drama*, op. cit., p. 138.
302 Cohen, op. cit., p. 126.
303 On a similar figure, though without reference to Shakespeare, see Hans Blumenberg, *The Legitimacy of the Modern Age*, op. cit., p. 35.
304 Jeremy Tambling, *Allegory and the Work of Melancholy. The Late Medieval and Shakespeare*, Amsterdam/New York, NY 2004, p. 204 and passim.
305 Francis Barker, *The Culture of Violence. Tragedy and History*, Manchester 1993, p. 31.
306 Benjamin, *The Origin of German Tragic Drama*, op. cit., p. 65.
307 Karl Kraus, 'Heinrich IV', *Die Fackel* 65, 1901, p. 29.
308 Karl Kraus, 'Sittlichkeit und Criminalität', *Die Fackel* 115, 1902, pp. 3–4.
309 Augustine, *Contra Faustum Manicheum*, op. cit., pp. 224/226.
310 Benjamin, 'Critique of Violence', op. cit., p. 242.
311 Ze'ev W. Falk, *Introduction to Jewish Law of the Second Commonwealth*, Leiden 1978, p. 15; Speyer, op. cit., p. 1168.
312 Foucault, op. cit., p. 46.
313 Benjamin, 'Critique of Violence', op. cit., p. 242.
314 Foucault, op. cit., p. 29.
315 Agamben, *Homo Sacer*, op. cit., p. 125.
316 Greenblatt, *Shakespearean Negotiations*, op. cit., p. 64.
317 Foucault, op. cit., p. 10.
318 Elias Canetti, *Crowds and Power*, translated by Carol Stewart, New York, NY 1962, pp. 231–234.
319 Kantorowicz, *The King's Two Bodies*, op. cit., pp. 314–317.
320 Anselm Haverkamp, *Shakespearean Genealogies of Power*, London/New York, NY 2011, p. 82.

321 Pye, *The Regal Phantasm*, op. cit., p. 125. In Shakespeare's dramas, it is not only Henry V who uses this much-discussed strategy (see e.g. *Henry V*, II. ii. 78–80); Richard himself takes the very same approach against Hastings:

> RICHARD: I pray you all, tell me what they deserve
> That do conspire my death with devilish plots
> Of damned witchcraft, that have prevail'd
> Upon my body with their hellish charms?
> HASTINGS: The tender love I bear your Grace, my lord,
> Makes me most forward in this princely presence,
> To doom th'offenders, whatse'er they be:
> I say, my lord, they have deserved death.
> RICHARD: Then be your eyes the witness of their evil.
>
> (III. iv. 59–67)

322 Foucault, op. cit., pp. 44–46.
323 Foucault, op. cit., p. 52. The issue was still discussed into the eighteenth century.
324 Kingsley-Smith, op. cit., pp. 9–10. This concept, by the way, was not removed from English Common Law until 1880. In Australia, it is still applicable, albeit seldom enforced.
325 Liza Picard, *Elizabeth's London*, New York, NY 2004, p. 249.
326 See section 1.2.
327 Vodola, op. cit., p. 191.
328 This is also the context for those legends that claim the corpses of excommunicates will not decompose so long as their ban is in force. (See Speyer, op. cit., p. 1165.)
329 Thomas, op. cit., p. 719.
330 Thomas, op. cit., p. 717.
331 See Marjorie Garber, *Shakespeare's Ghost Writers. Literature as Uncanny Causality*, New York, NY/London 1997.
332 Thomas, op. cit., p. 715.
333 Edward Halle, *The Union of the Two Noble and Illustre Famelies of Langcastre & Yorke*, London 1548, p. ii, quoted by Paola Pugliatti, *Shakespeare the Historian*, Basingstoke/London 1996, p. 29.
334 Christopher Pye, *The Vanishing. Shakespeare, the Subject and Early Modern Culture*, Durham, NC/London 2000, p. 31.
335 Especially for antiquity, see the detailed study by André Parrot, *Malédictions et Violations de Tombes*, Paris 1939.
336 Shakespeare's epitaph, Holy Trinity Church, Stratford-upon-Avon 1616, quoted by Stephen Greenblatt, 'General Introduction', op. cit., p. 45.
337 See especially Stephen Greenblatt, *Hamlet in Purgatory*, Princeton, NJ/Oxford 2001.
338 Thomas, op. cit., pp. 703/722.
339 Krishan Kumar, *The Making of English National Identity*, Cambridge 2003, pp. 105–106.
340 Quoted in Greenblatt, *The Norton Shakespeare*, op. cit., p. 3317.
341 Diehl, *Staging Reform, Reforming the Stage*, op. cit., pp. 120–121.
342 Diehl, *Staging Reform, Reforming the Stage*, op. cit., p. 123.
343 Thomas Nashe, 'Pierce Penniless his Supplication to the Devil', in *The Unfortunate Traveller*, London 1985, pp. 112–113.
344 Jacques Derrida, *Of Grammatology*, translated by Gayatri Spivak, Baltimore, MD [et al.] 1976, p. 305.
345 Ann Blair, *The Theater of Nature. Jean Bodin and Renaissance Science*, Princeton, NJ 1997, p. 168.
346 Steven Gallery, 'Dance of Death', in Robert Kastenbaum (ed.), *Encyclopedia of Death and Dying*, London/New York, NY 2001, p. 134.

347 Alistair Fox, 'Richard III's Pauline Oath. Shakespeare's Response to Thomas More', *Moreana* 57, 1978, 18.
348 Fox, ibid. pp. 13–19.
349 Greenblatt, *The Norton Shakespeare*, op. cit., p. 200. See also Sigmund Freud, *Die Traumdeutung*, Frankfurt a. M. 1991, p. 64.
350 See also section 1.7.
351 Freud, op. cit., p. 236.
352 Benjamin, *The Origin of German Tragic Drama*, op. cit., pp. 115–116. Translation slightly modified.
353 See for example Clemen, op. cit. p. 239.
354 Peter Saccio, *Shakespeare's English Kings. History Chronicle and Drama*, Oxford/New York, NY 2000, p. 183.
355 Clemen, op. cit., p. 301.
356 Tillyard, op. cit., p. 208.
357 Benjamin, *The Origin of German Tragic Drama*, op. cit., p. 223. See also Jeffrey Burton Russell, *The Prince of Darkness. Radical Evil and the Power of Good in History*, Ithaca, NY 1992, pp. 17–20.
358 Benjamin, *The Origin of German Tragic Drama*, op. cit., pp. 223–226.
359 Benjamin, *The Origin of German Tragic Drama*, op. cit., p. 223.
360 Agamben, *Homo Sacer*, op. cit., p. 19.
361 Benjamin, *The Origin of German Tragic Drama*, op. cit., p. 224.
362 Little, op. cit., p. 82.
363 Thomas, op. cit., pp. 36–45.
364 Hein, op. cit., p. 441.
365 "Significans quoniam non homini principaliter praeparatus est aeternus ignis, sed ei qui seduxit et offendere fecit hominem et inquam, qui princeps apostasiae est principi abscessionis et his angelis qui apostatae facti sunt cum eo; quem quidem iuste percipient etiam hi qui similiter ut illi sine paenitentia et sine regressu in malitiae perseverant operibus." Irenaeus of Lyon, *Adversus Haereses.* Book III, 23. 3, Freiburg 1995, S. 286.
366 Aquinas, op. cit. Supplement, Quaestio 21, Art. 2.
367 Aquinas, op. cit. Summa 2.2, Quaestio 76. 1.
368 Cox, op. cit., p. 27.
369 Benjamin, 'Critique of Violence', op. cit., p. 249.
370 See for example Russell, op. cit., pp. 167–170.
371 Thomas, op. cit., pp. 560–561.
372 Thomas, op. cit., p. 589.
373 Thomas, op. cit., pp. 559–560.
374 King James VI and I, 'To the Reader', in *Daemonologie*, Edinburgh 1597, quoted by Thomas, op. cit., p. 563.
375 Hobbes, op. cit., p. 425.
376 Pye, *The Regal Phantasm*, op. cit., pp. 56–57.
377 Russell, op. cit., p. 70.
378 Jeffrey Knapp, *Shakespeare's Tribe. Church, Nation and Theater in Renaissance England*, Chicago, IL/London 2002, p. 18.
379 Knapp, ibid. p. 116.
380 See for example Mephistopheles' effective utterance: "Why, this is hell, nor am I out of it." (I. iii. 78)
381 Cox, op. cit., p. 125.
382 Tillyard, op. cit., pp. 208–210.
383 See sections 1.4 and 1.5.
384 Benjamin, *The Origin of German Tragic Drama*, op. cit., p. 229.
385 See Gilles Deleuze, *Cinema 2: The Time-Image*, translated by Hugh Tomlinson and Robert Galeta, Minneapolis, MN 1989, p. 71.

386 Benjamin, *The Origin of German Tragic Drama*, op. cit., p. 228. Already in the Mystery Plays, by the way, Satan is depicted as a person of privilege, usually as a nobleman; his characteristic is excessive pride. (See Cox, op. cit., p. 22.)
387 See for example Grene, op. cit., pp. 127–128.
388 Clemen, op. cit., p. 10.
389 See for example Luther Link, *The Devil. A Mask without a Face*, London 1995.
390 Johann Wolfgang von Goethe, *Faust: A Tragedy*, translated by Walter Arndt, New York, NY/London 2001 [1335–1336].
391 Richard uses the same figure also in a monologue:

> RICHARD: Simple, plain Clarence, I do love thee so –
> That I will shortly send thy soul to Heaven –
> If Heaven will take the present at our hands.
>
> (I. i. 118–120)

392 Greenblatt, 'Shakespeare's World', op. cit., p. 19.
393 Benjamin, *The Origin of German Tragic Drama*, op. cit., p. 66.
394 Tillyard, op. cit., p. 208, paraphrasing James VI and I, op. cit., p. 79.
395 For example, even in his monologues he speaks of "dissembling nature" (I. i. 19).
396 See also section 1.7.
397 Benjamin, *The Origin of German Tragic Drama*, op. cit., p. 228.
398 Puttenham, op. cit., p. 196.
399 Benjamin, *The Origin of German Tragic Drama*, op. cit., p. 175.
400 Benjamin, *The Origin of German Tragic Drama*, op. cit., p. 229.
401 See Norman Cohn, *The Pursuit of the Millennium*, Oxford/New York, NY 1970, p. 300 about Humphrey Ellis' account of the perverting methods that the Ranters use and of their "Allegorical fancies."
402 Benjamin, *The Origin of German Tragic Drama*, op. cit., p. 230.
403 Benjamin, *The Origin of German Tragic Drama*, op. cit., p. 227.
404 Benjamin, *The Origin of German Tragic Drama*, op. cit., p. 230.
405 Carl Schmitt, *Hamlet or Hecuba: The Intrusion of the Time into the Play*, translated by David Pan and Jennifer Rust, New York, NY 2009, pp. 64–65.
406 It is a general phenomenon in *Richard III* that human characters serve as stage props, which is made explicit, for example, when Buckingham's calls the cleverly arranged bishops "props" (III. vii.94). As will have to be shown, later royal dramas draw upon the implications of this equivalence.
407 Benjamin, *The Origin of German Tragic Drama*, op. cit., p. 166.
408 Walter Benjamin, 'On the Concept of History', in *Selected Writings*, vol. IV, translated by Harry Zohn, Cambridge, MA 2006, p. 392.
409 Benjamin, *The Origin of German Tragic Drama*, op. cit., p. 166.
410 Dante, *The Inferno*, translated by Robert and Jean Hollander, New York, NY 2002, pp. 50–53 [3. 82–99].
411 See the translation of Mark 5, 15 in William Tyndale, *Tyndale's New Testament*, edited by David Daniell, New Haven, CT 1995, p. 68. The *King James Bible* does not use this expression.
412 Dante, op. cit., pp. 168–169 [9.34–9.54].
413 Aeschylus, *The Oresteia*, translated by Robert Fagles, New York, NY 1966, line 429.
414 Benjamin, 'Critique of Violence', op. cit., p. 249.
415 Benjamin, *The Origin of German Tragic Drama*, op. cit., p. 131.
416 Suggested by Christian Meier, *Die Entstehung des Politischen bei den Griechen*, Frankfurt a. M. 1995, pp. 194–197.
417 Benjamin, *The Origin of German Tragic Drama*, op. cit., p. 132.
418 Grene, op. cit., p. 157.

419 Seneca, 'Thyestes', in *Tragedies II*, translated by John G. Fitch, Cambridge/London 2004, pp. 232–239. Rossiter compares Seneca's Fury, esp. in her announcements of vengeance, with Margaret (Rossiter, op. cit., pp. 13–14).
420 Seneca, op. cit., pp. 313–323.
421 Hans Urs von Balthasar, *Theodramatik. Erster Band: Prolegomena*, Einsiedeln 1983, pp. 88/91.
422 Knapp, op. cit., p. 14.
423 Knapp, op. cit., pp. 2–3.
424 Foxe, op. cit., p. 57.
425 Kingsley-Smith, op. cit., pp. 21–22.
426 Plato, *Republic*, Books 6–10, translated by Chris Emlyn-Jones and William Preddy, Cambridge, MA 2013, Book X, 595a–608b.
427 Kingsley-Smith, op. cit., pp. 21–22.
428 Agnew, op. cit.
429 John Hall, *The Advancement of Learning*, Liverpool 1953, quoted by Agnew, op. cit., p. 97.
430 Cohen, op. cit., p.161.
431 Robert Weimann, *Zwischen Performanz und Repräsentation. Shakespeare und die Macht des Theaters*, Heidelberg 2000, p. 82.
432 Act of Parliament, 14 Elizabeth I, c. 5, in Tanya Pollard (ed.), *Shakespeare's Theater, A Sourcebook*, Malden, MA 2004, pp. 303–305.
433 Cohen, op. cit., p. 151.
434 Kingsley-Smith, op. cit., p. 24.
435 Greenblatt, *Will in the World*, op. cit., p. 162.
436 Thomas Heywood, *An Apology for Actors (1612)*, New York, NY 1941, pp. 1–2.
437 Greenblatt, *Shakespearean Negotiations*, op. cit., p. 64.
438 Raphael Holinshed, *Chronicles of England, Scotland, and Ireland*, vol. 4, London 1807/1808, p. 159, quoted by Pye, *The Regal Phantasm*, op. cit., p. 64.
439 Elizabeth I, *Collected Works*, Chicago, IL 2002, p. 189; James VI and I, op. cit., p. 49.
440 Kantorowicz, *The King's Two Bodies*, op. cit., pp. 46–47.
441 Ernst H. Kantorowicz, *Götter in Uniform, Studien zur Entwicklung des abendländischen Königtums*, Stuttgart 1998, pp. 164–165.
442 Greenblatt, *Shakespearean Negotiations*, op. cit., p. 64.
443 Stephen Orgel, *The Illusion of Power. Political Theater in the English Renaissance*, Berkeley/Los Angeles, CA/London 1975, p. 39.
444 Thomas, op. cit., p. 498.
445 Thomas, op. cit., p. 157.
446 Thomas, op. cit., p. 160.
447 Thomas, op. cit., p. 159.
448 Thomas, op. cit., p. 159.
449 Thomas, op. cit., p. 506.
450 On the concept of the absolute metaphor, see Hans Blumenberg, *Paradigms for a Metaphorology*, translated by Robert Savage, Ithaca, NY 2010, pp. 5, 14–17.
451 Agnew, op. cit., pp. 16–20.
452 Agnew, op. cit., p. 16.
453 Cohen, op. cit., p. 126.
454 See for example Cohen, op. cit., p. 73. See also section 1.6.
455 See section 1.2.
456 Thomas, op. cit., p. 579.
457 '*King Lear* and Harsnett's "Devil-Fiction"', in Stephen Greenblatt, *The Power of Forms in the English Renaissance*, Norman, OK 1982, p. 241.
458 Act of Parliament, 3 James I, c. 21, quoted by Kenneth Gross, *Shakespeare's Noise*, Chicago, IL/London 2001, p. 171.
459 Peter Ackroyd, *London. The Biography*, London 2000, p. 170.

460 Stephen Greenblatt, *Renaissance Self-Fashioning From More To Shakespeare*, Chicago, IL/London 1980, pp. 230–231.
461 "*King Lear* and Harsnett's "Devil-Fiction"", op. cit., p. 242.
462 John Langshaw Austin, *How To Do Things With Words*, Cambridge, MA 2003, p. 22.
463 See the Introduction.
464 Greenblatt, *Shakespearean Negotiations*, op. cit., pp. 112–113.
465 Richard Halpern, *The Poetics of Primitive Accumulation. English Renaissance Culture and the Genealogy of Capital*, Ithaca, NY/London 1991, p. 239.
466 Benjamin, *The Origin of German Tragic Drama*, op. cit., p. 119.
467 See section 1.4, referring to Iser, op. cit., pp. 66–67.
468 Russell West, *Spatial Representation and the Jacobean Stage from Shakespeare to Webster*, Basingstoke/New York, NY 2002, pp. 83–84.
469 Lacan, *The Psychoses*, op. cit., pp. 258–270.
470 Rossiter, op. cit., p. 16.
471 On the concept of the "simulacrum," see Deleuze, *The Logic of Sense*, op. cit., pp. 299/302.
472 This is probably the reason Richard counts him among the "simple gulls" (I. iii. 328).
473 Clemen, op. cit., p. 171.
474 Benjamin, *The Origin of German Tragic Drama*, op. cit., p. 157.
475 On this concept, see Jacques Lacan, *The Four Fundamental Concepts of Psychoanalysis. Seminar XI*, translated by Alan Sheridan, New York, NY/London 1978, pp. 267–276.
476 Iser, op. cit., p. 59.
477 See section 1.6.
478 See for example Clemen, op. cit., pp. 307–308.
479 See section 1.5.
480 Benjamin, *The Origin of German Tragic Drama*, op. cit., p. 188.

CHAPTER 2

King John and the ordeal of the bastard *commodity*

In *Richard III*, Shakespearean theater discloses ambiguities and aporias of the curse that impede its identification with fixed symbolic mandates. The play demonstrates that only one attitude can cope with these aporias: a sovereign irony that acknowledges the autonomous field of representation, defined by the endless sliding of the signifier, as the true sovereign. In *King John*, even this distanced position is absorbed into the theatrical representation and deconstructed on the spot: not only do the identifications fail, but also the de-identification proves to be problematic, in consequence of which every resultant *auto-da-fé* of the ironists opens up new ironies.

The starting position of *King John* resembles that of *Richard III*: no legitimate supremacy can be established in a politically volatile period. The cause of the difficulty in this case is a loophole in the regulation defining royal succession. The principle of primogeniture is the only uncontested principle of determining accession to the throne. But in this specific case, the claim of the youngest brother, John, conflicts with that of Arthur, the son of the middle brother. And this constellation confronts the aspirants with an open situation because no established rule of succession is applicable.[1] Neither the competitors themselves nor their supporters are fully convinced that their claim is legitimate; as Queen Eleanor admits to John:

> ELEANOR: Your strong possession much more than your right,
> Or else it must go wrong with you and me:
> So much my conscience whispers in your ear,
> Which none but heaven, and you, and I, shall hear.
>
> (I. i. 40–43)

One can observe, however, that the question of legitimacy is of only limited practical relevance: John's most tireless standard-bearer, the bastard Faulconbridge, does consider Arthur the legitimate king, for this reason calling even France's entrance into the war "honourable" (II. i. 585), since it is an act that justifies itself through Arthur's claim to the throne. But the fact that he declares John's dynastic legitimacy insufficient does not keep him from remaining his ally. It is not so much the law that upholds the sovereign's power but the loyalty of his allies and the speech act that makes this loyalty obligatory, namely the oath of allegiance. The multiple oaths sworn by France and Austria in support of Arthur and his mother Constance, vowing to defend Arthur's claim to the throne with their lives (e.g. in II. i. 19–31), for example, militarize the struggle for the accession to the throne. They turn France, that is, the French king Philip, into Arthur's deputy who in the latter's name can lay claim to the English territories and proclaim an oath of war against King John (II. i. 343–349). But the oath's position as the nucleus of supremacy soon proves problematic in this play, too. A steady sequence of oaths and their breaches structures the shifting power constellations that characterize the plot of *King John*. The elaborate oaths of France and Austria, which always appeal to God, are broken and replaced by vows of friendship between Philip and John (II. ii. 1) that are based on the matrimonial oath of fidelity between John's niece, Blanche, and Lewis, the Dauphin (II. i. 538–539). That the French king drops Arthur in return for John's sacrifice of the princess makes it obvious that Philip does not in fact defend Arthur's claim to the throne. Rather, from the start he pursues his own interests, which involve the English territories in the north of France. But the recently sworn oaths of loyalty between John and Philip are also broken when the papal legate Pandulph enters and insists on Philip's antecedent oath of loyalty to the church (III. i. 150–223). The consequent resumption of the military conflict leads to Arthur's captivity and death. This offers the English nobles an opportunity to break their feudal oath of loyalty to John and to replace it with an oath of loyalty to the dead Arthur (IV. iii. 62–73) that is in fact an oath to the French king. Subsequently, the English nobles and the Dauphin swear an oath of eternal loyalty. Not only the Eucharist secures this oath (V. ii. 6–7); it is also set down in writing (V. ii. 1–5). But these medial fortifications do not prevent both parties from breaking it; the French side will do so with a counter oath, sworn immediately thereafter and likewise with the guarantee of the Eucharist (V. iv. 13–20). The English side will replace it with a renewed oath of feudal loyalty to John (V. iv. 52–57) after he has renewed his broken oath in favor of papal supremacy (V. i. 1–24). Finally, after John's death, one more oath is sworn in support of the new king, his son Henry, and the play ends (V. vii. 101–107). In addition, numerous "internal oaths" support or subvert the public oaths (e.g. III. ii. 33 and V. i. 5–7). The abundance of the oath formulas seems to be proportional to the bigotry of those proclaiming them; hence, it does not come as a surprise that the name of one of the play's most prominent English noblemen is Lord Bigot. Shakespeare found this name in Holinshed, to be sure,[2] but uses it as a punning synecdoche: the modern denotation of "bigot" (hypocritical) was already known during the Elizabethan era. The word presumably derives from the oath formula "bi god."[3]

It is striking, in the developments summarized here, that oaths are consistently broken, but nonetheless never questioned in principle as a means of ascertaining legitimacy. In the cycle of oath-taking, oath-breaking, and oath renewal, betrayal functions as the structural principle that repeats the early modern *circulus vitiosus* in the relationship of legitimacy and obligation. It is through oaths that those swearing them in *King John* try to legitimate their positions. Theirs are oaths as defined by Augustine, to wit, promises that subject those who swear them to God as the supreme judge and thereby integrate them into God's kingdom as subjects. These oaths constitute as well as sanctify the feudal structure and especially establish the king as God's deputy.[4] In this function, the king assumes his place in the center of the feudal structure, i.e. a position that alone, especially in the ideology of the early modern era, can guarantee the binding power of oaths through its "fiat".[5] This opens a vicious circle in which the oath is the condition of legitimacy, but legitimacy also is the condition of the oath.

What can people rely on when founding oaths contradict one another? The problem becomes virulent at the moment when competitors jockey for the position of God's legitimate representative. John calls himself "God's wrathful agent" (II. i. 87), but so does Philip (II. i. 110–114). In *King John*, God acts only through representatives who contradict both other representatives and themselves,[6] thus reducing Him to the status of a hypothesis. What can legitimacy mean under these circumstances? This is the question at the center of the perpetual fluctuation in the struggle for the throne. John has little interest in the fine points of its theological and judicial dimensions; in the end he always invokes the rule of force. In contrast to Richard III, he presents himself as a proponent of *Realpolitik*. The legitimacy and succession conflict, John thinks at first, can be contained inside State borders; he must see to it that his conflict with Arthur/Philip is perceived as a territorial controversy between two States (see e.g. II. i. 207–234). But the problem of circular legitimacy involves also the idea of the State, insofar as it is nominally constituted by the oath. But the State is also the authority that demands these constitutive oaths. In the domain of the oath, the State's boundaries take shape and dissipate. Before the Reformation, the West European kingdoms can still be seen as provinces of Christendom unified under the Pope so that the conflicts among these States appear as civil wars.[7] And even in the seventeenth century the differentiation between an international and a civil war can often be made only retrospectively. The State borders in *King John* are extremely porous, a circumstance to which especially the abundance of French terms and names in the vocabulary of John's court calls attention, a noticeable but hitherto largely uncommented detail. In this way, the play continuously alludes to the fact that English nobility has itself been of French descent since the Norman Conquest. The English princess' name (as a grandchild of Eleanor of Aquitaine) is Blanche, and the constantly evoked heroic English *Überking* Richard I is almost exclusively called "*Coeur-de-Lion*" (I. i. 54/85/253, etc.). The Bastard originally has the same name as the French king Philip, after his knighting the same name as his father, the English king Richard. This natural "bastardization" of the languages, names, and bloodlines makes the Bastard's appeal to a folk spirit of Englishness all the more laughable.

In this meta-national conflict of interests the involved parties experiment with different methods of ascertaining sovereignty. The first possibility that offers itself for determining the monarch is to fall back on acclamation by the subjects. The focus of this attempt is Angiers, a French city in English hands that appears to occupy a threshold position. The citizens of Angiers witnessing the conflict from *above* are experimentally granted the role of a "sovereign people." They may elect their king by acclamation, though under the threat of incurring the wrath of the party not elected. And for this very reason they unbendingly reject the suggestion of becoming involved in the conflict:

> HUBERT: In brief, we are the King of England's subjects:
> For him, and in his right, we hold this town.
> JOHN: Acknowledge then the king, and let me in.
> HUBERT: That can we not; but he that proves the king,
> To him will we prove loyal: till that time
> Have we ramm'd up our gates against the world.
> JOHN: Doth not the crown of England prove the king?
> And if not that, I bring you witnesses,
> Twice fifteen thousand hearts of England's breed [. . .].
>
> (II. i. 267–275)

By referring to his troops, John explicitly lets it be known that he considers the question of legitimacy a question of power. But with the same killer argument Philip claims the recognition of the citizens (II. i. 278–280). The symmetry of the two parties becomes obvious through their similar, in part stichomythic utterances but also through an arrangement of the *personae* that places the English on the one, the French on the other side of the stage. The citizens of Angiers occupy the gallery. These citizens find themselves in a dilemma comparable to that of Buridan's ass:[8] they are willing to submit to the sovereign but unable to ascertain who is the sovereign. This is how Shakespeare shows a loophole in Elizabethan ideology that cannot be closed by conventional means. The Elizabethan doctrine of sovereignty, as developed for example in the *Homily against Disobedience and Wilful Rebellion* of 1570, states that subordination is the citizen's highest duty and rebellion the worst crime; even a bad ruler must be tolerated as punishment sent by God.[9] Aside from the theological aporias developed in *Richard III*, this ideology also raises the question to whom the subjects are to subjugate themselves, if two equally valid or equally unclear claims to sovereignty present a conflict. The "Tudor Doctrine" in this case is undecided and answers according to historical need.[10] The arrangement of the scene discreetly hints at the possibility that the Elizabethan audience might have the same problem as the citizens of Angiers: Hubert is placed on the gallery *above*, a location that playhouse technique can, depending on preference, attribute either to the stage or to the spectators' area.[11]

Since primogeniture, oath, and acclamation alone are obviously insufficient to achieve their purpose, the parties agree to settle the issue of who is to rule through trial by battle. (It would be worth a separate study to show how the notion of the ordeal in its various aspects floats through all of Shakespeare's royal dramas.) The ordeal is a divine judgment, that is to say, an eminently theatrical and elastic means of limiting conflicts, attributing guilt and creating consensus. Structurally, it functions like the oath but accelerates the fate that the oath postpones indefinitely: oaths appeal to God for judgment, ordeals stage the verdict. The ordeal is invoked above all because it relieves judicial authorities of responsibility and of making a decision, for example, in the interpretation of written laws.[12] Even more strongly than the oath, it directly activates fate, that is, "the demonic nature of the law" into which the subjects are inserted. During the Middle Ages the ordeal functions, Peter Brown writes, "as an instrument of consensus and as a theatrical device by which to contain disruptive conflict."[13] But this way of containing conflicts and creating consensus takes place in the twilight between lawmaking and law-preserving. The ordeal shows a law in action that is not a principle to protect from arbitrariness and to institute general order. It is, rather, an act of violence in which judgment and execution coincide. When divine judgment organizes a society, it exposes this society to religiously sanctioned lawmaking violence.

The trial by battle is not only one of the dominant forms of lawful judgment in early medieval England;[14] it also legitimates the king's rule. A regular part of every coronation ceremony is the appearance of a "King's Champion," who publicly declares his willingness to defend his sovereign's title by combat against any challenger.[15] In the late Middle Ages and early modern era the ordeal and the legal model that is based on it are increasingly scaled back in civilian life, and the clergy refuses to give the blessing required for its enactment. The arguments used against the ordeal identify it as a forced, institutionalized miracle and hence as a procedure "to tempt God."[16] During Shakespeare's time it is above all James I who picks up the motif and emphasizes that the ordeal has no basis in the New Testament.[17] This suppression of the ordeal in civilian life no doubt has something to do with the State's consolidation of its monopoly on violence: legal controversies are no longer to be settled through violent acts between the citizens.[18]

Instead, any question about legitimacies, even that about the king's own legitimacy, is surrendered to the king; pretenders to his office are by definition criminals. But the ordeal does survive in a number of defused civilian forms, for example, in the use of the Eucharist as divine judgment.[19] And it recurs also in the Calvinist doctrine in a different context insofar as Calvinism teaches that economic life essentially reveals a verdict rendered by God: wealth, the victory in the ordeal of economic life, is a sign of justification by God, poverty signifies damnation.[20] But while the model of trial by combat is being suppressed in the domestic realm, it openly remains in force in a conflict between States: medieval and early modern chronicles again and again use the commonplace of war as a synecdoche of the Last Judgment, when God decides the affairs of man.[21] Hence, every military conflict is declared a trial by combat; consequently, God is appealed to before battles as the one who dispenses a higher justice.[22] Since no other solution of the dilemma before the gates of Angiers emerges, everybody retreats to this rhetoric of the ordeal and to battle, the "dreadful trial of our kingdom's king" (II. i. 286).

King John is teeming with anachronisms, one of the most prominent being the fact that the military confrontation between "England" and "France" takes place under modern premises: combat here is a battle of technology and *matériel* in which armies of mercenaries (II. i. 66–71) and cannons (II. i. 37/210/251/382/461–462)—i.e. gun powder, at that time not yet used in Europe—play the decisive roles. This anachronism not only involves the audience;[23] it also undermines the rhetoric of the ordeal: battles of *matériel*, in contrast to ritualized sword fights, are rather more difficult to represent as acts of fate. The ordeal traditionally is not an internecine war in which a material superiority is deployed. It is, rather, a confrontation that moves toward the admission of defeat[24]—a speech act that both parties renounce in the situation before the gates of Angiers. Consequently, the subsequent battle produces no unequivocal decision since either party claims victory for itself (II. i. 300–324). Also the citizens of Angiers, who have observed the fight from a neutral position, still do not want to declare a victor (III. i. 325–328). Not even military force, in *Richard III* still the indubitable mark of a ruler, provides a dependable ultimate justification in *King John*. Battles decide nothing in this play. Their ends always remain subject to revisions, a fact which the crafty cardinal Pandulph formulates explicitly (III. iii. 121–122). Many citizens are inclined to hear God's voice in this apparently irrevocable draw (II. i. 368). Since the competing parties cannot agree to accept this proposition, the Bastard submits to them an alternate proposal that is directed against the position of the citizens as neutral observers:

> BASTARD: By heaven, these scroyles of Angiers flout you, kings,
> And stand securely on their battlements,
> As in a theatre, whence they gape and point
> At your industrious scenes and acts of death.
>
> (II. i. 373–376)

By referring to the battle as a spectacle put on for the citizens, he touches a secret nerve of the preceding speeches and actions: the trial by combat is an act of representation, and as such it is a dramatic act.[25] In order to terminate this artificial construction, the Bastard proposes to deal with the question of sovereignty in the radical manner of Clausewitz: he pleads for total war in the style of modernity, without ritual boundaries and without neutral observers:

> BASTARD: Do like the mutines of Jerusalem,
> Be friends awhile and both conjointly bend
> Your sharpest deeds of malice on this town. [. . .]
> I'd play incessantly upon these jades,
> Even till unfenced desolation
> Leave them as naked as the vulgar air. [. . .]
> How like you this wild counsel, mighty states?
> Smacks it not something of the policy?
>
> (II. i. 378–380/385–387/395–396)

But the historical parallel the Bastard quotes turns against him: he refers to Flavius Josephus' *Bellum Judaicum*, according to which the Roman siege of Jerusalem in AD 70 ended the civil war among the Jews. In fact, the "mutines of Jerusalem" were defending rather than attacking a city and, moreover, were utterly defeated. By recommending that the warring parties imitate them, the Bastard implicitly turns Philip and John not only into losers but even into impersonators of losers, despite the fact that he seemed to plead for the suspension of the theatrical situation. John nevertheless endorses the Bastard's plan with an emphatic oath formula and persuades France to accept the new strategy—one which is senseless from a military standpoint but symbolically seminal:

> JOHN: Now, by the sky that hangs above our heads,
> I like it well. France, shall we knit our powers
> And lay this Angiers even with the ground;
> Then after fight who shall be king of it? [. . .]
> PHILIP: Let it be so.
>
> (II. i. 397–400/408)

In this total legal dispute not only the object of the dispute is to be destroyed willfully, but also the neutral, independent position from which one might judge objectively is marked as something to be abolished. There is no neutral place of observation, no mediation between the parties that both sides do not consider disposable. A motif is formulated here that the following acts will repeat and vary: it is the impossibility of standing at a neutral distance in the conflicts between France and England. In contrast to preceding scenes (see e.g. I. i. 29–30) and starting in II. I, not only prophets will be attacked, maligned, and punished for their predictions (IV. ii. 147–157), but also messengers and ambassadors for their reports (II. ii. 36–41; V. v. 14, et al.). Due to the parallel between the position of Angiers' citizenry and that of the audience, such a shift implicitly also involves the spectators in this changed situation. Their neutral and external position relative to what transpires onstage is marked as similarly precarious.[26] A chasm opens in which lurk diverse shadows cast forth by modernity. An alternative, more traditional proposal by Hubert succeeds in sealing it up again—for the time being: the destruction of Angiers and the totalizing of the war's conduct is averted when the citizens instigate the sacrifice of the princess. This turn of events does not, to be sure, move the situation toward a good end. But at least it offers a less apocalyptic process of consolidating power by means of blood. The Dauphin's marriage to Blanche ends the mutual bloodletting in battle by uniting the bloodlines of the competing dynasties in a political marriage, thereby reconciling the claims of both parties, at least provisorily.

It becomes evident in this situation that Arthur and Constance are nothing to Philip but assets in his strategy to realize his own goals of arrogating British provinces in France. After he has been able to bargain for these territories as Blanche's dowry, he is ready to drop John's nephew. This turn of events as well is justified with sacral concepts and secured through holy loyalty oaths. But now the old functionaries of the legitimating sacral sphere object to the use of their language for purely functional purposes. The question of legitimacy is again problematized, this time from the perspective of the relationship between church and State, when the Pope interjects himself into scene III. i. and claims in his role as head of the church that it is his duty to impose a new order on what is taking place. The papal legate Pandulph enters and demands the installation of an archbishop, which John rejects, provoking an investiture struggle *en miniature* (III. i. 63–86). John's justification of his refusal to comply establishes a parallel between this situation and the Reformation:

> JOHN: Though you and all the kings of Christendom
> Are led so grossly by this meddling priest,
> Dreading the curse that money may buy out;
> And by the merit of vile gold, dross, dust,
> Purchase corrupted pardon of a man,
> Who in that sale sells pardon from himself;
> Though you and all the rest so grossly led
> This juggling witchcraft with revenue cherish,
> Yet I alone, alone do me oppose
> Against the pope, and count his friends my foes.
>
> (III. i. 88–97)

John's refusal vis-à-vis Pandulph is formulated in Protestant phrases and concepts: He calls himself the head of the English Church (III. i. 79–86) and the Pope a usurper and blasphemer. It is likewise in the rhetoric of the English Reformation that he calls the practice of ecclesiastical excommunication the source of papal power and hence the central object of his denunciation, stating that its insinuated commodity character ought to disqualify the practice.[27]

Through his solitary position as the only sovereign who has divine legitimacy and is not subject to the false Pope, John declares himself a kind of (triple-crowned) "Antipope," which again reflects the early Anglican view (articulated by Foxe, for example) of the English kings' superior position as elect rulers of an elect nation.[28] It is almost superfluous to point out how anachronistic this representation is. Canon law supported the papal claim to supremacy and was valid during the Middle Ages in all of Europe. Its *de facto* implementation, to be sure, required the co-operation of the secular institutions and hence varied from one country to the next, but nobody attacked canon law *per se*; possible conflicts questioned boundaries of responsibility but never the validity of canon law.[29] Shakespeare's representation of the conflict between Pandulph and John appropriates the traditional conflict and presents it as a prefiguration of the Reformation rather than as a dispute over prerogatives of power. In this way John becomes a figure anticipating Henry VIII; however, such a parallelization may contribute little to the latter's glorification.

Due to John's refusal to accede to the Pope, Pandulph pronounces upon him one of the curses whose legitimacy and effectiveness the former has just denied. Pandulph's curse does not pack the liturgical abundance of Margaret's curses, however, but remains unadorned and concise. It reduces excommunication to a political act; hence, he does not enumerate the spiritual consequences of his curse but exclusively its social repercussions:

> PANDULPH: Then, by the lawful power that I have,
> Thou shalt stand curs'd and excommunicate:
> And blessed shall he be that doth revolt

> From his allegiance to an heretic;
> And meritorious shall that hand be call'd,
> Canonized and worshipp'd as a saint,
> That takes away by any secret course
> Thy hateful life.
>
> (III. i. 98–105)

In order to emphasize more strongly the parallel to the ban decreed on Henry VIII and Elizabeth I, Shakespeare leaves an important point unmentioned: in the thirteenth century it was not only John who was excommunicated, but the interdict was also imposed on England.[30] It is to be assumed that Shakespeare acquits himself of ideological obligations with this abbreviated version: in the England of the early modern era, it was obligatory to denounce the papal practice of excommunicating monarchs, a demand still dutifully accepted by Hobbes:

> And because the sentence of excommunication, importeth an advice, not to keep company nor so much as to eat with him that is excommunicate, if a sovereign prince, or assembly be excommunicate, the sentence is of no effect. For all subjects are bound to be in the company and presence of their own sovereign, when he requireth it, by the law of nature [. . .].[31]

The ecclesiastical curse functions in this context as the negative of the political loyalty oath, as an explicit annulment of the alliances previously constituted in various crooked ways. Pandulph, in subjecting John to the ban, declares that the agreement between France and England has been cancelled, and he threatens Philip likewise with excommunication should he refuse to turn against John. In this dilemma, Philip defensively refers to the holy oaths that unite him and John, mentioning moreover the religious and familial bond that has brought their "inward souls" together through the marriage of Blanche and Lewis (III. i. 150–158). Would it not be a "jest with heaven" (III. i. 168) and an occasion for God's wrath if these oaths were broken immediately after they had been sworn? Pandulph does not accept these arguments and attempts to declare the ecclesiastical curse hegemonic by calling it "a mother's curse" (III. i. 183), using the customary metaphor that makes the church the mother of all Christians, and following traditional doctrine, based on the Bible, that the parental curse counts among the most effective execrations.[32] But with this metaphor he directly invokes again the authority of familial hierarchies, established through bonds of blood, even though he had just tried to deny their legitimacy when he repudiated Philip's argumentation. The official pronouncements in *King John* tend to be subverted by their own tropes; and this deputy of God carries on the duties of his office without paying much attention to this fact. In a subsequent longish speech, Pandulph seeks to prove the absolute priority of Philip's oath of loyalty toward the Pope:

> PANDULPH: O, let thy vow
> First made to heaven, first be to heaven perform'd.

That is, to be the champion of our church. [. . .]
It is religion that doth make vows kept,
But thou hast sworn against religion:
By what thou swear'st against the thing thou swear'st,
And mak'st an oath the surety for thy truth!
Against an oath the truth thou art unsure
To swear – swears only not to be forsworn! –
Else what a mockery should it be to swear?
But thou dost swear only to be forsworn,
And most forsworn, to keep what thou dost swear.
Therefore thy later vows against thy first
Is in thyself rebellion to thyself [. . .].

(III. i. 192–194/205–215)

Pandulph declares that religion alone, and hence the church, can guarantee that oaths are kept and that, moreover, it is the first recipient of oaths. This means that he defines the loyalty oath to the Church as a "primordial signifier."[33] From this logical and temporal priority he derives the claim that the secondary oath to John has no efficacy, since he who breaks an oath that guarantees the validity of oaths disqualifies every oath whatsoever. The cardinal, just like Philip, emphasizes the religious dimension of the oath, acting as though religion and oath were interdependent ("deep-sworn faith," III. i. 157, etc.). In this he plays with the two meanings of "faith" (III. i. 158), denoting belief but also the confidence that is required for the ratification of contracts/treaties and is established through them. Pandulph is equally shrewd in the way he handles the ambiguity of other terms, which seems to open up a strange dialectics. This strategic and casuistic employment of equivocations again poses parallels between the events in *King John* and the interconfessional conflicts of Shakespeare's time, insofar as the systematic abuse of casuistry and a doctrinaire approval of misleading equivocations were traditionally attributed to the Jesuits.[34] Pandulph's remark about the necessity of a primordial signifier nevertheless carries a certain power of persuasion, especially since John can only counter it with his belief in violence as the *de facto* final justification, a position that already has proven its insufficiency. Consequently, Pandulph succeeds in persuading Philip to abandon John, even if in the final analysis the cardinal's argumentation, like the earlier viewpoints, is reduced to absurdity—just more subtly so: the fact that he has to rely on equivocations already suggests that it is less his conclusions than his premises that are questionable. He bases the church's hegemony on its primordial status, which indirectly is a topic of the discussion. In other words, this hegemony is considered debatable and can be deemed dubious by the very fact that Pandulph takes recourse to familial metaphors. His argumentation is circular because in order to prove a priority, it must base itself on this very priority. But only the following scenes render a truly devastating verdict on the papal legate, who now *in praxi* stands for a modern, nearly Machiavellian conception of politics that shows little concern for final justifications. The cardinal invokes a process of legitimation that he invalidates through the strategies he has employed in its invocation.

Sigurd Burckhardt has analyzed how the medieval hierarchical structure collapses in *King John* when traditional primordial signifiers are suspended and when this structure is replaced by a different order whose norms and obligations are more fluid and conjectural.[35] This rupture also involves the problem of the curse. A fundamental problem of the interminable and indeterminable efficacy of the curse becomes virulent: illegitimate cursing cannot have an effect according to official doctrine, since a person whose concerns are illegitimate sins against God's decree; but it is a function of the act of cursing to call precisely this illegitimacy into question—hence the imperative to take tough measures against cursing. For this reason, the legitimacy of the oath and the curse, but consequently also the legitimacy of the law itself, are constantly in doubt. One indication of this fact is the dialogue between Pandulph and Constance after the cardinal has excommunicated John:

> CONSTANCE: O, lawful let it be
> That I have room with Rome to curse awhile!
> Good father cardinal, cry thou amen
> To my keen curses: for without my wrong
> There is no tongue hath power to curse him right.
> PANDULPH: There's law and warrant, lady, for my curse.
> CONSTANCE: And for mine too: when law can do no right
> Let it be lawful that law bar no wrong!
> Law cannot give my child his kingdom here,
> For he that holds his kingdom holds the law;
> Therefore, since law itself is perfect wrong,
> How can the law forbid my tongue to curse?
>
> (III. i. 105–116)

Constance claims the right of participating in the papal legate's curse as a layperson. But while Pandulph curses laconically and unceremoniously, she quotes the liturgical form of the ecclesiastical excommunication ceremony by her reference to the "Amen" response—as does Elizabeth in *Richard III*.[36] But she attributes the priest's role to herself and, to the cardinal, that of the congregation. This represents but one of the inversions in which Constance's utterances abound. Pandulph logically denies her the right to her own curses because he claims a monopoly, now as before, on representing primordial signifiers; whereupon Constance attacks the idea of the law *per se* and condemns the law, calling it the servant of violence ("he that holds his kingdom holds the law"). According to her disquisitions, the law is reduced to institutionalized injustice ("the law itself is perfect wrong.").[37] Since everybody has the right to do what is in his or her power to do, if the law is derived from power, her capacity to curse also grants her the right to curse. The theological implications of thus conflating commonwealth and state of nature are also unfolded by way of the curse: Constance reduces God to the function of dispensing justice as well as injustice. She portrays Eleanor as God's instrument that punishes Arthur for her own sins:

> CONSTANCE: I have but this to say,
> That he is not only plagued for her sin,
> But God hath made her sin and her the plague
> On this removed issue, plagued for her
> And with her plague; her sin his injury,
> Her injury the beadle to her sin,
> All punish'd in the person of this child,
> And all for her; a plague upon her!
>
> (II. i. 183–190)

Constance seems to insinuate a monstrous God who punishes the innocent and appoints the guilty as their executioners. But in this case her numerous appeals to valid law (II. i. 47/176, etc.) and to divine justice (II. i. 172; III. i. 33, etc.) would be senseless. Her argumentation is illogical and spins in a circle insofar as she never quite gives up the idea that there exists a justice superior to royal violence, even as she continues to insist on Arthur's right to the crown and repeatedly curses her enemies on this assumption (II. i. 190; III. i. 33–38). Constance positions herself in the dangerous zone between two contradictory conceptions of the law and consequently is ground down by them. Her attempts to find a way out of the dilemma of lost legitimacy are no more successful than those of the other *dramatis personae.*

King John deals with the aporias of ruling that become virulent after the dissolution of theologico-political universalism. This raises the question of what order the play proposes in this situation to take the place of old bonds. Burckhardt suggests that *King John* implicitly propagates "ties of blood" as the new bonding agent of society.[38] But this drama in fact allows even less hope in a solution by blood than *Richard III*. It reveals the loopholes in the rule of primogeniture as clearly as the ambiguity of the ordeal and other bloody acts. John speaks of "unreprievable condemned blood" (V. vii. 48):

> JOHN: There is no sure foundation set on blood [. . .].
>
> (IV. ii. 104)

And his son and successor designates the blood of the royal body politic as corrupt:

> HENRY: It is too late: the life of all his blood
> Is touched corruptibly [. . .].
>
> (V. vii. 1–2)

Instead, society is apparently held together by other forces. Problems of legitimacy in *King John* are always solved *de facto* when interests converge. Alliances are formed when their respective members pursue their own advantages. The new agent of social bonds turns out be self-interest, the striving for "commodity." In the late sixteenth century, "commodity" still signifies a convenience and a profit more than it suggests a material object, but the term's meaning begins to shift and during this interim covers all three significations.[39] Politics no less than religion seem to be in the service of "commodity": *King John* represents a crisis of representation in which the exchange of traditional signs of holy obligation and rank takes place according to the rules of a commodity transaction, as is made clear in the play and explicit in the Bastard's monologues:

> BASTARD: Mad world! mad kings! mad composition!
> John, to stop Arthur's title in the whole,
> Hath willingly departed with a part:
> And France, whose armour conscience buckled on, [. . .]
> As God's own soldier, rounded in the ear
> With that same purpose-changer, that sly divel,
> That broker, that still breaks the pate of faith,
> That daily break-vow, he that wins of all,
> Of kings, of beggars, old men, young men, maids, [. . .]
> That smooth-fac'd gentleman, tickling commodity [. . .].
> (II. i. 561–564/566–570/573)

Personified "commodity" appears as a universal "break-vow" and "broker" (which also suggests "pimp"). It suspends the binding force of traditional oaths while establishing commercial relationships. Its invocation by the Bastard oscillates ambivalently between encomium and invective, between moralizing didactic poem and its subversion, an oscillation that is amplified in the monologue's continuation, by the introduction of the next metaphor—"commodity" as "bias:"

> BASTARD: Commodity, the bias of the world,
> The world, who of itself is peised well,
> Made to run even upon even ground,
> Till this advantage, this vile drawing bias,
> This sway of motion, this commodity,
> Makes it take head from all indifferency,
> From all direction, purpose, course, intent [. . .].
> (II. i. 574–580)

The Bastard draws the conclusion that social interaction always follows the momentum of what promises the greatest personal convenience. Individual interests take the place of absolute obligations, and this situation obtains—in a retrospective view of history—from the beginning of the world: "commodity," to be sure, is depicted as the cause of all deviancy and perversion but, by virtue of these very characteristics, also as world-generating; and not only because the genitives in "bias of the world" and "sway of motion" can be read both as *subiectivi* and *obiectivi*. Consequently, "commodity" as a Lucretian cosmic *clinamen*[40] is actually deified:[41]

> BASTARD: And why rail I on this commodity?
> But for because he hath not woo'd me yet:
> Not that I have the power to clutch my hand,
> When his fair angels would salute my palm;
> But for my hand, as unattempted yet,
> Like a poor beggar, raileth on the rich. [. . .]
> Since kings break faith upon commodity,
> Gain, be my lord, for I will worship thee! (*Exit*)
>
> (II. i. 587–592/597–598)

On the one hand, "commodity" is demonized as a "divel" who misleads into disloyalty, on the other, it is worshipped as a deity. Appropriately, "commodity" has two bodies: it is both a material, attractive object of value ("gain") and an abstract medium in which society develops. The ambassador of "commodity" is money, which transforms the one form into the other: the "fair angels," a monetary unit frequently mentioned by Shakespeare, order the world into an operation area for general profiteering. Metaphysical connections are imposed upon economic relationships, but there is no longer any attempt at creating an ideological compromise as in *Richard III*. Emblems become trademarks, trademarks turn into emblems:

> BASTARD: Saint George, that swing'd the dragon, and e'er since
> Sits on's horse-back at mine hostess' door,
> Teach us some fence!
>
> (II. i. 288–290)

But "commodity" is not the only part-abstract, part-concrete entity that is anthropomorphized in *King John*. There is an abundance of personifications in the speeches of the *dramatis personae*, among which figurations of death and fate again play major roles.[42] This procedure of personification is complemented by the reification of persons: People are repeatedly described as things or as a conglomerate of objects and occasionally even assume the form of money. In the play's first half it is above all the Bastard who uses this metaphor:

> BASTARD: Because he hath a half-face, like my father!
> With half that face would he have all my land:
> A half-faced groat five hundred pound a year! [. . .]
> And if my legs were two such riding-rods,
> My arms such eel-skins stuff'd, my face so thin
> That in mine ear I durst not stick a rose
> Lest men should say 'Look, where three-farthings goes!'
>
> (I. i. 92–94/140–143)

The metaphor of money also extends to the description of linguistic utterances, as when Constance denounces the French king's oath as counterfeit money:

> PHILIP: By heaven, lady, you shall have no cause
> To curse the fair proceedings of this day:
> Have I not pawn'd to you my majesty?
> CONSTANCE: You have beguil'd me with a counterfeit
> Resembling majesty, which, being touch'd and tried,
> Proves valueless: you are forsworn, forsworn!
>
> (III. i. 22–27)

Money, as a socially binding convention and as a material object, shows a double aspect in Shakespeare's metaphorics: in the general form of the absolute metaphor of "commodity," it takes up a position between immanence and transcendence. It is symptomatic of this fact that coins are often equated with celestial messengers ("angels"):

> JOHN: (*To the BASTARD.*) And, ere our coming, see thou shake the bags
> Of hoarding abbots; imprisoned angels
> Set at liberty: the fat ribs of peace
> Must by the hungry now be fed upon:
> Use our commission in his utmost force.
>
> (III. ii. 17–21)

Here the metaphor is charged up once more with ideas of the Reformation: not only is robbery from the church justified as a deed pleasing to God, because it provides nourishment for the poor, i.e. for the impoverished state, but it is justified also for unleashing objectified transcendence in order to stimulate the God-pleasing circulation of money by freeing "angels" from the restrictions imposed by the church.[43] The Dauphin uses the same terminology when he presents the disloyal English aristocrats with the prospect of their joining in the pillage of England:

> LEWIS: Come, come; for thou shalt thrust thy hand as deep
> Into the purse of rich prosperity
> As Lewis himself: so, nobles, shall you all,
> That knit your sinews to the strength of mine.
> (*Enter PANDULPH.*)
> And even there, methinks, an angel spake [...].
>
> (V. ii. 60–64)

It remains unclear If Lewis' last remark already refers to Pandulph's entering. But he insinuates in any case that the announcements of the angel promise riches and that the rebellion of the English nobility is triggered more by the hope for gain than by a sense of outrage over Arthur's death. There is not one person in

King John who would actually withdraw from the sacred process of profiting from "commodity." Blanche points out ungraciously that even Constance is pursuing material interests with her execrations (III. i. 136–137), which nobody in *Richard III* would have thought fit to mention in front of Margaret. In *King John*, money is the convention that replaces the sacral speech acts and rituals—above all those of curses and blessings. The Bastard comments on this fact with the words:

> BASTARD: Bell, book, and candle shall not drive me back
> When gold and silver becks me to come on [. . .].
>
> (III. ii. 22–23)[44]

The juxtaposition of sacral obligations and money is not explained merely by the fact that money and blessings are structurally comparable as circulating, aporetic ordering powers. Both converge, for example, in the Calvinist commonplace of "being blessed with money," which is also a curse on the financially less fortunate.[45] Habermas calls this a "liquescence of the sacred"[46] in the contractual thinking of the seventeenth century, and it appears indeed that God's liquidity is enhanced in more senses than one under these circumstances.

The process of loading the concept of "commodity" with religious connotations is supplemented by loading the concept of "fortune" with economic ones. "Fortune" continues to signify fate and the godhead of fate (see e.g. II. i. 391–394 and III. iii. 119–120), but sometimes it is also used to signify property and convenience (as in I. i. 148). It is again Constance who combines both significations:

> CONSTANCE: But fortune, O,
> She is corrupted, chang'd and won from thee;
> Sh' adulterates hourly with thine uncle John,
> And with her golden hand hath pluck'd on France
> To tread down fair respect of sovereignty,
> And made his majesty the bawd to theirs.
> France is a bawd to fortune and King John,
> That strumpet fortune, that usurping John!
>
> (II. ii. 54–61)

These shifts in the concept of "fortune" are the manner in which the play integrates "commodity" into the fatefully overdetermined course of a world fallen and burdened with guilt. The absolute and absolutely incalculable entity that distributes "commodities" is historical time in its constant transformations, bawdily creating opportunities from its abundance. Time generates agreements that are temporary at best, and its successful followers anticipate that it will therefore dynamize any legal order. Time as καιρός is set above the declared oath, the ordeal, and primogeniture. What a person is and to what that person will be entitled depends on his resources of mind and property and on his ability to employ them decisively, i.e. to utilize time as "commodity." However, when time becomes the sole ordering principle of the world, it is inevitable that every victory, every faith and even every betrayal become endangered and ambiguous, because steadfast loyalty toward *de facto* existing structures may under many circumstances very well be definable as a betrayal of the demands made by time. Categories of right or wrong under these circumstances are applicable only with difficulty:

> SALISBURY: But such is the infection of the time,
> That, for the health and physic of our right,
> We cannot deal but with the very hand
> Of stern injustice and confused wrong.
>
> (V. ii. 20–23)

The awareness that every agreement is precarious and can be overtaken by events, and the resultant compulsion to use one's time well is what determines the actions of all protagonists in the play. There are frequent emphatic reminders that the decisive turns in history, the broken and the renewed oaths as well as the other political and military actions, depend on favorable opportunities:

> SALISBURY: we must embrace
> This gentle offer of the perilous time.
>
> (IV. iii. 12–13)

There will be only one favorable opportunity for the lords to desert John and for Lewis to conquer England:

> LEWIS: Have I not here the best cards for the game
> To win this easy match play'd for a crown?
> And shall I now give o'er the yielded set?
>
> (V. ii. 105–107)

Also the marriage of Blanche and Lewis is possible only at a particular time:

> ELEANOR: I see a yielding in the looks of France;
> Mark, how they whisper: urge them while their souls
> Are capable of this ambition,
> Lest zeal, now melted by the windy breath
> Of soft petitions, pity and remorse,
> Cool and congeal again to what it was.
>
> (II. i. 474–479)

All alliances that are advantageous for a time will also be quickly overtaken by the course of time, however, as will be the principles on which one had put one's trust. The legal standards of the protagonists are the result of temporary commodities, and not vice versa. For example, John and Eleanor (I. i) declare the Bastard his stepfather's legitimate heir despite his extramarital conception, since the law of primogeniture, they say, overrules any disinheriting Last Will of the father:

> JOHN: Sirrah, your brother is legitimate;
> Your father's wife did after wedlock bear him,
> And if she did play false, the fault was hers;
> Which fault lies on the hazards of all husbands
> That marry wives.
>
> (I. i. 116–120)

But a little later, in scene II. i, Eleanor herself refers to a directive in Richard I's Last Will in order to repudiate Constance's claims to Arthur's royal heritage:

> ELEANOR: Thou unadvised scold, I can produce
> A will that bars the title of thy son.
>
> (II. i. 191–192)

The most eager proponent of a complete accommodation to time is the Bastard, being in his very existence the result of a favorable opportunity that he himself justifies (I. i. 259–276). The same is true of his social position: he can be integrated into the community of nobles because the war against France is being prepared and the court for this reason needs soldiers of fortune and war profiteers who plan in this conflict "to make a hazard of new fortunes" (III. i. 71). The Bastard constantly refers to the "spirit of the time" and by his own confession is engaged in mimicking this entity:

> BASTARD: The spirit of the time shall teach me speed.
>
> (IV. ii. 176)

He generally recommends this kind of accommodation:

> BASTARD: For he is but a bastard to the time
> That doth not smack of observation [. . .].
>
> (I. i. 207–209)

But even this absolute adaptation to time does not solve the dilemma of lost sovereignty. This becomes obvious when the Bastard toward the end begins to dominate John and is entrusted by him with "the ordering of this present time" (V. i. 77). As the *de facto* sovereign the Bastard orders the king to behave like a king so that one might imitate him. But at the same time he orders him to adapt to time:

> BASTARD: Let not the world see fear and sad distrust
> Govern the motion of a kingly eye!
> Be stirring as the time, be fire with fire,

Threaten the threat'ner, and outface the brow
Of bragging horror: so shall inferior eyes,
That borrow their behaviours from the great,
Grow great by your example [. . .].

(V. i. 46–52)

But if the king himself is told to become the figure of the only sovereign power, namely time, then how is he expected to regiment its structure by his "fiat?" How, by the same token, can he imitate an order that he is meant to implement through his performatives? Under the circumstances of time's hegemony, the monarch's word cannot establish the legitimacy of an act, the true value of a statement, or the identity of an object with durable and binding force. John himself appears to admit as much by declining to be held responsible for his decrees and by attributing them to favorable circumstance:

JOHN: It is the curse of kings to be attended
By slaves that take their humours for a warrant
To break within the bloody house of life,
And on the winking of authority
To understand a law, to know the meaning
Of dangerous majesty, when perchance it frowns
More upon humour than advis'd respect [. . .]
How oft the sight of means to do ill deeds
Make deeds ill done! Hadst not thou been by,
A fellow by the hand of nature mark'd,
Quoted and sign'd to do a deed of shame,
This murther had not come into my mind [. . .].

(IV. ii. 208–214/219–223)

But how could Hubert not understand John's utterances as the law, since the king's word has the force of law? That the king always speaks as king is simply the "curse of kings" that defeats John with the curse that each of his utterances redistributes the sovereign curse. Once again the double relation of curse and royal dignity is reflected in the ambiguity of the genitive. But when the king and his utterances are that much determined by opportunities, only "fortune" is, in the final analysis, sovereign. To rule requires taking one's distance; the insinuation of an absolute dictatorship of time, however, makes any stable distance impossible since it renders every position insecure. In *Richard III*, at least Richard is making plans; in *King John*, the only thing left is to seize opportunities. John structurally fails the task of maintaining his dignity under these conditions, of determining the course of time by adapting to it. John is quick-witted, to be sure, as he shows in II. i, III. ii, and elsewhere; he also constantly pushes people to hurry (see I. i. 178–179), but this mimicry to the fleetingness of time does not in itself establish order. Instead, the king is drawn into a circular motion in which he chases after his already existing sovereignty and yet can affirm it only by repeating the old rites. Evidence of this failure is the double repetition of John's coronation

(IV. ii; V. i). The more firmly John wants to meld with his sovereign role, the more its precarious and theatrical status manifests itself:

> JOHN: Here once again we sit, once again crown'd,
> And look'd upon, I hope, with cheerful eyes.
> PEMBROKE: This "once again", but that your highness pleas'd,
> Was once superfluous: you were crown'd before,
> And that high royalty was ne'er pluck'd off [. . .].
> SALISBURY: Therefore, to be possess'd with double pomp,
> To guard a title that was rich before,
> To gild refined gold, to paint the lily,
> To throw a perfume on the violet,
> To smooth the ice, or add another hue
> Unto the rainbow, or with taper-light
> To seek the beauteous eye of heaven to garnish,
> Is wasteful and ridiculous excess.
> PEMBROKE: But that your royal pleasure must be done,
> This act is as an ancient tale new told,
> And, in the last repeating, troublesome,
> Being urged at a time unseasonable.
>
> (IV. ii. 1–5/9–20)

The complaints of the nobles thematize, in phrases such as the "ancient tale new told," that the "reenactment of the coronation" does not merely suggest a *coup de théâtre* but also retroactively puts John's first coronation into a dramatic, and hence questionable, light. Again the theatrical situation is injected into the diegetic plot, insofar as the coronation itself already appears as State theater and in this "hollowness" seems equivalent to the coronation on Shakespeare's stage.[47] A further dimension of this reenactment is added by the fact that Pembroke's phrase "in the last repeating, troublesome" seems to allude to the Elizabethan drama *The Troublesome Raigne of Iohn King of England*, which has been alternatively considered to be a plagiarism, or the model and predecessor, of Shakespeare's *King John*.[48] In the latter case, Shakespeare's drama itself would rank as an imitation in the fourth degree. In this emphatic artificiality John's "look'd upon, I hope, with cheerful eyes" also addresses the audience that lets the theater continue to function as a precarious instrument of legitimation. But within the diegetic schema of *King John*, theater can at best serve to limit the damage done, i.e. to uphold temporarily the aporias of an impossible sovereignty. John's court theater—just like the one before the gates of Angiers—is marked as an imperiled institution. In his third coronation, by Pandulph, it is spelled out in detail, moreover, that his performances are also subject to the law of "commodity." John characterizes the sovereign pronouncement of sovereignty by the cardinal (that in malicious irony takes place on Ascension Day) as an exchange transaction under time pressure:

> PANDULPH: Take again (*Giving back the crown.*)
> From this my hand, as holding of the pope,

Your sovereign greatness and authority.
JOHN: Now keep your holy word: go meet the French,
And from his holiness use all your power
To stop their marches 'fore we are inflam'd. [. . .]
Then pause not; for the present time 's so sick
That present med'cine must be minist'red [. . .].

(V. i. 2–7/14–15)

The use of "inflam'd" introduces here that absolute metaphor which by the end of the play will have replaced that of the *theatrum mundi* and that of "commodity": the metaphor of fire. It is completely absent in *Richard III*, but (together with that of the festering wound) defines large parts, and especially the last act, of *King John*. It is consistently connected with war, hatred, and the pains of hell but appears also as an attribute of royalty and in this function is above all associated with John:

BASTARD: Ha, majesty! how high thy glory towers
When the rich blood of kings is set on fire! [. . .]
You equal potents, fiery kindled spirits! [. . .]
Be stirring as the time, be fire with fire [. . .].

(II. i. 350–351/358; V. i. 48)

Furthermore, a conception of historical events that increasingly imposes itself on the protagonists is concentrated in this metaphor: fire appears in *King John* as the image of time itself and especially of urgent time (as in V. i. 48 but also II. i. 67 and V. iv. 24–25). The more fiery the king becomes in his mimicry of time, the more he seems to consume himself:

JOHN: France, I am burn'd up with inflaming wrath [. . .]
PHILIP: Thy rage shall burn thee up, and thou shalt turn
To ashes [. . .].
JOHN: This tyrant fever burns me up [. . .].
Within me is a hell [. . .]

(III. i. 266/270–271; V. iii. 14; V. vii. 46)

The clandestine point in using this metaphor, however, is the implication that the devouring fire of time not only destroys the *dramatis personae* themselves but also all traces they leave behind, any memory of them, and the symbolic legitimations that derive from these traces and this memory. From such a perspective, survival in written traditions or other forms of representation appears extremely questionable, a survival that other texts of Shakespeare describe as if it was a secular form of salvation.[49] This ploy is carried off by means of an allegorical figure that represents the actors in *King John* as frail juxtapositions of signs, becoming unreadable and withering away in the world's conflagration. The fires of Time turn the very medium on which they are inscribed into ashes: Melun compares himself before his death with the impression in wax melting from the fire

(V. iv. 22–25), John describes himself in his farewell speech as writing on a parchment turning to ashes:

> JOHN: There is so hot a summer in my bosom,
> That all my bowels crumble up to dust:
> I am a scribbled form, drawn with a pen
> Upon a parchment, and against this fire
> Do I shrink up.
>
> (V. vii. 30–34)

By his death the king enters into history, but the metaphors suggest that history itself can be destroyed like the parchment to which its immortal memory has been committed. History as a failing attempt at control falls prey to the metaphorical and literal flames; and what the conflagration has seized will return only as irretrievably lost.[50] Time is consequently the greatest destroyer and the only sovereign in the kingdom of "commodity." Hence, John in his last words refers to himself as nothing more than a "module of confounded royalty" (V. vii. 58), "confounded" in this context suggesting both "destroyed" and "accursed."[51] Everything in *King John* has been smitten with the curse of time, a highly dynamic curse beyond all fixed, liturgical forms, opening the view onto a general *auto-da-fé*. Quite naturally, the theater continues to represent itself as an institution that rescues dissolution from dissolving by representing the events of history on stage and thus apparently saving them from the fire. But in *King John*, this very act of representation also marks a precipitous fall into time in which theater itself is included. This fall can be understood as a figure of secularization,[52] inasmuch as *saecularisatio* has always meant the return into temporality (as in the release of the cleric from his order to the station of a "secular priest").[53]

In this sense, Shakespeare in all his plays secularizes theological-political references; it is the novelty of *King John* that this process becomes a problem for the theater medium itself: the citizens of Angiers as well as the theater audience are given a demonstration that the distance of the spectator, judge, or neutral reporter is constitutively in danger. All observers are involved and implicated in what they observe. There is no firm place of ironic distance, external to the events, hence, the theater no longer appears as a secret sovereign as it did in *Richard III*. Just like its decrepit kings, this theater is involved in developments it cannot control. Time that may have temporarily made the theater into a hegemonic power can also destroy this hegemony. This is how Shakespeare in his representation of social processes avoids establishing a reliable perspective. What, after all this, can it mean that England should to itself "rest but true" (V. vii. 118)? It is a demonstratively hollow statement, especially since Shakespeare's plot development leaves every opportunity unused to corroborate the Bastard's patriotic appeal that ends the play.[54] Due to this display of hollowness, *King John* has not been and is not now a spectacular success at the box office. The heritage trusts find it very difficult to assimilate this drama because it plays with the destruction of a past, in which their cosy historicisms seek to make themselves at home. Situated in the dead angle between the Histories and the pure Tragedies, *King John* marks, outside the loop of the York and of the Lancaster tetralogy, the end of the Histories—whether the play was written before the Lancaster tetralogy or not. (Since there exist no Quartos or other sources for *King John* that would precede the first Folio, one can only speculate about the time of its writing and first performance.)

The world of the High Middle Ages seems to be confronted with more modern problems in *King John* than the late medieval world of the York tetralogy. In the following discussion, it will be shown that the representation of the ancient world in *King Lear* grapples with specifically modern concepts that were developed in order to redress the theological-juridical dilemmas which were the subject of *King John*, and in this function have not been set to rest to this day.

Notes

1 Peter Saccio, *Shakespeare's English Kings. History, Chronicle and Drama*, Oxford/New York, NY 2000, p. 190.
2 See the Arden edition of *King John*, ed. by Ernst A. J. Honigmann, London 2001, p. 159.
3 Craig M. Carver, *A History of English in its Own Words*, New York, NY 1991, p. 114.
4 See Chapter 1, section 1.3.
5 In Constance's emphatic formulation, "a king's oath" is qualitatively different from an ordinary oath (II. ii. 7–10).
6 Sigurd Burckhardt, *Shakespearean Meanings*, Princeton, NJ 1968, p. 138.
7 Burckhardt, ibid. p. 62.
8 Burckhardt, ibid. p. 125.
9 John Griffiths (ed.), *Two Books of Homilies Appointed To Be Read in Churches*, Oxford 1859, pp. 550–553.
10 Burckhardt, op. cit., pp. 124–126. And Hobbes still does the same when he is confronted with the question of how one should deal with two competing claims to the position of sovereign in one country: *Leviathan*, Oxford 1998, pp. 470–475.
11 Andrew Gurr, 'The Shakespearean Stage', in *The Norton Shakespeare*, New York, NY/London 1997, p. 3287.
12 Peter Brown, *Society and the Holy in Late Antiquity*, Berkeley, CA 1982, p. 311.
13 Brown, ibid.
14 John Hamilton Baker, *An Introduction to English Legal History*, London 1979, p. 11.
15 Burckhardt, op. cit., p. 168.
16 Brown, op. cit., p. 308.
17 James VI and I, *Political Writings*, Cambridge 1993, p. 32.
18 See Robert Bartlett, *Trial by Fire and Water. The Medieval Judicial Ordeal*, Oxford 1986, pp. 124–126.
19 See Chapter 1, section 1.1.
20 Max Weber, *The Protestant Ethic and the Spirit of Capitalism*, translated by Talcott Parsons, New York, NY 1958, p. 171.
21 Burckhardt, op. cit., p. 171.
22 See Frederick H. Russell, *The Just War in the Middle Ages*, Cambridge 1979, p. 26. The motif appears in precisely this sense also in *Richard III*, when Richmond speaks of "bloody trial of sharp war" (V. ii. 16).
23 Phyllis Rackin, *Stages of History. Shakespeare's English Chronicles*, Ithaca, NY 1990, p. 99.
24 Brown, op. cit., pp. 313–314.
25 Also in a different context the Bastard refers to a trial by combat as theater, "harness'd masque and unadvised revel" (V. ii. 132).

26 A biography of Shakespeare tells of a recontextualization of theater property that confirms this threat: during the forced removal of the "playhouse" of the Lord Chamberlain's Men in the winter of 1598, the weapons arsenal that was part of the stage props belonging to Shakespeare's troupe is said to have been used, even though only as a threat, against the subordinates of Giles Allen, the owner of the lot. (James Shapiro, *1599. A Year in the Life of William Shakespeare*, New York, NY 2005, pp. 1–2.)

27 How strongly the hegemonic discourses of Elizabethan England associate the Pope with his power to curse can be seen in the fact that he is often called the "bull" and Catholics are called "calves" on account of his excommunication bulls. *King John* as well alludes to the terminology of these invectives. (III. 1. 125; see the Arden edition of the play, p. 66.)

28 On this see William Haller, *Foxe's Book of Martyrs and the Elect Nation*, London 1963.

29 Baker, op. cit., p. 111.

30 Saccio, op. cit., p. 196.

31 Hobbes, op. cit., p. 341.

32 On the doctrine of the especial effectiveness of parental curses, see Keith Thomas, *Religion and the Decline of Magic. Studies in Popular Beliefs in Sixteenth- and Seventeenth-Century England*, London 1991, pp. 603–604.

33 On this concept, see Jacques Lacan, *The Psychoses. Seminar III*, translated by Russell Grigg, London/New York, NY 1993, p. 267.

34 David Martin Jones, *Conscience and Allegiance in Seventeenth Century England. The Political Significance of Oaths and Engagements*, Rochester 1999, p. 89; Albert R. Jonsen and Stephen Toulmin, *The Abuse of Casuistry*, Berkeley, CA 1988, p. 164. This context may also explain Pandulph's occasionally confusing syntactical constructions.

35 Burckhardt, op. cit., pp. 116–143.

36 See Chapter 1, section 1.2.

37 Constance's accumulation of these and similar oxymora (see e.g. III. iii. 25–28) also appears to imitate the rhetorical strategies of the ex-queen Elizabeth in *Richard III*.

38 Burckhardt, op. cit., pp. 141–142.

39 Jean-Christophe Agnew, *Worlds Apart, The Market and the Theater in Anglo-American Thought, 1550–1750*, Cambridge, MA 1986, p. 78.

40 Lucretius, *De rerum natura*, translated by W. H. D. Rouse, Cambridge, MA 1982, II. 216–224/289–293.

41 The whole preceding sentence seems to accommodate itself also mimetically to this *clinamen* (swerve) by constantly retreating from itself grammatically: until its end, 22 lines later, the reader waits in vain for the predicate of "France" in line 564.

42 See for example II. i. 352–355/391–394; II. ii. 4–61; III. i. 44–47; III. iii. 119–120; V. ii. 58–59.

43 On this liberation, see for example Agnew, op. cit., pp. 44–46.

44 See also what Timon in *Timon of Athens* says about gold: "This yellow slave will knit and break religions, bless the'accursed" (IV. iii. 34–35).

45 Weber, op. cit., pp. 176–178 and passim.

46 Jürgen Habermas, *The Theory of Communicative Action*, vol. 2, *Lifeworld and System: A Critique of Functionalist Reason*, translated by Thomas McCarthy, Boston, MA 1987, p. 288. The book's translator renders the quote as "[the basic religious consensus] was set communicatively aflow."

47 Stylistically, the redundancy of Salisbury's similes also reflects his criticism of the ceremony's redundancy.

48 On this relationship, see Ernst A. J. Honigmann's preface to the Arden edition, op. cit., pp. xi–lxxv.

49 See Chapter 1, section 1.5.

50 On the figure of the fire of time and its non-signifyingly signifying ashes, see Jacques Derrida, *Schibboleth. Für Paul Celan*, translated by Wolfgang Sebastian Baur, Wien 2002, p. 98.

51 Thomas McAlindon, *Shakespeare's Tragic Cosmos*, Cambridge/New York, NY/Melbourne 1991, p. 1.
52 Rackin, op. cit., p. 9.
53 Hans Blumenberg, *The Legitimacy of the Modern Age*, translated by Robert M. Wallace, Cambridge, MA/London 1983, p. 19.
54 See also David Scott Kastan, *Shakespeare and the Shapes of Time*, Hanover, NH 1982, p. 53.

CHAPTER 3

King Lear and the naturalized state of exception

3.1 Cordelia and the problem of equity

In the first Folio, *King Lear* is not listed among the Histories but among the Tragedies. Since the drama takes place in pre-Christian times, about 800 BCE, *Lear* is not burdened with the theological and dynastic ballast of *Richard III* or *King John*: the relationships do not appear too complicated, there are no explicit references to the chain of Lear's ancestors, the constellation of persons is fairytale-like and pastoral rather than historical. But there are nevertheless arguments that justify linking *Lear* with the Histories, at least as their vanishing point. Besides the facts that genre boundaries in Shakespeare are fluid anyway, that the 1608 Quarto version of *Lear* is titled a "true chronicle history," and that a major source of the play is a work of medieval historiography, namely Geoffrey of Monmouth's *Historia Regum Britanniae*, *Lear* deals with the same themes of sovereignty and representation as the Histories, presupposes them, and is situated at their horizon. What has preceded the play in the historical dramas is the deconstruction of divine, transcendent law. *King Lear* adds to this a deconstruction of the overdetermined threshold figure of "natural law" as it is emerging in Shakespeare's time. It will be shown that this transition from the unfolding of divine law to the unfolding of natural law entails a dissolution of the boundaries that used to enclose the theatrical curse.

Robert Weimann reads *King Lear* as a drama that performs a failure of signs: the play marks the point where signs are no longer at the service of power and representation accordingly founders.[1] But it should be apparent from the last chapters that the failure of representation and the insufficiencies of signs are already problems of the Histories. Rather, it is *Lear's* originality to stage a failing attempt at deriving consequences from these problems, namely to let language and judicature orient themselves toward a law that inheres in the course of the world. The concept of "nature," whose impressive ambiguities and overdeterminations, particularly in the early modern era, C. S. Lewis has convincingly expounded,[2] provides this project with its fateful focal point: the *Natura* which contrasts with the transcendent world of the divine yet is itself deified, which represents the most particular as well as the most general, the human and the inhuman, the perfect and the deficient, seems to offer jurisdiction a new form of support with whose help the law can adjust to the paradoxes of sovereignty instead of being overwhelmed by them.

That Shakespeare's dramas, especially *King Lear*, often allude to the conceptual language of natural law can be explained by the fact that his contemporaries, especially those of the higher estates, are discussing proto-Hobbesian "natural law" intensively.[3] It is an enormously intricate and multifunctional concept with a long history that derives its origin from the Aristotelian notion of φύσει δίκαιον. Aristotle is considered the founding father of natural law in the ancient world, even though his comments on this topic are brief and inconclusive. There is no Aristotelian concept of natural law; there are only scattered remarks.[4] The most prominent one can be found in his *Nicomachean Ethics*:

> What is politically just divides into the natural and the legal: the natural being what has the same force everywhere, and does not depend on a decision whether to accept it or not, the legal what in the beginning makes no difference whether enacted or not, but when enacted *does* make a difference [. . .].[5]

Aristotle further states that natural law gives everyone his due, hence is to be equated with justice. Cicero appropriates this concept and ontologizes it: in *De legibus* he writes that human law is part of a more comprehensive law that operates in nature and is identical with the principle of reason governing the world.[6] Roman jurisprudence partially adopts this idea and modifies it: digests of the *corpus iuris civilis* are influenced by the Ciceronian concept of natural law.[7] Among the authors of the digests, the Roman jurist Paulus embraces the idea of natural law most confidently. According to him, equity justly allots to all people what they are justly entitled to. This justice, however, has not been codified anywhere; as a quasi-transcendental law, it is partially realized in civil legislations without being identifiable with them. Natural law, then, becomes relevant only if the justice of civil law is called into doubt.[8] Natural law in this sense is not a system but an agency that intervenes correctively on a case-by-case basis, supplementing the written form of positive law.

This construction is translated into an explicitly Christian context by scholastic philosophy, especially that of Thomas Aquinas. Thomas theologizes the *lex naturalis*: according to the *Summa Theologica*, the law has four stages: first, God's eternal law (*lex aeterna*) that exists in the divine spirit and governs the world. This supreme law is only partially knowable to man; the knowable part is called *lex naturalis*, natural law. This law implies above all the right to pursue the good: all things toward which man has a natural inclination (*inclinatio naturalis*), primarily self-preservation, procreation, social life and the recognition of God, are components of natural law, within the limits imposed on these inclinations by reason.[9] Hence, the root of natural law would be the feeling of desire and aversion, qualified by intellect. By applying natural law, man can distinguish between good and evil. Human law (*lex humana*), that is primarily codified, positive law, originates because man must endeavor to derive positive laws from natural law and to apply them. Of assistance here is divine law (*lex divina*), which is not identical with God's eternal law but is rather the revealed, Biblical law that is meant to guide human reason.[10] This also justifies referring to the Bible as a source of laws. This very influential categorization attributes to the positive order of law the role of interpreting natural law; natural law is the rule to which human law must accommodate itself,[11] hence it is the law of law, a meta-law, as it were. Worldly law, according to the *Summa* and other medieval texts, imitates natural law. It adds particular points to the latter, but these particular aspects must mirror the general law of nature, must be an application of the general law to a specific place at a specific time.[12] Consequently, positive law is an application and imitation of natural law. The lawmaking, legislating sovereign becomes the relay station mediating between these two variables.[13] Through his mediation, this construction also serves to legitimize positive law as an echo of God's voice. In this context, Thomas declares monarchy to be the best, because the most harmonious form in the sense of natural law,[14] using here the sacralized analogy of the head that rules over the body.[15]

However, there are also contravening references to an immediate implementation of natural law, i.e. God directly punishing deviations from the natural order.[16] Some recalcitrant sinners, including monarchs, are miraculously executed by natural phenomena, such as the famous divine lightning bolt striking the culprit out of a blue sky. A large number of legends and anecdotes testify to such divine acts.[17] The curse is affiliated with this idea of natural law in that it articulates executions such as these. The invocation of natural law, understood in this sense, facilitates the constitution of extra-institutional tribunals such as when, for example, the injured party accuses and curses the transgressor in a private or public place (such as a market square or the main street).[18] But God's judgment, even when invoked in this manner, must be interpreted, and different parties may read it differently or refuse to acknowledge it.

During the Reformation, diverse attempts are made to tie the concept of natural law to new practices of inwardness. Many reformers perceive it primarily as the articulation of an interior, controlling agency; Philipp Melanchthon, for example, declares that the "voice of conscience," which proclaims the same ethical commandments to all human beings, proves the existence of natural law. Thus, he employs a circular logic by presupposing what would have to be proved, namely that conscience does indeed announce the same commandments to everyone.[19] But only insofar as conscience amounts to a social phenomenon, established, for instance, by State ceremonies of confessions and oaths,[20] is such an alignment of interests really incontestable. Contemporary English jurisprudence, by contrast, attempts directly to approximate natural to positive law. Many a jurist since the Reformation (Christopher St. German, for example) has considered English Common Law an amplification of natural law. This makes good sense primarily because Common Law is not an altogether coherent and consistent system of jurisprudence and its laws and procedures do not represent two independent factors but are connected by way of "precedent."[21] In the early modern discourse that engages with Common Law, St. Thomas's division of the law into four parts is tendentially avoided for obvious reasons. Instead, increasing attention is paid to Aristotle's concept of equity, which blurs the scholastic differentiation.[22] Already medieval judges in England occasionally follow less the letter of the law than what they see as its spirit and inner sense, and they justify this approach by referring to equity (ἐπιείκεια) which in the *Nicomachean Ethics* is explained rather laconically.[23] Aristotle defines equity as the correction of a law that is defective due to its universality. But equity corrects positive law in the interest of natural law since it accords to everyone what is rightfully his or hers by nature.[24] As early as 1468, the concept of equity is used most frequently in connection with the jurisdiction of the Court of Chancery. This court was authorized by the monarch to countermand the inevitable imperfections of positive law.[25] In this function, it was empowered to decide cases without recourse to precedents and to cancel decisions of other courts if they did not appear to agree with the principle of equity. The Court of Chancery, in other words, functioned as a resource of equity and was firmly established in this position around 1500.[26]

During Tudor times, the law is already perceived as a corpus of rules that is to be applied to facts; however, the Chancellor and the Court of Chancery are not concerned with this general law but with particular cases. It is the Chancellor's task to decide them according to his conscience. His verdict, rendered according to the principle of equity, demands faith in its adequateness, which must in the end be a blind faith. It is can be discerned that natural law assumes the role of a Derridean supplement in this context: it is a means for correcting and supplementing positive law but it is also its universal source. It is the most general, but also the most specific law; it frames positive law and is itself framed by it. The "nature" that natural law invokes is a system of cosmic order and, concurrently, the individual, corrective measure of finite human life. That these two factors are identical or at least compatible is the central wager of early modern natural law.

The identification of natural law and equity reduces the former to a methodological guideline according to whose rules law can be revised.[27] It is deontologized insofar as equity is not treated as an independent corpus of law but presupposes common law and supplements it in a subordinate function.[28] Attempts are made throughout the seventeenth century to formulate a true system of natural law as an alternative. But it is not until the 1630s that the great era of natural law theoreticians, such as Grotius, Hobbes and Pufendorf, begins. In contrast to the earlier natural law, theirs is systematic; it claims to derive a coherent, general scheme of natural laws from first principles.[29] During Shakespeare's time, theoretical discussion had not yet attained this level. Instead, the king's double body is all the more fervently inserted into the gap between positive and natural law: the monarch is seen as the incarnation of justice.[30] It is the king who ultimately presides over the Court of Chancery; the Chancellor is but his deputy, one of whose titles is "Keeper of the King's Conscience."[31] James I in particular intensively grappled with the resultant questions about the natural rights of kings. More than any other English monarch of the early modern era, he is a propagator and proponent of natural equity, which he defines in the customary Aristotelian way: it gives "euery one that which is meetest for him."[32] Hence, the king represents natural order within society; "nature" is an ideological key concept for James. However, when he addresses his son in *Basilikon Doron* as "Natural Successour," even this familial relationship must be supplemented by a curse that qualifies natural kinship:

> To conclude then, I charge you, as euer yee thinke to deserue my Fatherly blessing, to follow and put in practise, as farre as lyeth in you, the praecept hereafter following. And if yee follow the contrary course, I take the Great GOD to record, that this Booke shall one day bee a witnesse betwixt mee and you; and shall procure to bee ratified in Heauen, the curse that in that case here I giue unto you. For I protest before that Great GOD, I had rather not bee a Father, and childlesse, then bee a Father of wicked children.[33]

Once more, James invokes God as supreme judge,[34] this time in order to secure the legally not completely codifiable process of the *translatio imperii* through the power of a sacred curse. That the *Basilikon Doron* is addressed to his son and only indirectly to the rest of his subjects can be considered symptomatic insofar as James generally tends to conceptualize the situation of governance with the help of a family metaphor. He equates the relationship between king and subjects with that between father and children.[35] Thus, the former as well as the latter cannot be based on positive, codified laws but only on reciprocal natural obligations.[36] In keeping with this analogy, the parental authority to pronounce a prophetic curse is transferred to the king and his representatives:

> O inuert not the order of nature, by iudging your superiours in your owne particular! But assure your selfe, the blessing or curse of the Parents, hath almost euer a Propheticke power ioyned with it: and if there were no more, honour your Parents, for the lengthning of your owne dayes, as GOD in his Law promiseth. Honour also them that are *in loco Parentum* vnto you, such as your gouernours, up-bringers, and Praeceptours: be thankefull vnto them and reward them, which is your dewtie and honour.[37]

In James' conception of nature, "body natural" and "body politic" merge. Under Edward II, the doctrine of the king's two bodies had been invoked in order to legitimate opposition to the monarch, on the grounds that the oath of allegiance had been sworn to the king as "body politic" and not to the king as an individual. On the occasion of *Calvin's Case*, even the traditionalistic Chief Justice Lord Edward Coke in 1609 explicitly rejects this thesis as "damnable and damned consequent" and states that the loyalty oath is due the royal person in its "natural capacity."[38] The obedience the subject owes the sovereign is, according to Coke, a natural obligation, a law of nature. Again, reference is made to the continuity of royal "blood," i.e. to the continuous line of descent as the marker of legitimacy.[39] Together with the royal bodies, the speech acts constituting sovereignty also move into the context of nature and become echoes of a pre-existing natural law: for James the "oath of allegiance" is merely "the profession of their naturall Allegiance to their Soueraigne," the ritual confirmation of existing obligations.[40] In further disquisitions on *Calvin's Case*, Coke reiterates his conviction that the king is "a natural liege lord and his people natural liege subjects." The positive laws only prescribe the form that this natural alliance assumes, he writes; hence, swearing an oath only serves to confirm an already existing duty of loyalty.[41] This form of the oath ceremony by which the subject affirms existing quasi-familial obligations recalls the familial contest instituted by Lear which is meant to serve as the redundant affirmation of a land distribution that has already been decided on. In Lear's contest, parental and royal power do in fact coincide since the participating subjects are the king's daughters; this arrangement obviously favors an argumentation in terms of natural law, and thus its deconstruction appears all the more definitive.

Natural law in the early seventeenth century is a phantasm which fills in the gaps in the legal order occupied by the sovereign and thereby justifies their continuing existence. In this function it assumes an important role in Stuart ideology; in particular, it is supposed to connect cosmic order and social order via the person of the monarch. Hobbes and his latent integration of the state of nature into the state of the commonwealth[42] can *mutatis mutandis* still be understood best in this context: according to Agamben, Hobbesian sovereign violence is the incorporation of the state of nature (differently defined as "war of all against all") into society; this incorporation creates a zone of indistinction between nature and culture, violence and law:

> It is important to note that in Hobbes the state of nature survives in the person of the sovereign, who is the only one to preserve its natural *ius contra omnes*. Sovereignty thus presents itself as an incorporation of the state of nature in society, or, if one prefers, as a state of indistinction between nature and culture, between violence and law, and this very indistinction constitutes specifically sovereign violence.[43]

Agamben goes on to say that, through the suspension of the law in the state of exception which the Hobbesian sovereign incarnates, the legal order includes within itself that which eludes it, i.e. life.[44] In the person of the sovereign, law coincides with reality. This coincidence can be interpreted in different ways: one might say that the law is constantly realized under these circumstances; but one could also say with Agamben that it becomes unimplementable. In either case, it cannot be formulated, it prohibits or commands nothing.[45] Benjamin has already formulated a similar thought in the *Trauerspielbuch*, stating that it is the *telos* of the Baroque sovereign, who is typified in tragic drama as a tyrant, to let the order of nature and the order of law coincide:

> The function of the tyrant is the restoration of order in the state of exception: a dictatorship whose utopian goal will always be to replace the unpredictability of historical accident with the iron constitution of the laws of nature.[46]

The play *King Lear* enacts precisely this royal utopia as well as its disastrous failure. In this play, Shakespeare unfolds and hyperbolizes the necessary paradoxes and overdeterminations of Jacobean natural law theory as well as those of Tudor ideology.[47] *Lear* achieves this by way of an experiment in which the utopia of sovereignty invoked by Benjamin is representatively implemented. The core theme of the drama is the idea of a sovereign decree as the institutionalization of natural order, that is, as the alignment of affective inclinations, natural processes and social obligations. Right from the opening dialogue between Kent and Gloucester, the relation between natural inclination and social obligation takes centre stage:

> KENT: I thought the King had more affected the Duke of Albany than Cornwall.
> GLOUCESTER: It did always seem so to us: but now, in the division of the kingdom, it appears not which of the dukes he values most, for qualities are so weighed that curiosity in neither can make choice of either's moiety.
> (I. i. 1–6)

With this utterance, Gloucester already lets it be known that in the court's official ideology royal "affection" is assumed to be codependent with his subjects' "value" or "qualities." It seems evident to the speaker that the affects the sovereign extends in *inclinatio naturalis* to his noblemen are directly proportionate to their qualities. A world is presupposed in which the king gives his affection to the most worthy, and therefore the person so affected is *per definitionem* justified in his position. This means, one is confronted with a world in which the sovereign affect constitutes the symbolic order. (Besides, his utterance indicates that Lear—contrary to the principle of primogeniture—has already distributed the parts of the country among his three heirs before the play begins. Hence, the ensuing love contest is intended as a purely formal ceremony in which the king's familial subjects will meekly accede to his sovereign decision.) The focus of the dialogue soon shifts from the national family to Gloucester's closer relatives and hence from the Lear plot to the Gloucester plot:

> KENT: Is not this your son, my lord?
> GLOUCESTER: His breeding, sir, hath been at my charge. I have so often blushed to acknowledge him that now I am brazed to 't.
> KENT: I cannot conceive you.
> GLOUCESTER: Sir, this young fellow's mother could; whereupon she grew round-wombed, and had, indeed, sir, a son for her cradle ere she had a husband for her bed. Do you smell a fault?
> (I. i. 7–15)

In a well-established Shakespearean manner, the locution "breeding at my charge" consists of two interweaving and mutually supportive ambiguities: if one reads "breeding" as "rearing" and "charge" as "expenses," the phrase would imply that

Gloucester has taken care of Edmund during the latter's childhood. If "breeding" is interpreted as "procreating" and "charge" as "task," however, then Edmund's begetting itself is declared an obligation that Gloucester has fulfilled as a sort of "natural imperative." That this imperative is somewhat contrary to positive law, however, is suggested when Gloucester contrasts Edmund with Edgar, the "son by order of law" (I. i. 18). Gloucester's utterances are full of equivocations whose slipperiness he obviously enjoys. He continues in this attitude when he brings the double meaning of "conception" into play. Throughout these equivocations Gloucester, partly in earnest, partly in jest, treats inclination and obligation as equivalents. Clandestinely, this rhetorical production of equivalencies also points to the idea that man's natural inclinations are, within the bounds of reason, the expression of a non-codified law. Lear's kingdom seems to be subject to the unwritten commandment to enjoy. Gloucester, protected by his social status, in this context uses the idea of natural law in order to ironically justify his transgressions as commandments he has received from a superior law, quasi from a sexual state of exception. The question of his responsibility is thereby suspended, or rather shifted: Gloucester, in this as in other scenes, tends to attribute responsibility for the situation to those below him, in this case to Edmund himself ("this knave came something saucily to the world before he was sent for," I. i. 20–21). He distances himself from his son with the same formulation with which he acknowledges him; for this purpose, he devises another ambiguous commandment that includes its own transgression: "the whoreson must be acknowledged" (I. i. 22–23). This simultaneous acknowledgement and rejection seems to define Edmund's subject status. He grows up in a double bind[48] which integrates him into society as his father's son but also keeps him in the position of an outsider as a "whoreson." Gloucester's remark: "He hath been out nine years, and away he shall again" (I. i. 30–31), furthermore suggests that Edmund is not an acknowledged and regular member of Gloucester's household, but that, depending on his father's whims, he is occasionally called to join the court and is then sent away again. This formulation in the passive voice once more affords Gloucester the opportunity to ambiguously represent Edmund as the active agent of his dislocations so that Gloucester himself can remain unnamed as their true cause. The figure of inclusive exclusion by which Edmund is subordinated to his father appears as the necessary complement of the self-sublating natural law to which Gloucester claims to be answerable. This abject status is presumably the reason why Edmund hates his father so fervently. But it will be shown in the following discussion that Edmund, by the opportunistic revenge he takes on his father, actually proves his successor in spirit.

Kent, for his part, responds rather half-heartedly to Gloucester's amusement (I. i. 16–17). He does play with the ambiguity of "issue" and "proper," but his pun sounds forced when compared with Gloucester's witticisms. Kent appears to be uncomfortable in this situation, that is at least suggested by the fact that his remarks become ever shorter and more distanced. When Gloucester presents Edmund to Kent, the latter reacts with the words: "I must love you, and sue to know you better" (I. i. 29). His "must" establishes the distance he maintains from

Edmund throughout the play. In Kent's utterance, the affection is also represented like an obligation but in this case the hierarchy of affect and duty is reversed. With him, affect appears to be derived from obligation and not vice versa. Even during the last act, Kent and Gloucester, among others, will mostly be occupied with using the same discourse strategies in order to distance themselves from tragic situations. Thus, the first 30 lines of *Lear* elliptically introduce the themes that define major parts of the drama; and this is done in the engaging tone of a comedy that makes the audience its accomplices. After this short, informal exposition Lear's entrance starts a longer and more ceremonious development:

> LEAR: Meantime we shall express our darker purpose.
> Give me the map there. Know that we have divided
> In three our kingdom; and 'tis our fast intent
> To shake all cares and business from our age,
> Conferring them on younger strengths, while we
> Unburdened crawl toward death.
>
> (I. i. 35–40)

Whereas Kent and Gloucester primarily have used expositives in their dialogue, the mode now shifts toward exercitives: Lear almost exclusively gives orders ("attend," "give me," "tell me"). He even turns a piece of information into a command by introducing it with "know that." It is as if he needed the constant repetition of the decisive speech act of sovereign power[49] to assure himself continuously of his own sovereignty. Moreover, Lear refers to himself as "we", using the *pluralis maiestatis*. That is a conventional but significant gesture: he speaks of himself as of a corporation to whose wishes he merely gives expression. The "shall" in "we shall express our darker purpose" also hints at an imperative to which he himself is subjected. In the same vein he often uses the passive voice to describe his own actions ("here are to be answered," I. i. 48), as if these were uncontrollable events in which he merely participates. Accordingly, in Lear's metaphors faculties such as his "intent" appear personified and in interaction with the *dramatis personae*; his performatives allegorize his intentions and passions:

> LEAR: We have this hour a constant will to publish
> Our daughters' several dowers, that future strife
> May be prevented now.
>
> (I. i. 42–44)

Similarly to Richard II, Lear uses an abundance of ceremonious performatives and surrounds himself with their protection. But even more strongly than Richard he gives the impression of being inhibited and suffocated by them, as if he felt ill at ease in the face of their incalculable and sovereignly independent existence, which cannot be clearly separated from his own life. He seems to think that his decrees are so definitive and powerful as to determine the future with the inevitability of a natural law, both in preventing "future strife" and in rendering his allotments irrevocable: "to thine and Albany's issue be this *perpetual*" (I. i. 66–67, emphasis added); "to thee and thine hereditary *ever* remain this ample third of our kingdom" (I. i. 79–80, emphasis added). In his characterization, the royal person to whose intentions he constantly refers appears so static and immutable ("our fast intent," "a constant will") as if it were located outside of all spatial and temporal contingencies. Lear postulates a Lear beyond Lear, a second linguistic body of the king, who would be a truly unlimited, absolute ruler and himself, as it were, a natural law. But, by way of contrast, he also minds the mortality and affectivity of his natural body and takes care of it by expressing the desire to "crawl unburdened toward death." This natural body's impermanence, moreover, seems to have an effect on the timelessness of his eternal body in that he does not simply refer to his "constant will," but to "this hour a constant will." Just as the term "nature" uneasily amalgamates a divine, eternally creative power and its fallen, passive products,[50] so the "two natures" of the king's body become indistinguishable in an overdetermined "Natural body." Through this implicit, arduously concealed collapse of the sovereign's two bodies into one another, the sovereign becomes his own big Other, but he thereby also loses any connection with the other outside of this self-relation; every other becomes for him a metonymy of the manifold monarch.[51] This loss is symptomatically revealed by his custom of addressing the men exclusively as metonymies of his own or adjoining territories: "Gloucester," "Cornwall," and "Albany" as well as "the vines of France and milk of Burgundy."

The official ceremony Lear inaugurates in I. i is subject to similar implosions: his abdication is not really an abdication, or rather is a somewhat mysterious one. On the one hand, he does announce "to shake all care and business from our age," but, on the other hand, he affirms that he will "retain all th' addition to a king" (I. i. 136–137). His rite seems to constitute an act of State that is designed to add a further attribute to his regality, namely dominion through a natural eminence that is so total that it absolves him of actually ruling. Through a sovereign abdication, Lear surrenders himself and his country to an unrestricted natural law. In the words of the Fool, Lear plays "bo-peep" (I. iv. 168) with himself. This self-effacing act of State is supplemented by the division of the kingdom in a contest that is no contest: the realm, as mentioned, has been divided into three parts by the time the drama begins, and these are to be allotted each to one daughter, or rather their husbands. Strictly speaking, the ceremony will not even effect a real division because the territorial boundaries that Lear has drawn will be almost instantly rejected by his heirs.[52] What actually occurs is merely the representation of a partition by drawing new boundaries on a map (I. i. 63), like the unification of Scotland and England under James which also mainly took place on paper at first. It might be worth pursuing this parallel between Lear and James, as has been occasionally done before.[53] James, who after Elizabeth's death has become king of both England and Scotland, likes to see himself as the unifier of Britain. Lear would then be a kind of anti-James: while James is the first king of Britain, Lear is the last. But in another respect, Lear is closer to James than the latter would like to admit, as becomes evident by the way the daughterly love contest is defined:

> LEAR: Tell me, my daughters [. . .]
> Which of you shall we say doth love us most,
> That we our largest bounty may extend
> Where nature doth with merit challenge.
>
> (I. i. 48/51–53)

Again, the drama touches upon a problem of natural law, this time that of natural virtue ("merit") which Lear identifies with love. Since antiquity and especially during the early modern age, the semantics of love oscillates in that it positions love as an impassioning affect beyond morality, while also declaring it the natural epicenter of the moral good.[54] It is not only Lear who tries to align his double regality with this double entendre; a general tendency exists in the English Renaissance, especially since Elizabeth, to add a touch of verbal eroticism to the relationship between monarch and subject.[55] While in the Middle Ages the subject is bound to the king primarily by moral and legal obligations, the discourse about this allegiance changes during the Renaissance: the monarch is frequently described as a subject and object of love and as such stands both inside and outside the law. It was mentioned before that the early modern English monarchs, due to their variously precarious positions, must to a high degree rely on their personal charisma and on the emotionally tinged devotion of their retainers. In this situation, Elizabeth finds intelligent ways of claiming the affection of her subjects; in speeches she describes her relationship to the English people in terms that border on the erotic and passionate:

> Yet I do not thank for that nor for all the rest so much as for this: that after twenty-eight years' reign I do not perceive any diminition [sic] of my subjects' good love and affection towards me. This is the thing I most joy in and that wherein I take my greatest comfort, and without which I would not desire to live; for then life should be a death unto me [. . .].
>
> I must needs say and confess that there was never prince more bound to his people than I am to you all. I can but acknowledge your great love and exceeding care of me to be such as I shall never be able to requite, having but one life, except I had as many lives as you all. But I will never forget it while I shall breathe. [. . .]
>
> I do assure you there is no prince that loveth his subjects better, or whose love can countervail our love. There is no jewel, be it of ever so rich a price, which I set before this jewel – I mean your loves. For I do more esteem it than any treasure or riches, for that we know how to prize.[56]

After his accession James tries to use similar language but is clearly less successful than his female predecessor both in rhetorical and in political terms, which may have to do with the fact that he ties his declaration of love more strongly to a concept of duty:

> So my Soueraigntie obligeth mee to yeeld to you loue, gouernment and protection: Neither did I euer wish happinesse to my selfe, which was not conjoyned with the happinesse of my people.[57]

This regal discourse remains ambiguous above all insofar as the *inclinatio naturalis* that it propagates is meant to consolidate a hierarchical legal relation, whereas the declared willingness to transgress socially imposed boundaries is an indispensable part of the repertory of rhetorical formulas that express amorous proclivity. It is only with juridical contortions that this political phantasm can be sustained, and James's familialism is one of them. In the case of Lear, the absurdity of the *topos* is somewhat mitigated, since the inferiors who subject themselves to him by their declarations of love are also his daughters and thus seem to be connected to him in a closer and more natural relation. But in what follows, Lear will have to implicitly acknowledge what the decreed contest was meant to conceal: the symbolic character of paternity:[58]

> GONERIL: Sir, I love you more than word can wield the matter,
> Dearer than eyesight, space and liberty,
> Beyond what can be valued, rich or rare,
> No less than life, with grace, health, beauty, honour,
> As much as child e'er loved, or father found,
> A love that makes breath poor and speech unable,
> Beyond all manner of so much I love you.
>
> (I. i. 55–61)

Goneril adapts to Lear's project to let convention and affection coincide by citing conventions of passionate affectivity. Her speech accumulates traditional *topoi* of love poetry, assonances with sonnets by Shakespeare and Donne being discernible. She depicts love as a traumatizing force that strikes the lover with the inability to express it in words. The absolute transcendence of her proclaimed love suggests a kind of negative erotology which connects the language of mysticism with the courtly ideal of love: her affection is described as something that transcends not only words ("more than words can wield the matter," "that makes breath poor and speech unable") but also what is beyond words ("beyond the manner of so much I love you").

The love declaration refers to a sublime affective motion that occurs in a place beyond language and beyond acts while it allows the speaker to ensconce herself within these very words: Goneril's evocation of a transcendent emotive sphere excludes *a priori* all obligations and active manifestations of her love because in their finiteness and contingency they could only be perceived as qualifying constraints. Hence, the love Goneril promulgates cannot effectuate any realization outside of this promulgation itself. It is precisely this impossible substantiation that Regan declares to be her own accomplishment in love:

> REGAN: In my true heart
> I find she names my very deed of love:
> Only she comes too short, that I profess
> Myself an enemy to all other joys
> Which the most precious square of sense possesses,
> And find I am alone felicitate
> In your dear highness' love.
>
> (I. i. 70–76)

Inevitably, Regan's proclaimed transgressive and absolute subjugation assumes incestuous traits, carrying her to the point of rejecting any bodily pleasure that is not incited by the father. Insofar as "dear highness' love" can be read both as an objective and as a subjective genitive, this locution implies a phantasmatic union in absolute desire while remaining dependent on the language it disparages and claims to surpass.

It is striking that Cordelia in her asides at first also emphasizes the transcendence of her affection and the deficiency of words in affairs of the heart. At times, she even uses the same terminology as her sisters: "What shall Cordelia speak? Love, and be silent. [. . .] I am sure my love's more ponderous than my tongue. [. . .] I cannot heave my heart into my mouth" (I. i. 62/77–78/91–92). A paraphrase of these monologic asides in her official declaration should therefore satisfy Lear. Why, then, does she reply "nothing" when Lear demands that she outdo her sisters? Lear's request, as indicated, is a double bind: on the one hand, the daughters are told to inscribe themselves into a quasi-feudal symbolic system, on the other, they are to demonstrate an affection that transcends these feudalistic bonds; thus, they are told to colonize the field beyond obligatory speech acts by way of a speech act. Regan and Goneril handle this demand according to protocol by pretending that symbolic bond and affect are, if not identical, then perfectly synchronized. After having been ordered to top her sisters, Cordelia articulates what remains suppressed in this phantasm:

> CORDELIA: I love your majesty
> According to my bond, no more nor less.
>
> (I. i. 92–93)

Turning the protestations of her sisters upside down, Cordelia's utterance posits an obligation as the upper and lower limit of her passion and thus insists on a operative separation between affect and law which the whole ceremony was designed to circumvent. Geoffrey Hartmann calls Cordelia's "nothing" a "curse" inasmuch as it sabotages the familial, *qua* divine, blessing.[59] The decisive point in this context is that Cordelia's curse articulates that the symbolic order divides and splits her and that *mutatis mutandis* it also splits Lear. Her curse reveals an inherent bisection in the subject addressed as well as in the subject speaking. Emphasizing that she endangers her "fortunes" (to which we will return in section 3.5), Lear demands of Cordelia to close this gap again:

> LEAR: How, how, Cordelia? Mend your speech a little,
> Lest you may mar your fortunes.
>
> (I. i. 94–95)

Instead of acceding to this ultimately impossible demand, Cordelia enlarges upon her remark about the formalization of emotions which necessarily conditions commitment by describing her love, Lear's love, and the love of her sisters as limited symbolic resources which circulate in a web of reciprocal obligations:

> CORDELIA: Good my lord,
> You have begot me, bred me, loved me. I
> Return those duties back as are right fit,
> Obey you, love you and most honour you.
> Why have my sisters husbands, if they say
> They love you all?
>
> (I. i. 95–100)

The problem arising from this economization is not so much that Cordelia's confession of love fails to come off as sufficiently exuberant, but that it implies the separation of Lear's two bodies: the declaration denies to Lear his role as the big Other, as the incarnation of the transcendent, inexhaustible source of good and bad gifts as whom Lear admonished Cordelia to acknowledge and love him. Also Cordelia's question about her sisters' husbands must provoke Lear who understands all *personae* as metonymies of his own person. As a defense reaction, Cordelia's curse triggers an elaborate, pseudo-pagan counter-curse from Lear by which he attempts to reassert his endangered position:

> LEAR: Let it be so. Thy truth then be thy dower,
> For by the sacred radiance of the sun,
> The mysteries of Hecate and the night,
> By all the operation of the orbs
> From whom we do exist and cease to be,
> Here I disclaim all my paternal care,
> Propinquity and property of blood,
> And as a stranger to my heart and me
> Hold thee from this forever.
>
> (I. i. 109–117)

In performative contradiction, this expulsion presupposes what it is meant to deny: that even blood ties ("propinquity and property of blood") are linguistically mediated relationships that can be established and dissolved by decree.[60] It is already apparent at this stage that Lear, with his curses and conditional self-imprecations, expels not only the accursed but also his own person from his royal presence. The curse splits the execrated daughter in inclusive exclusion but it does the same to the curser who denies his kinship with the accursed even as his own curse testifies to it. With a proclamation of his fealty, Kent interrupts this ceremony:

> KENT: Royal Lear,
> Whom I have ever honoured as my king,
> Loved as my father, as my master followed [. . .].
>
> (I. i. 140–142)

But immediately after this protestation of deference Kent questions Lear's authority as ruler, father, and king and addresses him in a rather undiplomatic manner as "thou" and "old man." Once more, the problem is not so much that Kent demands against protocol for the distribution of land to be revoked (I. i. 150/165). Instead, it consists of the seemingly supplementary circumstance that he disputes the king's capacity to perform effective speech acts:

> LEAR: Now by Apollo –
> KENT: Now by Apollo, King,
> Thou swear'st thy gods in vain.
>
> (I. i. 161–162)

That this attack on his perlocutionary power is what enrages Lear the most, he emphasizes in his banishment of Kent, an act safeguarded by further oaths:

> LEAR: Hear me, recreant, on thine allegiance, hear me:
> That thou hast sought to make us break our vows,
> Which we durst never yet, and with strained pride
> To come betwixt our sentences and our power,
> Which nor our nature, nor our place can bear,
> Our potency made good, take thy reward.
> Five days we do allot thee for provision,
> To shield thee from disasters of the world,
> And on the sixth to turn thy hated back
> Upon our kingdom. If on the next day following
> Thy banished trunk be found in our dominions,
> The moment is thy death. Away! By Jupiter,
> This shall not be revoked.
>
> (I. i. 168–180)

A hitherto largely uncommented peculiarity can be seen in the fact that this banishment occurs in the first place, and is subsequently accepted as legally valid: insofar as Lear has already abdicated, it should be Albany's or Cornwall's prerogative to judge Kent or at least to approve of Lear's verdict. Besides this additional indication that Lear's resignation is not a real resignation, his utterance seems paradoxical for yet another reason: he calls Kent a traitor ("recreant"), but at the same time orders him to listen "on his allegiance." But if Kent were a traitor, it would not be sensible to appeal to his loyalty, and if he were loyal, it would make no sense to call him a traitor. Again, the figure of inclusive exclusion can be discerned in the relations between the characters. But rather more interesting for the present question is Lear's rationale for banishing Kent: he accuses Kent of having tried to make him violate his oath ("sought to make us break our vows") and thereby to uncouple his speech from his power, i.e. to question his natural performative force ("to come betwixt our sentences and our power"). That Lear sees the oaths he himself has sworn as instruments in his execution of performative power seems perplexing at first: usually, these speech acts appear in Shakespeare's plays as problematic means of disciplining their speakers;[61] in other words, they serve as performative utterances that do not create sovereign authority but its opposite, symbolic submission. For example, an oath founds the fealty of a vassal to his liege lord, and this fealty enables Lear to address Kent as his subject: the "allegiance" Lear demands is based on Kent's "oath of allegiance." The ability to perjure himself is even a sign of sovereignty for Henry V. For Lear, however, the bond established by his oath seems to have a vital function: both his nature and his position become suspect when the efficacy of his vows is called into doubt or when he is asked to break them ("which nor our nature, nor our place can bear"). By his oaths, Lear apparently affirms and restores the sound relationship between his nature and his place, i.e. between his mortal and his immortal body. Through the ligatures of his oaths (extending and varying his coronation oath), he keeps his sovereign body in shape despite the contradictory concepts of nature squirming and squabbling inside it. Hence, he supplements his curse with another oath on Kent's banishment ("By Jupiter, this shall not be revoked") that has no comprehensible function other than to make Lear vouch for his own statement before himself.

When marrying off Cordelia, Lear still employs an intrinsically contradictory rhetoric: on the one hand, he stresses that he has dissolved all bonds that tie him to Cordelia, so that she is now "a stranger to my heart and me" (I. i. 116), completely unrelated to him, "for we have no such daughter" (I. i. 264–265). But, on the other, she remains closely attached to him insofar as attributes like "adopted to our hate" (I. i. 204) and "dowered with our curse" (I. i. 205) emphasize their persisting kinship. Again, inclusive exclusion becomes the determining figure in a relation between parent and child. France reacts to this situation by eroticizing the position of the ostracized. His own words attest that the fire of his passion is fanned by Cordelia's expulsion: "'Tis strange that *from* their cold'st neglect my love should kindle to inflamed respect" (I. i. 256–257, emphasis added). And he describes his future spouse as "most rich being poor, most choice forsaken and most loved despised" (I. i. 252–253). According to these utterances his love, or at least its paroxysm, depends on Cordelia's newly allotted position as the discarded, inverted image of Lear's sovereignty. The preceding love contest has raised the question of how the supposed absolute transcendence of love can be integrated into the firm symbolic "bonds" that constitute society; a convincing answer could not be found. France marks a provisional escape from this dilemma by declaring his love for a person who has fallen out of her former sphere and is standing on the threshold between social existence and non-existence. This move is not free from a latently sadistic component that lets the own abundance of power be mirrored in the powerlessness of the loved object—France emphasizes her status as "cast away" (I. i. 255) and "thrown to my chance" (I. i. 258) without mentioning that their marriage amounts to a political windfall for him in that it will legitimate his interference in English politics. (The parallel with the Dauphin's marriage to the English king's granddaughter Blanche in *King John* has rarely been drawn. But it might be read as an implicit commentary on this scene.) Nonetheless, France suggests a solution that does not conceal or suppress the problem of political affectivity. But for this suggestion he seems to pay the price of his own transcendentalization, for he entirely vanishes from the play after his declaration; only his name remains. He leaves behind a dilemma that continues to confront all the *dramatis personae*; for in this initial scene the fatal aporias of natural law have merely been introduced, but not yet explored.

3.2 Goneril and Regan within the liberties of nature

Lear's abdication in favor of his own natural eminence puts the British kingdom under the rule of nature, presuming there *is* a legal order inherent in nature. But a problem soon becomes virulently apparent, namely that there's no consensus whatsoever on the statutes of this order. Almost all characters (Lear, Gloucester, Kent, Cornwall, Regan, Cordelia, Albany, France, and Edmund) enlist nature's help with competing and often contradictory aims. Consequently, nature seems to contend with itself, without ever satisfying the claims of her numerous adherents. For example, Albany (like Lear) uses organicist metaphors in order to refer to a judgment by nature on nature, triggered by Goneril's and Regan's turn against their father:

> ALBANY: That nature which contemns its origin
> Cannot be bordered certain in itself.
> She that herself will sliver and disbranch
> From her material sap perforce must wither,
> And come to deadly use.
>
> (IV. ii. 33–37)

In *Lear*, even divinities seem to be nothing more than henchmen of the supreme, most ambivalent godhead "Nature."[62] Especially Albany, Gloucester, and Kent, but also Edgar, assign to the gods the role of avenging guarantors of the familial order *qua* natural order:

> EDGAR: The gods are just and of our pleasant vices
> Make instruments to plague us [. . .].
>
> (V. iii. 168–169)

According to Gloucester, even demons participate in executing this jurisdiction: for example, he threatens Regan with the revenge of the Fury[63] as a reinstatement of parental authority:

> GLOUCESTER: but I shall see
> The winged vengeance overtake such children.
>
> (III. vii. 64–65)

It is assumed that transgressions against the cosmic order inevitably call down punishments and that the gods are responsible for this disciplining. Spontaneous killings and mutilations are consequently considered manifestations of divine judgment. Albany, for one, perceives the news of Cornwall's death as confirmation of the world's good organization:

> ALBANY: This shows you are above,
> You justicers, that these our nether crimes
> So speedily can venge.
>
> (IV. ii. 79–81)

But Albany's utterances also reveal that "nature" takes on a double role in these argumentations: it functions as a personified cosmic system of order but also as a measure of man's limited life. It is insinuated that both aspects are identical or at least compatible, but this insinuation entraps Kent and others in paradoxical formulations, for example in the storm of III. iv, when he tries to persuade Lear to seek shelter in the hovel:

> KENT: The tyranny of the open night's too rough
> For nature to endure.
>
> (III. iv. 2–3)

Kent anthropomorphizes and politicizes the forces of nature as tyrants and, by contrast, conceives of suffering man as a natural phenomenon. Nature (*natura naturata*) in this formulation is described as passively exposed to its own power (*natura naturans*), true to its etymology that derives "nature" from the Latin passive "natus," i.e. "that which has been born."[64] In *Lear's* concept of nature, supreme power and abject impotence seem to coincide:

> GLOUCESTER: Though the wisdom of Nature can reason it thus and thus, yet nature finds itself scourged by the sequent effects.
>
> (I. ii. 104–106)

Between the natural order and the natural products subjugated to it, mediation is effected with the help of metaphors whose metaphoricity is suppressed. As mentioned earlier, the most prominent of these metaphors is Lear himself: Ernst Kantorowicz several times calls the doctrine of the king's two bodies a metaphor.[65]

The collapsed "two natures" of the sovereign reduplicate the discursive double role of the concept of nature. In addition, an abundance of derivatives clusters around this metaphor and complements its cohesive function as needed. A particularly salient example of this, already prominent in *Richard III*, is the comparison of the king with the sun, emphasizing the transcendental uniqueness and sublime dominion of each. According to Benjamin, this comparison is characteristic of the seventeenth century,[66] and during Shakespeare's time it is indeed used frequently by other dramatists associated with his troupe and also, for instance, by Francis Bacon.[67] In *Lear*, however, the metaphorization of the celestial bodies is pushed to the limit of its explanatory capability and becomes a heuristic instrument. It is by way of this construction that astrology comes into play as a system of natural order that explicates how constellations of celestial bodies relate to social constellations, and vice versa. It is Kent who most persistently cites the stars as forces determining the course of terrestrial events; for instance, he identifies the noblemen as those "that their great stars throned and set high" (III. i. 22–23). Since he insists on society's fundamental stability, he also appeals to the stability of the stellar metaphor that "celestializes" sovereignty and thereby justifies it:

> KENT: It is the stars,
> The stars above us govern our conditions [. . .].
>
> (IV. iii. 33–34)

The constant use of planetary and stellar metaphors (as Lear's curse on Cordelia, quoted above, illustrates, I. i. 109–117) is intent on endowing the events at court with an air of transcendence. From this purpose springs the attempt to affirm a course of the world in which all elements of society would be in their right place, in which they would follow their eternally predestined orbit; nature, State, and godhead would for this very reason be reconciled and united in harmony. What is missing in this intellectual construct is any sublunar sense of the genuinely unpredictable and non-identical. For this reason, the protagonists at times resemble certain psychotics described by Lacan, who minimize the operationality of their speech by identifying with celestial bodies: "What they have identified with is an image where every gap, every aspiration, every emptiness of desire is lacking."[68] First and foremost, this image of a perfect plenitude without discrepancy attracts and guides Lear, who tries to assume the place of the big Other; but it also acts as a center of gravity whose force is communicated to all characters of the drama. They very seldom consider the possibility that something might differ *in* its assigned place; and that is what keeps the protagonists entrenched in their circular paths. In general, the *dramatis personae* find it difficult to distinguish between position and person; for example, they often seem incapable of recognizing themselves and one another after a loss of their social position. This incapacity is particularly pronounced in Gloucester and Lear, who do not seem to recognize Edgar and Kent in their disguises despite their increasing intimacy. Lear and Gloucester stumble through the darkness of misapprehension that is caused not only by overwhelming shame[69] but also by the fact that they always perceive culture as nature.[70] The drama's catastrophes are exacerbated by this presumed conformity; it soon becomes apparent to all protagonists that they are on a collision course with the forces of nature as well as with each other. This circumstance renders tangible that a sovereignty underpinned by astrology entails a paradox: the harmonious, universal and eternal order of nature that this worldview affirms involves a self-destructive fatality, for it is also a hermeneutics of planetary catastrophes. The astrological model of thought leads into a vicious circle that in turn can be projected into the sky as the fatal wheel of destiny. An "unnatural" nature seems to turn against itself. The most significant emblems of this calamity in *King Lear* are eclipses of the sun and moon that figure as indicators of social disorder:

> GLOUCESTER: These late eclipses in the sun and moon portend no good to us. [. . .] Love cools, friendship falls off, brothers divide: in cities, mutinies; in countries, discord; in palaces, treason; and the bond cracked 'twixt son and father.
>
> (I. ii. 103–104/106–109)

Edmund echoes Gloucester when he introduces the curse into this context:

> EDMUND: I am thinking, brother, of a prediction I read this other day, what should follow these eclipses. [. . .] I promise you, the effects he writes of succeed unhappily, as of unnaturalness between the child and the parent, death, dearth, dissolutions of ancient amities, divisions in state, menaces and maledictions against King and nobles, needless diffidences, banishment of friends, dissipation of cohorts, nuptial breaches and I know not what.
>
> (I. ii. 140–141/143–149)

The *fatum* as unnatural nature triggers the curse of the subjugated; in this curse, the indistinguishability of nature and anti-nature is given expression by the *natura naturata.*

As if the sovereign had to assimilate himself mimetically to the portentous solar and lunar eclipses so as not to endanger the parallelization between society and cosmic order, Lear through his "abdication" enacts the metaphorical equivalent of a conjunction of sun and moon that brings about an eclipse: The close association between Lear and the sun is admittedly never directly questioned over the course of the drama, but it is increasingly supplemented by his implicit identification with the moon (as ruler over the sublunar and hence natural world[71]). After his abdication, Lear sets himself, like the moon, on a "monthly course" in "due turn:"

> LEAR: Ourself by monthly course,
> With reservation of an hundred knights

> By you to be sustained, shall our abode
> Make with you by due turn [. . .].
>
> (I. i. 133–136)

Even before his transformation into the "lunatic King" (III. vii. 46), Lear's inconstancy "that ebbs and flows by the moon" is emphasized again and again with astrologically connotative formulations:

> GONERIL: You see how *full of changes* his age is. The *observation* we have made of it hath not been little.
>
> (I. i. 290–291, emphasis added)

Nevertheless he also takes good care to maintain his status as the helio-center of society and to defend it against competitors, above all against Cornwall, who begins to rise to his own solar altitude as early as the second act. Kent at first uses the comparison in a speech addressed to Cornwall with polemical and parodic intent:

> KENT: Sir, in good Faith, or in sincere verity,
> Under th' allowance of your great aspect,
> Whose influence, like the wreath of radiant fire
> On flickering Phoebus' front –
>
> (II. ii. 103–106)

But a little later, Gloucester suggests the same thing quite earnestly:

> GLOUCESTER: My dear lord,
> You know the fiery quality of the Duke,
> How unremovable and fixed he is
> In his own course.
>
> (II. ii. 280–283)

It is presumably the use of these solar metaphors that induces Lear to react so irritably to Gloucester's remark:

> LEAR: Vengeance, plague, death, confusion!
> Fiery? What quality? [. . .]
> "Fiery"? The fiery Duke, tell the hot Duke that –
>
> (II. ii. 284–285/293)

But at first Lear has no problem with being eclipsed or even with being the eclipse himself. After the "abdication," he chooses the twilight as his proper element, which does not devalue but rather exalts him. From out of the dark, he can operate all the more mightily. This is indicated in I. iv: admittedly, Lear's first utterances during his first entrance after the "distribution of land" are commands, just like before: "Let me not stay a jot for dinner; go, get it ready" (I. iv. 8). His orders in this scene differ from those in I. i. only by two technicalities: that he gives them not in blank verse but in prose and that he no longer uses the *pluralis maiestatis*.[72] Apart from the command, however, Lear utilizes another speech act which is no less significant for his status at this point: he not only gives orders, but also asks numerous questions: "What art thou?" (I. iv. 9), "What dost thou profess?" (I. iv. 11), "What wouldst thou?" (I. iv. 22), "Dost thou know me, fellow?" (I. iv. 26), etc. A question is a speech act that establishes an indeterminate power relationship; it demands of the person addressed to justify himself and to explain his position while that of the questioner remains in the dark, unquestioned, and hence more authoritative. This is the reason why in many dictatorial systems and subsystems (the police and some bureaucracies, for instance) constant interrogations take place for the sake of interrogation.[73] The unending repetitions of more or less senseless questionings are a form of torture. They establish asymmetrical, invasive relationships that require no clearly delimited boundaries of power. Lear has abdicated without abdicating and thereby has maneuvered himself into an opaque twilight situation in which his power is to be kept free of concrete obligations. He considers the symbolic *terrain vague* that he has entered his new domain; interrogations are speech acts that are ideally suited to this situation.

Yet questions such as "Where's my daughter?" and "Who put my man in the stocks?" also run the risk of remaining unanswered by addressees who do not acknowledge the power relation implicit in them. Oswald's "So please you" (I. iv. 45) confronts Lear with such a refusal. It amounts to a reinterpretation, supported by Goneril, of I. i as a genuine abdication. Lear experiences this refusal as a traumatic event to which his questions can respond with nothing more than a redundant echo: "He would not?" (I. iv. 54), "Sayst thou so?" (I. iv. 61), "Did you?" (II. ii. 389). It is obvious that he is losing initiative. In order to master this situation, he tries at first to make even his trauma look like something he himself had induced ("a most faint neglect of late, which I have rather blamed as mine own jealous curiosity," I. iv. 66–68). Afterwards, he returns to questioning: in response to his question "Who am I, sir?" (I. iv. 76), Lear obviously expects to hear from Oswald that he is the king. But the fact that he needs to ask already indicates the ambiguity of the situation. However, Oswald's answer ("My lady's father," I. iv. 77) instead situates Lear's identity in a secondary, derivative position. He vests him with a title that depends on Goneril's status as Oswald's mistress. Thereupon Lear and Kent apply physical force, the last resort on which Lear's sovereign power can rely. For Lear, this beating is a punishment of a insubordinate and a "service" Kent owes (I. iv. 92); for Goneril, appearing on the scene forthwith, it amounts to a "riot" (I. iv. 194). Like their father, Goneril and Regan constantly set themselves up as sovereign representatives of the law of nature. Under the auspices of *inclinatio naturalis*, they constantly designate their own desire as "convenience" and "wisdom" and declare everything that stands in its way as a transgression. Since I. iii, Goneril has complained that

Lear's knights are rebellious, and in this context she also describes Lear's behavior as transgressive:

> GONERIL: By day and night he wrongs me. Every hour
> He flashes into one gross crime or other
> That sets us all at odds.
>
> (I. iii. 4–6)

The unresolved question of power in this situation posits itself as question of definition: by calling Lear criminal and his knights rebellious, Goneril implies that Lear has indeed abdicated completely, is no longer a sovereign, and for this reason is now subject to the law. Since he is no longer entitled to the use of force, his "lawmaking" acts mark him only as a person "who still would manage those authorities that he hath given away" (I. iii. 18–19). Goneril's appearance reintroduces the blank verse to scene I. iv, replacing the previous prose and adding a sense of ceremony to the situation. Exactly what ceremony is involved here is not immediately apparent since Goneril gives to her speech acts the form of factual expositives:

> GONERIL: Not only, sir, this your all-licensed fool,
> But other of your insolent retinue
> Do hourly carp and quarrel, breaking forth
> In rank and not to be endured riots. Sir,
> I had thought by making this well known unto you
> To have found a safe redress, but now grow fearful
> By what yourself too late have spoke and done,
> That you protect this course and put it on
> By your allowance; which if you should, the fault
> Would not scape censure, nor the redresses sleep,
> Which in the tender of a wholesome weal
> Might in their working do you that offence
> Which else were shame, that then necessity
> Will call discreet proceeding.
>
> (I. iv. 191–204)

In this scene, all her essential speech acts are implicit ones: by calling the violent actions of his liegemen "riots" and her own vassals "their betters" (I. iv. 248), she posits Lear's deposition and her own enthronement, thereby giving Lear a latent command to abdicate once and for all. It is to her strategic advantage that they both are moving in the performative twilight which Lear has installed. By keeping her speech acts veiled, she also makes them seem irrefutable; they do not even appear to be acts but references to facts beyond language that have been in effect since time immemorial. In other words, she applies the administrative, bureaucratic strategy of representing controversial issues as always already decided. A further administrative strategy, popular at the latest since Jacobean times, complements this procedure: She allegorizes the situation by personifying abstractions and values, and has them enter into interactions of their own: "The shame itself does speak for instant remedy" (I. iv. 237–238), and, more elaborately: "the fault would not scape censure, nor the redress sleep, which [...] might do you that offence [...] that then necessity will call discreet proceeding" (I. iv. 199–204). In her allegorical representation, it is not Goneril and Lear who act but "fault," "shame," "redress," and, last but not least, "necessity." This is how she keeps responsibility away from her and declares herself a passive tool of processes and necessities that transcend her. Even so, Lear is made to understand unmistakably who now decides on his state of exception in his stead:

> GONERIL: I would you would make use of your good wisdom,
> Whereof I know you are fraught, and put away
> These dispositions which of late transport you
> From what you rightly are.
>
> (I. iv. 211–214)

Goneril builds herself up as the person with sufficient knowledge on Lear, i.e. with the power of definition that allows her to assign him his status. Her behavior is perfidious not least because *de facto* she assigns him no status at all, treating him both condescendingly and submissively ("I do beseech you to understand my purposes aright," I. iv. 229–230). Goneril takes advantage of the fact that Lear has created an undefined, eclipsed space for himself. She acknowledges this space as her sphere of activity but can operate in it all the more freely since she has the control over the power of definition, supported by executive force.[74] Lear reacts to this obvious assault with perplexity, still speaking in prose:

> LEAR: Are you our daughter? [...] Does any here know me? This is not Lear. Does Lear walk thus, speak thus? Where are his eyes? [...] Who is it that can tell me who I am?
>
> (I. iv. 209/217–218/221)

Lear continues to be in the default mode of permanent interrogation, but a new urgency can be detected in his questions; he no longer controls them. He cannot at the same time recognize Goneril as his natural child and retain his status as king—both aspects understood in the strict sense of the word: "For by the marks of sovereignty, knowledge and reason, I should be false persuaded I had daughters" (I. iv. 223–225). His dual identity comes into question. As in Cordelia's case, he solves the problem by expelling the unnatural daughter. Relapsing into blank verse, he announces the termination of his parental relationship with Goneril as well as his departure to the house of his last daughter, Regan ("Yet have I left a daughter" I. iv. 246). However, this departure turns out to be a rather complicated process. First, Lear rhetorically elaborates his announcement. Then he orders his liegemen to leave the scene, and they obey. In this context, he also several times addresses himself, or, rather, his several selves: "O Lear, Lear, Lear!" (I. iv. 262). Next, he curses

Goneril, leaves the stage, returns, curses her again, and only then exits for good. His redundant delay tactics indicate perplexity but also his inclination (discussed earlier) to remain in an ambiguous situation, on the threshold of inclusive exclusion. Analogously, his rhetorical figures come across as arrested, too: like Goneril, he addresses personified abstractions, for example "Ingratitude, thou marble-hearted fiend, more hideous when thou show'st thee in a child than the sea-monster" (I. iv. 251–253) and "O most small fault, how ugly didst thou in Cordelia show" (I. iv. 258–259). But these entities remain inactive because Lear's invocations remain elliptical: the subjects of his sentences are in each case given only attributes, but no actions. Whereas Goneril's allegorical figures interact directly with each other in a transcendental law court, by speaking, transgressing, calling up, punishing, and not getting away from each other, Lear's figures remain stuck in immobility. It seems that they are defeated by their own dynamics, which can also be said of the royal curse that follows his invocations:

> LEAR: Hear, Nature, hear, dear goddess, hear:
> Suspend thy purpose if thou didst intend
> To make this creature fruitful.
> Into her womb convey sterility,
> Dry up in her the organs of increase,
> And from her derogate body never spring
> A babe to honor her. If she must teem,
> Create her child of spleen, that it may live
> And be a thwart disnatured torment to her.
>
> (I. iv. 267–275)

Lear appeals to deified (traditionally female) Nature as executrix of his curse. But it comes somewhat as a surprise that he unequivocally orders her to implement the punishment: he does not pray, he commands. It is a strange way to deal with a divinity, but it can be explained by her contradictory status: that active nature, when the need arises, is also passively submissive to Lear, follows logically from his conflation of two concepts of nature. Nature so addressed has lost all her distinctive attributes. She no longer embodies harmonious proportions and cosmic order but, on this occasion, also their opposites. As the power of sickness, sterility, and monstrosity, nature is directed to produce something unnatural ("disnatured"). Like Albany's cannibalistic "monsters of the deep" (IV. ii. 51), she is to be subject and object of the curse at the same time. But this curse is both paradoxical and redundant since nature and anti-nature are indistinguishable from the beginning, if nature includes her own perversion, as exemplified by Lear's daughters (II. ii. 467). This turns the natural curse, irresolvably oscillating between powerlessness and absolute power, into the redundant articulation of a fate already intrinsic to nature. In this respect, Lear's curse is also a strategy of accommodation. Through his curse, he attempts to secure for himself a new sovereign position in the "general curse" of nature. Nature as "that which has been born" can no longer be discerned from the curse that subverts nature and to which Lear lends his voice.

Consequently, he repeatedly uses the image of filiation as an excrescence of parasitical flesh, of progeny as tumor:

> LEAR: But yet thou art my flesh, my blood, my daughter,
> Or rather a disease that's in my flesh,
> Which I must needs call mine. Thou art a boil,
> A plague sore, or embossed carbuncle
> In my corrupted blood.
>
> (II. ii. 410–414)

In this representation, Goneril is herself the monstrosity, "a thwart disnatured torment." But Lear and Goneril cannot be separated from one another: her flesh is his wound. Therefore, the curse he emits also affects Lear's body. When he has banished Cordelia in scene I. i, Lear has implicated himself in his curses by reinforcing them with oaths. Although Lear does not supplement the curses he lays on Goneril in this way, neither in I. iv nor in II. ii, they reveal the suicidal component of the curse even more clearly. His divine judgment assumes the shape of a stormy assault on his own eyes, his own virility, and his own flesh:

> LEAR: Blasts and fogs upon thee!
> Th'untented woundings of a father's curse
> Pierce every sense about thee. Old fond eyes,
> Beweep this cause again, I'll pluck ye out,
> And cast you with the waters that you loose
> To temper clay.
>
> (I. iv. 291–296)

William Empson has analysed the teeming ambiguities enfolded in the genitive construction of "Th'untented woundings of a father's curse pierce every sense about thee":

> The *wounds* may be cause or effect of the *curse* uttered by a *father*; independently of this, they may reside in the *father* or his child. The curse, indeed, might be uttered *against* the father by the child, and certainly the king would have meant this if he had thought of it. All the meanings arrived at by permuting these versions make up one single-minded *curse*; any pains Lear has felt or is still to feel, any pains Cordelia has felt or is still to feel, as an effect or cause whether of this *curse* on Goneril or of his previous *curse* on Cordelia, or of Goneril's implied curses on him, all these give him good reason for *cursing* Goneril with the same pains in return; and if any pains in Goneril are to be cause or effect of any of these *cursings*, so much the better, let them *pierce* her. These pains are already all that he can foresee from the *cursing of fathers*; they, therefore, mean also "all the curses that a father *can* impose on his child."[75]

This sentence, nearly inexhaustible in its destructive abundance, offers even more interpretive possibilities: for example, the "curse" may also be linked to the "untented woundings of a father" as a *genitivus subiectivus*, suggesting that these woundings are pronouncing the curse, in analogy to the personal accusations proclaimed by the torn-out hairs of his beard with which Gloucester tries to threaten Regan (III. vii. 38–39). Painful injuries float between speaker and addressee; or rather, the persons circulate among the injuries: curses and wounds seem to be substances; Lear, Cordelia, and Goneril merely their *modi*. At this point, Lear abandons any point of reference that would make it possible to delimit the curse strategically, to monopolize it and thereby to keep it compatible with political order in the accepted sense. The curse becomes the symptom of an implosion of all social relations. It opens up as a kind of black hole in the symbolic field, an active void that devours both the guilty and the innocent.

The same scene is repeated between Regan and Lear in II. ii after Lear—speaking in blank verse, as before—has demanded of her the "offices of nature" (II. ii. 367). Like her sister, Regan refuses these services, justifying herself by invoking the frailty of Lear's natural body. Her reference to his age and the mental decline presumably resulting from it disqualifies his utterances *a priori* and saves her the trouble of any further discussion:

> REGAN: O, sir, you are old:
> Nature in you stands on the very verge
> Of her confine. [...] Give ear, sir, to my sister;
> For those that mingle reason with your passion
> Must be content to think you old, and so –
> But she knows what she does.
>
> (II. ii. 335–357/422–425)

The *topos* is taken up by the arriving Regan and enables the daughters to put up an effective blockade of Lear's executive power. This strategy is first designated a "revolt" by Lear (II. ii. 278), but then prompts him once more to reinterpret the adversities that confront him as results of his own sovereign decision. When that also proves futile, he engages in a tenacious struggle for the remnants of his dignity, and then in new execrations. The curses Lear pronounces in this scene are clearly more decentered than those of the first act. He no longer calls on personified Nature or on planetary divinities as executors and guarantors of his curse but addresses singular, concrete natural phenomena, such as bad weather, unhealthy climates, flashes of lightning and fogs:

> LEAR: All the stored vengeances of heaven fall
> On her ingrateful top! Strike her young bones,
> You taking airs, with lameness! [...]
> You nimble lightnings, dart your blinding flames
> Into her scornful eyes! Infect her beauty,

You fen-sucked fogs, drawn by the powerful sun
To fall and blister!

(II. ii. 351–357)

There is no longer a central authority from which the teeming punishments of nature originate. Instead, sources for execrations are now seen to be omnipresent in nature.

Lear's curses, therefore, become more rich and concrete, and hence more poetic. In places, they are reminiscent of nature poetry striving for sublimity. This modification of his curses turns Lear into a kind of proto-Romantic, effecting a secularizing shift he himself comments on:

LEAR: I do not bid the thunder-bearer shoot,
Nor tell tales of thee to high-judging Jove.

(II. ii. 416–417)

Lear's turn toward the decentered and the particular is caused by his circumstances: precisely because power in his kingdom is increasingly represented as dark and intangible, its marginal manifestations become all the more important.[76] Having lost his overt eminence, he has to cling all the more doggedly to the remaining palpable fetishes of his distinction; this also becomes apparent in the haggling over Lear's liegemen who keep dropping off on their own anyway. This quarrel is purely symbolic, for when Lear enters Gloucester's house, he is no longer accompanied by the hundred knights for which he persistently demands billets and board from Regan (see II. ii. 252–261). The symbolic nature of the dispute dawns on Lear during the course of their verbal altercation, as his reaction to Regan's question: "What need you one follower?" demonstrates:

LEAR: O, reason not the need! Our basest beggars
Are in the poorest thing superfluous;
Allow not nature more than nature needs,
Man's life is cheap as beast's. Thou art a lady;
If only to go warm were gorgeous,
Why, nature needs not what thou gorgeous wear'st,
Which scarcely keeps thee warm.

(II. ii. 453–459)

Surprisingly, Lear expostulates that a man's worth and position are determined by the surplus he has at his command, i.e. by that part of his property that does not satisfy mere natural needs. The regal garments the princess wears, for example, set her apart from her subjects, and in that respect they have a supplementary social function besides the elementary purpose of protecting her from the cold. Even beggars, analogously, own "superfluities" they don't need for survival, even if they are "poorest things." Every social distinction comes about through the play of significant surplus, which is a symbolic entity above all. The supplement is a sign that marks people's position in the State. And this is how Lear perceives his liegemen.

The symbolic supplement, however, is an entity whose structuring function he had steadfastly denied and suppressed before, through the obligatory gesture of directly equating State and nature—a gesture that denies its own metaphorical character. Hence his observation marks a decisive turn of the drama, compared to which all of Lear's later conversions, as will have to be shown, appear unimportant. The restoration of his ability to rule with the help of distinguishing signs will consequently be the goal to which Lear clings with steadfast determination for the rest of the drama, despite continuously failing at it. By refusing his sovereign daughters the submission *qua* dissolution of his shrinking retinue, he drops out of the prevailing order and is no longer part of the sovereign household, and thus no longer part of the State. In this situation he carries out his intent to participate unconditionally in the fight of nature against nature, making this the mark of his distinction:

> LEAR: Rather I abjure all roofs and choose
> To wage against the enmity o'th'air [. . .]!
>
> (II. ii. 397–398)

His first action after his expulsion is to amplify his curses on the stormy heath, at the same time in harmony with nature and in opposition to it, as one of his last remaining liegemen is the first to point out:

> KNIGHT: Contending with the fretful elements;
> Bids the wind blow the earth into the sea,
> Or swell the curled waters 'bove the main,
> That things might change or cease; tears his white hair,
> Which the impetuous blasts with eyeless rage
> Catch in their fury and make nothing of,
> Strives in his little world of man to outscorn
> The to and fro conflicting wind and rain [. . .].
>
> (III. i. 4–11)

According to this description, Lear's utterances are suffused with ambivalence: he orders the tempest to intensify and thereby to cause either another Great Flood or the Apocalypse ("change or cease"), as if their difference were irrelevant. His appeals imply his total submission, even an acquiescence to his own extinction, anticipating the great catastrophe through acts of auto-aggression ("tears his white hair"), as if he were indeed the "pattern of all patience" (III. ii. 37). But nonetheless, he also strives to exercise executive power, to compete ("contending") with the elements, to surpass ("outscorn") nature, and thus to reaffirm the surplus of humankind.

In the following scene, the contradictions in his curses stand out even more prominently: Lear calls himself the slave of the storm's powers (III. ii. 19), but by commanding them, he also positions himself above them:

> LEAR: Blow winds and crack your cheeks! Rage, blow!
> You cataracts and hurricanoes, spout

> Till you have drenched our steeples, drowned the cocks!
> You sulphurous and thought-executing fires,
> Vaunt-couriers of oak-cleaving thunderbolts,
> Singe my white head! And thou, all-shaking thunder,
> Strike flat the thick rotundity o'the world [. . .]!
>
> (III. ii. 1–7)

Once more, Lear orders nature to execute a cosmic disaster. But just like the others, this curse is simultaneously redundant and excessive: the flashes of lightning and torrents of water he evokes are already coming down, so the disaster appears to be in full progress.[77] As in I. iv, nature is being positioned against itself, cosmic natural forces against human nature. It is not clear, however, which side of the frontline is to be considered that of humanity, since Lear not only converses with the destructive forces of nature but also anthropomorphizes them (furnishing them with "cheeks" and a "belly", III. ii. 14); they figure as metaphorical ordering forces that are nonetheless meant to extinguish order, a situation that is analogous to the ambiguities of the adjective "thought-executing," which leave open whether the flashes of lightning execute annihilating thoughts, annihilate the thoughts themselves, annihilate with the speed of thoughts, or all of the above at the same time:

> LEAR: Crack nature's moulds, all germens spill at once
> That make ingrateful man!
>
> (III. ii. 8–9)

The goal of this curse appears to be the destruction of the fixed natural forms which generate man. But this annihilation of nature through nature is imaginable only if a constant surplus is imagined to exist within nature, an inherent excessive propensity for violence beyond its eternal self-preservation. By this detour, Lear returns to the idea of apocalyptic justice:

> LEAR: Let the great gods
> That keep this dreadful pudder o'er our heads
> Find out their enemies now. Tremble, thou wretch,
> That hast within thee undivulged crimes,
> Unwhipped of justice. Hide thee, thou bloody hand,
> Thou perjured, and thou simular of virtue
> That art incestuous. Caitiff, to pieces shake,
> That under covert and convenient seeming
> Has practised on man's life. Close pent-up guilts
> Rive your concealing continents and cry
> These dreadful summoners grace. I am a man
> More sinned against than sinning.
>
> (III. ii. 49–60)

The Apocalypse is a last resort of the faith that a just law inheres in creation. Lear refers to a chastising tribunal that is hidden but already beginning to unveil itself in the shape of the storm. The form of his speech is reminiscent of an apocalyptic penitential sermon about the impending Day of His Wrath, especially since he no longer addresses weather phenomena but the people subjected to them ("wretch," "caitiff," perjured," etc.). But this sermon only holds out the prospect of punishment for sinners and does not promise any complementary reward for the righteous. And even that contradicts all of Lear's previous pronouncements. He declares the storm to be the harbinger of cosmic retribution even though he has just affirmed (and will continue to affirm) that the tempest is either indifferent toward the law or explicitly unjust; therefore, it batters the speaker first and foremost, despite the fact that he is relatively innocent ("more sinned against than sinning"). Lear addresses rain, wind, thunder, and fire not only as tools for the expiatory destruction of "ungrateful man;" he also sees them as servile underlings of his malignant daughters—as if the storm were merely an extension of the perverse cosmos it is meant to obliterate. Lear's appeals and metaphorizations continuously cancel themselves out: first the storm is addressed as the king's avenger, then as his daughters' helper; in one moment it is an indifferent force, in the next a penalizing agency, at the same time anthropomorphous and inhuman. And Lear himself both fights against nature and on its behalf. A paradoxical conception of *Natura* lets all distinctions collaborate. There is only one attribute that all these conceptions of nature and all their representatives do share: they are all auto-aggressive powers of extermination. Annihilating force appears as the ultimate authority in Lear's curses. But by preaching this power, Lear does nothing but radicalize the dilemma of I. iv: the doomsday that Lear evokes is perpetually taking place already. The world's course is the world's end. Lear's curse thus merely articulates the omnipresent disaster that he seems to oppose. His problem is that, in the final analysis, the juridical system and societal order cannot be established through reference to a natural order beyond the law and constituent of the law. Such an order is not demonstrable in a world of contingencies; instead, the nature by which the law justifies itself is always the law's own metaphoric construction.[78] Yet the system of laws cannot be justified through its pure self-referentiality either: by positivistically accepting as valid law whatever the law deems to be law, it becomes indistinguishable from pure violence. Lear as *lex animata* loses not merely his collapsing dual body; he loses all coherence beyond the metaphysical certainty of a primordial violence. Since this violence has no limits and thus not even an object outside itself, it must turn upon itself. This circularity expresses itself in the abounding metaphors of auto-aggression, such as flagellation, cannibalism, and autophagy:

> LEAR: Is it not as this mouth should tear this hand
> For lifting food to't?
>
> (III. iv. 15–16)

Under these circumstances, the exercise of power must appear as inherently self-destructive. Lear will admit even this conclusion into his regal ethos. Consequently, he propagates self-punishment as an appropriate way to treat the generatively teeming flesh of man "preying on itself like monsters of the deep." But instead of enacting this practice himself, beyond tearing out his hair, he declares it as realized in Edgar's representation of "Poor Tom":

> LEAR: Is it the fashion that discarded fathers
> Should have thus little mercy on their flesh?
> Judicious punishment, 'twas this flesh begot
> These pelican daughters.
>
> (III. iv. 71–74)

Lear integrates Edgar, who strikes himself (III. iv. 60–61), into his new phantasm as "the thing itself" (III. iv. 104), turning him into the emblem of perverse, nihilating nature. Under Lear's gaze, Edgar appears as a creature appropriate to nature, in whose inhuman, destructive processes human beings are actively involved. In this, he resembles the naked "Timon of Athens", according to Benjamin:

> Shakespeare portrays inhuman figures [. . .] and says: Nature would produce such a creature if she wished to create something befitting the world as your kind have fashioned it, something worthy of it. Such a creature is Timon [. . .].[79]

And on the heath Lear proclaims "Poor Tom" to be just such a creature. But not even in the role he plays does Edgar correspond to the image Lear creates of him for his own use.[80] Their encounter is a failure anyhow. Following an established practice, Lear extends his empathy only to those he considers his metonymic derivatives. Even his prayer to all that labor and are heavy laden is to be seen in this context (III. iv. 28–32). He notices others, as he has always done, only when they are virtually identical:

> LEAR: Have his daughters brought him to this pass?
> Couldst thou save nothing? Wouldst thou give 'em all? [. . .]
> (*to EDGAR*) Now all the plagues that in the pendulous air
> Hang fated o'er men's faults light on thy daughters.
> KENT: He hath no daughters, sir.
> LEAR: Death, traitor! Nothing could have subdued nature
> To such a lowness but his unkind daughters.
>
> (III. iv. 62–63/66–70)

The curse on Edgar's daughters, followed by the condemnatory "Death, traitor!," indicates that Lear does not let go of his aspirations to natural executive power, even though such power may be nothing but the mask of raw violence. Lear never intends to actually abdicate; instead, he engages in ever new mental sorties to constitute new forms of sovereignty. For this purpose, he undertakes various experiments in the execution of natural law. All these experiments in the maintenance of his sovereignty end in aporias, which has not kept centuries of Shakespeare critics from projecting various timely ideologies into most of them as Lear's edifying insights. At first, Lear simply imitates conventional jurisdiction by improvising a unsuccessful tribunal against his daughters: two chairs representing Regan and Goneril are called to appear before a commission, presided over by two common law judges appointed by the king and supplemented by a Court of Chancery judge—the composition customary during the seventeenth century.[81] Hence Lear addresses Edgar as "robed man of justice" (III. vi. 36), Kent as "o' the commission" (III. vi. 38), the Fool as "yoke-fellow of equity" (III. vi. 37). Does this trial of defendants *in effigie* signify the omnipotence of Lear's jurisdiction or his powerlessness?[82] At any rate, it is not the only show trial in the play, and like all other proceedings in *King Lear* it is parodic in one sense or another. For this very reason, equity retains its significance in all of them.

When Lear reappears, near Dover in IV. vi, he is still preoccupied with the same project of expanding his sovereignty. And as before, he refers to his authority as to a natural phenomenon:

> LEAR: No, they cannot touch me for coining. I am the king himself.
> EDGAR: O thou side-piercing sight!
> LEAR: Nature's above art in that respect. There's your press-money.
> (IV. vi. 83–87)

It is to be assumed and has become a stage tradition that in this scene he distributes pebbles as means of payment, in analogy to his self-coronation with weeds. The king continues to insist on his royal prerogative to create money. His approbation indicates the value of things and persons as much as his mint vouches for the value of his money.[83] However, scholarly literature offers surprisingly few comments on the purpose for which Lear apparently uses the money he has created:

> LEAR: There's your press-money. That fellow handles his bow like a crow-keeper: draw me a clothier's yard. Look, look, a mouse: peace, peace, this piece of toasted cheese will do't. There's my gauntlet, I'll prove it on a giant. Bring up the brown bills. O, well flown, bird, i' the clout, i' the clout!
> (IV. vi. 86–92)

In this scene, Lear is farther away than ever from any form of abdication and crypto-Christian forgiveness. Evidently, he is reorganizing the jurisdiction as well as the financial and military affairs of his dominion whose ability to function has proved to be noticeably deficient on the heath during the storm. The king is obviously engaged in the bio-political reconstitution, recruitment, and drilling of his army, "for I lack soldiers" (IV. vi. 115). In his description of his troops he uses ambiguous terms that can refer to weapons and soldiers as well as to animals and their habitats: the "brown bills" can be those of birds but also halberds and halberdiers; "troop of horse" can designate both an army of horsemen and a "troupe of horses;" and "crow-keeper" may not be just a scarecrow but also refer to a crow which serves as a guard. In this vein, "bird" is not only an avian animal, but also a synonym for arrow, an ambiguity supported by a second one that results from the homophony of "clout" as the goal of the arrow and "cloud" as a possible location of the flying bird. The troop seems to be augmented with the enlistment of the mouse in which cheese is used as earnest payment. Besides the image of the female centaurs (IV. vi. 122), the later reference to the watchdog also continues the motif that there is no clear distinction between the world of animals and that of humans. Even the dog has social authority by virtue of his integration into a hierarchical and conflictive system:

> LEAR: Thou hast seen a farmer's dog bark at a beggar? [. . .] And the creature run from the cur – there you mightst behold the great image of authority: a dog's obeyed in office.
>
> (IV. vi. 150–151/153–155)

Already in the first act, Lear has understood sovereign power as the incorporation of the state of nature into society, creating a zone in which nature and culture, affect and law are indistinguishable. Now he insinuates that this zone is omnipresent: for him, natural processes and social conflicts dissolve in a comprehensive, absolute metaphor of struggle (*Kampf*). This conflation makes it impossible to arrive at a valid moral judgment about the world inasmuch as all deeds express sovereign and conflictive nature as a universal characteristic. This leads Lear to proclaim that everybody is free of sin: "None does offend" (IV. vi. 164). But it does not follow from this dispensatory gesture that Lear stops his tirades; on the contrary, he gains a new target for his old diatribes. The sin he henceforth attacks is the dishonesty which denies the universal struggle by feigning cordiality and virtue (IV. vi. 96–104/116–125/156–163). Being virtuous is by definition hypocrisy because if sin does not exist, then virtue does not exist either. Instead of advocating universal reconciliation, Lear with perfect logic persists in envisioning victory in the cosmic struggle by any means necessary and plans the murder of his self-proclaimed successors:

> LEAR: It were a delicate stratagem to shoe
> A troop of horse with felt. I'll put it in proof
> And when I have stolen upon these son-in-laws,
> Then kill, kill, kill, kill, kill, kill!
>
> (IV. vi. 180–183)

Therefore, the forgiveness that Lear announces remains empty (in analogy with that of the church). It cannot and will not constrain the all-pervasive cutthroat competition since it acquits struggle itself and forms a part of it. This makes Lear's verdicts of damnation as well as his sermons appear not so much incoherent as increasingly redundant. Even the victory he envisions means little, since it cannot change this fundamental structure. Under these circumstances, all his performances lead to absurdity:

> LEAR: I am even
> The natural fool of fortune.
>
> (IV. vi. 186–187)

After Lear has surrendered, unprotected, to the idea that the general order of nature and the particular order of law are mutually dependent, he has fallen into the chasm that separates them and was only provisionally patched up with an assortment of ideologemes. Through his fall, he abandons his world to the domination of unchained, naturally sovereign bodies. From the beginning, the governance of Goneril, Cornwall, Regan, and their minions presents itself as the rule of privileged *natural bodies.* The overdetermined concept of nature advocated by the so-called villains of the play differs little from that of Lear, Gloucester, and Kent. This is clearly observable in Edmund's prayer to *Natura* personified:

> EDMUND: Thou, Nature, art my goddess; to thy law
> My services are bound. Wherefore should I
> Stand in the plague of custom, and permit
> The curiosity of nations to deprive me?
> [. . .] Why brand they us
> With base? With baseness, bastardy? Base, base?
> Who in the lusty stealth of nature take
> More composition and fierce quality
> Than doth within a dull stale tired bed
> Go to the creating of a whole tribe of fops
> Got 'tween a sleep and wake. Well, then,
> Legitimate Edgar, I must have your land. [. . .]
> Now gods, stand up for bastards!
>
> (I. ii. 1–4/9–16/22)

It seems that Edmund, in contrast to Lear, sets the concept of nature against that of convention. He contrasts "nature" with "custom;" his nature, then, lies beyond the institutions whereas Lear's includes them. But all the same, Edmund proceeds from the premise that nature has a law: he equates nature and drive as *inclinatio naturalis* ("lusty stealth of nature"), derives from this equation his superiority over the "fop" Edgar, and from this deduces his legal claim, secured by his version of natural religion, to Gloucester's land; in order to succeed in this claim, he proceeds not, as one may expect, with prejuridical violence but by the manipulation of conventions. Inasmuch as he also calls for fairness and equity, he is not all that different from Lear; their valuations are partly based on opposite assumptions, but they structure the world homologously. The diminishing difference between them is prefigured in the conversation of Gloucester *naturans* with

Kent *naturata* at the beginning of the play. Edmund's statement "All with me's meet that I can fashion fit" (I. ii. 182) could also be Gloucester's credo; even in this respect he is his father's son.

Like Edmund and Gloucester, Cornwall, Goneril, and Regan also use conventions and decrees manipulatively in order to satisfy natural inclinations. Their desire is the valid law; they act as tools of this desire. This transgressivistic sovereignty of the new generation allows them strategic infringements of traditional symbolic obligations. During the first two acts, for instance, Goneril, Regan, and Cornwall pretend to be indisposed in order to brush off the diverse claims Lear makes on them. A supposed weakness of their nature entitles them to this transgression of etiquette:

> GONERIL: When he returns from hunting,
> I will not speak with him; say I am sick.
>
> (I. iii. 8–9)

> LEAR: Deny to speak with me? They are sick, they are weary,
> They have travelled all the night?
>
> (II. ii. 277–278)

The *body natural* can thus be used as an instrument of power that will help to defer the question about the constitution of the *body politic*. At first, Lear plays along; after all, it was he himself who introduced the appropriate overdeterminations into the official political discourse by representing his own "unburdening" in I. i as a politically advisable action:

> LEAR: No, but not yet, maybe he is not well;
> Infirmity doth still neglect all office
> Whereto our health is bound. We are not ourselves
> When nature, being oppressed, commands the mind
> To suffer with the body. I'll forbear,
> And am fallen out with my more headier will
> To take the indisposed and sickly fit
> For the sound man.
>
> (II. ii. 294–301)

This arrangement can be read as evidence that the new sovereigns' natural bodies immediately constitute the new body politic, once the kingdom has been allocated in their favor. Especially Cordelia's sisters turn into Ubuesque figures of a legislative power that has grotesquely short-circuited. According to Foucault,[84] such power is an integral part of modern State constitutions:

> GONERIL: Say if I do, the laws are mine, not thine.
> Who can arraign me for't?
>
> (V. iii. 156–157)

The natural bodies of Regan and Goneril appear to be machines for the infinite production of demands; their emphatically insatiable neediness is apparent as early as I. i, where they complain even about developments that are to their own benefit, i.e. the disinheritance and expulsion of Cordelia and the exile of their adversary Kent (I. i. 292–302). Nothing fills their avaricious eyes ("still soliciting eye," I. i. 233), and for this reason they constantly install judicial double binds that put the subjects of their law *a priori* in the wrong and thus make their work of administration easier. In this connection Goneril even propagates preventive punishment of the innocent:

> GONERIL: Fools do those villains pity who are punished
> Ere they have done their mischief.
>
> (IV. ii. 55–56)

Lear's heirs institute an exceptional jurisdiction that they clearly make contingent on their pleasure and displeasure (III. vii. 4–6). Not only the love Regan proclaims in I. i but also her proclaimed will to carry out the law in exemplary fashion overflows all empirical bounds:

> REGAN: all vengeance comes too short
> Which can pursue the'offender.
>
> (II. i. 88–89)

A permanent state of exception becomes established after Lear's downfall in which juridical forms cave in before the new sovereigns' emotions ("a courtesy to our wrath," III. vii. 26). It soon becomes abundantly clear that this exceptional justice is massively libidinous. Especially Regan appears to favor legal sadomasochistic practices. The fact that Kent is put in the stocks and Gloucester is tied to a chair and tortured seems to involve her affections even more strongly than those of her husband:

> CORNWALL: Fetch forth the stocks!
> As I have life and honour, there shall he sit till noon.
> REGAN: Till noon? Till night, my lord, and all night too.
>
> (II. ii. 130–132)

> CORNWALL: Bind him, I say –
> REGAN: Hard, hard. O, filthy traitor!
>
> (III. vii. 31–32)

During Gloucester's interrogation, Regan permanently asks questions whose answers she claims to know already (III. vii. 43), thereby establishing, as the daughter of her father, a senseless juristic ritual that serves to humiliate the legal subject. Cornwall, Goneril, and Regan are perverse in Lacan's sense because they undertake to institutionalize the satisfaction of the big Other.[85] Like Lear, they undertake to administratively represent the Other in its place and deny their own split by methodically imposing it on other subjects.[86] This outspoken sadism emerges from Lear's groundbreaking conception of natural law; his heirs provide a service to the sovereign natural body by turning themselves into instruments of the *jouissance* that dominates and in the end overwhelms them.[87] Their *inclinatio naturalis* finally makes them lose even that which Goneril calls her "hateful life" (IV. ii. 87).

In *King Lear*, the struggle for legitimacy that defines Shakespeare's Histories assumes the form of a grotesque quarrel about natural rightfulness in which all parties ruin themselves without reaching a final verdict. In the course of this process, the curse is dislocated from the traditional theologico-juridical contexts that kept its aporias exploitable. Even at the end of the drama, there is no new containment of the proliferating curse and no solution to the problem of natural rights on the horizon; rather, the problem becomes ever more urgent in ever new spheres of life. Even in this respect *Lear* is in accord with Benjamin's definition of *Trauerspiel* as a trial indefinitely adjourned with a charge only partially dealt with and a verdict postponed to an unforeseeable future.[88]

3.3 Kent in internal banishment

Although one might associate the legal practice of banishment in England above all with the Middle Ages, the early modern era does not abolish it but merely reforms the punishment. During the sixteenth century, it is true, the traditional forms for sentences of banishment, which derive from canon law (especially "abjuration"), are repealed step by step or grow obsolete. But at the same time numerous royal statutes ("acts") introduce new forms and objects of banishment. For example, all gypsies are expelled from England by statute in 1562, all Jesuits in 1585, and all "recusants"[89] in 1592; all relapsing beggars and vagabonds as well as unlicensed players and actors are banished in 1597.[90] In addition to the "acts," Elizabeth promulgates royal proclamations denying sojourn in England to Anabaptists, the Irish, blacks, and others.[91] According to Elizabethan jurisdiction, those banished must leave her jurisdiction under threat of the death penalty. Banishment forces them from the judicature of the State to the indeterminate status of an exile. Official pronouncements often declare this expulsion to be a provision for returning the banished persons to the place that suits their nature. This applies to certain beggars and vagabonds but also to the forcefully repatriated Irish.[92] Banishment is considered not only a punishment but also a contribution towards maintaining the natural order, which apparently requires the State's jurisdiction to implement it.

In many medieval and early modern discourses that refer to biblical tradition, curse and banishment merge smoothly into one another. Deuteronomy 27 and 28 in particular are often quoted whenever the curse is intended to constitute not only the law of a community but also, as ban in the sense of banishment, a territory subjugated to said law. The ban guarantees the homogeneity of the country, which the sovereign represents as proprietor and "supreme landlord."[93] He secures the identity of the State and its boundary markers, keeping the body politic clean of latent subversions and unnatural contaminations.[94] The excluding curse also establishes the internal boundaries within the State's territories and safeguards them: the boundaries between subjects' private freeholds depend on the approbation of the sovereign and his representatives.[95] Regarding official written records, it is first and foremost in land grants and similar documents that ecclesiastical curses appear.[96] As an example, a curse included in the deed of an Anglo-Saxon land donation might be quoted:

> And Archbishop Wulfhelm and all the bishops and abbots who were there assembled excommunicated from Christ and from all the fellowship of Christ and from the whole of Christendom anyone who should ever undo this grant or reduce this estate in pasture or in boundary. He shall be cut off and hurled into the abyss of hell for ever without end. And all the people who stood by said "So be it, Amen."[97]

A combination of curse and boundary marking reminiscent of Deuteronomy 27.17 can also be found in the not quite extinct English custom of "beating the bounds." During this annual Ascension Day ceremony a group of royal officials or clergymen together with the youths of a parish paces out the boundary markers of the neighborhood. The youngsters beat the stones with branches, and sometimes their heads are knocked against the stones so as to imprint them on their memory. The priest, meanwhile, pronounces prospective curses on those who ignore the border markings and modify them ("cursed be he who moveth our boundary"), and blesses those who respect them.[98] Like certain ecclesiastical processions,[99] the royal "progresses" *mutatis mutandis* can be seen as variations of this custom: in the sixteenth century, the monarch's processions through the country involve inspections of urban and harbor fortifications at the kingdom's border and of similar outposts.[100]

Only a sovereign who can enforce the binding validity of boundaries can be the final authority to order changes of such boundaries as, for example, their extension through military actions.[101] During Shakespeare's time attempts are made not only to redraw the external borders of the English State (e.g. in Scotland and Ireland) and to keep these borders flexible at sea (especially in the conflict with Spain); but internal borders, too, are secretly in a state of flux. Under the Tudors and Stuarts, England increasingly becomes private property. This is due to the development of capitalistic enterprises that, in part through monopolies granted by the crown, accumulate considerable fortunes; but it is due also to the "enclosures," i.e. the privatization of common land by landlords, effecting the "so-called primitive accumulation."[102] What takes place is a largely illegal process of land acquisition. But since the monarch (*qua* genuine proprietor of this land) opposes its transfer only sporadically, no help is to be expected from the royal jurisdiction. The smallholders who before had farmed common lands by customary law lose the basis of their existence when this land is privatized and enclosed. The proletarization of the expropriated in turn contributes to the increase in power of the emerging *haute bourgeoisie*.[103] Under the banner of the inviolability of private property, the State's territory ever more becomes a commodity—a development for which Lear's land distribution could likewise be a metaphor (as will be shown in section 3.5).

Official texts of the early modern era show that biblical *topoi* shape the discourse about exile. Beyond justifying expulsion from one's country as a legal process by referring to biblical passages, a general connection between lawmaking and banishment can be observed. In this context, the primary source of quotations is the Book of Genesis, which often combines banishment and the lawmaking curse.[104] Prominent examples are the expulsion from Paradise (3. 14–24) and the ban on Cain (4. 11–16). But even clandestine self-descriptions of exiles make use of these same religiously sanctioned discourses.[105] For example, connecting the political practice of banishment with the biblical expulsion from Paradise revitalizes a *topos* popular in Christian rhetoric that posits the world as mankind's place of banishment *per se*. Consequently, exile is seen as nothing other than an evident expression of the *conditio humana*.[106] Alternatively, the time away from home is also understood (with the help of Matthew 24. 21) as an apocalyptic "time of tribulation" comparable to the Israelites' wanderings in the desert; life in exile can therefore be considered an ascetic, redemptive experience. Already in Republican Rome, *exilium* is an ambiguous concept that denotes both the more or less voluntarily chosen emigration and the one imposed by a court of law. This ambiguity also characterizes the English terms "exile" and "banishment."[107] It enables exiles to represent their status, depending on circumstances, as a voluntary act and thereby to revaluate it. Partly in imitation of Cicero. who in an essay about his banishment states that all values of the republic—and that means, the republic itself—have gone into exile with him,[108] oftentimes a person banished for political or religious reasons resorts to inverting his banishment and portraying those who have banished him as the true apostates and exiles. This inversion also figures in Shakespeare's dramas, most prominently in *Coriolanus*, where the central figure, after his expulsion from Rome, turns against the assembly of citizens exclaiming "I banish you" (*Coriolanus*, III. iii. 127). The mutual repudiation is based on a divergent definition of the concept of State in this case. Analogously, John of Gaunt remarks to Bolingbroke in *Richard II*: "Think not the King did banish thee, but thou the King" (I. iii. 268–269). These formulations hint at the problem that the imposition of exile as punishment for disloyalty can lead both to the consolidation and to the division of the State. They also suggest that an excess of contradictory banishments, i.e. of drawing contradictory boundary lines, can confuse the structures of political authority along with territorial outlines.

Exclusion from the realm appears in *Lear* also as a self-sublating procedure. Kent reacts to the announcement of his expulsion much like Coriolanus by exclaiming: "Freedom lives hence and banishment is here" (I. i. 182), as if not he but the rest of the court had been expelled. In I. iv, the Fool picks up the same motif: "Why, this fellow has banished two on's daughters and did the third a blessing against his will" (I. iv. 100–102), suggesting that not Cordelia on the continent but Goneril and Regan are in exile. The term "banishment" in this context implies primarily that the territory of the British State itself has passed into a time of conflict and inclusive exclusion insofar as the king, its ruler, has relinquished the task of ruling. There no longer exists a British sovereign who could reliably define the shape of his realm by legislation. The metonymies that have structured Lear's world are thus made inapplicable. British territorial integrity begins to dissolve, "wars 'twixt the dukes of Cornwall and Albany" as a synonym of this dissolution announce themselves as early as the second act (II. i. 11–12; III. i. 19–21). Due to this development as well, the difference between the boundaries of the State and those of the noble Houses collapses more and more—a collapse that can be observed not only in the Houses of Cornwall and Albany but also in the House of Gloucester:

> CURAN: You have heard of the news abroad? – I mean the whispered ones, for they are yet but ear-kissing arguments.
> EDMUND: Not I; pray you, what are they?
> CURAN: Have you heard of no likely wars toward 'twixt the dukes of Cornwall and Albany?
>
> (II. i. 7–12)

The word "abroad" in this dialogue unfolds a symptomatic ambiguity, for it can mean both "in a foreign country" and "beyond the borders of the house, in public." The impending tribal wars are prevented only by the French invasion, but not even this incursion comes altogether from without, since a British king's daughter leads it in the name of the British king ("our aged father's right," IV. iv. 28). In several respects, the distinctions between familial, interfamilial and intergovernmental conflict remain blurred. Consequently, the "external" threat only unites Cornwall and Albany insufficiently: the official armistice between the two Houses does not keep Albany from declaring his solidarity with the English deserters who have joined the French army ("others whom the rigour of our state forced to cry out," V. i. 22–23); neither does it prevent Goneril from approving of Cornwall's death ("One way I like this well," IV. ii. 84) and from murdering Regan. With the progressive unmaking of the king's central authority, the kingdom seems to dissolve irretrievably between the frontlines of new Houses; betokening, indeed, a "death on [Lear's] state" (II. ii. 301). Nothing remains but the parodistic pretensions to a kingdom. In Dover, Lear dismisses the reference to an England under his rule as nothing more than a bad joke:

> LEAR: Am I in France?
> KENT: In your own kingdom, sir.
> LEAR: Do not abuse me.
>
> (IV. vii. 76–77)

The decay of State boundaries logically results in an erosion of the subjectivities produced by the power of the State.[109] The general expulsion and deterritorialization brings about the desubjectivation or splitting of the *dramatis personae*.[110] This phenomenon can be explained in part by the fact that the protagonists define themselves through their position in the kingdom and their vested rights and properties. (The Fool, Kent, and Edgar occasionally make this explicit.) Above all, the nobles understand themselves in reference to the territories assigned to them; consequently, they are named exclusively after their dominions. In *Richard III* and *King John*, the nobles have first names besides their titles: Hastings is also Lord William, Derby is also Lord Stanley, France is also Philip. In *Lear*, by contrast, Gloucester becomes nameless when his title is transferred to Edmund. If the liegemens' substance is determined by the territories, positions, and privileges they hold, then this is all the more true of the king who owns his land and represents it at the same time.[111] The monarch and his territory mutually represent each other and thus are bound together in a reciprocal relationship. Therefore, it is only logical that Lear and his kingdom should disintegrate together.

Its deterritorialization turns Lear's kingdom into a mirage, a comprehensive simulacrum. Under these circumstances, only the exile is in a position appropriate to the situation, since he can complement the dissolution of the territory with his own uprooting. Consequently, the banished in *Lear* do not try to leave the country but rather work to integrate themselves into the events by taking on a new, self-contradictory mandate. These attempts produce eminently theatrical stratagems: the exiles Kent and Edgar disguise themselves and assume new identities so that they can stay in the country and survive. They invent new names and new biographies for themselves as well as new garments and manners of speaking—that is to say, they enact themselves as a theatrical spectacle. It is a distinguishing feature of other Shakespearean dramas as well that exile is an experience that characters can master through the art of drama, that is, through the dramatic use of language, bodies, and props. (Two examples are Rosalind in *As You Like It* and Viola in *Twelfth Night*.)[112] A feature particular to *Lear*, however, is the excess with which these internal exiles become occupied by their assumed roles; their mask seems to develop its own rousing dynamic.

Particularly Kent, after he has assumed his servant role, turns out to be an expert in meta-theatrical legalities:

> KENT: If but as well I other accents borrow
> That can my speech diffuse, my good intent
> May carry through itself to that full issue
> For which I razed my likeness.
>
> (I. iv. 1–4)

His reference to "borrowed accents" implies that "Caius" speaks in a regional dialect. Across the board, banishment forces Kent into a mimesis that gives him a more intensive contact with the vernacular, with local customs ("to eat no fish," I. iv. 17),[113] and with the countryside from which he has nominally been excluded. Numerous further instances could exemplify this fact: for instance, after the "razing of his likeness" Kent seems altogether more intimately informed than the ruling princes about the course of political events in the country. One often wonders where all his information may come from (see e.g. II. ii. 45; III. i. 19–29; IV. vii. 87–89). Edgar also works hard to acquire a similar intimacy with England's countryside, some of his speeches making him sound like a proto-Romantic nature poet and precursor to Wordsworth[114] or Burns.[115] (In IV. vi, he is disguised as a peasant and speaks the Yorkshire dialect.) A further paradox of the inclusive exclusion within a decomposing kingdom thus becomes apparent: banishment associates the banished all the more closely with the land and the local idiom rather than driving them into zones beyond their country and their native language. The dissolution of the territories and the expulsions complementing it are thus also processes of linguistic transformations: proliferating idioms encroach on the universal language of court and temple, poetic condensations supplant their protocol. In the impending Babylonian confusion, the banished actors use xenoglossia, the only forms of expression equal to the moment.

Supporting his performance as a meta-actor is Kent's apparent awareness of being a *dramatis persona*, and hence of being subject to the laws of drama. As early as the middle of the play, his aim ("dear cause," IV. iii. 52) becomes obvious: he wants to bring about a conciliatory denouement by the end of the play, a reversal that would be capable of turning tragedy into comedy. Symptomatic of this is his refusal to heed Cordelia's exhortation to take off his disguise:

> KENT: Pardon, dear madam;
> Yet to be known shortens my made intent.
> My boon I make it that you know me not
> Till time and I think meet.
>
> (IV. v ii. 8–11)

But the anagnorisis he has in mind founders on Cordelia's death and Lear's resultant lack of interest in Kent's split identity (V. iii. 280–288). Kent/Caius is denied his "promised end" and the restitution of his univocal identity through Shakespeare's obliteration of traditional dramatic forms.[116]

Kent turns into a paradoxical, split figure in yet another sense: he claims simultaneously the privileged position of the nobleman and the subordinate one of the footman. His new position of playacting exile permits him to shift to and fro between the role of master and servant, and so to incarnate the mime's social ambiguity. For example, he vituperates Oswald in II. ii as "a base, proud, [...] beggarly, three-suited-hundred-pound, filthy, worsted-stocking knave [...]; one-trunk-inheriting slave" (II. ii. 14–18). These formulations suggest that he reproaches Oswald most of all for trying to influence the politics of his masters despite his inferior status, his low birth (see also "mongrel," II. ii. 21), and his insufficient supply of "commodities" that exhibit wealth (see also II. ii. 71 ff.). In all this, Kent demonstrates a class conceit that sounds all the more grotesque as he in fact occupies a station lower than Oswald's in his role of Caius. This vacillating relationship to his roles and his incognito seem to offer to the exile peculiar pleasures, which dominate Kent even as he announces to serve the king (II. ii. 126). This is made obvious not least by the fact that his deeds frequently work to Lear's disadvantage, as when Kent in II. ii. insults and attacks not only Oswald but also Edmund (II. ii. 44–45), Regan, and Cornwall:

> KENT: Sir, 'tis my occupation to be plain:
> I have seen better faces in my time
> Than stands on any shoulder that I see
> Before me at this instant.
>
> (II. ii. 90–93)

Kent is put in the stocks because, as Lear's representative, he has made diverse somewhat presumptuous attempts to act with executive authority, some of which he later tries to whitewash (II. ii. 251–252). It is this punishment that sets off the great confrontation between Lear and his daughters in which the monarch loses his last symbolic support. In this way, Kent contributes to an escalation of the situation; the role he had assumed develops its own, fatal dynamic that speeds up the kingdom's collapse rather than impeding it.

What new perspectives become available to people who have been expatriated in this manner? Does their dislocation allow them a new, freer view of things? The exiled, play-acting Edgar at first thinks it does:

> EDGAR: Yet better thus, and known to be contemned
> Than still contemned and flattered. To be worst,
> The lowest and most dejected thing of fortune,
> Stands still in esperance, lives not in fear.
> The lamentable change is from the best,
> The worst returns to laughter. Welcome then,
> Thou unsubstantial air that I embrace;
> The wretch that thou hast blown unto the worst
> Owes nothing to thy blasts.
>
> (IV. i. 1–9)

Edgar tries his hand at stoicism by characterizing the *conditio humana* as a state of general repudiation ("to be contemned") whose universality is revealed only to him who has nothing left to lose and hence leads a life devoid of fear. Because he no longer owes the cruel world any possessions or a secure place to live, and has therefore become independent of it, he expects the cosmos to expose its pellucid depths to his view. But he can think only of conventional allusions to the image of the "wheel of fortune"[117]—widely used since Cicero—when he tries to describe it metaphorically, suggesting that his worldview will require radical revisions. Subsequently, Edgar finds that fate knows no natural turning points, not even a nadir of destitution:

> (*Enter GLOUCESTER, led by an Old Man.*)
> EDGAR: But who comes here? My father, poorly led? [. . .]

> O gods! Who is't can say "I am at the worst"?
> I am worse than e'er I was. [...]
> And worse I may be yet; the worst is not
> So long as we can say "This is the worst."
>
> (IV. i. 10/27–30)

Because the excluded always remains embedded into what is included,[118] banishment and curse are interminable and therefore operations that can be infinitely intensified. Therefore, a stoicism that attempts to adjust to the worst case in matters of jurisdiction does not assume a tenable position, but a pose. With this representation of Edgar, Shakespeare turns a martyr drama into an aborted metatheater.[119] It is specifically as a stoic that Edgar remains an actor caught up in a simulacrum. Thus even the metaphysical safety of a martyr's death is denied him: besides Albany, he is almost the sole survivor of the drama. Does a path of political action lead out of this general exile and its Babylonian confusion? Do Cordelia and her campaign, for instance, offer an opportunity to restore the kingdom and the decomposing concept of nature? Her vassals seem to think so:

> GENTLEMAN: Thou hast one daughter
> Who redeems nature from the general curse
> Which twain have brought her to.
>
> (IV. vi. 201–203)

According to this ambiguous formulation, Cordelia's mission would be both military and religious, "twain" apparently referring to Goneril and Regan but also to Adam and Eve, who are responsible for the "general curse" on nature, i.e. the expulsion from Paradise. The Gentleman is neither the first nor the last one who tries to reinterpret Lear's drama as a salvation history: even Cordelia herself uses biblical allusions to justify her invasion as a holy war:

> CORDELIA: O dear father,
> It is thy business that I go about; [...]
> No blown ambition doth our arms incite,
> But love, dear love, and our aged father's right:
> Soon may I hear and see him.
>
> (IV. iv. 23–24/27–29)

Cordelia calls the restitution of her father the primary goal of her war, alluding to the phrase "my father's business" from Luke 2. 49. The Christian subtext implies that her work of salvation also involves her messianic self-sacrifice. She no longer acts "according to her bond," but transcends all fulfillments of duty under the banner of sacrificial love. That this absolute love becomes the cause of a war points back to the dilemma of affirmatively transgressive affections treated in I. i

Cordelia lets herself be captivated by the rhetoric of a messianic politics in which affect and nature seem to be in harmony:

> CORDELIA: All blest secrets,
> All you unpublished virtues of the earth,
> Spring with my tears.
>
> (IV. iv. 15–17)

The problem with her attitude is that the family dispute, as well as Goneril's and Regan's rule by nature, are merely symptoms ("furnishings," III. i. 29) of a theologico-political dilemma that dissolves transcendence and immanence into one uncomfortable entity. Cordelia's religiously secured affection does not show her a way out of this situation because she also short-circuits nature with martial law. Therefore, Cordelia is thrown back to perpetuating *Lear's* metaphors of cosmic struggle:

> CORDELIA: Had you not been their father, these white flakes
> Did challenge pity of them. Was this a face
> To be opposed against the warring winds?
> To stand against the deep dread-bolted thunder,
> In the most terrible and nimble stroke
> Of quick cross-lightning?
>
> (IV. vii. 30–35)

As Lear does on the heath, Cordelia describes the storm as a cosmic war of the elements. In her locutions, even pity is something that can be challenged ("these white flakes did challenge pity on them"), just as her own loving pity leads to military challenges.[120] She thus *nolens volens* reaffirms the vicious circle of nature that structures the play. All of this goes to show that even the reconciliation of Lear and Cordelia in IV. vii does not offer the country a way out of its problems. Perpetuating the Christian subtext as well as its subversion, the scene focuses on the mutual forgiveness of father and daughter, an act of mercy that appears to be the antidote to their mutual execrations in I. i Derrida has extensively elaborated the paradoxes of forgiveness by demonstrating, for instance, that only what is unforgivable can be forgiven.[121] The problem is that forgiveness, on account of its equally paradoxical structure, can suspend within itself the contradictions of the symbolic system that express themselves symptomatically in the curse, but cannot overcome them. Repentance and forgiveness are not denounced *per se* in *Lear*; the play only demonstrates that they are symbolic actions that neither reconstitute political orders nor are able to resolve the double binds that lock the gates of heaven. Their act of mutual forgiveness merely leads the forgiver and the forgiven back to the situation where the event that requires forgiveness occurred, and burdens them additionally with the full array of its consequences, superposing itself on the original and still malignant dilemma whose repression has triggered the curse.[122]

But nevertheless, Lear attempts to reconstruct his sovereignty even with the help of forgiveness. Since his previous attempts—through the implementation of natural law—ended in aporias, after the military defeat he envisions a place where he could retain his sovereign subjectivity by acknowledging Cordelia with a constantly renewed forgiveness and a love that transcends all contingencies. That is to say, he once again lays claim to the transcendent form of her love that Cordelia refused him in I. i, but which circumstances now force her to give.[123] And once more Lear tries to spin the defeat of his party into an act posited by him. By analogy to I. i, he sovereignly renounces his sovereignty, but this time with the gesture of a saint and clearly in a language with a more strongly religious imprint:

> LEAR: Come, let's away to prison;
> We two alone will sing like birds i'th'cage.
> When thou dost ask me blessing I'll kneel down
> And ask of thee forgiveness. So we'll live
> And pray, and sing, and tell old tales, and laugh
> At gilded butterflies, and hear poor rogues
> Talk of court news; and we'll talk with them too –
> Who loses and who wins, who's in, who's out –
> And take upon's the mystery of things
> As if we were God's spies.
>
> (V. iii. 8–17)

His effusion suggests that so long as Lear and Cordelia maintain a contact that transcends all their other responsibilities, even prison is but an environment that makes monastic remoteness and intimacy possible. At the non-place of their shared cell, the ritual drama of their reciprocal self-denials ("sacrifices," V. iii. 20), which also takes on Eucharistic traits, can be enacted: Their endless repetition shall serve to fill the time left to them both. In this situation, Lear translates sovereignty into a sovereign irony toward contingencies. Like Edgar, he tries to take a distanced, purely observing position ("God's spies"), affording him a view from nowhere with a somewhat priestly orientation.[124] Lear fends off those who will disturb this arrangement with an appropriate supplementary curse: "The good-year[125] shall devour them, flesh and fell" (V. iii. 24). But as in *King John* so in *Lear*, there is no position from which to observe political problems at a distance, as Cordelia's murder strikingly demonstrates. Inasmuch as the acknowledgment of Cordelia and their mutual love has since IV. vii been the medium of Lear's new sovereignty, the definitive loss of his daughter throws Lear back into the self-destructing, unlimited realm of nature where he loses himself. Lear's loss, in turn, makes it impossible for the other exiles like Kent and Edgar to return to their former position.[126] Since Lear can have no legitimate successor and since the old structures cannot be reconstructed, the State's territory remains barred.

The sequence of loss of status, flight into exile and restitution, incorporating an ostentatiously exhibited differentiation between nature and culture, reconciled in a phantasmatic synthesis of the lower and the upper classes, is characteristic of pastoral.[127] *Lear* rejects this form: in the exile of its protagonists there certainly occurs a phantasmatic synthesis of society and nature, respectively of lower- and upper-class people. But it is a synthesis that is clearly marked, first, as a pure phantasm and, second, as anything but harmonious. When, third, the dislocated figures begin endeavoring to return from their banishment, their homeland nonetheless remains irrevocably lost. There is no return out of the half-world synthesized from nature, family and State. All survivors remain exiles in the "uncanny," stranded in a "different scene," "*ein anderer Schauplatz.*"[128]

3.4. Edgar and the *benedictio vacui*

The origin of all early modern blessings and benediction ceremonies is biblical; blessing plays no role in the pagan cultures of Greece and Rome.[129] This is also attested indirectly in the German word for blessing, "*Segen*," which is etymologically derived from "signum,"[130] i.e. the sign of the cross, and translates the Old Testament "berakah" (בְּרָכָה), a term that the Septuagint and the New Testament, for lack of a pagan equivalent, render as εὐλογία, "praise." The benediction appears as the structural counterpart of the execration insofar as it creates community through inclusion rather than exclusion. In essence, it is the integrating act of recognition, acceptance or readmission of a person in a community that is predominately conceived as familial. The blessing is given[131] as a sign of belonging, both in the interactions among humans and in their exchanges with God, who is figured as the primordial giver of blessings (Genesis 1. 28) and hence as their transcendent source. According to this dichotomy, the forms of the benediction may be roughly divided into a primary, vertical and a secondary, horizontal blessing: the former comes from the world's Lord and Father to his faithful servants, while the latter is directed toward equals, occasionally even towards superiors. In the following discussion, the first will be called paternal, the second, fraternal. The fraternal blessing affirms the reciprocity of relationships within a community; the paternal, by contrast, their hierarchy. In the family, the father, along the patrilineal lines of descent, confers the latter upon his successor. (See, e.g. Gen. 27–28; Sirach 3. 8–9.)

In the State, metaphorically understood as one large family under a representative of God the Father, the paternal blessing comes from the prince. With this blessing, the sovereign dispenses authority and recognition on his progeny as much as on his subjects, and thereby reaffirms his dynastic and his political superiority. The blessing of the country's father, by preserving the State and his "House," unites nature and politics by doubly securing bloodlines. Good health and fruitfulness in various forms are mentioned again and again as an effect of this blessing. Accordingly, in Elizabethan and Jacobean England the king as God's deputy commands a special power to bless that is thought to be effective against illnesses and especially against scrofula, the "king's evil." Talk of this healing ability of the monarch plays a legitimating role throughout the sixteenth century. Various legends about Elizabeth's healing power are cited as proof that the papal Bull of

Excommunication has failed to actually depose the queen.[132] That God approves of the monarchs' status is evidenced by the latter's effective benediction, so that this act can legitimate its own authority.

Like the execration, so the benediction appears as a fetishized, paradoxical act that representatively stages a transcendent creative authority with whose help it claims to structure the world. The blessing operates paradoxically by producing a homogeneity and similitude between the giver and the recipient of the benediction which it presupposes at the same time—analogously to the curse that both creates an exclusion and presupposes it. Both the curse and the blessing unfold a vicious circle in whose endless circuit they perpetuate themselves. The churches have institutionalized this paradox by integrating the blessing into both the Catholic and the Protestant liturgy. It appears most explicitly at the end of the mass, when the priest or pastor pronounces God's blessing on the congregation, often adding to it the sign of the cross (*signatio crucis*). Most of the benedictory formulas used in this context are derived from the Aaronic blessing (Num. 6. 24–26), also used in the Jewish worship service.[133] It is noticeable that they all are kept significantly shorter than the liturgical execratory formulas listed in Chapter 1, section 1.2: they are empty formulas that will be filled by an open shared future. Aside from this brief closing benediction, however, blessings also interweave with other parts of the worship service. The Lord's Supper above all is to be understood as an act of benediction that institutes the bloodlines of Christian brotherhood. For this reason, Paul calls the chalice of the Eucharist the "cup of blessing" (1 Cor. 10. 16; see also Matthew 26. 26). In this context, an additional etymological connection between blessing and blood may be suggested by the fact that the verb "to bless" seems to be derived from Germanic "*blothisojan*" (to mark with blood).[134]

The blessing affirms that the person blessed is integrated into the social system, and it also delineates the area in which the curse unfolds, marking its boundaries. As for example the Eucharist makes evident, curse and blessing feed on each other; they do not represent two different acts but one act with two facets, in that exclusion and inclusion are interdependent in it. Ecclesiastical benediction ceremonies are therefore also seen as exorcistic acts that can expel evil spirits.[135] Analogously, the blessing that the dead pronounce upon Richmond in *Richard III* supplements their curse on Richard (V. iii. 119–177).[136] The blessing legitimates the one to the same degree that the curse delegitimates the other; it is remarkable how often not only the dead but also his mother and the nobles bless Richmond:

> BLUNT: God give you quiet rest tonight [. . .].
> STANLEY: Fortune and victory sit on thy helm! [. . .]
> I, by attorney, bless thee from thy mother [. . .].
> Be valiant and speed well.
>
> (V. iii. 39/80/84/103)

Last but not least, there are repeated allusions in *Richard III* (e.g. IV. ii. 94–96) to a scene in *3 Henry VI* in which Henry VI lays his hand in blessing on the future Henry VII (see *3 Henry VI*, IV. vii. 68 ff.).

During the early modern era and particularly in Protestant Europe, the fraternal blessing shows a marked increase over the paternal one. In part, this development vindicates itself biblically: the New Testament promises the universalizing of Abraham's blessing through Christ's sacrifice (Gal. 3. 14); hence, a universal call to blessing goes out to all Christians (Rom. 12. 14). This propagates the view that it is less the curse of the highest dignitaries that one must fear than the imprecation of those who have suffered injustice, especially if they are indigent.[137] The benediction of the destitute carries special weight insofar as they are said to be figurations of Christ, in allusion to Matthew 25. 40 ("Verily I say unto you, inasmuch as ye have done it unto one of the least of these my brethren, ye have done it unto me"). This view in no way changes the practice of occasionally condemning the imprecation of the helpless and needy as witchcraft[138] and, especially among the Puritans, of preaching polemically against it and against blessings as an either redundant or misguided weapon lifted from the arsenal of the "Pope's playhouse."[139] In Elizabethan England, benediction and execration alike are a precarious variable.

In *King Lear*, the blessing is rather less frequently in evidence than the curse; but when it does occur, it is as an obviously empty speech act. The fraternal as well as the paternal blessing are marked as ineffective ("hollow and void"). After the first scene, there is no longer a clearly discernable political or religious community anyway into which the blessed one could be received. For this reason, blessings become private affairs and are used only outside of State ceremonies: as a family benediction, as a blessing of the patriarchal "House," or as a fraternal blessing conferred among friends and allies. But, even in this context, it seems to be employed only in order to ironically accentuate its comprehensive ineffectiveness: everything blessed is either already lost or will be lost soon. That Kent, for example, exclaims: "The gods reward your kindness" (III. vi. 5) to bless Gloucester, does not keep the latter from having his eyes gouged out for this very "kindness" in the very next scene. And even though Lear on his way to prison promises his constant benediction to his youngest daughter and Albany's "The gods defend her" (V. iii. 254) additionally affirms this blessing, Cordelia will be dead when she is carried on to the stage a little later. Blessings in *Lear* occur as nothing but the persisting relic of a collapsed transcendence: its own specter, as it were.

Analogously to the way that curses, oaths, and prophecies function in Shakespeare's dramas, the semiotic evacuation of the blessing also effects its representation as a speech act that, precisely because of its ineffectiveness, can take over new functions in a theatrical context. Within the diegetic action of *Lear*, this appropriation for the theater is taken on by Edmund, who in his role of Poor Tom certainly insists most tenaciously on blessings. As an internal exile, he claims fraternal reciprocity by way of benedictions, which constitutes part of his role as indigent beggar and *imitator Christi*:

> EDGAR: The country gives me proof and precedent
> Of Bedlam beggars, who, with roaring voices,

> Strike in their numbed and mortified bare arms
> Pins, wooden pricks, nails, sprigs of rosemary;
> And with this horrible object, from low farms,
> Poor pelting villages, sheepcotes and mills,
> Sometime with lunatic bans, sometime with prayers,
> Enforce their charity.
>
> (II. ii. 184–191)

The term "prayers" here refers to blessings that complement "bans," i.e. curses. In Edgar's words, the performative forces of curse and blessing seem bound together. It is implicit in his role, as defined by these two speech acts, that his discursive power as a beggar depends on impotence and destitution. When Edgar mimes the possessed, blessing beggar–exorcist, he merely intensifies the theatrical component of mendicancy; for the beggars he wants to imitate have themselves already taken up roles, according to Edgar's description. They also arouse compassion not so much through their objective misery but through its dramatic intensification, which combines self-flagellation with sacral speech acts. Because of this duplication, Edgar, in pursuing his meta-theatrical efforts, loses sight of the boundary between reality and play in occasionally surprising ways. But it is precisely this loss that enables him to unobtrusively inhabit the no-man's-land between nature and culture that Lear's kingdom has become. Edgar represents himself as a man from whom all culture has been subtracted ("the basest and most poorest shape [. . .] brought near to beast," II. ii. 178–180), but nonetheless he is the figure who most often regurgitates various chunks of cultural products, constantly spitting out scraps of benedictory incantations, Bible quotes, aphorisms, poems, epics, fairy tales, anti-Catholic tracts, demonologies, and iconologies. Lear accordingly calls him an "unaccomodated man," "the thing itself," and "a poor, bare, forked animal" (III. iv. 104–106) but also a "most learned justicer" (III. vi. 21), "noble philosopher" (III. iv. 168), a "good Athenian" (III. iv. 176), and "learned Theban" (III. iv. 153). This contradictory characterization seems appropriate insofar as Edgar in his play-acting (analogously to Lear's own efforts) tries to synthesize nature and culture. But whereas Lear intends to achieve this synthesis by means of a compulsory political program, Edgar limits himself to justifying and affirming his own marginal position through its public evocation. In his role of "natural man," Edgar must therefore also function as "master of arts" and "master of ceremonies," an imposed mission which seems to anticipate that of the Romantics.[140] His speech acts derive their ambivalence from this task. Examples are the exorcizing benedictory and protective spells that define his role most prominently, such as:

> EDGAR: Swithold footed thrice the wold;
> He met the nightmare and her nine foal,
> Bid her alight and her troth plight,
> And aroint thee, witch, aroint thee.
>
> (III. iv. 117–120)

This "kind of charm against demons"[141] cites a popular narrative form:[142] Its ceremonious exorcism apparently is to be effected through the description of another ceremonious exorcism, as if an action that is recalled with the help of a fixed formula were carried out a second time. But using a form whose effectivity stems from narration immediately raises the problems inherent in any representation that conflates times and places—problems with which any reflection on theatrical blessings has to come to terms. The problems appear to be all the more urgent as the charm itself collapses the timeframe imposed by the diegetic action: the name "Swithold" refers to St. Swithin or Withold,[143] which is a living anachronism in Lear's nominally pre-Christian kingdom. Insofar as the saint is an anachronism, hence without a distinct place in time and without a definable identity, he personifies the theater's untimely regime. By the power of his speech he can request an oath from the demonic apparition ("her troth plight") and thus bind it to his commanding, exorcising word. But this bond is null and void inasmuch as the ambivalence and indefinability of the conjured apparition can stand up to those of the theatrical saint; its ambiguous designation already indicates this dilemma: "Nightmare" may designate a bad dream but also the nightmare with her foals, weighing down her victim as an incubus or succubus.[144] The charm's ambiguity allows the apparition to keep oscillating between reality and unreality and between second and third person, and thus to remain elusive, preserving her uncanny status which the charm was supposed to overcome in the first place. The execution of the exorcism seems to be reduced to self-parody. The same applies to the charm with which Edgar exorcises the dogs that Lear hallucinates:

> EDGAR: Tom will throw his head at them: avaunt, you curs!
> Be thy mouth or black or white,
> Tooth that poisons if it bite;
> Mastiff, greyhound, mongrel grim,
> Hound or spaniel, brach or him,
> Or bobtail tyke or trundle-tail,
> Tom will make him weep and wail;
> For with throwing thus my head,
> Dogs leap the hatch and all are fled.
> Do, de, de, de. *Cessez!* Come, march to wakes and fairs and market towns.
> (III. vi. 62–72)

In imitation of the demons whose body parts are detachable and who can therefore disintegrate into their own *membra disiecta*,[145] Edgar announces that he will throw his own head at the demon dogs. His confrontation with the fiends thus includes entering into a mimetic relationship with them, or rather with their non-existence. (Incidentally, it is remarkable that this procedure is meant to banish the demons to markets and other commercial hubs, as if these were the appropriate locations for ambiguous "foul fiends." Section 3.5 will indirectly return to this issue.) Edgar dissolves the demonic being into language, but he also incorporates it. Like Richard III, he is a threshold figure who, adopting the persona of the exorcizing actor, both subverts the old belief and safeguards it.[146] By appropriating the ruins of protective and consecrating charms, he demonstrates the ambiguous function and performative strength of the theater: as he plays a man possessed ("whom the foul fiend vexes," III. iv. 59), he seems to become increasingly possessed by his role, both as a man possessed, and as an exorcist. The role he assumes gradually develops its own dynamic; consequently, he elaborates his cover story beyond any pragmatically sensible degree and for a time quite plainly identifies with its self-destructive, quasi-sovereign synthesis of nature and culture. His mask absorbs his face. Perhaps this fact also contributes to explaining his mysterious behavior toward Gloucester in Act IV. In Lear's world of phantasms, their very oscillation between reality and unreality links not only Edgar, but also his "foul fiends," with nature. The way Poor Tom depicts them, the demons have no separate sphere of influence; rather, this sphere seems to be coextensive with open nature:

> EDGAR: Who gives anything to Poor Tom? Whom the foul fiend hath led through fire and through flame, through ford and whirlpool, o'er bog and quagmire; that hath laid knives under his pillow and halters in his pew; set ratsbane by his porridge, made him proud of heart, to ride on a bay trotting horse over four-inched bridges, to course his own shadow for a traitor.
>
> (III. iv. 50–56)

In this and related passages, the demons are associated with sublime natural phenomena: storms, conflagrations, maelstroms, and various desolate landscapes. Edgar's proto-Romantic prose poem describes the demonism of wild nature as a fascinating force of annihilation in which the sublime has the effect of a strange attractor. However, the "fiends" who supply this attraction merely lead the subject deeper into a precarious situation instead of annihilating it. While they certainly more than hint towards dangerous objects and circumstances, they still keep these suggestions inconclusive and vague: shall his forced ride across extremely narrow bridges, the rat poison by his plate, the knife under his pillow, the noose on the pew, etc. induce him to suicide or murder, or some other act of furor? What remains equally unclear is the motivation of this demonic will to destruction: are the "foul fiends" the executors of a divine judgment? (It is worth remembering that Clarence in *Richard III* also calls the hellish Furies "foul fiends.") Or might they perhaps be executioners in the service of the Court of Chancery? For Edgar's demons can also be understood as paranoid figurations representing real agents of public order that *de facto* pursue him, Gloucester, and Lear.[147] This diffuse ambiguity of the natural demons leaves the question of their legitimacy unanswerable. This fact is also taken up and worked out in Edgar's enactments: as a cover story, he first constructs a moral tale that would explain his desolate condition and his possessed state:

> LEAR: What hast thou been?
>
> EDGAR: A serving-man, proud in heart and mind, that curled my hair, wore gloves in my cap, served the lust of my mistress' heart and did the act of

> darkness with her; swore as many oaths as I spake words and broke them in the sweet face of heaven. One that slept in the contriving of lust and waked to do it. Wine loved I deeply, dice dearly; and, in woman, out-paramoured the Turk: false of heart, light of ear, bloody of hand; hog in sloth, fox in stealth, wolf in greediness, dog in madness, lion in prey.
>
> (III. iv. 82–92)

Edgar describes himself as a decadent youth from a better family whom God punished for his licentious conduct with destitution, dementia (delirium tremens?, syphilis?) and other scourges. And he does not forbear to derive edifying lessons from his fate:

> EDGAR: Take heed o'the foul fiend; obey thy parents, keep thy word justly, swear not, commit not with man's sworn spouse, set not thy sweet-heart on proud array. [. . .] Let not the creaking of shoes, nor the rustling of silks, betray thy poor heart to woman. Keep thy foot out of brothels, thy hand out of plackets, thy pen from lenders' books, and defy the foul fiend.
>
> (III. iv. 78–80/92–96)

In this list of commandments, the solicited moral behavior consists first, in respect for the traditional obliging word ("keep thy word justly, swear not") and, second, in the avoidance of sexuality—which is clearly marked as fetishistic by profuse references to female apparel such as "rustling of silks," "gloves in my cap," "creaking of shoes," and "plackets." Edgar displays himself as an erstwhile lecher and traitor and hence as the subject of a terrifying broadside ballad. Thus, he parodies not only his own demonic possession but also conventional morality, which seeks to appraise the individual's position in the world as either the reward or as the just penalty for his past deeds. For the plot of *Lear* contradicts these moralizing rationalizations insofar as no immoral, profligate acts of Edgar are identified that might be considered the cause of his factually desolate situation; rather, he finds himself pursued, poor and at the edge of insanity on account of an intrigue instigated by Edmund. In this respect, Edgar parodies morality, personifying the insufficiency of moralizing explanations of the world, whether he is aware of this or not. That he probably realizes it is shown by his (once more anachronistic and parodic) turn at the end of III. iv, where, along with an epic and a fairy tale, he amalgamates a lofty Christian-nationalist mission and a monstrous thirst for blood:

> EDGAR: Childe Rowland to the dark tower came,
> His word was still "Fie, foh and fum,
> I smell the blood of a British man."
>
> (III. iv. 178–180)

The formula of a monstrous giant from an early version of *Jack and the Beanstalk* is put into the mouth of the hero of the Songs of Roland (i.e. of Charlemagne's nephew and/or a son of King Arthur).[148] Insofar as the noble knight in this epic fragment assumes the speaking part of a monster that heroes like him are generally called upon to slay, the representation of the good is blended with that of evil so that the paladin becomes indistinguishable from the ogre. Man's monstrosity can no longer be restricted to specific roles and transgressions. The genres of epic, broadside ballad and fairy tale thus collapse: it is no longer possible to tell edifying stories about winners and losers.

It is also no longer possible to give a meaningful blessing: Edgar's countless fraternal benedictions are quite evidently powerless and empty, just like those of the other characters. But in contrast to the others, Edgar accentuates this emptiness so that it appears to be the blessing's real object and driving force. He pronounces, for example, the benediction "Bless thee from whirlwinds, star-blasting and taking" (III. iv. 58) in the midst of a storm whose winds already pummel both its speaker and his listener ("this contentious storm invades us to the skin," III. iv. 6–7) and which Lear interprets as a cosmic, arbitrary force. At this point, Edgar does not even bless the endangered and the marginalized anymore, but only those already beyond blessing.[149] This becomes even more obvious in other situations: Edgar twice blesses the king's "five wits" (III. iv. 56–57/III. vi. 56) shortly before Kent tersely summarizes Lear's condition with the words: "His wits are gone" (III. vi. 84). The void occupying the place of a missing entity seems to be the only adequate object of Edgar's empty blessing. The same strategy can be discerned in his "Bless thee, master" (IV. iv. 41/66) vis-à-vis Gloucester, who in Act IV has definitively lost his lordly position, and, most pointedly, in his "Bless thy sweet eyes, they bleed" (IV. i. 56–57) on Gloucester's gouged-out eyes. Once more evoking the etymological connection between "bless" and "bleed," a congregation of desolation is founded on attributes that only in their state of destruction can give and accept blessings.

Why does Edgar bless only that which—like "wits" and "eyes"—must be absent in order for the conditions of pronouncing the benediction to come about at all? Stephen Greenblatt has explicated in "Shakespeare and the Exorcists" that Edgar's sacral speech acts cannot simply be reduced to self-parodies. In Greenblatt's reading, Edgar's performance is motivated by the insight that "evacuated" rituals, which have become meaningless but are still enacted and cherished, produce better effects than uncontested and saturated ones, but also better effects than the total absence of rituals.[150] The requisite containment of ceremony is accomplished by the theater, whose representative in the play is Edgar's metatheater, itself clearly marked as empty. In this connection, Greenblatt presumes Shakespeare's enlightened crypto-Catholicism, since he is primarily interested in Edgar's exorcisms as specifically Catholic acts.[151] But what seems more relevant to the problem of blessings is Greenblatt's suggestion that Edgar might be read as Shakespeare's inscription of himself into his own text:[152] the theater's contained compromise formations "evacuate" ceremonies but also preserve and repurpose them.[153] This ironic appropriation is ambiguous and can be read differently depending on the spectator's point of view, because its irony always points in several directions; contrary positions can find themselves confirmed by it. The theater thus functions as a double fraud, but one that emphasizes its own fraudulence and thus can clear a new, more complex path to truth by way of its metaphorization.[154] And it is through this honest and potentially productive fraud that Shakespeare and Edgar secure their own survival. This theory also implies that the theater of the early modern era has anything but an unequivocally secularizing effect: the evacuation of rites in the theater does not entail their abolition; rather, they become fetishized in new ways. According to the psychoanalytical definition, fetishistic objects and practices are distinguished by the fact that they incarnate and thus perpetuate a faith that is simultaneously acknowledged as fallacious. In this way, a mourner may, for example, simultaneously deny and acknowledge the death of a loved one.[155] The constant "*Je sais bien, mais quand même* . . ." employed by the fetishist erects a protective barrier against both undiluted faith and the reality that contradicts this faith.[156] Now, as Edgar's case makes evident, the fraternal blessing of vacuity is exactly the form that the fetishization of empty benedictions must assume in a theatrical context. Edgar treats emptiness as a unifying power of benediction that, like the action of the theatrical plot, is both effective and at the same time inconsequential. Deliberately, he seeks out deprivation as an ally: "Welcome then, thou unsubstantial air that I embrace" (IV. i. 6–7). And while he treats nothingness as something, this absence does indeed develop an unexpected productivity, for example in form of the saved and saving "happy hollow:"

> EDGAR: I heard myself proclaimed,
> And by the happy hollow of a tree
> Escaped the hunt.
>
> (II. ii. 172–174)

Stanley Cavell suggests that in a certain way even Gloucester's empty eye sockets save Edgar and his fetishism.[157] Edgar does not vanish like France; indeed he, or rather the void with which he aligns himself, develops a dynamic which keeps him out of reach of both friend and foe. Near Dover he uses dramatic means to set up before Gloucester the image of a salvific emptiness that, for its part, turns out to be "hollow and void"—and can work as a provisional rescue precisely for this reason (IV. iv. 1–74). Edgar's attempt to enter a beneficent alliance with the void even prompts him to identify with it; he makes verbal efforts to merge into nothingness: "Edgar I nothing am" (II. ii. 192). Once again, in this formulation the person is reduced to a mode:[158] since he as Edgar is nothing anymore, nothing becomes Edgar's essence—and becomes his name after his own name has been lost (V. iii. 119). In this excessive, anticipatory compliance toward nothingness, emptiness appears as sovereign and determines the way Edgar relates to both nature and culture. But the salvation it brings no longer seems to include a transcendent promise of bliss; instead, it appears to be reduced to naked survival at best, i.e. to the bare life of the inclusively excluded. Hence Edgar, on the occasion of his duel with Edmund, does refer to a higher justice—but as he describes it, this justice does not bring about the triumph of the just; instead, as a negative capacity, it merely surrenders all things to their warranted destruction (V. iii. 168–169). He conceives the “promised end” of the Apocalypse as a pure “horror” (V. iii. 262). It is only logical that his attempt to re-establish the bloodlines is a catastrophic failure: in an effort to close his metatheater, Edgar surprisingly demands a regularly hierarchical, paternal benediction from his father once more. But this blessing eludes him since Gloucester dies from the anagnorisis that would have made it possible:

> EDGAR: I asked his blessing and from first to last
> Told him our pilgrimage. But his flawed heart,
> Alack, too weak the conflict to support,
> ‘Twixt two extremes of passion, joy and grief,
> Burst smilingly.
>
> (V. iii. 194–198)

Like the other characters, Edgar remains incapable of reaccommodating himself to a comprehensive, paternalistic order, because this lordly structure cannot be reconstructed after Lear’s symbolic collapse.[159] The paternal as well as the royal blessing are no longer available in his new world, which is dynamically and provisionally organized around a void; and the fraternal benediction is reduced to a speech act that not only supplements the curse but has become altogether indistinguishable from it.

3.5 The Fool and the bonds of fate

In sixteenth- and seventeenth-century England, the medium of money liberates itself from most of its ritual and juridical shackles. It increasingly structures social interaction without having to safeguard itself through recourse to other media; money enjoys, as it were, its *coming-out*. As a result, the discourse of many a contemporary elevates economic transactions to the status of a paradigm of all social intercourse.[160] This also means that the transition from coins to paper money and book money, a process directed but not initiated by the State, makes money appear ever more abstract and immaterial.[161] However, while this revalorization and diffusion of money-mediated exchange is taking place, there is no contemporary economic theory adequate to these complex developments, since Shakespeare’s time does not yet possess an advanced conceptual language for economics.[162] To develop a science of economics beyond mere τέχνη is a theoretical project that, in the sixteenth and early seventeenth century has only begun to take shape, for instance in the preparatory work contributed by Bacon[163] and Hobbes.[164] Before then, reflections on a country’s economy did not even claim to delimit a research area of its own, and accordingly no attempt was made to authoritatively conceptualize terms such as “price,” “market,” or “commodity.”[165] Economic theory remained subordinate to the discourse on ethics and theology. The earliest economic texts are characterized by this subordination and therefore concentrate on the desirable containment and control of the market[166] (which seems to form a strange parallel with the displacement of the ordeal from the State's internal sphere onto international affairs).[167] These rudiments of theory consistently fall back on traditional (above all Aristotelian) commonplaces; for this reason, they appear in retrospect as self-contradictory, self-destructive projects.[168] Into this vacant conceptual space, a provisional metaphor is quickly inserted, as is also true for example in the case of natural law.[169] A large number of discourses (which at first remain largely independent of the explicit theories of natural law) attempts to deal with the borderless open market by using metaphors taken from nature. Hence the market appears as human nature, or respectively as what is naturally appropriate for man.[170] This soon opens an infinite regress: a theory of the market develops that claims to be based on nature, but at the same time nature is frequently theorized with reference to the market. Thus, an absolute metaphor is created, with which the world in its monetary liquidity can admittedly not be controlled, but with which it can at least be described.[171] This metaphorization of the interaction between commodities and money seems to hold out the promise an all-encompassing calculus, if both of them are allowed to circulate freely—a calculus that enables both society and human nature to pursue their appropriate development while relating them to each other. (In the eighteenth century, Adam Smith will claim it as his achievement to have provided the theoretical redemption of this promise.)[172] But under the conditions of early capitalism, the envisioned calculation remains a chimera, because the very structure of trade relations makes the participants incalculable to each other: within the market, any concrete calculation must assume the reverse calculation on the part of the other, hence it must take into account that he may be dissembling and masking his true intentions. Mutual opacity and personal indifference are, according to Georg Simmel, the conditions that make effective trade possible.[173] Monetary and trade relationships connect the partners in a reciprocity that establishes itself on the grounds of their mutual deceivability.[174] In business relationships, "brotherhood" and "otherhood" mutually refer to one another.[175] The actors of commerce (*die Handelnden*) enter the market as they would a theater; for them the market is experienced both as nature and as a dramatic institution.[176] Thus, in ontologizing the act of dissemblance in representation, one also poses the question of the difference between reality and imitation. This consideration is thematized early by Francis Bacon, for instance, who—in anticipation of Pascal—remarks that in mimetically assuming a posture, one at times also assumes the emotion associated with it; this means that, through the artificial manipulation of external appearances, one can also change one's inner life, respectively internal "nature."[177] Man becomes indistinguishable from his mask; his representation becomes his identity. Under these circumstances, "nature" must be thought anew; it appears that in the absence of firm, traditional connections, a new space has opened up, but one that is defined by the overdetermination of potential and virtual connections.

The *coming-out* of the market and the resultant dynamization and virtualization of the social field also enhance the significance of written contracts.[178] The contract in this context is frequently understood as the basic building block of a natural society.[179] Accordingly, natural-right equity begins to function as the legal norm that favors the contractual forms preferred by the market: merchants in sixteenth-century England mostly try to have their cases tried under the royal legislature of the Court of Chancery (*equity law*) and its offshoots (e.g. *admiralty law*) because these authorities are generally more open-minded toward their commercial concerns and the new forms of contractual law than the representatives of common law.[180] Analogously, the importance of the Roman *ius civilis* increases on the Continent as early as the late Middle Ages, to the detriment of canon law. This may be due to the fact that an oral contract is accorded a different status in each legal system: canon law obligates the parties involved to fulfill the terms of their contract even if these are based on a purely oral agreement. In Roman law by contrast, the promise, *nudum pactum*, is not actionable; an additional piece of objective evidence, either written material or a security, is needed. This understanding of what a contract requires proves to be more appropriate in a market where a contractual exchange is not an additional determinant within a pre-existing network of familial, territorial, communal or professional ties, but arises as an independent social relationship, separate from other connections.[181] For obligatory speech acts to be successful, it is increasingly necessary to formulate und keep written documents. One may even ask if their transcription is not in fact the decisive performative act. On account of his logocentrism, for which Derrida has faulted him,[182] Austin himself does not extensively deal with this question, but some of his examples imply that he accepts acts of writing as legitimate performative acts. One of the first performatives he lists may exemplify this: "'I give and bequeath my watch to my brother' – as occurring in a will."[183] According to this statement, written contractual agreements are performative acts, and not merely their written protocols. This conception implies that the promise as the fundamental regulator of object relations and of social connections can itself become an object in the contract. This increasing importance of contractual law accompanies the emerging dominance of book money and paper money, since money too is ever more often perceived as a contract between seller, buyer, and bank.[184] It should be remembered that, according to a conceptualization that has been popular since the early modern age and that was developed in all its ramifications by Hobbes, even the law of the commonwealth is understood to be an overarching form of the contract.[185] Hobbes derives both the form of the contract and of the law from a primordially represented oath;[186] and perhaps it is not accidental that the structured openness of the latter is analogous to that of the money form.[187]

Through the oath, the contract is connected with the curse; during the Middle Ages contracts are often secured by the conditional self-execration of both parties. Mostly due to insufficient legal security, early medieval sales contracts, as well as deeds of conveyance or donation, seldom include legal sanctions in case of breach of contract; instead one finds prospective curses and warnings that those committing such a breach would "fall victim to the wrath of hell" and would suffer the same eternal torments as the traitor Judas.[188] In this way, the contract is inscribed into the context of divine law; its resultant integration into the practice of the Eucharistic ordeal has already been discussed.[189] During the Renaissance, when a contract is not sufficiently secured by law, it is made a general practice to supplement the obligatory proclamation of the fear of God with one's proclaimed respect for interpersonal obligations, which is the cardinal prerequisite for any from of trade: creditworthiness slowly comes to supplement the *credo*. Subsequently, a system of (written or unwritten) agreements will guarantee the preservation of contracts, and no businessman can afford to be caught transgressing its boundaries.[190] This shift of orientation has an effect on theology in turn: in Puritan "covenant theology," which is nearly hegemonic in early seventeenth-century England, the relationship between God and believer is conceived as a special form of trade agreement.[191] Accordingly, religious doctrine down to its details is interpreted in terms of contract law[192] so that, for instance, baptism and the Eucharist are imagined as figures of a contractual ratification.[193] Victoria Kahn has shown that this mixing of sacred and economic variables is made possible by the supposition of man's infinite debt owed his creator.[194] (On this point, historical research seems to confirm Benjamin's notion of capitalism as the religion of irredeemable *Schuld*—both guilt and debt.)[195] Even if one may question some of Max Weber's theses about the connection between Protestantism and capitalism: the modern social order, which is based on trade and contracts, retains a cultic tint from these religious contaminations, which indicates that this order is anything but a purely goal-oriented affair of instrumental rationality. Thus the establishment of the contract's hegemony during the formative decades of capitalism does not entail that the curse and the oath are being deprived of their power by the spread of a skeptical pragmatism that would characterize the secularizing modern age. Rather both of them, along with the contract, free themselves of old hierarchical and ritual contexts and diffuse themselves across the entire symbolic field in reified form. The curse enters economic life and afflicts its subjects with a diffuse guilt (that is only bearable in this diffusion).[196]

It has already been developed in Chapter 1, section 1.7 and Chapter 2 that Shakespeare's dramas enact the ways in which the market transforms social obligations according to its own laws and that the dramas assume an ambiguous attitude toward emerging economic structures in which they nevertheless participate. The official morality of the plays, concurring with prevalent taste, often denounces economizing developments that define the conditions of the Elizabethan playhouse itself, insofar as these originated in the theater's commodification.[197] The dramas come to embrace the problems of social representation under these schizophrenic circumstances, which reflect a fundamental dichotomy of the early modern situation: *King Lear* as well as *King John* and *Richard III* stage the interaction of theologico-political with economic discourses, in part conflictual, in part mutually bastardizing. In this way, Shakespeare transmutes the ceremonies of kingship's transcendent legitimation into the commodity form; his theater explicates their mutual contamination.

In *Lear*, this contamination is uncompromisingly forced to its logical conclusion. A patent symptom of this state of affairs is the ambiguity inherent in the concept of "fortune," already quite evident in *King John* and playing an even more prominent role in *Lear*.[198] "Fortune"—in the polysemantic sense of fate, goddess of destiny, good luck, commodity, monetary assets, situation in life, and social status—enters the stage as the ruler of the crypto-capitalist *theatrum mundi*.[199] It is Lear who introduces the term by referring to his daughters' inheritances as their "fortunes" (I. i. 94). Nearly all characters move in the field of tension opened by this conceptual ambiguity, an environment in which the word's meanings become more and more blurred and interwoven. An example is the Fool's remark about "unfortunate beggars" (IV. vi. 68):

> FOOL: Fortune, that arrant whore,
> Ne'er turns the key to the poor.
>
> (II. ii. 242–243)

A remark made by Edmund, without doubt a soldier of fortune, becomes doubly ambiguous since it links a polysemic stroke of fate with a polysemic justice: "How malicious is my fortune, that I must repent to be just?" (III. v. 9–10). The motivation for these semantic blurrings can again be discerned in the circumstance that in *King Lear* a subject appears defined by the objects and the privileges it has at its disposal.[200] The name makes the person, and possessions make the name. The treatment of another semantic field points to the complementary figure of a sovereign performative attribution of status and value: in the land distribution ceremony,[201] the "price" (value), "prize" (reward), and "praise" (honor, esteem) of Lear's subjects meld seamlessly. When they are combined, these three define the love contest as a process not only of naturalization but also of value creation, *qua* appreciation of the valuable:

> REGAN: I am made of that self metal[202] as my sister,
> And *prize* me at her worth. [. . .]
> LEAR: When she was dear to us, we did hold her so,
> But now her *price* has fallen. [. . .]
> FRANCE: This is most strange,
> That she who even but now was your best object,
> The argument of your *praise*, balm of your age,
> The best, the dearest, should in this trice of time
> Commit a thing so monstrous, to dismantle
> So many folds of favor.
>
> (I. i. 69–70/197–198/214–219, emphasis added)

The sovereign's approbation ("praise") apparently indicates the value of things and persons ("price"); the vassal is an object of value ("a proclaimed prize," IV. vi. 222) to be appraised by it. Lear does not proceed arbitrarily in his evaluation: rather, he takes inventory before distributing the land, "where nature does with merit challenge" (I. i. 53) in order to have the attribution of material value coincide with the inner value of the *inclinatio naturalis*. The basis of "merit," as Lear declares in a loop of reciprocity, is the confession of love by the person requiring approval

(I. i. 51): to wit, the degree to which the subject herself approves of her sovereign and hence of the natural social contract. By virtue of its self-reinforcement, the reciprocity inherent in this love appears to open an unlimited potential for free value creation; for upon its foundation Lear generates riches via obliging speech acts as if his words of praise could increase the worth of things. This arrangement becomes manifest, for example, in his description of the land he distributes: he relentlessly exaggerates its splendor, using every superlative of "rich," "plenteous," "ample" and "opulent" (I. i. 63–65/79–86), as if he could upgrade the country with his hymnic word alone. Lear designates as the inexhaustible source of his country's wealth his eternal, overflowing word that is engaged in a loving dialogue with his subordinates. The benefits of this mutual and limitless affect must be to the advantage of the "jewels of our father" (I. i. 270), Regan and Goneril, whose cheaply proclaimed obedience towards Lear's emotional demands also symbolically subjects them to his exuberant coining. However, they are both fully aware that the property he is about to distribute is finite; Lear is the only one who never appears to recognize this limitation. Even after the storm on the heath, he generates wealth through his sovereign word: "There's your press-money" (IV. vi. 86–87). It has already been mentioned that his "they cannot touch me for coining" (IV. vi. 83), spoken near Dover, implies that, in analogy to his coronation with weeds, he is distributing pebbles or the like as means of payment.[203] But the same scene reveals an incoherence in Lear's discourse: he claims for himself the power to freely create money and to circulate it, but he also thunders against the power of wealth, which after all should logically be considered nothing but the extension of his own power:

> LEAR: Through tattered clothes small vices do appear;
> Robes and furred gowns hide all. Plate sin with gold,
> And the strong lance of justice hurtless breaks;
> Arm it in rags, a pigmy's straw does pierce it.
>
> (IV. vi. 160–163)

Here at the latest it becomes apparent that this sovereign has a schizophrenic relationship with wealth: the king may be its source, but wealth continues to be a transferable instrument of power that threatens to slip from his grasp and overwhelm him. The sovereign's word freely determines the value of persons and things; but on the other hand, this value manifests in the world as an independent force, a limited resource in nature that furnishes the laws of social interaction from the start.

The figure in the drama who analyzes the processes of value generation in greatest detail is Lear's "shadow," the Fool. He makes his first appearance immediately after money is used as a prop for the first time, i.e. when Kent thrashes Oswald off the stage and Lear hands him "earnest" for this and future services. At the moment when money changes hands, the Fool appears, exclaiming "Let me hire him too" (I. iv. 93) and presenting Kent with his fool's cap, apparently both as a means of payment and as the *insignium* of his trade. It is already symptomatic that the Fool designates Lear's as well as his own transaction as a "hiring," whereas Kent and Lear use "service" with its stronger feudal connotation; but the presentation of the cap itself also indirectly revaluates the preceding action in accordance with a more modern order of values. The Fool's duplicating gesture suggests that remuneration for more or less violent "services," even as it defines feudal relations, is *per se* not a feudal act at all: anybody with money or possessions can bring it off. The moment the Fool appears, he insists on the economic foundation of social relationships and he will henceforth not desist from judging persons with the help of the quantitative concepts of property and profit ("so much the rent of his land comes to," I. iv. 131–132). In his various pieces of advice, he thematizes first and foremost the necessity of keeping house with limited resources, most prominently in the rhymed speech to Lear which seems to resonate with the early sixteenth-century's ideology of proto-mercantilism:[204]

> FOOL: Have more than thou showest,
> Speak less than thou knowest,
> Lend less than thou owest. [. . .]
> Set less than thou throwest,
> Leave thy drink and thy whore,
> And keep in-a-door,
> And thou shalt have more
> Than two tens to a score.
>
> (I. iv. 116–118/121–125)

This sermon must fall on deaf ears because the king, as an absolute ruler whose loving word provides him with an endlessly flowing cornucopia of riches, is inclined to absolute rather than relative judgments. Thus in his parables, the Fool insists in vain that relationships of property and exchange, as well as the deceptions implicit in them are the forces which determine social life (see e.g. "Nuncle, give me an egg and I'll give thee two crowns," I. iv. 148–149, but also I. iv. 310–313; II. ii. 238–243; III. ii. 27–30). It is curious that the play's reception seems to be afflicted with a comparable deafness: the secondary literature usually takes the Fool to represent traditional wisdom and the earthy popular voice which proclaims timeless truths,[205] even though Shakespeare misses no opportunity to characterize the Fool as a modernist. The Fool acts as a skeptical court economist, and in this role he uses a proto-mercantilist language which is neither traditional nor timeless but at best is marked as untimely by the diegetic frame. The Fool, for example, is the only character in *Lear* who uses concepts such as "rent" (I. iv. 131) and "monopoly" (I. iv. 146). In section 3.6, we will briefly return to the question of what is "untimely" about the Fool and his worldview; it should only be pointed out here that the Fool as a good economist relies less on eternal than on future knowledge ("This prophecy Merlin shall make, for I live before his time," III. ii. 95–96), and that the theater, likewise an "untimely," inauthentic medium, provides the appropriate frame for this reliance.[206] The well-known "Prophecy of Merlin" to which the Fool alludes here (and which was already quoted in Chapter 1, section 1.4) Shakespeare found in the *Historia Regum Brittaniae* by Geoffrey of Monmouth that is also the source for Lear's own legend.[207] In his reference to Merlin, the Fool thus also refers indirectly to his own textuality and to that of his dialogue partners. In another passage, the Fool lets it be known even more explicitly that a person and his or her untimely notation are interdependent, and even to this affirmation he adds an economistic punchline:

> FOOL: Now thou art an O without a figure; I am better than thou art now. I am a fool, thou art nothing.
>
> (I. iv. 183–185)

The words "O without a figure" may allude to the fact that Lear only retains the power for creaturely screaming but not for performative speaking with social relevance. Consequentially, his penultimate words in the Quarto version are "O, o, o, o," (V. iii. 308). But above all, "an O without a figure" refers to a zero without preceding number. This interpretation is reinforced when the Fool in the same breath calls Lear a "nothing." But the zero is not simply nothing, but also a central example of the fact that, contrary to Lear's assertion (I. i. 90; I. iv. 130), "something will come from nothing." Zero represents a nothing, resp. an absence, and thereby creates and occupies a semiotically relevant space, in most cases a position in the decimal system, which constitutes itself through this occupancy.[208] That has its consequences: if we, to take the simplest example, write a zero behind a one, the latter advances in the decimal system by one step; this means that through the zero we add the nine to the one. This notation of the Fool is also in advance of his diegetic time: even in Shakespeare's time, the number zero might almost be considered a recent innovation in Western Europe; it is absent during the high Middle Ages, let alone during pagan antiquity. Instead, Roman numerals were used, which have no sign for zero.[209] It is only in the late Middle Ages that the number zero is adopted from the Arabs, its introduction representing a decisive step in the history of economics. The development of capitalism would have been impossible without this adoption, or at least would have proceeded quite differently:[210] try to calculate interest with Roman numerals and you will see that without the decimal system it is virtually impossible to effectively conduct the diverse financial transactions on which modern economic life depends.[211] The introduction of zero and the decimal system based upon it, then, is one of the prerequisites for the accumulation of capital that secures the financial supremacy of some European merchant families (such as the Fuggers and the Medici) over princely dynasties. The resultant dependence of many princes on many a merchant changes Europe's social structure fundamentally, and hardens many confessional or pseudo-confessional fronts during the Reformation.[212] The Fool as a premature economist and showman maintains—like Edgar's Poor Tom—a close relationship with this virulent, active nothing and therefore notices that, despite Lear's assertion to the contrary, the destinies of an entire world can be made out of the zero (in co-operation with the "wooden O" of *Henry V*, I. i. 13), namely that of capitalism. Lear has become a mythical founding father of this world by having given the sovereignty of natural inclinations a free hand in his kingdom. For this reason the Fool calls Lear not only a "nothing" and a zero, but also uses other tropes of emptiness like "shadow" (I. iv. 222) and "shelled peascod" (I. iv. 190). In this way he suggests that it is precisely Lear's confidence in the hierarchical world order of feudalism that has initiated its replacement by the order of money. Lear's self-contradictory discourse identifies him, on the one hand, as the mouthpiece of eternal decrees and infinite abundances; on the other hand, it claims to merely exert a kind of command that renders itself superfluous and is no more than regulative. Hence it appears as the repressed, schizophrenic foundational discourse of a type of capitalism that steadily and sovereignly lets human nature take its course.

It has already been pointed out in section 3.2 that, after Lear's ambiguous abdication, neither he nor any of the other *dramatis personae*, who are driven or swept along by the "great wheel of fortune," take the position of the sovereign in the traditional sense. Instead, the protagonists often refer either to natural effects, inherent necessities, or objects as the powerful determinants of their fateful behavior. In this context, Douglas Bruster has developed the thesis that stage props are given a progressively more important role during the time of Shakespeare's literary activity (c. 1590–1610). Their capacity to generate identities and restructure affects demands greater and greater attention. According to Bruster, this development reflects an interest, increasing with the expansion of capitalism, in the money form and in the circulation of the "commodities" it governs.[213] Bruster further demonstrates that in Elizabethan and Jacobean dramas (in contrast to ancient tragedies) the props consistently outnumber the actors on stage.[214] In *Lear*, the approximately 20 speaking parts require more than twice as many movable objects. The actors are surrounded and determined by things, some of which influence the course of events in unforeseen ways; especially representational and circulating props, among them various letters and moneys, decide some of the most important turns of the story.[215] The contractual letter in particular plays a significantly larger role than in, for example, *King John*, a play structured almost exclusively by the aporias of sacral oral oaths (*nudum pactum*).[216]

Deserving of mention in this context is Benjamin's concept of the "fatal stage prop" (*das fatale Requisit*) that in the tragedy of fate and the mourning play incarnates the curse cast on a noble family.[217] Fateful destiny, which arises from the curse and the resulting guilt-ridden subjugation to a fallen nature, involves in the *Trauerspiel* (again in contrast to ancient tragedy) not only persons but also emblematic objects. Acting as substitutes for the dead, inanimate objects appear as carriers of the curse; their insistent presence at the place "where guilt has been incurred" Benjamin reads as "a sign of the approach of death."[218] The capitalist world of commodities offers this insistence a broad field of activity, as Benjamin shows, for example, in his analysis of Baudelaire's poetry.[219] But the field of commodities tends to coincide with that of fatal props well before the nineteenth century: as Benjamin himself shows, the circulation of debt-incurring stage properties and curse-ridden emblems in the *Trauerspiel* is from the beginning subject to the law of a comprehensive circular convertibility—a controvertibilty which has obvious parallels in an economic sphere ruled by the markets' early modern *coming-out*. This significant parallel is formulated almost explicitly by Benjamin's statement on the general exchangeability of the emblems in baroque allegoresis, in which everything can express everything else.[220] Benjamin did not explicate the coincidence of both forms in his book on German tragic drama, but his later works can be of help in the analysis of its significance for Shakespeare's *Trauerspiel*, thereby opening new perspectives on various circulating props in *Lear*.

The props most relevant but also most fatal in this context are no doubt the numerous letters that function mostly as bonds (*Schuldverschreibungen*): they are contracts and contractual offers, that is, letters affirming reciprocal obligations and debt relations. This impression is intensified by the fact that hostile parties often intercept (or appear to intercept—as in I. ii) these letters on their way to their intended recipient. Their purloinment moves them into a new position, but also assigns them a new value in the play for power: when they are in the "wrong" hands, they change from a sign of reciprocal obligation into evidence of a contaminating guilt.[221] Once more Shakespeare integrates a condition of the theater into the dramatic plot itself, this time by representing a misdirection of props that have already "gone astray" by making their way into the theater;[222] and he seems to imply that their true purpose is not their arrival at their intended place but a deviation due to all manner of contingencies. Despite their volatile status, the letters determine decisive events of the plot, most of the time making things worse and further splitting the kingdom into competing parties. The paths and effects of the altogether eight important letters in *Lear* will demonstrate this: the forged letter 1 from Edgar to Edmund that is "intercepted" by its proper addressee, Gloucester, initiates Edgar's persecution and expulsion; letters 2 and 3, sent by Lear and Goneril to Regan, get into each other's way as do their messengers, contributing decisively to the breach between Lear and his daughters (I. iv; II. ii). Letters 4 and 5 that Kent and Cordelia write to one another establish an alliance of enemies of the new order (II. ii; III. i; IV. iii); letter 6 that Cordelia or France sends to Gloucester is passed on to Cornwall by Edmund, which results in Gloucester's blinding and Edmund's advancement (III. iii; III. v). Letter 7 from Goneril to Edmund is the one Regan tries to intercept, but Edgar steals it instead and passes it on to Albany, leading to Goneril's fall and indirectly to the death of both sisters, Edgar's reinstatement, and Edmund's death (IV. v; IV. vi; V. i; V. iii). Letter 8, the letter of execution drafted by Edmund and Goneril, is directly presented to the Captain; since a belated attempt by the remaining court society to intercept this document fails, it causes Cordelia's and indirectly also Lear's death, with its unforeseeable consequences (V. iii). This enumeration makes it sufficiently clear that the circulating letters do indeed tragically determine broad stretches of the plot and of the shifting positions within it, but also that their rhizomatically entangled paths do not proceed from or converge toward a central point. (By contrast, the various written decrees in *Richard III* at least nominally go back, directly or indirectly, to the royal personages of Edward IV, Richard III and

Henry VII, as the last wills in *King John* to various kings of France and England.) The letters in *Lear* are thus no sovereign decrees; they are business letters. In several cases, one can actually speak of murderous business proposals ("If our father would sleep till I waked him, you should enjoy half his revenue for ever," I. ii. 52–53; "If thou dost as this instructs thee, thou dost make thy way to noble fortunes," V. iii. 29–31). All letters, moreover, envision a redistribution of power; they are focused on creating new political and/or familial alliances as well as dissolving old ones. Through the political perspectives they open up in this way, the letters revaluate the legitimacy of sender and recipient as well as their capacity to conduct business: through their anticipation of new power constellations, the various letters enact virtual, mutually incompatible royal dramas. The fatal epistolary props in *Lear* therefore affirm less a deprivation of the present by demonically insistent pasts (as is the case in traditional dramas of fate) than a splintering of the present into incompatible future-oriented simulacra, under the influence of various "vile-drawing biases."[223] The letters thus develop a dynamic that no subject can control. They constitute an unstable system of competing, floating alliances into which the actual existence of the kingdom (i.e. the sum of values attributed by Lear) dissipates. Lear's influence on this field of virtualities is reduced to an irritation: sovereign power is no longer capable of organizing the destinies of the community—they elude it. In the aberrant contractual letters secured by natural law, some contours of the bourgeois economic world can already be discerned.[224]

In *Lear*, the new contractual forms and processes of liquidation penetrate the old discourses of sovereign representation and jurisdiction. Because of this contamination, the status of many letter props leaves the impression of an irritating transitionality; from a pragmatic as well as from a formal legal standpoint they seem unjustifiable and superfluous. Only the combination of both viewpoints illuminates the dynamic at work in their distribution. A good example is the incriminating document that Edmund gives to the Captain in V. iii:

> EDMUND: Come hither, captain, hark:
> Take thou this note. Go, follow them to prison.
> One step I have advanced thee. If thou dost
> As this instructs thee, thou dost make thy way
> To noble fortunes. [. . .] Thy great employment
> Will not bear question: either say thou'lt do't,
> Or thrive by other means.
>
> (V. iii. 27–31/33–35)

Does Edmund in this situation act in his arrogated position as Albany's proxy? (V. i. 63–64). But if his note is meant to be an official order of execution, why does Edmund buttress it with the offer of a bribe? Furthermore, why does he need a cover story about a suicidal Cordelia if her execution is supposed to be a juridical act (V. iii. 250–253)? Edmund also calls the "note" a "writ" (V. iii. 243), a term used during Shakespeare's time for directives issued by the Crown: "writs" are usually administrative decrees of the monarch pertaining to a specific case, which thereafter become part of common law. In other words, they are law-positing decrees of the sovereign.[225] But in this case they are not issued by a sovereign but by a prospective sovereign (V. i. 69–70) and his prospective spouse (V. iii. 250–251); the murders of Lear, Cordelia and Albany are still preparations for Edmund's accession to the throne. That the "writ" will have been executed is therefore a condition of its retrospective legitimacy. The killing of Cordelia oscillates between a lawful execution and an illegal murder with predatory intent, so long as Edmund's status remains unclear. Consequently, the status of Edmund's written claim wavers between that of a fatal sovereign decree and a dubious promissory note for "noble fortunes" with uncertain backing. The sovereign sphere can no longer be neatly differentiated from market events and their modernized contractual forms. The letters conjoin both, and for this reason they function as over-determined, "impossible" supplements that implement the curse as an active "nothing."[226]

3.6 *Storm still* and the perpetual downfall of the last judgment

The Christian curse delivers the accursed to a divine judgment that it announces in bypassing the present for the eternal suspension of a future perfect tense.[227] The maledictory utterance cites both the primordial, world-structuring and also the final, history-ending verdict on the *massa damnata*. The canonic treatments of this issue reveal that the curse is meant to retain this Janus-faced aspect even at the day of the Last Judgment: at the end of time, damnation still is to be accomplished by referring to itself as to a process that has been in effect since time immemorial. Matthew 25. 41 may once again serve as an example; in this passage, Christ announces the Last Judgment, along with his own brief address to the damned: "Depart from me, ye cursed, into everlasting fire, prepared for the devil and his angels."[228] On the one hand, the Last Judgment implements the reprobation of all sinners, but, on the other hand, this condemnation has already been achieved from the very beginning of time: according to Paul and especially Augustine, it constitutes an integral part of God's primordial election of grace.[229] The doctrine of predestination, in emphasizing that creation and damnation are equiprimordial, perpetuates a disguised Gnostic heritage of Christianity.[230] During the Reformation—as in early Christianity—this doctrine occasionally is complemented with the idea that a "pneumatic," who knows how to read the signs, can see the Last Judgment as an event ever present in historical time.[231] To this belief, the everyday course of the world appears as the constant and secret enactment of God's judgment. Hence the Apocalypse is not only situated at the unattainable end of history and contrasts with it as its other, but it is also identical with history.

The Church attempts to bridge this discrepancy in the apocalyptic discourse by pushing the Last Judgment away into a "long-term indeterminacy."[232] The *ecclesia militans*, functioning as a temporary substitute for the *ecclesia triumphans*,[233] in its self-assertion institutionalizes the plea "*pro mora finis*," i.e. for the postponement of the end.[234] At the same time, ecclesiastical jurisdiction since Tertullian presents itself as a mitigating allegory of the Day of His Wrath, i.e. as the "the highest anticipation of the judgment to come."[235] This reference to God's judgment as a removed but supplementing double adds a certain flexibility to ecclesiastical jurisdiction. In order to keep it in reserve in this way, the church curtails any discussion of the Apocalypse with the categorical comment that it "will come like a thief in the night" (1 Thess. 5. 2). The Anglican Church of the sixteenth and seventeenth centuries, due to its still precarious legitimacy, makes special efforts to keep apocalyptic speculations within close limits. In its lectionary, for example, readings from the Revelation of John are not given a place.[236] Performances of the Last Judgment in the Mystery Plays of many a community are also reduced and often prohibited in the sixteenth century.[237]

In numerous movements of the early modern age that the State churches seek to suppress, Protestant sectarians (again in parallel to late antiquity) reaffirm the immediate expectation (*Naherwartung*) of the Apocalypse. They evade the contradiction implicit in the idea of a Last Judgment by "acting it out."[238] In England, this tradition of apocalyptic deviance extends from the Lollards of the late Middle Ages to the Ranters of the Civil War.[239] Especially the Ranters accord the ritual curse a central place in their ceremonies; their malediction functions as the performative that instantaneously separates the sheep from the goats. In the vein of other impersonators,[240] the Ranter William Franklin for instance takes on the role of the returned, triumphant Messiah and assigns subsidiary roles in his drama to his followers: one of them impersonates a destroying angel, "sent forth to curse the earth," another plays "a healing angel charged with healing those whom his companion had cursed."[241] This example already demonstrates that the Last Judgment inexorably dissolves into its allegorizing representation, if one tries to force its realization.[242] The Apocalypse, like the proclamation of the Hobbesian Leviathan, has a dramatic structure and can only be acted out.[243] It is mostly for this reason that Ranters are regularly attacked in Anglican cautionary pamphlets as perverting the Bible, "wresting it from the true sense thereof by [. . .] Allegorical fancies."[244]

In general, the treatment of eschatological themes in seventeenth-century England appears to be strongly affected by a development that Benjamin describes as the baroque fall from the state of grace into the state of nature: whereas during the Middle Ages the ephemerality of the world and of its creatures was still a mere episode in the history of salvation, during the Baroque an ambiguous "disappearance of eschatology" occurs; the natural transience of the human creature and its environment is now largely considered an unconditional *conditio humana*, and it is only through this transience itself that redemption can be expected.[245] This naturalization of the Last Things promotes the melancholy immersion in the things of the world, for which allegoresis is the appropriate method.[246] But toward the end of the *Trauerspielbuch*, Benjamin furnishes the description of this melancholic absorption with a dialectical punchline that, he claims, saves Baroque allegoresis from its surrender to the fallen world: the baroque allegorist is not forced to lose himself irretrievably in a bad infinity[247] and in melancholy, for the Golgothan expanse of ruins to which the world reduces itself for him can itself also be understood allegorically. Evanescence itself thus becomes an allegory of resurrection. Even the last debris can refer to something beyond it, and is therefore always identifiable as merely penultimate and negligible. In characterizing this reversal, Benjamin employs an apocalyptic rhetoric that situates itself on the threshold of theology.[248] But is this turn toward the resurrection not subverted by the argumentation he had previously developed? Satan, evil, death, and sin can certainly be understood allegorically, even as allegories of their own negligibility; but this does not entail that their opposites, God, life, the good, and virtue, would be capable of establishing the framing, stable reality that is able to contain them. It is after all the disintegration of such a direct and confident relation to the world of resurrection that Benjamin sees as the cause of baroque melancholic absorption.[249] Apparently, he wants to rescue intellectual insight from itself by means of a final dialectical reversal. But once theology has been set on the slippery slope of allegory, the former can no longer provide a firm schema for the latter; the inner Apocalypse leads back to the mortality of all things natural. And for this reason it is also impossible to reconvert psychological, semiotic, or epistemological terms into messianic ones, since the result would immediately be subjected to the allegorical corrosion of the melancholy gaze. *King Lear* plays out precisely this circumstance in the figure of a perpetual apocalypse of the apocalypse. As mentioned previously (e.g. in section 3.2), the encompassing "nature" that unfolds in *Lear* does not conform to the schemata of a customary eschatology; however, in their quest for a legal order that is inherent in nature the play's protagonists end up rediscovering the paradoxes of the Divine Judgment. For reasons that can partly be attributed to the intensification of censorship since 1606,[250] Judgment Day in Shakespeare's play only makes its presence felt in the form of two remnants: on the one hand, as a pattern of allusions to an alternative, transcendent court of law (see e.g. IV. ii. 47–51), and, on the other, as the ghost image of a series of executions that claim divine approbation for themselves (see e.g. V. iii. 229–231). Even so, it is remarkable how frequently eschatological motifs and phrases are used; over long periods the play resembles an echo chamber in which the premonitory voices of biblical prophets reverberate. A not even exhaustive listing of apocalyptic images from John's Revelation that are quoted in *Lear* can be found, for instance, in Joseph Wittreich's *Image of that Horror*:

> the mystery of the seven stars [...], the cracking thunder and catastrophic earthquakes, the eclipse of sun and moon, the wheel of fire, the lake of darkness, the sulphurous pit, the wrathful dragon, the prince of darkness, the black angel, [...] even the monsters of the deep and the imagery of defiled and fresh garments.[251]

But despite the assertions made by Wittreich and numerous other commentators, all of this adds up to no more than a debris of citations that fails to coalesce into a humanistic reconstruction of apocalyptic motives. The correspondences of diction and tone are numerous and obvious, but they fail to reveal any coherent theological subtext to the drama; rather, their incompatibility emphasizes its fragmentation. Every time, an eschatological perspective seems to open, it turns out to be a feint, for example when *King Lear* occasionally thematizes its own status as a play and as an allegory, meta-theatrically demonstrating the porousness of the border between drama and reality. For with the help of these two techniques the drama repeatedly alludes to the theologically informed metaphor of the *theatrum mundi* ("This great stage of fools," IV. vi. 179), whose traditional use in the Middle Ages refers all events to the Day of Judgment.[252] But the collapse of its theological frame disqualifies even this reference to the apocalypse as a commonplace that constantly shifts along the slippery slope of representation. Hence, the apocalypse cannot be referenced on stage as a final vanishing point and moral ultimatum, but merely as an allegory. When Shakespeare, according to Benjamin, dissolves the cosmos into infinity,[253] then it is the bad infinity of a *mise en abyme*, at least in *Lear*. In Lear's proliferating curses of Act III, apocalyptic prophecies are short-circuited with creation myths, as in Gnostic cosmologies; the world's formation and its end collapse into each other insofar as they are both manifestations of a destructive nature.[254] As an active "nothing," Lear's boundless curse sends the signs of present, past, and future careening into each other. The Fool's prophecy on the heath makes this collapse explicit:

> FOOL: I'll speak a prophecy ere I go:
> When priests are more in word than matter,
> When brewers mar their malt with water,
> When nobles are their tailors' tutors,
> No heretics burned but wenches' suitors;
> When every case in law is right,
> No squire in debt, nor no poor knight;
> When slanders do not live in tongues,
> Nor cut-purses come not to throngs,
> When usurers tell their gold i' the field,
> And bawds and whores do churches build,
> Then shall the realm of Albion
> Come to great confusion:
> Then comes the time, who lives to see't,
> That going shall be used with feet.
> This prophecy Merlin shall make, for I live before his time.
>
> (III. ii. 79–96)

This prophecy (appearing for the first time in the 1623 Folio) is often emended by editors, most of whom place "Then shall the realm of Albion/ Come to great confusion" behind "No heretics burned but wenches' suitors," i.e. between the predictions that appear to describe a deplorable state of affairs, and those that strike the editors as descriptions of the future Kingdom of God.[255] The prophecy is thus given an immediately obvious meaning, but this also deprives it of its salient point, namely the ambiguous fusion of satire and utopia in which the terrible state of the world and the implementation of the God-given law meld smoothly into one another, first in the initial ten, then in the final four lines. What, for instance, does it ultimately say about the epoch that prostitution builds churches in it, "bawds and whores do churches build?" Does this phrase suggest the atonement of the whores and procuresses, or the Babylonian degeneration of the church? Or does the Fool introduce here a Blakean allegorical image of the interdependence of virtue and vice? The collapse of theologico-juridical categories erases the clear distinction between the Last Judgment and the activities of the *massa damnata*. As such it marks the disappearance of any point of reference that would allow to delimit and monopolize the curse. In a situation like this, the curse has neither a tangible, univocal content nor a comprehensible function that might be appropriated: it no longer institutes but only "de-poses" (*entsetzt*)[256] without furthering anyone's political interests. The execrations of Lear and Edgar on the heath, which are symptomatic of this state of affairs, appear to mimic the storm as a violent force that cannot be put to the service of any speaker. Between sense and nonsense, the decomposing curse of the protagonists oscillates as mere noise, as if it were itself merely a gust of the storm.[257] In a passage that Foakes in the Arden edition calls "presumably deliberate 'mad' nonsense,"[258] Edgar, reversely, assigns to the storm a voice that formulates demonic or demon-dispelling words, wavering between sense and nonsense, as it blasts through the void in a Christian symbol:

> Edgar: Still through the hawthorn blows the cold wind, says suum, mun, nonny, Dauphin my boy, my boy, *cessez!* Let him trot by. (*Storm still.*) (III. iv. 96–98)

The passage ironically alludes to the popular belief that Christ's crown of thorns had been plaited of hawthorn and that hawthorn for this reason protects from storm and demons. There is a corresponding passage, for example, in *The Travels of Sir John Mandeville*:

> And you must know that Our Lord, the night He was captured, was led into a garden, and was there sharply interrogated; and there the Jews mocked Him and set a Crown on His head [. . .] And that crown was made of branches of hawthorn; and therefore the hawthorn has many virtues. For he who carries a twig of it on him, no thunder nor any kind of storm may harm him; and no evil spirit may come into the house or any other place where it is.[259]

But Edgar's voice from the hawthorn, just as Lear's curses, formulates neither an ultimate truth nor a timelessly valid precept; it expresses only their overdetermined absence. "Nature" in *Lear* is reduced to exactly this endless collapse of apocalyptic figures, to a perpetual nemesis of nemesis that Shakespeare's early modern curse articulates. Its force can therefore unfold only in allegory, in the representational space of the theater and its meta-theater, exposed to bad infinity.

The *dramatis personae* do not endure the de-position that results from this aporetic situation after the storm has subsided; they fall back into more conventional, partly immanentist theologico-political interpretations of the events. Lear, for example, tries after the storm to get a firm foothold in a post-apocalyptic position: when he awakens in the French camp near Dover, he identifies himself as one of the damned, tied to a hellish wheel of fire, perceiving Cordelia as a saved, blessed soul (IV. vii. 45–48). Even after their mutual forgiveness, the king persists in this unorthodox position beyond judgment; he fantasizes to be a self-sacrificial victim who henceforth, as "God's spy," stands outside the natural history of earthly powers which reduces itself to a sequence of disasters for him (V. iii. 8–26). But Edmund will soon demonstrate to Lear by the example of Cordelia that judgment in the new Britain is not altogether a thing of the past and that there is no neutral, ironic position which would allow for real distance from the political events. Lear's successor, Albany, is thrown off balance by this as well: at first, he makes a point of interpreting and performing the events on the political stage as prefigurations of the Last Day. This is also how he masks his inability to decide on them; to this end he arranges, for instance, to exhibit the corpses of Goneril and Regan as a representation of divine judgment:

> ALBANY: Produce the bodies, be they alive or dead.
> (*GONERIL'S and REGAN'S bodies brought out.*)
> This judgment of the heavens that makes us tremble
> Touches us not with pity.
>
> (V. iii. 229–231)

Together with Albany *militans*, the spectator could at this point in the plot plausibly accept the reconciliation of Lear and Cordelia, the death of Goneril, Regan, and Edmund as well as the rehabilitation of Edgar and Kent as a grand synecdoche signifying the punishment of the reprobate and the redemption of the blessed. But subsequently some further exhibits are added to the display of the dead which do not conform to the schema of Albany's divine comedy: Lear's last entrance supplements Albany's happy ending with a second ending, and parodies it. History has forced its way into Lear's post-historical play, and along with Cordelia has sacrificed Lear's own self-sacrifice on the altar of progress, thus robbing him of his last symbolic support. In his resultant lament, Lear instructs his subjects to unleash a cosmic storm in which their voices figure as winds and their tears as rain:

> LEAR: Howl, howl, howl! O, you are men of stones!
> Had I your tongues and eyes, I'd use them so
> That heaven's vault should crack: she's gone for ever.
> I know when one is dead and when one lives;
> She's dead as earth.
>
> (V. iii. 255–259)

It remains unclear whether this storm of affects is intended to break the vault of the heavenly kingdom to pieces in order to usher in the triumphant revenge of the transcendent forces or their definitive death plunge. At any rate, it is noteworthy that Lear's expression "dead as earth," in spite of the religious concepts he had invoked only a moment before, appears to foreclose the possibility of Cordelia's celestial life after her death as a martyr. That Lear only addresses secular resuscitation attempts, but no longer an afterlife in the beyond, does not entail that the drama would also abandon its various apocalyptic motifs, however. On the contrary: parodic references to the biblical idea of the Divine Judgment condense and multiply after this turning point. Lear's "Howl" itself echoes the prophetic writings especially of Isaiah, in which the exhortation to weep and wail regularly introduces the announcement of an impending divine punishment (see e.g. also Jeremiah 25. 34, Ezekiel 21. 12/30. 2–3 and James 5. 1):

> Howl ye; for the day of the LORD is at hand; it shall come as a destruction from the Almighty. [. . .] Howl, O gate; cry, O city; thou, whole Palestina, art dissolved: for there shall come from the north a smoke, and none shall be alone in his appointed times.
>
> (Isaiah 13. 6/14. 31)

Lear's specific connection with Isaiah can be established not only by way of various other rhetorical assonances.[260] For instance, Geoffrey of Monmouth, Shakespeare's source, explicitly approximates the lifetimes of both men.[261] And the Elizabethan lectionary assigned a reading from Isaiah for the day of Lear's first performance at court, the Feast of Stephen in 1606.[262] Against this background, it does not seem all too extravagant to discern a travesty of the English Tersanctus from Isaiah 6. 3 in Lear's triple "Howl!"—particularly since both in its original context and in its citation in Revelation 4. 8 the exclamation "Holy, holy, holy" introduces an impending divine judgment. In the Anglican liturgy, it is fittingly integrated into the Eucharistic prayer.[263] Lear celebrates a ruined, inverted mass, holding in his hands the senselessly sacrificed body of a redeemer whose return is not to be expected (V. iii. 306–307).

The surviving nobles comment on this last act of Lear with a further allusion to the questionable apocalypse and its dispersion in representation, i.e. in its "image":

> KENT: Is this the promised end?
> EDGAR: Or image of that horror?
>
> (V. iii. 261–262)

Insofar as these questions can also be read as a commentary on the play's unexpected, detraditionalized ending, they indirectly thematize the consequences of the perpetual nemesis for the dramatic form.[264] The protagonists seem to be aware that they are approaching the end of *King Lear* and that this end does not conform to expectations since the drama has already gone beyond the customary schema of both comedy and tragedy.[265] Because the persons are now moving within incompatible simulacra,[266] a convincing conclusion is no longer possible; neither is a closure of the dramatic form. Kent and Edgar try nonetheless to reconnect the play to classical poetics and to force a concluding anagnorisis, whereupon Lear utters his last curse: "A plague upon you murderers, traitors all" (V. iii. 267). Just like the preceding execrations, this curse erases the distinction between friend and foe; and indeed, it reaches only those who think of themselves as Lear's friends and vassals since all his declared enemies are already dead. Kent's second attempt to reveal his identity to Lear and so to re-establish old loyalty ties and dramatic conventions takes an even more unsatisfactory turn: his king does indeed recognize him this time, but this recognition remains a matter of indifference to him despite Kent's carefully prepared climax (V. iii. 280–287). Once again the use of a basic dramatic element seems only to demonstrate that it cannot fulfill its traditional function in a state of general fragmentation. The loss of the obligatory familial, political, theological, and aesthetic bonds causes Lear's insurmountable mourning, an inverted reflection of the universal and empty amnesty he had proclaimed during his encounter with Gloucester in IV. vi. By the definite loss of his daughter he is cast out into the destructive, boundless realm of nature and loses himself in it; his utterances suggest that he finds himself neither in heaven nor in hell but back in a nature that is but a vast absence, an active, nihilating nothing (V. iii. 304–307). A revelation capable of transcending this extinction fails to materialize, much as Lear may hang on Cordelia's lip. Once more a condemnatory "nothing" issues from these lips, a response which the drama's reception has interpreted in various ways, skimming off its semantic surplus value. His gaze turned in Cordelia's direction, Lear dies with a final command on his lips that keeps a final insight inaccessible even as he emphatically points to it:

> LEAR: Do you see this? Look on her: look, her lips,
> Look there, look there! (*He dies.*)
>
> (V. iii. 309–310)

Lear attaches no predicate to Cordelia's lips; it is quite uncertain if his deathly affect is due to the fact that he believes his daughter to be alive again. In its pure indexical persistence, his utterance is neither true nor false, neither delusional nor disillusioned, neither apocalyptic nor anti-apocalyptic. His perplexing command remains an enigma that, while it does not unfold any fatal consequences, also has no illuminating effect on anybody in the "cheerless, deadly darkness."[267] In dying, Lear conveys no message that his vassals might comprehend. Franco Moretti sees the specifically modern character of Elizabethan and Jacobean tragedy in the fact that it portrays a sovereign's traumatic decomposition which those around him can neither understand nor come to terms with.[268] *King Lear* provides the most comprehensive evidence for this thesis: in this mourning play, the conceptualizations that have kept the king's rule intelligible and perpetuated it are delivered to decay along with him. After the unraveling of the social net in the course of Lear's naturalizations, no restitution of the monarchy's God-given legal order can be convincingly claimed. It is precisely through this traumatic liquidation that this order has proved itself unsustainable and self-destructive. For, as shown in the preceding chapters, it is the theologico-semiotic dilemmas associated with the traditional idea of sovereignty that have made Lear's natural law reform a desideratum. Among the corpses strewn across the stage, never to be revived, lies the decomposed cadaver of immortal sovereignty. It is surprising in this context how little attention has been paid to the fact that, according to Geoffrey of Monmouth, Lear is the legitimate successor of Britain's primal father, Brutus. As such, he is a patriarch of the archaic royal house from which the Tudors also claim to be descended. This means that the death of Lear and of all his legitimate heirs, which Shakespeare has inscribed into history, also turns this extinguished dynasty (whose last representative bequeathed the English crown to the incumbent King James) into a collection of usurpers or spectral bastards.

In the noise of the stage, the curse has perpetuated itself ever since. Whereas in ecclesiastical rites it functions as the representation of lawmaking violence within the juridical order, it retains this position in Shakespeare's dramas as a voided form whose references to transcendent or mythic authorities tend to self-destruct. But the ritual curse does not dissolve on account of this transformation; it continues to take effect latently, as the trace of an unlocalizable trauma in the social field, without ever claiming an intelligible content or unequivocal purposes. It is worth asking whether the curse in this deterritorialized state has not remained a factor in the (self-)constitution of the modern subject: "Perhaps it is this state of the diffuse flocculation of hatred which saturates the call for the destruction of being in us."[269] At the least, the curse represents a part of Europe's cultural heritage, a mortgage on representation that must still be reckoned with. It is the deconstructive unfolding of the curse's aporetic structure that has enabled Shakespeare to integrate its articulation into the exchange of commodities and to derive a profit from it under the conditions of the early modern era. The uncontained, disintegrated curse has thus been fitted to the modern stage, and the stage to it: the dramatist presents a black hole in the symbolic order; and this hole is at once invoked by the theater and sublated in its ban, so as to perpetuate the theatrical profession. It is above all the mass media that in our time seem to siphon off surplus value from this cultural capital by gearing their marketing strategies to the reproduction, coordination, and exorcism of traditional social traumas. One would have to investigate in another study to what degree their products retain and perfect the techniques of keeping the curse latent that were first developed on the English stage of the sixteenth and seventeenth centuries.

Notes

1 Robert Weimann, *Zwischen Performanz und Repräsentation. Shakespeare und die Macht des Theaters*, Heidelberg 2000, p. 137.
2 Clive S. Lewis, *Studies in Words*, Cambridge 1960, pp. 24–74.
3 George W. Keeton, *Shakespeare's Legal and Political Background*, London 1967, p. 67.
4 Merio Scattola, *Das Naturrecht vor dem Naturrecht. Zur Geschichte des* ius naturae *im 16. Jahrhundert*, Tübingen 1999, pp. 9/21.
5 Aristotle, *Nicomachean Ethics*, translated by Christopher Rowe, Oxford 2002, p. 169 [1134b 18–20].

6 See Scattola, op. cit., pp. 25–27.
7 Scattola, op. cit., p. 37.
8 Scattola, op. cit., p. 119.
9 Thomas Aquinas, *Summa Theologica* Summa 2.1, Quaestio 94.2.
10 Aquinas, ibid. Summa 2.1, Quaestio 91.
11 Aquinas, ibid. Summa 2.1, Quaestio 95.2.
12 See also Ernst H. Kantorowicz, *Gods in Uniform. Selected Studies*, Locust Valley 1965, pp. 355–356.
13 Ernst H. Kantorowicz, *The King's Two Bodies, A Study in Mediaeval Political Theology*, Princeton, NJ 1997, p. 136.
14 Aquinas, op. cit. Summa 2.1, Quaestio 105.1.
15 Aquinas, op. cit. Summa 3, Quaestio 8.6.
16 See Alexandra Walsham, *Providence in Early Modern England*, Oxford 1999, p. 26.
17 Keith Thomas, *Religion and the Decline of Magic. Studies in Popular Beliefs in Sixteenth- and Seventeenth-Century England*, London 1991, pp. 92–94.
18 Thomas, ibid., p. 605.
19 Scattola, op. cit., pp. 42–43.
20 See Chapter 1, section 1.3.
21 John Hamilton Baker, *An Introduction to English Legal History*, London 1979, p. 147.
22 David Martin Jones, *Conscience and Allegiance in Seventeenth Century England. The Political Significance of Oaths and Engagements*, Rochester 1999, p. 39.
23 Baker, op. cit., p. 181.
24 Aristotle op. cit. [1137a 31–1138a 3].
25 Baker, op. cit., pp. 89–90.
26 Baker, op. cit., p. 181.
27 Scattola, op. cit., p. 119.
28 Baker, op. cit., p. 99.
29 Scattola, op. cit., p. 215.
30 See Kantorowicz, *The King's Two Bodies*, op. cit., p. 415 and Gregor Braungart, 'Der Tod des Körpers des Herrschers. Begräbnisrituale als Zeichenprozesse', in Erika Fischer-Lichte (ed.), *Theatralität und die Krisen der Repräsentation*, Stuttgart/Weimar 2001, p. 31.
31 Robert Bucholz and Newton Key, *Early Modern England 1485–1714. A Narrative History*, Malden, MA 2004, p. 47.
32 James VI and I, *Political Writings*, Cambridge 1993, p. 45.
33 James VI and I, ibid. pp. 2–3.
34 See Chapter 1, section 1.4.
35 James VI and I, op. cit., p. 65.
36 See also William Cobbett and Thomas Howell (eds), *A Complete Collection of State Trials*, vol. 6, London 1809, p. 596, quoted by Jones, op. cit., p. 73.
37 James VI and I, op. cit., p. 47.
38 Edward Coke, *Reports*, Dublin 1792–1793, quoted by Kantorowicz, *The King's Two Bodies*, op. cit., p. 317.
39 Jones, op. cit., pp. 72–73.
40 James VI and I op. cit., p. 98.
41 Edward Coke, *The Declarations*, London 1659, p. 587, quoted by Jones, op. cit., p. 70.
42 See Chapter 1, section 1.3.
43 Giorgio Agamben, *Homo Sacer. Sovereign Power and Bare Life*, translated by Daniel Heller-Roazen, Stanford, CA 1998, p. 35.
44 Using the terminology of systems theory, Rainer M. Kiesow censures this Agambenian (and Benjaminian) notion of natural law. Kiesow asserts that Agamben's thought itself perpetuates a modernized version of natural law theory by criticizing the indistinction of life and law as tendentially catastrophic. Since Agamben, he says, cannot derive this criticism from the law so criticized, he supposes an ethically obliging "ought" that is its superior and is derivable from nothing other than from the nature of things themselves;

and that is said to be the "blind spot" in Agamben's conceptions. (Rainer M. Kiesow, 'Ius sacrum. Giorgio Agamben und das nackte Recht', *Rechtsgeschichte. Zeitschrift des Max-Planck-Instituts für europäische Rechtsgeschichte* 1, 2002, p. 61.) However, even if occasional splinters of natural law ideas are interspersed in Agamben's argumentation (owing primarily to his Benjaminian terminology), it is false to speak in this context of an unbroken continuation for the simple reason that *Homo Sacer* includes a genealogical critique of early modern natural law (see Agamben, *Homo Sacer*, op. cit., pp. 34–38/105–107). Agamben analyzes a paradox that is inherent in concepts of natural law, for example that of Hobbes. He tries to take the paradox to its limit, thereby raising valid questions about modern notions of legitimacy. Kiesow's legal positivism tries to avoid these questions, which it neither wants to raise nor is able to answer—for instance, by removing the sovereign declaration from the realm of law into that of politics, unconvincingly assuming to have thereby solved the problem. (Kiesow, op. cit., p. 59.)

45 Giorgio Agamben, *The Time That Remains. A Commentary on the Letter to the Romans*, translated by Patricia Dailey, Stanford, CA 2005, pp. 104–107.

46 Walter Benjamin, *The Origin of German Tragic Drama*, translated by John Osborne, London/New York, NY 1998, p. 74. Translation modified.

47 That *King Lear* is concerned with early modern conceptions of natural law has already been noted by several scholars, but has been analyzed too briefly or too schematically. John Danby's rigorous dualism of a "new" and an "old" concept of nature seems to have provided the uncertain foundation for many subsequent studies: Danby distinguishes a medieval-scholastic natural law, which sustains a society living in harmony with itself and with its traditions, from a modern natural law, which refutes traditions and conventions as artificial and replaces them with the struggle of all against all. In this schema, Lear represents the traditional natural law of the theologian Richard Hooker, whereas Edmund prefigures Thomas Hobbes. Consequently, Danby places the author of *Lear* firmly on the side of an idealized medieval Christianity. (John F. Danby, *Shakespeare's Doctrine of Nature. A Study of* King Lear, London 1975.) Robert White simplifies the issue even more than Danby by equating natural law with the ideal of justice incarnate in Cordelia, expressing an altruistic "inner voice". With the help of rather crude parallels he insinuates that Edmund and Hobbes, by contrast, represent a legal positivism à la Kelsen. (Robert S. White, *Natural Law in English Renaissance Literature*, Cambridge 1996, pp. 185–215.) That the frontlines between the parties inside and outside the play are considerably less distinct and unequivocal will have to be developed in the following discussion. William Elton has already written a historically more precise analysis of the complexities inherent in the theologico-juridical ideologies determining the drama. But as concerns natural law, he has largely retained Danby's binary frame. (William R. Elton, *King Lear and the Gods*, Lexington, KY 1988, pp. 126–130.) Only Paul Shupack and Nigel Smith have in fact stepped out of Danby's shadow. Shupack shows particularly clearly, against the historical background of the way "Natural Law," "Common Law," and "Divine Right of Kings" are intertwined, ambiguities and conflations of the drama that raise questions both about medieval and about modern concepts of natural law. (Paul M. Shupack, 'Natural Justice and King Lear', *Cardozo Studies in Law and Literature* 9, 1997, 67–105. Nigel Smith, 'Forms of Kingship in King Lear', in Linda Cookson and Brian Loughrey (eds), *Critical Essays on King Lear*, London 1988, pp. 31–42.)

48 On the concept of the "double bind", see Gregory Bateson, *Steps to an Ecology of Mind*, Chicago, IL/London 2000, p. 201 f.

49 Marcus Twellmann, *Das Drama der Souveränität*, München 2004, pp. 59–82.

50 Lewis, op. cit., p. 40.

51 On the difference between the little other and the big Other, see Jacques Lacan, 'The Instance of the Letter in the Unconscious, or Reason since Freud', in *Écrits. The First Complete Edition in English*, translated by Bruce Fink, New York, NY/London 2006, pp. 436–437. On the ambiguous coincidence of the latter with the eternal "order of

the world" see Jacques Lacan, *The Psychoses. Seminar III*, translated by Russell Grigg, New York, NY/London 1993, p. 74.
52 See section 3.3.
53 See for example Joseph Wittreich, '*Image of that Horror*'. *History, Prophecy, and Apocalypse in King Lear*, San Marino, CA 1984, pp. 22–24.
54 Niklas Luhmann, *Love as Passion: The Codification of Intimacy*, Stanford, CA 1998, pp. 48–49/67–68/110–111 and passim.
55 Christopher Pye, *The Regal Phantasm*, London/New York, NY 1990, pp. 33–37.
56 Elizabeth I, *Collected Works*, Chicago, IL 2002, pp. 186/198/337.
57 James VI and I, op. cit., p. 161; see also the remark on "fatherly loue" towards his subjects on p. 31.
58 See also Lacan, *The Psychoses*, op. cit., p. 320.
59 Geoffrey Hartmann, *Saving the Text*, London 1981, pp. 129–130.
60 The protagonists of *King Lear* also demonstrate in other scenes that patrilinear families are not natural entities but constituted through speech acts, and hence dissolvable symbolic structures. This fact is symptomatically demonstrated in Edgar's expulsion (GLOUCESTER: I never got him, II. i. 78) but also in Edmund's adoption by Cornwall (CORNWALL: Thou shalt find a dear father in my love, III. v. 24–25).
61 See Chapter 1, section 1.3.
62 However, this does not make Lear's kingdom pagan, as one can deduce from the numerous phrases with strong Christian connotations to which we will return later. Britain under Lear is pagan only in the sense in which diverse works of Renaissance literature are pagan: both repress their Christian heritage and constantly have to face the return of the repressed.
63 In this context, it is of interest that, at the latest since Heraclitus, the Erinyes are considered to be in charge of enforcing the laws of nature: "The sun will not overstep his measures. Else the Furies, the ministers of justice, will find him out." ("Ἥλιος οὐχ ὑπερβήσεται μέτρα·εἰ δὲ μή, Ἐρινύες μιν Δίκης ἐπίκουροι ἐξευρήσουσιν." Heraclitus, Fragment 94. See Daniel W. Graham (ed.), *The Texts of Early Greek Philosophy: The Complete Fragments and Selected Testimonies of the Major Presocratics*, vol. 1, Cambridge 2010, p. 165.)
64 Wolfgang Pfeifer (ed.), *Etymologisches Wörterbuch des Deutschen*, München 1995, p. 913.
65 Kantorowicz, *The King's Two Bodies*, op. cit., pp. 26/446.
66 Benjamin, *The Origin of German Tragic Drama*, op. cit., p. 67.
67 For example in Francis Bacon, 'The Charge Touching Duels', in *Major Works*, Oxford/New York, NY 2002, p. 307.
68 Jacques Lacan, *The Ego in Freud's Theory and in the Technique of Psychoanalysis. Seminar II*, translated by Sylvana Tomaselli, New York, NY/London 1988, p. 238.
69 See Stanley Cavell, 'The Avoidance of Love. A Reading of King Lear', in *Disowning Knowledge in Seven Plays of Shakespeare*, Cambridge 2003, pp. 48–49/58–59.
70 See also sections 3.3 and 3.4.
71 Lewis, op. cit., p. 40.
72 Neither Lear's daughters nor their husbands use the *pluralis maiestatis* either.
73 On this topic, see Aron Ronald Bodenheimer, *Warum? Von der Obszönität des Fragens*, Stuttgart 1984.
74 She depends on Lear's twilight since her father has made it a point not to entrust her and Regan but their husbands with the "execution" of the kingdom (I. i. 137–140).
75 William Empson, *Seven Types of Ambiguity*, London 1991, p. 89.
76 See Hans Blumenberg, 'Anthropologische Annäherung an die Aktualität der Rhetorik', in *Wirklichkeiten in denen wir leben*, Stuttgart 1981, p. 120.
77 It should be noted, however, that the storm in *Lear* does not inflict tangible damage on anyone; it is other people who bring about the demise of the *dramatis personae*, and not fire, water, and lightning.

78 See also Paul W. Kahn, *Law and Love. The Trials of King Lear*, New Haven, CT/London 2000, p. 10.
79 Walter Benjamin, 'Karl Kraus', in *Selected Writings*, vol. II. ii, translated by Edmund Jephcott, Cambridge, MA 2005, p. 449.
80 See section 3.4.
81 W. Moelwyn Merchant, *Lawyer and Actor*, Edinburgh 1962, pp. 107/122, quoted by Kahn, op. cit., p. 188.
82 See Richard Halpern, *The Poetics of Primitive Accumulation. English Renaissance Culture and the Genealogy of Capital*, Ithaca, NY/London 1991, p. 240.
83 See section 3.5.
84 Michel Foucault, *Abnormal. Lectures at the Collège de France, 1974–1975*, translated by Graham Burchell, New York, NY 2003, pp. 11–13.
85 Jacques Lacan, 'Kant with Sade', in *Écrits. The First Complete Edition in English*, translated by Bruce Fink, New York, NY/London 2006, pp. 645–668.
86 Lacan, 'Kant with Sade', ibid., p. 651.
87 Lacan, 'Kant with Sade', ibid., p. 652 and passim.
88 Benjamin, *The Origin of German Tragic Drama*, op. cit., p. 137.
89 I.e. subjects who refuse to participate in the Anglican worship service.
90 Jane Kingsley-Smith, *Shakespeare's Drama of Exile*, Basingstoke/New York, NY 2003, pp. 9–11. These statutes, by the way, were implemented by the Star Chamber, which generally applied the principles of common law, and not by the Court of Chancery (ibid. p. 10).
91 Kingsley-Smith, ibid. p. 11.
92 Kingsley-Smith, ibid. pp. 12–13.
93 Ken MacMillan, *Sovereignty and Possession in the English New World. The Legal Foundations of Empire, 1576–1640*, Cambridge/New York, NY 2006, pp. 3–4 and passim.
94 See also Jonathan Gil Harris, *Foreign Bodies and the Body Politic. Discourses of Social Pathology in Early Modern England*, Cambridge/New York, NY 1998, pp. 3–4 and passim.
95 On "Landnahme" (land appropriation) as the basis of civil property law, see Carl Schmitt, *The Nomos of the Earth in the International Law of the Jus Publicum Europaeum*, translated by Gary Ulmen, New York, NY 2003, pp. 56–66.
96 Brenda Danet and Bryna Bogoch, 'Whoever Alters This, May God Turn His Face from Him on the Day of Judgment', *Journal of American Folklore* 105 (416), 1992.
97 Danet and Bogoch, ibid. p. 142.
98 A. E. Crawley, 'Cursing and Blessing', in James Hastings (ed.), *Encyclopedia of Religion and Ethics*, vol. 4, Edinburgh 1911, p. 371.
99 On the parallel between Corpus Christi processions and "beating the bounds," see Sara Beckwith, 'Ritual Theatre and Social Space in the York Corpus Christi Cycle', in Barbara Hanawalt and David Wallace (eds), *Bodies and Disciplines. Intersections of Literature and History in Fifteenth-Century England*, Minneapolis, MN 1996, p. 74.
100 Mary Hill Cole, *The Portable Queen. Elizabeth I and the Politics of Ceremony*, Amherst, MA 1999, p. 155.
101 Schmitt, op. cit. See note 7.
102 Karl Marx, *Capital. A Critique of Political Economy*, vol. 1, London/New York, NY 1990, pp. 877–895.
103 Marx, ibid. p. 744. See also Halpern, op. cit., pp. 71–73.
104 Kingsley-Smith, op. cit., p. 176.
105 Kingsley-Smith, op. cit., p. 176.
106 Kingsley-Smith, op. cit., p. 16.
107 Kingsley-Smith, op. cit., p. 14.
108 Marcus Tullius Cicero, 'Paradoxa Stoicorum IV', in *De Oratore III*, London 1942, p. 283, quoted by Kingsley-Smith, op. cit., p. 143.

109 On the State's production of subjectivity, see for example Michel Foucault, *Discipline and Punish. The Birth of the Prison*, translated by Alan Sheridan, New York, NY 1978, p. 34.
110 See also sections 3.2 and 3.4.
111 Schmitt, op. cit., pp. 143–145.
112 See Kingsley-Smith, op. cit.
113 Joan Fitzpatrick, *Food in Shakespeare. Early Modern Dietaries and the Play*, Aldershot/Burlington, VT 2007, p. 28.
114 William Wordsworth, 'The Thorn', in *The Major Works*, Oxford/New York, NY 2000, pp. 59–66.
115 Robert Burns, 'A Winter Night', in *Complete Poems and Songs*, Oxford/New York, NY 1971, pp. 246–248.
116 See section 3.6. See also Barry B. Adams, *Coming to Know. Recognition and the Complex Plot in Shakespeare*, New York, NY 2000, p. 241.
117 Marcus Tullius Cicero, 'Against Piso', in *Ten Speeches*, translated by James E.G. Zetzel, Indianapolis, IN/Cambridge 2009, p. 243.
118 Agamben, *Homo Sacer*, op. cit., p. 38.
119 See Benjamin, *The Origin of German Tragic Drama*, op. cit., p. 74 on the connection between stoicism and the martyr's tragedy in *Trauerspiel.*
120 Maynard Mack, *King Lear in Our Time*, London 1966, p. 89.
121 Jacques Derrida, 'Hostipitality' in Jacques Derida, *Acts of Religion*, edited and translated by Gil Anidjar, New York, NY/London 2002, p. 385.
122 J. J. Lawlor, *The Tragic Sense of Shakespeare*, London 1960, p. 175, quoted by Ivor Morris, *Shakespeare's God. The Role of Religion in the Tragedies*, London 1972, p. 56.
123 Cavell, op. cit., pp. 68–72.
124 In this attempt, the flight into transcendence is once more short-circuited with a flight into open nature, at least insofar as the metaphors Lear uses are largely taken from the animal world ("birds," "butterflies," "foxes").
125 Oxford; Folio: "good years." According to the *Oxford English Dictionary*, the "goodyear" is "some undefined malefic power or agency." (See the Arden edition of the play, edited by R. A. Foakes, London 2001, p. 366.)
126 Kingsley-Smith, op. cit., p. 134.
127 William Empson, *Some Versions of Pastoral*, New York, NY 1974.
128 See Sigmund Freud, 'The "Uncanny"', in Sigmund Freud, *Writings on Art and Literature*, translated by Alix Strachey, John Strachey and Alan Tyson, Stanford, CA 1997, pp. 193–233. See also Sigmund Freud, *Die Traumdeutung*, Frankfurt a. M. 1991, p. 64.
129 Bernhard Maier, 'Segen und Fluch I', in Gerhard Müller (ed.), *Theologische Realenzyklopädie*, vol. 31, Berlin/New York, NY 2000, p. 75.
130 Pfeifer, op. cit., p. 1269.
131 "Berakah" can also mean "present" or "gift" (as in 1 Sam. 25. 27). See Timo Veijola, 'Segen und Fluch II', in Gerhard Müller (ed.), *Theologische Realenzyklopädie*, vol. 31, Berlin/New York, NY 2000, p. 76.
132 Thomas, op. cit., p. 231.
133 Bernhard Lang, *Sacred Games. A History of Christian Worship*, New Haven, CT/London 1997, p. 118.
134 John A. Simpson and Edmund S. C. *Weiner* (eds), *The Oxford English Dictionary*, vol. 2, Oxford 1989, p. 281.
135 Thomas, op. cit., p. 32.
136 See Chapter 1, section 1.5.
137 Thomas, op. cit., pp. 604–605.
138 Thomas, op. cit., p. 611.
139 Thomas, op. cit., p. 59.
140 See for example Howard Abrams, *The Mirror and the Lamp. Romantic Theory and the Critical Tradition*, Oxford 1971, pp. 218–225.

141 See R. A. Foakes's Arden edition of the play, London 2001, p. 280.
142 See for example Don C. Skemer, *Binding Words: Textual Amulets in the Middle Ages*, University Park, PA 2006, pp. 105–107.
143 See the Arden edition of the play, op. cit., p. 280 and Stephen Greenblatt (ed.), *The Norton Shakespeare*, New York, NY/London 1997, p. 2400.
144 See Ernest Jones, *On the Nightmare*, New York, NY 1971.
145 See for example Jeffrey Jerome Cohen, *Medieval Identity Machines*, Minneapolis, MN 2003, p. 149.
146 Stephen Greenblatt, *Shakespearean Negotiations*, Berkeley/Los Angeles, CA 1988, p. 126.
147 On a similar naturalizing figuration of executive power, see Anika Lemaire, *Jacques Lacan*, London 1977, pp. 231–233.
148 See the Arden edition of the play, p. 284 and Leon Harold Craig, *Of Philosophers and Kings*, Toronto 2001, p. 383.
149 Kenneth Gross, *Shakespeare's Noise*, Chicago, IL/London 2001, p. 185.
150 Greenblatt, *Shakespearean Negotiations*, op. cit., p. 127.
151 Greenblatt, *Shakespearean Negotiations*, op. cit., pp. 121–122.
152 Greenblatt, *Shakespearean Negotiations*, op. cit., p. 127.
153 Greenblatt, *Shakespearean Negotiations*, op. cit., p. 126.
154 Greenblatt, *Shakespearean Negotiations*, op. cit., p. 127.
155 Sigmund Freud, 'Fetishism', in *The Standard Edition of the Complete Psychological Works of Sigmund Freud*, vol. xxi, translated by James Strachey, London 1953, pp. 152–157.
156 Octave Mannoni, 'Je sais bien, mais quand même . . .', in Slavoj Zizek (ed.), *Jacques Lacan. Critical Evaluations in Cultural Theory*, London/New York, NY 2003, pp. 125–144.
157 Cavell, op. cit., pp. 55–57.
158 See section 3.2.
159 See sections 3.3 and 3.6.
160 Jean-Christophe Agnew, *Worlds Apart. The Market and the Theater in Anglo-American Thought, 1550–1750*, Cambridge, MA 1986, pp. 4 ff.
161 Karl Appuhn, 'Tools for the Development of the European Economy', in Guido Ruggiero (ed.), *A Companion to the Worlds of the Renaissance*, Oxford/Malden, MA 2002, pp. 271–273.
162 Agnew, op. cit., pp. 9–10.
163 Andrea Finkelstein, *Harmony and the Balance. An Intellectual History of Seventeenth-Century English Economic Thought*, Ann Arbor, MI 2000, pp. 96/128–129.
164 Finkelstein, ibid. pp. 19–20/104–106.
165 Alessandro Roncaglia, *The Wealth of Ideas. A History of Economic Thought*, Cambridge 2005, p. 23.
166 Finkelstein, op. cit., pp. 246/249.
167 See Chapter 2.
168 Finkelstein, op. cit. and passim.
169 On the need for metaphors in such cases, see Hans Blumenberg, 'Licht als Metapher der Wahrheit. Im Vorfeld der philosophischen Begriffsbildung', in *Ästhetische und metaphorologische Schrifen*, Frankfurt a. M. 2001, p. 139. See also section 3.1.
170 Agnew, op. cit., p. 88.
171 Agnew, op. cit., pp. 57–100.
172 Adam Smith, *The Wealth of Nations*, New York, NY 2003.
173 Georg Simmel, *The Philosophy of Money*, translated by Tom Bottomore and David Frisby, Boston, MA 1978, p. 303.
174 Indeed, willful deception and money seem to be intrinsically related in the civil law of early modern times. See Simmel, ibid., p. 368.
175 Agnew, op. cit., p. 68.

176 Agnew, op. cit., p. 202. See also Chapter 1, section 1.7.
177 Francis Bacon, *Advancement of Learning*, Whitefish, MT 1994, p. 125.
178 See Chapter 1, section 1.3.
179 See for example Gerald Hartung, 'Zur Genealogie des Versprechens', in Manfred Schneider (ed.), *Die Ordnung des Versprechens*, München 2005, p. 283.
180 Michael E. Tigar and Madeleine R. Levy, *Law and the Rise of Capitalism*, New York, NY 2000, pp. 203/207.
181 Tigar and Levy, ibid. pp. 142–143.
182 Jacques Derrida, *Limited Inc*, translated by Samuel Weber, Evanston IL 1988, pp. 19–20.
183 John Langshaw Austin, *How to Do Things with Words*, Cambridge, MA 2003, p. 5.
184 See Joseph Vogl, '1797. Geld als Versprechen', in Manfred Schneider (ed.), *Die Ordnung des Versprechens*, op. cit., pp. 313–329.
185 Karl Schuhmann, 'Die Theorie des Versprechens bei Thomas Hobbes', in Manfred Schneider (ed.), *Die Ordnung des Versprechens*, op. cit., pp. 99–101.
186 Thomas Hobbes, *Leviathan*, Oxford 1998, p. 94.
187 See Hannah Arendt, *The Origins of Totalitarianism*, New York, NY 2004, pp. 186–196.
188 Tigar and Levy, op. cit., p. 71; Danet and Bogoch, op. cit., S. 132–165.
189 See Chapter 1, section 1.1.
190 Thomas, op. cit., pp. 77–78; see also p. 80.
191 Agnew, op. cit., p. 138.
192 Victoria Kahn, *Wayward Contracts. The Crisis of Political Obligation in England 1640–1674*, Princeton, NJ 2004, p. 50.
193 Kahn, *Wayward Contracts*, ibid. p. 54.
194 Kahn, *Wayward Contracts*, ibid. pp. 50 ff.
195 Walter Benjamin, 'Capitalism as a Religion', in *Selected Writings*, vol. I, translated by Rodney Livingstone, Cambridge, MA 1996, pp. 288–291.
196 Simmel, op. cit., pp. 291–293.
197 See Russell West, *Spatial Representation and the Jacobean Stage from Shakespeare to Webster*, Basingstoke/New York, NY 2002, pp. 83/106.
198 "Fortune" and its grammatical derivatives are mentioned 17 times in *King John*, and 26 times in *King Lear.*
199 See for example I. i. 250/280; I. ii. 48/119; IV. vi. 172/187/217/224/229; V. i. 47; V. iii. 6/31/42/130/163/278.
200 See section 3.3.
201 Peter Stallybrass, 'The Value of Culture and the Disavowal of Things', in Henry S. Turner (ed.), *The Culture of Capital. Property, Cities, and Knowledge in Early Modern England*, New York, NY/London 2002, p. 275.
202 Quarto; Folio: "mettle."
203 See section 3.2.
204 On this ideology, see Finkelstein, op. cit., p. 96.
205 See for example Margot Heinemann, '"Demystifying the Mystery of the State", *King Lear* and the World Upside Down', in Catherine M. S. Alexander (ed.), *Shakespeare and Politics*, Cambridge 2004, pp. 163–164, and Reginald A. Foakes, 'Introduction', in *King Lear* (Arden edition), London 2001, p. 58.
206 See also Greenblatt, *Shakespearean Negotiations*, op. cit., p. 117.
207 Geoffrey of Monmouth, *The History of the Kings of Britain*, translated by Lewis Thorpe, London 1966, pp. 81–86; see also Foakes, op. cit., p. 94.
208 Charles Seife, *Zero. The Biography of a Dangerous Idea*, New York, NY 2000; Robert Kaplan, *The Nothing That Is. A Natural History of Zero*, Oxford/New York, NY 1999.
209 Seife, op. cit., pp. 11/55.
210 Seife, op. cit., pp. 79–81.
211 See Sybille Krämer, 'Rationalismus und künstliche Intelligenz. Zur Korrektur eines Mißverständnisses', *Künstliche Intelligenz* 7, 1993, p. 32.

212 See for example Carter Lindberg, *The European Reformation*, Malden, MA/Oxford 1996, pp. 38/81/118.
213 Douglas Bruster, 'The Dramatic Life of Objects in the Early Modern Theatre', in Jonathan Gil Harris and Natasha Korda (eds), *Staged Properties in Early Modern English Drama*, Cambridge/New York, NY 2003, p. 89.
214 Bruster, ibid. pp. 78–81.
215 For a listing of these props, see Frances Teague, *Shakespeare's Speaking Properties*, London/Toronto 1991, pp. 185–186.
216 See Chapter 2.
217 Benjamin, *The Origin of German Tragic Drama*, op. cit., pp. 131–132.
218 Benjamin, *The Origin of German Tragic Drama*, op. cit., p. 132.
219 Benjamin, 'Central Park', in *Selected Writings* IV, translated by Edmund Jephcott, Cambridge, MA 2006, pp. 168/173.
220 Benjamin, *The Origin of German Tragic Drama*, op. cit., p. 175.
221 On the motif of the purloined letter "transporting" guilt, and the structures it constitutes, see also Lacan, *The Ego in Freud's Theory and in the Technique of Psychoanalysis*, op. cit., pp. 191–205.
222 See Chapter 1, section 1.7.
223 It might be mentioned here that something similar is true of the "future in the instant" of *Macbeth* which is also mediated by a letter (see Anselm Haverkamp, *Shakespearean Genealogies of Power*, London/New York, NY 2011, pp. 84–85).
224 On a similar figure, see Joseph Vogl, *Kalkül und Leidenschaft. Poetik des ökonomischen Menschen*, Zürich/Berlin 2004, pp. 129–132.
225 Baker, op. cit., pp. 50–51.
226 Against this background, Gloucester's utterance "If it be nothing, I shall not need spectacles" (I. ii. 35–36) turns out to have been quite to the point.
227 See Introduction.
228 "Πορεὺεσθε ἀπ` ἐμοῦ οἱ κατεραμένοι εἰς τὸ πῦρ τὸ αἰώνιον τὸ ἡτιομασμένον τῷ διαβόλῳ καὶ τοῖς ἀγγέλοις αὐτοῦ."
229 See for example Romans 9. 14–23; Augustine, *Logik des Schreckens. De diversis quaestionibus ad Simplicianum I.2*, Mainz 1990.
230 Hans Blumenberg, *The Legitimacy of the Modern Age*, translated by Robert M. Wallace, Cambridge, MA 1983, pp. 135–136.
231 Blumenberg, *The Legitimacy of the Modern Age*, ibid. p. 43.
232 Blumenberg, *The Legitimacy of the Modern Age*, ibid. p. 42.
233 Kantorowicz, *The King's Two Bodies*, op. cit., p. 291.
234 Blumenberg, *The Legitimacy of the Modern Age*, op. cit., p. 600, note 6.
235 "Summumque futuri iudicii praeiudicium," Tertullian, *Apologeticum* 39.4, quoted by Blumenberg, *The Legitimacy of the Modern Age*, op. cit., p. 44/600.
236 Jeremy Tambling, *Allegory and the Work of Melancholy. The Late Medieval and Shakespeare*, Amsterdam/New York, NY 2004, p. 174.
237 See for example Richard Beadle and Pamela M. King (eds), *York Mystery Plays. A Selection in Modern Spelling*, Oxford/New York, NY 1999, pp. vi/267 ff.
238 On the concept of "acting out," see Lacan, *The Psychoses*, op. cit., p. 80.
239 Thomas, op. cit., pp. 166 ff. The term "Ranter" is pejorative; the group of "Ranters" is largely defined by the antagonism of those who gave them this name. (Andrew Hopton, *Introduction*, in Abiezer Coppe, *Selected Writings*, London 1987, p. 5.)
240 See Chapter 1, section 1.7.
241 Norman Cohn, *The Pursuit of the Millennium*, Oxford/New York, NY 1970, p. 300.
242 Thomas, op. cit., pp. 202–203.
243 On this, see Wolfgang Iser, 'Die Präsenz des Endes, King Lear – Macbeth', in Karlheinz Stierle and Rainer Warning (eds), *Das Ende. Figuren einer Denkform. Poetik und Hermeneutik XVI*, München 1996, p. 365.
244 Humphrey Ellis, *Pseudochristus*, London 1650, quoted by Cohn, op. cit., p. 300.

245 Benjamin, *The Origin of German Tragic Drama*, op. cit., p. 81.
246 See Chapter 1, section 1.6.
247 On this concept, see Georg Wilhelm Friedrich Hegel, *The Science of Logic*, translated by George Di Giovanni, Cambridge 2010, p. 109.
248 Benjamin, *The Origin of German Tragic Drama*, op. cit., pp. 231–232.
249 Benjamin, *The Origin of German Tragic Drama*, op. cit., pp. 79–80.
250 See Gross, op. cit., p. 171.
251 Wittreich, op. cit., p. 96.
252 Benjamin, *The Origin of German Tragic Drama*, op. cit., p. 77.
253 Walter Benjamin, 'Shakespeare: Wie Es Euch Gefällt', in *Gesammelte Schriften*, vol. 2. ii, Frankfurt a. M. 1991, pp. 610–611.
254 Gross, op. cit., pp. 177–178.
255 See for example Greenblatt, *The Norton Shakespeare*, op. cit., and the New Cambridge edition (Jay L. Halio (ed.), *The Tragedy of King Lear*, Cambridge 1992).
256 On the concept of "Entsetzung" ("de-posing" or "de-positing"), see Werner Hamacher, 'Afformative, Strike: Benjamin's Critique of Violence', in Andrew E. Benjamin, Peter Osborne (eds), *Walter Benjamin's Philosophy: Destruction and Experience*, London/New York, NY 1994, pp. 110–138. See also Walter Benjamin, 'Critique of Violence', in *Selected Writings*, Michael Jennings (general ed.) vol. I, translated by Edmund Jephcott, Cambridge, MA 1996, pp. 252–253, where Edmund Jephcott renders "Entsetzung" as "suspension." The term here refers to the opposite of "Setzung" (positing).
257 On the political dimension of mere noise, see Jacques Attali, *Noise: The Political Economy of Music*, translated by Brian Massumi, Minneapolis, MN 1985.
258 See the Arden edition, p. 278.
259 John Mandeville, *The Travels of John Mandeville*, London 1983, p. 48.
260 See for example Isaiah 11. 15/17. 13/28. 2/29. 6/32. 11.
261 Geoffrey of Monmouth, op. cit., p. 87.
262 Wittreich, op. cit., p. 118.
263 John E. Booty (ed.), *The Book of Common Prayer 1559. The Elizabethan Prayer Book*, Charlottesville, VA/London 2005, p. 262.
264 See Greenblatt, *Shakespearean Negotiations*, op. cit., p. 124.
265 See Cavell, op. cit., pp. 110/114.
266 See sections 3.3 and 3.5.
267 Howard Felperin, *Shakespearean Representation*, Princeton, NJ 1977, p. 105.
268 Franco Moretti, '"A Huge Eclipse": Tragic Form and the Deconstruction of Sovereignty', in Stephen Greenblatt (ed.), *The Power of Forms in the English Renaissance*, Norman, OK 1982, p. 19.
269 Jacques Lacan, *Freud's Technical Writings. Seminar I*, translated by John Forrester, New York, NY/London 1991, p. 277.

Bibliography

Abrams, Howard, *The Mirror and the Lamp. Romantic Theory and the Critical Tradition*, Oxford 1971.
Ackroyd, Peter, *The Life of Thomas More*, London 1998.
— , *London. The Biography*, London 2000.
Adams, Barry B., *Coming to Know. Recognition and the Complex Plot in Shakespeare*, New York, NY [et al.] 2000.
Aeschylus, *The Oresteia*, translated by Robert Fagles, New York, NY [et al.] 1966.
Agamben, Giorgio, *Homo Sacer. Sovereign Power and Bare Life*, translated by Daniel Heller-Roazen, Stanford, CA 1998.
— , *The End of the Poem. Studies in Poetics*, translated by Daniel Heller-Roazen, Stanford, CA 1999.
— , *Means Without End: Notes on Politics*, translated by Vincenzo Binetti and Cesare Casarino, Minneapolis, MN 2000.
— , *The Time that Remains. A Commentary on the Letter to the Romans*, translated by Patricia Dailey, Stanford, CA 2005.
Agnew, Jean-Christophe, *Worlds Apart. The Market and the Theater in Anglo-American Thought, 1550–1750*, Cambridge, MA 1986.
Albrecht, Christoph, *Einführung in die Liturgik*, Göttingen 1995.
Althusser, Louis, 'Ideology and Ideological State Apparatuses', in *Lenin and Philosophy and Other Essays*, translated by Ben Brewster, New York, NY/London 1971.
Anonymous, *The Curse of Popery and Popish Princes to the Civil Government and the Protestant Church of England*, London 1716.
Appuhn, Karl, 'Tools for the Development of the European Economy', in Guido Ruggiero (ed.), *A Companion to the Worlds of the Renaissance*, Oxford/Malden, MA 2002.
Aquinas, Thomas, *Summa Theologica*, translated by Fathers of the English Dominican Province, London, 1915–1924.
Arendt, Hannah, *The Origins of Totalitarianism*, New York, NY 2004.
Aristotle, *Topica*, translated by E. S. Forster, Cambridge, MA 1989.
— , *Nicomachean Ethics*, translated by Christopher Rowe, Oxford 2002.
Assmann, Jan, 'When Justice Fails. Jurisdiction and Imprecation in Ancient Egypt and the Near East', *Journal of Egyptian Archaeology* 78, 1992.
Attali, Jacques, *Noise: The Political Economy of Music*, translated by Brian Massumi, Minneapolis, MN 1985.
Augustine, *Logik des Schreckens. De diversis quaestionibus ad Simplicianum I.2*, Mainz 1990.
— , *Contra Faustum Manicheum. Libri 1–19, XIV/1*, Rome 2004.
Austin, John Langshaw, *How To Do Things With Words*, Cambridge, MA 2003.

Bacon, Francis, *Advancement of Learning*, Whitefish, MT 1994.
—, 'The Charge Touching Duels', in *Major Works*, Oxford/New York, NY 2002.
Baker, John Hamilton, *An Introduction to English Legal History*, London 1979.
Balthasar, Hans Urs von, *Theodramatik. Erster Band: Prolegomena*, Einsiedeln 1983.
Barion, Hans, 'Exkommunikation', in Kurt Galling (ed.), *Die Religion in Geschichte und Gegenwart. Handwörterbuch für Theologie und Religionswissenschaft*, vol 2. Tübingen 1958.
Barker, Francis, *The Culture of Violence. Tragedy and History*, Manchester 1993.
Bartlett, Robert, *Trial by Fire and Water. The Medieval Judicial Ordeal*, Oxford 1986.
Bateson, Gregory, *Steps to an Ecology of Mind*, Chicago, IL/London 2000.
Beadle, Richard and King, Pamela M. (eds), *York Mystery Plays. A Selection in Modern Spelling*, Oxford/New York, NY 1999.
Beckwith, Sara, 'Ritual Theatre and Social Space in the York Corpus Christi Cycle', in Barbara Hanawalt and David Wallace (eds), *Bodies and Disciplines. Intersections of Literature and History in Fifteenth-Century England*, Minneapolis, MN 1996.
—, *Signifying God. Social Relation and Symbolic Act in the York Corpus Christi Plays*, Chicago, IL/London 2003.
Belgrader, Michael, 'Fluch, Fluchen, Flucher', in Kurt Ranke (ed.), *Enzyklopädie des Märchens*, vol. 4, Berlin/New York, NY 1984.
Benjamin, Walter, 'Shakespeare: Wie Es Euch Gefällt', in *Gesammelte Schriften*, vol. 2. ii, Frankfurt a. M. 1991.
— , 'Capitalism as Religion', in *Selected Writings*, Michael Jennings (general ed.) vol. I, translated by Rodney Livingstone, Cambridge, MA 1996.
— , 'Critique of Violence', in *Selected Writings*, vol. I, translated by Edmund Jephcott, Cambridge, MA 1996.
— , 'Fate and Character', in *Selected Writings*, vol. I, translated by Edmund Jephcott, Cambridge, MA 1996.
— , *The Origin of German Tragic Drama*, translated by John Osborne, London/New York, NY 1998.
—, 'Karl Kraus', in *Selected Writings*, vol. II. ii, translated by Edmund Jephcott, Cambridge, MA 2005.
— , 'Central Park', in *Selected Writings*, vol. IV, translated by Edmund Jephcott, Cambridge, MA 2006.
— , 'On the Concept of History', in *Selected Writings*, vol. IV, translated by Harry Zohn, Cambridge, MA 2006.
Beth, Karl, 'Fluch', in Hanns Bächtold-Stäubli (ed.), *Handbuch des deutschen Aberglaubens*, vol. 2, Berlin/Leipzig 1930.
Bettenson, Henry (ed.), *Documents of the Christian Church*, second edition, Oxford [et al.] 1967.
Beza Vezelius, Theodorus, *Volumen Tractationum Theologicarum I*, Geneva 1570.
Blair, Ann, *The Theater of Nature. Jean Bodin and Renaissance Science*, Princeton, NJ 1997.
Blake, Norman Francis, *Shakespeare's Language. An Introduction*, London/Basingstoke 1983.
Blanchot, Maurice, *Le livre à venir*, Paris 1959.
Blumenberg, Hans, 'Anthropologische Annäherung an die Aktualität der Rhetorik', in *Wirklichkeiten in denen wir leben*, Stuttgart 1981.
— , *The Legitimacy of the Modern Age*, translated by Robert M. Wallace, Cambridge, MA/London 1983.
— , *Die Lesbarkeit der Welt*, Frankfurt a. M. 1986.

—, 'Prospect for a Theory of Nonconceptuality', in *Shipwreck with Spectator. Paradigm of a Metaphor for Existence*, translated by Stephen Rendall, Cambridge, MA/London 1997.

—, 'Licht als Metapher der Wahrheit. Im Vorfeld der philosophischen Begriffsbildung', in *Ästhetische und metaphorologische Schrifen*, Frankfurt a. M. 2001.

—, 'Sprachsituation und immanente Poetik', in *Ästhetische und metaphorologische Schriften*, Frankfurt a. M. 2001.

—, *Paradigms for a Metaphorology*, translated by Robert Savage, Ithaca, NY 2010.

Bodenheimer, Aron Ronald, *Warum? Von der Obszönität des Fragens*, Stuttgart 1984.

Boethius, *Consolatio Philosophiae*, Cambridge, MA 2008.

Bohlender, Matthias, *Die Rhetorik des Politischen. Zur Kritik der politischen Theorie*, Berlin 1995.

Booth, Wayne C., *A Rhetoric of Irony*, Chicago, IL/London 1975.

Booty, John (ed.), *The Book of Common Prayer 1559. The Elizabethan Prayer Book*, Charlottesville, VA/London 2005.

Braungart, Gregor, 'Der Tod des Körpers des Herrschers. Begräbnisrituale als Zeichenprozesse', in Erika Fischer-Lichte (ed.), *Theatralität und die Krisen der Repräsentation*, Stuttgart/Weimar 2001.

Brown, Kate E. and Kushner, Howard I., 'Eruptive Voices: Coprolalia, Malediction, and the Poetics of Cursing', *New Literary History* 32, 2001.

Brown, Peter, *Society and the Holy in Late Antiquity*, Berkeley, CA 1982.

Bruster, Douglas, 'The Dramatic Life of Objects in the Early Modern Theatre', in Jonathan Gil Harris and Natasha Korda (eds), *Staged Properties in Early Modern English Drama*, Cambridge/New York, NY 2003.

Bucholz, Robert and Key, Newton, *Early Modern England 1485–1714. A Narrative History*, Malden, MA [et al.] 2004.

Burckhardt, Sigurd, *Shakespearean Meanings*, Princeton, NJ 1968.

Burns, Robert, 'A Winter Night', in *Complete Poems and Songs*, Oxford/New York, NY 1971.

Cabantous, Alain, *Geschichte der Blasphemie*, translated by Bernd Wilczek, Weimar 1999.

Calvin, Johannes, *Auslegung des Römerbriefes und der beiden Korintherbriefe*, translated by Gertrud Graffmann et al., edited by Otto Weber et al., Neukirchen-Vluyn 1960.

—, *Institution of the Christian Religion [1536]*, translated by Ford Lewis Battles, Atlanta, GA 1975.

Canetti, Elias, *Crowds and Power*, translated by Carol Stewart, New York, NY 1962.

Carus, Paul, *The Bride of Christ. A Study in Christian Legend Lore*, Chicago, IL 1908.

Carver, Craig M., *A History of English in its Own Words*, New York, NY 1991.

Cavell, Stanley, *Philosophical Passages. Wittgenstein, Austin, Derrida*, Oxford/Cambridge, MA 1995.

—, 'The Avoidance of Love. A Reading of King Lear', in *Disowning Knowledge in Seven Plays of Shakespeare*, Cambridge [et al.] 2003.

Charnes, Linda, *Notorious Identity. Materializing the Subject in Shakespeare*, Cambridge/London 1993.

Cicero, Marcus Tullius, 'Paradoxa Stoicorum IV', in *De Oratore III*, London 1942.

—, 'Against Piso', in *Ten Speeches*, translated by James E.G. Zetzel, Indianapolis, IN/Cambridge 2009.

Clemen, Wolfgang, *Kommentar zu Shakespeares Richard III. Interpretation eines Dramas*, Göttingen 1969.

Cobbett, William and Howell, Thomas (eds), *A Complete Collection of State Trials*, vol. 6, London 1809.

Cohen, Jeffrey Jerome, *Medieval Identity Machines*, Minneapolis, MN 2003.

Cohen, Walter, *Drama of a Nation. Public Theater in Renaissance England and Spain*, Ithaca, NY/London 1985.
Cohn, Norman, *The Pursuit of the Millennium*, Oxford/New York, NY 1970.
Coke, Edward, *The Declarations*, London 1659.
—, *Reports*, Dublin 1792–1793.
Cole, Mary Hill, *The Portable Queen. Elizabeth I and the Politics of Ceremony*, Amherst, MA 1999.
Cooper, Jean C., *Dictionary of Christianity*, Chicago, IL 1996.
Corbett, Margery and Lightbown, R. W., *The Comely Frontispiece: The Emblematic Title-Page in England 1550–1660*, London 1979.
Cox, John D., *The Devil and the Sacred in English Drama 1350–1642*, Cambridge/New York, NY 2000.
Craig, Leon Harold, *Of Philosophers and Kings*, Toronto [et al.] 2001.
Crawley, A. E., 'Cursing and Blessing', in James Hastings (ed.), *Encyclopedia of Religion and Ethics*, vol. 4. Edinburgh 1911.
Danby, John F., *Shakespeare's Doctrine of Nature. A Study of King Lear*, London 1975.
Danet, Brenda and Bogoch, Bryna, 'Whoever Alters this, May God Turn His Face from Him on the Day of Judgment', *Journal of American Folklore* 105 (416), 1992.
Dante, *The Inferno*, translated by Robert and Jean Hollander, New York, NY 2002.
Davies, Eleanor, *Prophetic Writings*, edited by Esther S. Cope, Oxford/New York, NY 1995.
Davies, Michael, 'The Transubstantial Bard. Shakespeare and Catholicism', in Douglas Burnham and Enrico Giaccherini (eds), *The Poetics of Transubstantiation. From Theology to Metaphor*, Aldershot/Burlington, VT 2005.
Deleuze, Gilles, *Cinema 2: The Time-Image*, translated by Hugh Tomlinson and Robert Galeta, Minneapolis, MN 1989.
—, *The Logic of Sense*, translated by Mark Lester with Charles Stivale, New York, NY 1990.
Demosthenes, *On the False Embassy (Oration 19)*, translated by Douglas M. MacDowell, New York, NY 2000.
Derrida, Jacques, *Of Grammatology*, translated by Gayatri Spivak, Baltimore, MD [et al.] 1976.
—, 'Declarations of Independence', translated by Tom Keenan and Tom Pepper, *New Political Science* 15, 1986.
—, *Limited Inc*, translated by Samuel Weber, Evanston, IL 1988.
—, *Acts of Religion*, translated by Gil Anidjar et al., New York, NY/London 2002.
—, *Schibboleth. Für Paul Celan*, translated by Wolfgang Sebastian Baur, Wien 2002.
Diehl, Huston, *Staging Reform, Reforming the Stage. Protestantism and Popular Theater in Early Modern England*, Ithaca, NY/London 1997.
Dietzfelbinger, Ernst, (ed.), *Das Neue Testament, Interlinearübersetzung Griechisch-Deutsch*, Neuhausen 1998.
Dohi, Yumi, *Das Abendmahl im spätmittelalterlichen Drama*, Frankfurt a. M. 2000.
Donne, John, *The Sermons of John Donne*, vol. 6, Berkeley, CA [et al.] 1984.
—, 'The Curse', in *The Complete English Poems*, London [et al.] 1996.
Douglas, Mary, *Purity and Danger*, London 1966.
Dryden, John, *The Poems of John Dryden*, vol. 5, Harlow 2005.
Elizabeth I, *Collected Works*, Chicago, IL 2002.
Ellis, Humphrey, *Pseudochristus*, London 1650.
Elton, William R., *King Lear and the Gods*, Lexington, KY 1988.
Empson, William, *Some Versions of Pastoral*, New York, NY 1974.
—, *Seven Types of Ambiguity*, London 1991.

Evans, Malcolm, *Signifying Nothing. Truth's True Contents in Shakespeare's Texts*, Hemel Hempstead 1989.

Evans, William, Granger, Thomas and Hammond, Anthony (eds), *A Collection of Statutes Connected with the General Administration of the Law*, vol. 4. London 1836.

Falk, Ze'ev W., *Introduction to Jewish Law of the Second Commonwealth*, Leiden 1978.

Felman, Shoshana, *The Scandal of the Speaking Body. Don Juan with J. L. Austin, or Seduction in Two Languages*, translated by Catherine Porter, Stanford, CA 2003.

Felperin, Howard, *Shakespearean Representation*, Princeton, NJ 1977.

Finkelstein, Andrea, *Harmony and the Balance. An Intellectual History of Seventeenth-Century English Economic Thought*, Ann Arbor, MI 2000.

Fitzpatrick, Joan, *Food in Shakespeare. Early Modern Dietaries and the Play*, Aldershot/Burlington, VT 2007.

Foakes, Reginald A., 'Introduction', in William Shakespeare *King Lear*, London 2001.

Foucault, Michel, *The Order of Things. An Archaeology of the Human Sciences*, New York, NY 1970.

—, *The History of Sexuality*, vol. I, *An Introduction*, translated by Robert Hurley, New York, NY 1978.

—, *Discipline and Punish. The Birth of the Prison*, translated by Alan Sheridan, New York, NY 1979.

—, 'The Subject and Power', in Hubert L. Dreyfus and Paul Rabinow (eds), *Michel Foucault: Beyond Structuralism and Hermeneutics*, Chicago, IL 1983.

—, *Dits et Écrits II. 1976–1988*, edited by Daniel Defert and François Ewald, Paris 1994.

—, *Abnormal. Lectures at the Collège de France, 1974–1975*, translated by Graham Burchell, New York, NY 2003.

Fowler, W. Warde, 'The Original Meaning of the Word "Sacer"', *Journal of Roman Studies* 1, 1911.

Fox, Alistair, 'Richard III's Pauline Oath. Shakespeare's Response to Thomas More', *Moreana* 57, 1978.

Foxe, John, *The Acts and Monuments of John Foxe*, vol. 5, London 1877.

Freud, Sigmund, 'Fetishism', in *The Standard Edition of the Complete Psychological Works of Sigmund Freud*, vol. xxi, translated by James Strachey, London 1953.

—, 'Negation', in *The Standard Edition of the Complete Psychological Works of Sigmund Freud*, vol. xix, translated by James Strachey, London 1953.

—, *Die Traumdeutung*, Frankfurt a. M. 1991.

—, 'The "Uncanny"', in Sigmund Freud, *Writings on Art and Literature*, translated by Alix Strachey, John Strachey and Alan Tyson, Stanford, CA 1997.

Friesenhahn, Ernst, *Der politische Eid*, Darmstadt 1979.

Gallery, Steven, 'Dance of Death', in Robert Kastenbaum (ed.), *Encyclopedia of Death and Dying*, London/New York, NY 2001.

Garber, Marjorie, *Shakespeare's Ghost Writers. Literature as Uncanny Causality*, New York, NY/London 1997.

Geoffrey of Monmouth, *The History of the Kings of Britain*, translated by Lewis Thorpe, London [et al.] 1966.

Geulen, Eva, *Giorgio Agamben zur Einführung*, Hamburg 2005.

Girard, René, *Violence and the Sacred*, translated by Patrick Gregory, Baltimore, MD 1977.

Goethe, Johann Wolfgang von, *Faust: A Tragedy*, translated by Walter Arndt, New York, NY/London 2001.

Goodland, Katharine, *Female Mourning and Tragedy in Medieval and Renaissance Drama*, Aldershot/Burlington, VT 2005.

Graham, Daniel W. (ed.), *The Texts of Early Greek Philosophy: The Complete Fragments and Selected Testimonies of the Major Presocratics*, vol. 1, Cambridge 2010.

Green, Richard Firth, *A Crisis of Truth. Literature and Law in Ricardian England*, Philadelphia, PA 2002.

Greenblatt, Stephen, *Renaissance Self-Fashioning From More To Shakespeare*, Chicago, IL/London 1980.

— (ed.), *The Power of Forms in the English Renaissance*, Norman, OK 1982.

—, *Shakespearean Negotiations*, Berkeley/Los Angeles, CA 1988.

—, 'Towards a Poetics of Culture', in H. Aram Veeser (ed.), *The New Historicism*, London/New York, NY 1989.

—, 'Remnants of the Sacred in Early Modern England', in Margareta de Grazia, Maureen Quilligan and Peter Stallybrass (eds), *Subject and Object in Renaissance Culture*, Cambridge/New York, NY 1996.

—, 'Shakespeare's World', in Stephen Greenblatt (ed.), *The Norton Shakespeare*, New York, NY/London 1997.

—, *Hamlet in Purgatory*, Princeton, NJ/Oxford 2001.

—, *Will in the World*, New York, NY/London 2004.

Gregory I, *Morals in the Book of Job*, Oxford 1844.

Grene, Nicholas, *Shakespeare's Serial History Plays*, Cambridge 2002.

Griffiths, John (ed.), *Two Books of Homilies Appointed To Be Read in Churches*, Oxford 1859.

Gross, Kenneth, *Shakespeare's Noise*, Chicago, IL/London 2001.

Gurr, Andrew, 'The Shakespearean Stage', in *The Norton Shakespeare*, New York, NY/London 1997.

Habermas, Jürgen, *The Theory of Communicative Action*, translated by Thomas McCarthy, Boston, MA 1984–1987.

— , 'Discourse Ethics: Notes on a Program of Philosophical Justification', in *Moral Consciousness and Communicative Action*, Cambridge, MA 1990.

Halio, Jay L. (ed.), *The Tragedy of King Lear*, Cambridge 1992.

Hall, John, *The Advancement of Learning*, Liverpool 1953.

Haller, William, *Foxe's Book of Martyrs and the Elect Nation*, London 1963.

Halpern, Richard, *The Poetics of Primitive Accumulation. English Renaissance Culture and the Genealogy of Capital*, Ithaca, NY/London 1991.

Hamacher, Werner, 'Afformative, Strike: Benjamin's Critique of Violence', in Andrew E. Benjamin and Peter Osborne (eds), *Walter Benjamin's Philosophy: Destruction and Experience*, London/New York, NY 1994.

— , 'Wilde Versprechen', in Manfred Schneider (ed.), *Die Ordnung des Versprechens*, München 2005.

Harris, Jonathan Gil, *Foreign Bodies and the Body Politic. Discourses of Social Pathology in Early Modern England*, Cambridge/New York, NY 1998.

Hartmann, Geoffrey, *Saving the Text*, London [et al.] 1981.

Hartmann, Wilfried, *Der Investiturstreit*, München 2007.

Hartung, Gerald, 'Zur Genealogie des Versprechens', in Manfred Schneider (ed.), *Die Ordnung des Versprechens*, München 2005.

Haverkamp, Anselm, *Latenzzeit*, Berlin 2004.

—, *Metapher. Die Ästhetik in der Rhetorik*, München 2007.

—, *Shakespearean Genealogies of Power*, London/New York, NY 2011.

Hazlett, Ian, *The Reformation in Britain and Ireland. An Introduction*, London/New York, NY 2005.

Hedrick, Charles W., *History and Silence. Purge and Rehabilitation of Memory in Late Antiquity*, Austin, TX 2000.
Hegel, Georg Wilhelm Friedrich, *The Science of Logic*, translated by George Di Giovanni, Cambridge 2010.
Hein, Kenneth, *Eucharist and Excommunication. A Study in Early Christian Doctrine and Discipline*, Bern/Frankfurt a. M. 1973.
Heinemann, Margot, '"Demystifying the Mystery of the State", *King Lear* and the World Upside Down', in Catherine M. S. Alexander (ed.), *Shakespeare and Politics*, Cambridge [et al.] 2004.
Heywood, Thomas, *An Apology for Actors (1612)*, New York, NY 1941.
Hobbes, Thomas, *Leviathan*, Oxford [et al.] 1998.
Holinshed, Raphael, *Chronicles of England, Scotland, and Ireland*, vol. 4, London 1807/1808.
Holst-Warhaft, Gail, *Dangerous Voices. Women's Laments and Greek Literature*. London 1992.
Holzem, Andreas, 'Eid und Eidschwörer. Wahrheitssuche und Loyalitätsverpflichtung im frühneuzeitlichen Sendgericht', in Stefan Esders and Thomas Scharff (eds), *Eid und Wahrheitssuche. Studien zu rechtlichen Befragungspraktiken in Mittelalter und früher Neuzeit*, Frankfurt a. M. 1999.
Hooker, Richard, *On the Laws of Ecclesiastical Polity*, Cambridge [et al.] 1989.
Hopton, Andrew, 'Introduction', in Abiezer Coppe, *Selected Writings*, London 1987.
Irenaeus of Lyon, *Adversus Haereses*, Book III, Freiburg [et al.] 1995.
Iser, Wolfgang, *Staging Politics: The Lasting Impact of Shakespeare's Histories*, translated by David Henry Wilson, New York, NY 1993.
—, 'Die Präsenz des Endes, King Lear – Macbeth', in Karlheinz Stierle and Rainer Warning (eds), *Das Ende. Figuren einer Denkform. Poetik und Hermeneutik XVI*, München 1996.
James VI and I, *Political Writings*, Cambridge 1993.
Jones, David Martin, *Conscience and Allegiance in Seventeenth Century England. The Political Significance of Oaths and Engagements*, Rochester 1999.
Jones, Ernest, *On the Nightmare*, New York, NY 1971.
Jonsen, Albert R. and Toulmin, Stephen, *The Abuse of Casuistry*, Berkeley, CA [et al.] 1988.
Jowett, John, 'Introduction', in William Shakespeare, *The Tragedy of King Richard III*, Oxford/New York, NY 2000.
Kahn, Paul W., *Law and Love. The Trials of King Lear*, New Haven, CT/London 2000.
Kahn, Victoria, *Wayward Contracts. The Crisis of Political Obligation in England 1640–1674*, Princeton, NJ 2004.
Kamps, Ivo, *Historiography and Ideology in Stuart Drama*, Cambridge/New York, NY 1996.
Kantorowicz, Ernst H., *Gods in Uniform. Selected Studies*, Locust Valley, NY 1965.
—, *The King's Two Bodies, A Study in Mediaeval Political Theology*, Princeton, NJ 1997.
—, *Götter in Uniform, Studien zur Entwicklung des abendländischen Königtums*, Stuttgart 1998.
Kaplan, Robert, *The Nothing That Is. A Natural History of Zero*, Oxford/New York, NY 1999.
Kastan, David Scott, *Shakespeare and the Shapes of Time*, Hanover, NH 1982.
Keats, John, 'Letter to George and Tom Keats, December 1817,' in *The Major Works*, Oxford 2001.
Keeton, George W., *Shakespeare's Legal and Political Background*, London 1967.
Kenyon, John P. (ed.), *The Stuart Constitution 1603–1688. Documents and Commentary*, second edition, Cambridge [et al.] 1986.

Kiesow, Rainer Maria, 'Ius sacrum. Giorgio Agamben und das nackte Recht', *Rechtsgeschichte. Zeitschrift des Max-Planck-Instituts für europäische Rechtsgeschichte* 1, 2002.

Kingsley-Smith, Jane, *Shakespeare's Drama of Exile*, Basingstoke/New York, NY 2003.

Klahr, Detlef and Sommer, Wolfgang, *Kirchengeschichtliches Repetitorium*, Göttingen 1994.

Klein Maguire, Nancy *Regicide and Restoration. English Tragicomedy 1660–1671*, Cambridge 1992.

Knapp, Jeffrey, *Shakespeare's Tribe, Church, Nation and Theater in Renaissance England*, Chicago, IL/London 2002.

Kolmar, Lothar, *Promissorische Eide im Mittelalter*, Kallmünz 1989.

Körntgen, Ludger, *Königsherrschaft und Gottes Gnade*, Berlin 2001.

Krämer, Sybille, 'Rationalismus und künstliche Intelligenz. Zur Korrektur eines Mißverständnisses', *Künstliche Intelligenz* 7, 1993.

Kraus, Karl, 'Heinrich IV', *Die Fackel* 65, 1901.

—, 'Sittlichkeit und Criminalität', *Die Fackel* 115, 1902.

Kselman, John S., 'Curse and Blessing', in Paul J. Achtermeier (ed.), *Harper's Bible Dictionary*, San Francisco, CA 1985, p. 198.

Kumar, Krishan, *The Making of English National Identity*, Cambridge [et al.] 2003.

Lacan, Jacques, *The Four Fundamental Concepts of Psychoanalysis. Seminar XI*, translated by Alan Sheridan, New York, NY/London 1978.

—, 'Hamlet', translated by Franz Kaltenbeck, Susanne Hommel and Michael Turnheim, *Wo Es War. Eine Veröffentlichung des Freudschen Feldes* 2, 1986.

—, *The Ego in Freud's Theory and in the Technique of Psychoanalysis. Seminar II*, translated by Sylvana Tomaselli, New York, NY/London 1988.

—, *Freud's Technical Writings. Seminar I*, translated by John Forrester, New York, NY/London 1991.

—, *The Psychoses. Seminar III*, translated by Russell Grigg, London/New York, NY 1993.

—, 'The Instance of the Letter in the Unconscious, or Reason since Freud', in *Écrits. The First Complete Edition in English*, translated by Bruce Fink, New York, NY/London 2006.

—, 'Kant with Sade', in *Écrits. The First Complete Edition in English*, translated by Bruce Fink, New York, NY/London 2006.

Lang, Bernhard, *Sacred Games. A History of Christian Worship*, New Haven, CT/London 1997.

Lawlor, J. J., *The Tragic Sense of Shakespeare*, London 1960.

Lemaire, Anika, *Jacques Lacan*, London 1977.

Lévi-Strauss, Claude, *Le Totémisme aujourd'hui*, Paris 1965.

Lewis, Clive S., *Studies in Words*, Cambridge 1960.

Lindberg, Carter, *The European Reformation*, Malden, MA/Oxford 1996.

Link, Luther, *The Devil. A Mask without a Face*, London 1995.

Lipsius, Justus, *Von der Bestendigkeit* [*De Constantia*], translated by Andreas Viritius, Stuttgart 1965.

Little, Lester K., *Benedictine Maledictions. Liturgical Cursing in Romanesque France*, Ithaca, NY/London 1993.

Livy, *History of Rome*, vol. IX (Books xxxi–xxxiv) Cambridge 1967.

Lohfink, Norbert, 'Moab oder Sichem – Wo wurde Dtn. 28 nach der Fabel des Deuteronomiums proklamiert?', in F. García Martínez and A. Hilshorst (eds), *Studies in Deuteronomy. In Honor of C. J. Labuschagne on the Occasion of his 65th Birthday*, Leiden/New York, NY/Cologne 1994.

Lucretius, *De rerum natura*, translated by W. H. D. Rouse, Cambridge, MA 1982.

Luhmann, Niklas, 'Die Theorie der Ordnung und die natürlichen Rechte', *Rechtshistorisches Journal*, Heft 3, 1984.

—, *Love as Passion: The Codification of Intimacy*, Cambridge 1986.

—, *Law as Social System*, Oxford/New York, NY 2004.

Luther, Martin, 'To the Christian Nobility of the German Nation Concerning the Reform of the Christian Estate', in *Luther's Works*, vol. 44, Philadelphia, PA 1966.

—, 'Kirche und Gemeinde', in *Luther deutsch*, vol. 9, Göttingen 1991.

—, 'Treatise on Good Works', in *Luther's Works*, vol. 44, Philadelphia, PA 1966.

—, 'Concerning Excommunication', in *The Smalcald Articles*, in Robert Kolb and Timothy J. Wengert (eds), *The Book of Concord. The Confessions of the Evangelical Lutheran Church*, Minneapolis, MN 2000.

—, *Briefwechsel*, vol. 10, Weimar 2002.

McAlindon, Thomas, *Shakespeare's Tragic Cosmos*, Cambridge/New York, NY/Melbourne 1991.

Mack, Maynard, *King Lear in Our Time*, London 1966.

MacMillan, Ken, *Sovereignty and Possession in the English New World. The Legal Foundations of Empire, 1576–1640*, Cambridge/New York, NY 2006.

Maier, Bernhard, 'Segen und Fluch I', in Gerhard Müller (ed.), *Theologische Realenzyklopädie*, vol. 31, Berlin/New York, NY 2000.

Mandeville, John, *The Travels of John Mandeville*, London [et al.] 1983.

Mannoni, Octave, 'Je sais bien, mais quand même . . .', in Slavoj Zizek (ed.), *Jacques Lacan. Critical Evaluations in Cultural Theory*, London/New York, NY 2003.

Manthe, Ulrich, *Geschichte des römischen Rechts*, München 2000.

Marin, Louis, *Food for Thought*, translated by Mette Hjort, Baltimore, MD/London 1997.

Marlowe, Christopher, 'Doctor Faustus', in David Bevington, Lars Engle, Katharine Eisaman Maus and Eric Rasmussen (eds), *English Renaissance Drama, A Norton Anthology*, New York, NY/London 2002.

Marx, Anthony W., *Faith in Nation. Exclusionary Origins of Nationalism*, Oxford/New York, NY 2003.

Marx, Karl, *Capital. A Critique of Political Economy*, vol. 1, London/New York, NY [et al.] 1990.

Maurer, Wilhelm, 'Exkommunikation', in Kurt Galling (ed.), *Die Religion in Geschichte und Gegenwart. Handwörterbuch für Theologie und Religionswissenschaft*, vol. 2, Tübingen 1958.

Meier, Christian, *Die Entstehung des Politischen bei den Griechen*, Frankfurt a. M. 1995.

Meineke, Eckhard, 'Fluch', in Johannes Hoops (ed.), *Reallexikon der Germanischen Altertumskunde*, vol. 9, Berlin/New York, NY 1995.

Merchant, W. Moelwyn, *Lawyer and Actor*, Edinburgh 1962.

Miller, J. Hillis, *Speech Acts in Literature*, Stanford, CA 2001.

Monfrin, Françoise, 'Anathema', in Philippe Levillain (ed.), *The Papacy. An Encyclopedia*, London 2001.

Montagu, Ashley, *The Anatomy of Swearing*, Philadelphia, PA 2001.

Montrose, Louis Adrian, '"Eliza, Queene of Shepheardes" and the Pastoral of Power', in Arthur F. Kinney and Dan S. Collins (eds), *Renaissance Historicism. Selections from 'English Literary Renaissance'*, Amherst, MA 1987.

Moretti, Franco, '"A Huge Eclipse": Tragic Form and the Deconstruction of Sovereignty', in Stephen Greenblatt (ed.), *The Power of Forms in the English Renaissance*, Norman, OK 1982.

Morris, Ivor, *Shakespeare's God. The Role of Religion in the Tragedies*, London 1972.
Muir, Edward, *Ritual in Early Modern Europe*, Cambridge 1997.
Müller, Heiner, *Shakespeare Factory 1*, Berlin 1996.
Murray, James Augustus Henry, Bradley, Henry [et al.] (eds), *The Oxford English Dictionary*, first edition, vol. 2, Oxford 1933.
Nashe, Thomas, 'Pierce Penniless his Supplication to the Devil', in *The Unfortunate Traveller*, London [et al.] 1985.
Newcombe, David Gordon, *Henry VIII and the English Reformation*, London/New York, NY 2003.
Ogden, Daniel, 'Binding Spells: Curse Tablets and Voodoo Dolls in the Greek and Roman Worlds', in Bengt Ankarloo and Stuart Clark (eds), *Witchcraft and Magic in Europe*, vol. 2, *Ancient Greece and Rome*, London 1999.
Orgel, Stephen, *The Illusion of Power. Political Theater in the English Renaissance*, Berkeley/ Los Angeles, CA/London 1975.
Parrot, André, *Malédictions et Violations de Tombes*, Paris 1939.
Peacham, Henry, *The Garden of Eloquence*, Historisch-kritische Einleitung, Transkription und Kommentar by Beate-Maria Koll, Frankfurt a. M. 1996.
Pfeifer, Wolfgang (ed.), *Etymologisches Wörterbuch des Deutschen*, München 1995.
Picard, Liza, *Elizabeth's London*, New York, NY 2004.
Pitkin, Hanna Fenichel, *The Concept of Representation*, Berkeley, CA/London 1967.
Plato, *Republic*, Books 6–10, translated by Chris Emlyn-Jones and William Preddy, Cambridge, MA 2013.
Pollard, Tanya (ed.), *Shakespeare's Theater, A Sourcebook*, Malden, MA [et al.] 2004.
Pratt, Mary Louise, *Toward a Speech Act Theory of Literary Discourse*, Bloomington, IL/ London 1977.
Prüm, Regino von, *Libri*, Leipzig 1840.
Prodi, Paolo, 'Der Eid in der europäischen Verfassungsgeschichte', in Paolo Prodi and Elisabeth Müller-Luckner (eds), *Glaube und Eid. Treueformeln, Glaubensbekenntnisse und Sozialdisziplinierung zwischen Mittelalter und Neuzeit*, München 1993.
— , *Das Sakrament der Herrschaft. Der politische Eid in der Verfassungsgeschichte des Okzidents*, Berlin 1997.
Pugliatti, Paola, *Shakespeare the Historian*, Basingstoke/London 1996.
Puttenham, George, *The Arte of English Poesie*, Kent, OH 1970.
Pye, Christopher, 'The Sovereign, the Theater, and the Kingdome of Darknesse: Hobbes and the Spectacle of Power', in Stephen Greenblatt (ed.) *Representing the English Renaissance*, Berkeley, CA [et al.] 1988.
—, *The Regal Phantasm*, London/New York, NY 1990.
—, *The Vanishing. Shakespeare, the Subject and Early Modern Culture*, Durham, NC/London 2000.
Questier, Michael, *Conversion, Politics and Religion in England 1580–1623*, Cambridge [et al.] 1996.
Rackin, Phyllis, *Stages of History. Shakespeare's English Chronicles*, Ithaca, NY 1990.
Ramsay, G. D. (ed.), *John Isham. Mercer and Merchant Adventurer*, Northampton 1962.
Richardson, Henry G., 'The English Coronation Oath', *Speculum* 24, 1949.
Roncaglia, Alessandro, *The Wealth of Ideas. A History of Economic Thought*, Cambridge [et al.] 2005.
Rossiter, Arthur Percival, *Angel with Horns and Other Shakespeare Lectures*, London 1961.
Russell, Frederick H., *The Just War in the Middle Ages*, Cambridge [et al.] 1979.

Russell, Jeffrey Burton, *The Prince of Darkness. Radical Evil and the Power of Good in History*, Ithaca, NY 1992.
Saccio, Peter, *Shakespeare's English Kings. History, Chronicle and Drama*, Oxford/New York, NY 2000.
Scattola, Merio, *Das Naturrecht vor dem Naturrecht. Zur Geschichte des ius naturae im 16. Jahrhundert*, Tübingen 1999.
Schmidt, Heinrich R., 'Die Ächtung des Fluchens durch reformierte Sittengerichte', in Peter Blickle (ed.), *Der Fluch und der Eid. Die metaphysische Begründung gesellschaftlichen Zusammenlebens und politischer Ordnung in der ständischen Gesellschaft*, Berlin 1993.
Schmitt, Carl, *Political Theology. Four Chapters on the Concept of Sovereignty*, translated by George Schwab, Cambridge/London 1985.
— , *The Nomos of the Earth in the International Law of the Jus Publicum Europaeum*, translated by Gary Ulmen, New York, NY 2003.
—, *Constitutional Theory*, translated by Jeffrey Seitzer, Durham, NC/London 2008.
— , *Hamlet or Hecuba: The Intrusion of the Time into the Play*, translated by David Pan and Jennifer Rust, New York, NY 2009.
Schottroff, Willy, *Der altisraelitische Fluchspruch*, Neukirchen-Vluyn 1969.
Schuhmann, Karl, 'Die Theorie des Versprechens bei Thomas Hobbes', in Manfred Schneider (ed.), *Die Ordnung des Versprechens*, München 2005.
Schulte Beerbühl, Margrit, *Deutsche Kaufleute in London*, München 2007.
Seife, Charles, *Zero. The Biography of a Dangerous Idea*, New York, NY 2000.
Seneca, 'Thyestes', in *Tragedies II*, translated by John G. Fitch, Cambridge/London 2004.
Sessions, William A., *Henry Howard. The Poet Earl of Surrey. A Life*, Oxford [et al.] 2001.
Shakespeare, William, *The First Folio of Shakespeare. The Norton Facsimile*, second edition, edited by Charlton Hinman, New York, NY/London 1996.
— , *The Norton Shakespeare*, edited by Stephen Greenblatt, New York, NY/London 1997.
— , *King John*, edited by Ernst A. J. Honigmann, London 2001.
— , *King Lear*, edited by Reginald A. Foakes, London 2001.
— , *Richard III*, edited by Anthony Hammond, London 2002.
Shapiro, James, *1599. A Year in the Life of William Shakespeare*, New York, NY 2005.
Shupack, Paul M., 'Natural Justice and King Lear', *Cardozo Studies in Law and Literature* 9, 1997.
Sidney, Philip, 'The Defense of Poesy', in Gavin Alexander (ed.), *Sidney's 'Defense of Poesy' and Selected Renaissance Literary Criticism*, London 2004.
Simmel, Georg, *The Philosophy of Money*, translated by Tom Bottomore and David Frisby, Boston, MA 1978.
Simpson, John A. and Weiner, Edmund S. C. (eds), *The Oxford English Dictionary*, vol. 2, Oxford 1989.
Skemer, Don C., *Binding Words: Textual Amulets in the Middle Ages*, University Park, PA 2006.
Smith, Adam, *The Wealth of Nations*, New York, NY 2003.
Smith, Nigel, 'Forms of Kingship in King Lear', in Linda Cookson and Brian Loughrey (eds), *Critical Essays on King Lear*, London 1988.
Sommerlath, Ernst, 'Abendmahl', in Kurt Galling (ed.), *Die Religion in Geschichte und Gegenwart. Handwörterbuch für Theologie und Religionswissenschaft*, vol.1, Tübingen 1957.
Speyer, Wolfgang , 'Fluch', in Theodor Klauser (ed.), *Reallexikon für Antike und Christentum*, vol. 7, Stuttgart 1969.
Spinoza, Benedict de, *Theological-Political Treatise*, translated by Michael Silverthorne and Jonathan Israel, Cambridge 2007.

Staley, Vernon (ed.), *The First Prayer Book of King Edward VI*, London 1903.

Stallybrass, Peter, 'The Value of Culture and the Disavowal of Things', in Henry S. Turner (ed.), *The Culture of Capital. Property, Cities, and Knowledge in Early Modern England*, New York, NY/London 2002.

Steible, Mary, 'Jane Shore and the Politics of Cursing', *SEL. Studies in English Literature 1500–1900* 43 (1), 2003.

Stein, Jürgen, 'Excommunication', in Erwin Fahlbusch, Jan Milič Lochman, John Mbiti, Jaroslev Pelikan and Lukas Vischer, *The Encyclopedia of Christianity*, vol. 1, Grand Rapids, MI 2001.

Steinhauer, Fabian, 'Gestaltung des Rechts: Agamben', in Sonja Buckel, Ralph Christensen and Andreas Fischer-Lescano (eds), *Neue Theorien des Rechts*, Stuttgart 2006.

Sterne, Laurence, *Tristram Shandy*, New York, NY/London 1980.

Tambling, Jeremy, *Allegory and the Work of Melancholy. The Late Medieval and Shakespeare*, Amsterdam/New York, NY 2004.

Taubes, Jacob, *The Political Theology of Paul*, translated by Dana Hollander, Stanford, CA 2004.

Teague, Frances, *Shakespeare's Speaking Properties*, London/Toronto 1991.

Thomas, Keith, *Religion and the Decline of Magic. Studies in Popular Beliefs in Sixteenth- and Seventeenth-Century England*, London 1991.

Thür, Gerhard, 'Oaths and Dispute Settlement in Ancient Law', in Lin Foxhall and Andrew D. E. Lewis (eds), *Greek Law in its Political Setting*, Oxford 1996.

Tigar, Michael E. and Levy, Madeleine R., *Law and the Rise of Capitalism*, New York, NY 2000.

Till, Dietmar, 'Execratio', in Gert Ueding (ed.), *Historisches Wörterbuch der Rhetorik*, vol. 3, Tübingen 1996.

Tillyard, E. M. W., *Shakespeare's History Plays*, London 1959.

Twellmann, Marcus, *Das Drama der Souveränität*, München 2004.

Tyndale, William, *Tyndale's New Testament*, edited by David Daniell, New Haven, CT 1995.

Veijola, Timo, 'Segen und Fluch II', in Gerhard Müller (ed.), *Theologische Realenzyklopädie*, vol. 31, Berlin/New York, NY 2000.

Vodola, Elisabeth, *Excommunication in the Middle Ages*, Berkeley/Los Angeles, CA/London 1986.

Vogl, Joseph, *Kalkül und Leidenschaft. Poetik des ökonomischen Menschen*, Zürich/Berlin 2004.

—, '1797. Geld als Versprechen', in Manfred Schneider (ed.), *Die Ordnung des Versprechens*, München 2005.

Wahl, François, 'Die Philosophie diesseits und jenseits des Strukturalismus', in François Wahl (ed.), *Einführung in den Strukturalismus*, Frankfurt a. M. 1973.

Walsham, Alexandra, *Providence in Early Modern England*, Oxford [et al.] 1999.

Wannenwetsch, Bernd, 'Liturgy', in Peter Scott and William T. Cavanaugh (eds), *The Blackwell Companion to Political Theology*, Malden, MA 2004.

Weber, Max, *The Protestant Ethic and the Spirit of Capitalism*, translated by Talcott Parsons, New York, NY 1958.

Weimann, Robert, *Zwischen Performanz und Repräsentation. Shakespeare und die Macht des Theaters*, Heidelberg 2000.

West, Russell, *Spatial Representation and the Jacobean Stage from Shakespeare to Webster*, Basingstoke/New York, NY 2002.

White, Peter, *Predestination, Policy and Polemic: Conflict and Consensus in the English Church from the Reformation to the Civil War*, Cambridge [et al.] 1992.

White, Robert S., *Natural Law in English Renaissance Literature*, Cambridge [et al.] 1996.
Wickham, Glynne, *Shakespeare's Dramatic Heritage*, London 1969.
Winwood, Ralph, *Memorials of Affairs of State*, vol. 3, London 1725.
Wittreich, Joseph, *'Image of that Horror'. History, Prophecy, and Apocalypse in King Lear*, San Marino, CA 1984.
Wordsworth, William, 'The Thorn', in *The Major Works*, Oxford/New York, NY 2000.
Zaller, Robert, *The Discourse of Legitimacy in Early Modern England*, Stanford, CA 2007.
Zizek, Slavoj, *The Sublime Object of Ideology*, London 1989.

Index

For Product Safety Concerns and Information please contact our EU representative GPSR@taylorandfrancis.com
Taylor & Francis Verlag GmbH, Kaufingerstraße 24, 80331 München, Germany

www.ingramcontent.com/pod-product-compliance
Lightning Source LLC
LaVergne TN
LVHW011119300926
849160LV00008B/446
* 9 7 8 0 4 1 5 7 0 4 2 2 9 *